AP TEST CHANGES / 2020 AND BEYOND

Because of school district closures across the U.S. in response to the global COVID-19 pandemic, the 2019/20 AP school year came to an unexpected halt in March 2020. At that point, educators and students across the country had to scramble to finish up the year and prepare for AP exams.

Here at McGraw Hill, the *5 Steps to a 5* team has received numerous questions and concerns about what this means for AP courses and exams moving forward. So, whether your personal test-taking plans in Spring 2020 were directly impacted or you will be sitting for your first AP test in 2021, you are likely experiencing anxiety and uncertainty about the future.

Here are some of the most frequently asked questions regarding 2020/2021 AP Exams:

What happened to the Advanced Placement exams in May 2020?

There were big changes. When the pandemic hit, the College Board (who creates and administers AP exams nationwide) was forced to pivot and administer at-home tests. So, the traditional AP exams did not take place, and new versions were offered online. Prior to testing dates, College Board provided a detailed breakdown of the content that would be covered on each revised exam, allowing for what students were unlikely to have covered in class due to school closures.

How were test-takers impacted? What was the test-taking experience like?

For the first time ever, AP exams were given online. Students took modified 45-minute, web-based, free-response exams, and they were allowed to use their books and notes during the tests. Each test was administered in open book/open note format, and there were no multiple-choice questions at all. Students were able to take the exam on any device (a computer, tablet or a smartphone). Alternatively, students were allowed to submit a photo of their handwritten work.

For the AP Chinese Language and Culture exam, the following changes took place:

- Only Units 1-4 were covered (2020) instead of Unit 1-6 (normal).
- Only the free-response questions of conversation and cultural presentation were tested.
- Students received an email indicating that they could download a free World Language Exam App on May 11th, 2020 and were encouraged to download the app to use the practice mode before the exam.

Is this *5 Steps* guide relevant and up-to-date?

Yes! Everything in this book is reflective of the current course and exam as it was originally designed. The *5 Steps* team strives to keep all information relevant and as up-to-date as possible, both in print and online.

What will happen in May 2021?

Your guess is as good as ours. We're hopeful that next year's test format will return to the complete form as created by the College Board, but at the time of this guide's publication, things remain fairly uncertain. However, whether the AP exams return to the original format, follow the 2020 online model, or something entirely new - we have you covered! We'll be updating our materials whenever any new information becomes available, and will make every effort to revise our digital resources as quickly as possible.

Most importantly, look for regular updates on the College Board website for the latest information on your course at **apcentral.collegeboard.org**. This will be your resource for the most up-to-date information on AP courses.

5 STEPS TO A 5™

AP Chinese
Language and Culture

Third Edition

JianMin Luo

McGraw Hill

New York Chicago San Francisco Athens London Madrid
Mexico City Milan New Delhi Singapore Sydney Toronto

1 2 3 4 5 6 7 8 9 10   LHS   25 24 23 22 21 20

ISBN 978-1-260-46814-4 (book and MP3 disk set)
MHID 1-260-46814-3 (book and MP3 disk set)

ISBN 978-1-260-46815-1 (book for set)
MHID 1-260-46815-1 (book for set)

e-ISBN 978-1-260-46817-5
e-MHID 1-260-46817-8

The series editor was Grace Freedson and the project editor was Del Franz.

Series interior design by Jane Tenenbaum.

ABOUT THE AUTHOR

JianMin Luo teaches AP Chinese at One Schoolhouse online and Chadwick School. She has been serving as an AP reader, an instructional designer, a book author, and an editor for a variety of educational institutions and associations in the United States and China. JianMin Luo received her M.Ed. in Curriculum and Instruction from Seattle University, and she specializes in assessment design and test-prep teaching.

CONTENTS

ACKNOWLEDGMENTS

I would like to express my gratitude to everyone for contributing to the success of this book: Lisa Podbilski, for being with me along the journey of Chinese teaching; Grace Freedson and Grace Freedson's Publishing Network, for giving me this opportunity; Qimin Zhang, for his collaboration of building a vocabulary bank aligning with the new course description; Del Franz, for his outstanding wisdom and insightful work put into this book; Garret Lemoi; Anya Kozorez; and Sylvia Rebert, project manager, and her editing team at Progressive Publishing Alternatives. I would also like to thank my students, colleagues, and administrators of Chadwick School and One Schoolhouse for their support all along.

In addition, many thanks to the suggestions from my book users. I hope this new edition will continue supporting students to succeed, aligning with the updated AP Chinese Language and Culture Course and Exam Description, effective fall 2019.

INTRODUCTION: THE FIVE-STEP PROGRAM

Welcome!

Not too long ago, you agreed to enroll in AP Chinese. Maybe the idea of becoming fluent in Chinese sounded pretty good or maybe a respected teacher encouraged you to challenge yourself and you agreed. Or maybe you just wanted to really impress college admissions officers! Whatever, you find yourself here, flipping through a book that promises to help you culminate this experience with the highest of honors—a 5 in AP Chinese. Can this be done without this book? Sure, there are many excellent teachers of Chinese out there who teach the class well and prepare their students so that every year some of them get a 5. But, the truth is that for the majority of students in your shoes, the proven strategies to approach each type of question, comprehensive review, and realistic practice exams in this book will make it much easier for you to achieve that goal.

Organization of the Book: The Five-Step Program

You will be taking a comprehensive exam this May. You want to be well prepared so that the exam takes on the feel of a command performance, not a trial by fire. Following the Five-Step Program is the best way to structure your preparation. Here are the five steps:

Step 1: Set Up Your Study Program

You need to get to know the exam—what's on it and how it's structured—so there are no surprises on test day. Understanding the test is the first step in preparing for it. Chapter 1 answers your questions about the test. And you need a plan—that's the focus of Chapter 2. Step 1 gives you the background and structure you will need before you even start to review and practice for the exam.

Step 2: Determine Your Test Readiness

Your study program should *not* include trying to cram absolutely everything about Chinese into your head a few weeks before the test; it can't be done. Instead, you'll need to assess your strengths and weaknesses and prioritize what you need to work on. The diagnostic test in Chapter 3 will help you do just that. This test will also show you what you're up against; it's a complete test just like the actual test you'll face in May. After you evaluate your performance on the test-like exam, you'll have a good idea of what you really need to work on to improve your performance. In addition, throughout this book are self-evaluation worksheets that will help you analyze how you're doing and, based on that analysis, offer suggestions as to what you can do to improve.

Step 3: Develop Strategies for Success

Chapter 4 is all about developing effective strategies to approach each of the types of questions found on the AP Chinese Language and Culture exam. Sure, you've been listening to general test-taking advice and have been taking multiple-choice standardized tests practically your whole life. But the chapter in this section contains strategies for the specific types of questions found on the exam—both multiple choice and free response. Having effective strategies is the key to doing well; in the rest of the chapters, you'll practice applying the strategies to the questions you'll encounter on the test.

Step 4: Review the Knowledge You Need to Score High

Chapters 5 through 11 contain comprehensive practice for the questions and topics found on the AP exam. You'll practice applying the strategies you learned in Step 3 to the tasks of listening, reading, writing, and speaking that are included on the test. Each chapter focuses on a particular question type or task. Chapter 5 deals with the listening rejoinders, in which you have to listen to a short conversation and pick the statement that most logically follows in the conversation. Chapter 6 involves listening to different types of audio selections and then answering questions that check your listening comprehension. In Chapter 7 you'll read different selections and answer questions that check your reading comprehension. The next four chapters relate to the four types of free-response questions on the exam. In Chapter 8 you'll practice writing a story based on four drawings. Chapter 9 provides practice reading an e-mail message and then writing a response. Chapter 10 focuses on taking part in a simulated conversation that involves speaking answers to questions you hear. Finally, Chapter 11 will help you prepare for the cultural presentation you'll need to make.

Step 5: Build Your Test-Taking Confidence

In this step you'll check your preparation by testing yourself using two full-length practice tests that closely reflect what you'll encounter in the actual test. Complete explanations for the answers are provided so you can learn from your mistakes. It's a good idea to read the explanations not only for the questions you got wrong, but also for the questions you weren't sure of or simply happened to guess correctly.

Graphics Used in This Book

To help you locate important and practical ideas, strategies, and tips, you'll see several icons placed in the left-hand margin of this book. We use these icons:

 This icon indicates a very important concept or fact that you should not pass over.

 This icon calls your attention to an important strategy.

 This icon alerts you to a tip that you might find useful.

 This icon indicates a listening passage that is provided on the accompanying CD-ROM.

Let's get started!

STEP 1

Set Up Your Study Program

CHAPTER 1

What You Need to Know About the AP Chinese Language and Culture Exam

IN THIS CHAPTER

Summary: This chapter provides the information you need to know about the AP Chinese exam, including how the test is administrated, how it is scored, and other basic test-taking information.

Key Ideas

✪ Most colleges award credit for a score of 4 or 5.
✪ The AP Chinese exam tests four skills of listening, speaking, reading, and writing. These skills are weighed equally in your final score.
✪ Your final score is based on the range of a converted composite score.
✪ You need to pay attention to the facts specifically required for the AP Chinese exam.

Background Information

The AP Chinese Language and Culture exam was first administered in 2007 with 3,261 exam takers (363 of whom were students of non-Chinese heritage). The number of students who take the exam has grown rapidly to 14,892 in 2019. Of these, 4,894 are students of non-Chinese heritage.

Frequently Asked Questions About the AP Chinese Language and Culture Exam

Here are the answers to the most important questions students (and parents) often ask about the exam.

Why Take the AP Chinese Language and Culture Exam?

First, taking the exam will help you to stand out in the college admission process. It demonstrates not only your commitment to academic excellence but also your determination to take one of the most rigorous high school courses available.

Second, it provides a way of getting college credit before you begin college. Most colleges and universities accept a 4 or 5 score for credit for their Chinese language course. Getting this credit in advance provides you with more time and flexibility in course selection in college, and more opportunities to pursue a double major, study abroad, or move into a more advanced Chinese course. Putting yourself through a year of pressure, stress, and challenge is also a great life experience to gain the skills to excel in college learning and the challenges beyond college.

What Is New About the AP Chinese Exam?

The College Board developed the new AP Chinese Course and Exam Description (CED) and the online platform of AP Classroom, effective fall 2019. The guides of six units/ themes are thoroughly covered in CED, including the suggested thematic course content and skills, the curriculum building and instructional strategies, the authentic resources, and the recommended sequencing and pacing in teaching. Eight skills categories are provided to identify what students should know and be able to do across the three modes of communication. When building your knowledge foundation, you should focus on these six themes: Families and Communities, Public and Personal Identities, Beauty and Aesthetics, Science and Technology, Contemporary Life, and Global Challenges. You don't need to follow the sequence of six themes in learning. Using this book will help you revisit the knowledge and skills in a spiral way.

What Is the Format of the Exam?

The AP Chinese Language and Culture exam is divided into two sections: multiple-choice questions and free-response questions. The following tables summarize the format of the AP Chinese exam.

Section I: Multiple Choice (70 questions, 50% of the final score)

SECTION I	QUESTION TYPE	KNOWLEDGE AND SKILLS	WEIGHT
Part A: Listening (20–30 minutes)	**Rejoinders:** 10–15 questions (Response time: 5 seconds per question)	These questions test the interpersonal communication skills of including using set phrases and social formulae to communicate opinion, attitude, intent, etc.	10% of the total score
	Listening Selections: 15–20 questions (Response time: 12 seconds per question)	These questions test the interpretive communication skills of listening comprehension, inference, and the application of introductory cultural knowledge based on various stimuli of notes, announcements, voice messages, reports, etc.	15% of the total score
Part B: Reading (60 minutes)	**Reading Selections:** 35–40 questions	These questions test the interpretive communication skills of reading comprehension, inference, and the application of introductory cultural knowledge based on a variety of stimuli of letters, e-mails, signs, advertisements, brochure, stories, news articles, etc.	25% of the total score

Section II: Free Response (four tasks, 50% of the final score)

SECTION II	QUESTION TYPE	KNOWLEDGE AND SKILLS	WEIGHT
Part A: Writing (30 minutes)	**Story Narration:** 1 question (15 minutes)	This question tests presentational communication skills: Students narrate a story based on four pictures.	15% of the total score
	E-mail Response: 1 question (15 minutes)	This question tests interpersonal communication skills: Students read an e-mail and respond to it.	10% of the total score
Part B: Speaking (11 minutes)	**Conversation:** 6 questions (Response time: 20 seconds per question)	These questions test interpersonal communication skills: Students respond appropriately to six questions in conversation.	10%
	Cultural Presentation: 1 question (Preparation time: 4 minutes; presentation time: 2 minutes)	This question tests presentational communication skills: Students describe and explain the significance of a Chinese cultural practice or product.	15%

Who Writes the AP Chinese Language and Culture Exam?

The College Board, a nonprofit educational organization is responsible for the exam. The College Board formed an AP Chinese Task Force to create an outline for the course and draft the exam specifications. An AP Chinese Development Committee is responsible for refining the course outline, finalizing the exam specifications, writing the exam questions, and so on.

The whole effort involves many education and testing professionals and students from the college and high schools. There are a large number of multiple-choice questions pretested and evaluated. The committee chooses those questions that fit the criteria of accuracy, clarity, and appropriateness with only one possible answer. A similar process is applied to create free-response questions and the corresponding scoring guidelines, which are designed, modified, pretested, and refined to allow the AP Chinese readers to evaluate student responses appropriately and equitably. In short, the AP Chinese exam is researched, created, evaluated, and refined by qualified professionals in this field.

Who Grades My AP Chinese Language and Culture Exam?

While the multiple-choice questions are scored by computer, a group of Chinese teachers and college professors gather together to score the free-response section of each exam in June of every year. Each of these AP readers is assigned to grade one of the questions only. They normally spend the first day getting trained to be the expert on their assigned question. Each day, the scoring of a random set of answers from each AP reader is compared to that of the "table leaders" to make sure that different readers are scoring in the same way. The table leaders also embed a prescored question in each set of 20 samples to make sure that some readers are not given significantly higher or lower scores than others. During this process, the students' answers are absolutely anonymous since each student is assigned a number rather than a name. If, by any chance, a reader thinks the answers he or she is reading is from one of his or her own students, the reader will pass the scoring responsibility to another reader. All of these measures are taken to maintain a consistent and unbiased scoring of that single question.

How Is My Final Score Determined, and What Does It Mean?

Based on your performance, the weighted scores from Sections I and II are added together and converted to a composite score. The detailed method used for doing this is provided at the end of Chapter 3. Once your exam has been scored, the composite score will be converted to an AP score that ranges from 1 to 5. The score ranges listed below are estimated (2019 AP Chinese exam). Because the conversion of raw scores changes based on the specific test given each year, it is not guaranteed that this table will apply exactly to your test.

- Score 5: Composite score range 101–120
- Score 4: Composite score range 91–100
- Score 3: Composite score range 75–90
- Score 2: Composite score range 61–74
- Score 1: Composite score range 0–60

AP SCORE	LETTER GRADE	INDICATION (FOR COLLEGE CREDIT)
5	A	Extremely Well Qualified
4	B	Well Qualified
3	C	Qualified
2	D	Possibly Qualified
1	F	No Recommendation

All of the reporting of scores to test takers is usually completed by the middle to the end of July.

How Do I Register, and How Much Does It Cost?

First, the best resource of information on registration and costs is the official website of the College Board: https://www.collegeboard.com.

Starting in school year 2019 to 2020, if you are enrolled in an AP Chinese course, your school's AP coordinator will guide you to complete the registration procedure. You'll need to join in your class section online in order to register for the exam. Then the AP coordinator will collect fees and order the exam materials for you. This will generally happen in the fall, so be sure to check with your teacher or AP coordinator.

If your school does not administer the AP Chinese exam or if you are homeschooled, you will need to take the exam at a participating school. You should contact AP Services for Students to get the contact information of the local AP coordinators who accept outside students no later than September 4, and make sure that your testing can be arranged by October 4. In 2019, the fee for taking the Chinese Language and Culture exam was $94 for each exam; this fee tends to go up a little each year. Students who demonstrate financial need may receive a fee reduction.

Keep in mind that you can always contact the coordinator of the AP program at your school or the school where your AP exam will be administered if you have any questions.

What Should I Bring to the Exam?

On exam day you need:

- A valid government- or school-issued photo ID to bring with you to the exam.
- Your school code or, if you do not have a school code, the international/self-study code given to you.
- Several pencils and an eraser.
- A watch to monitor your time and a coat in case the temperature of a computer lab is too low.

What Should I *Not* Bring to the Exam?

It is a good idea to leave the following items out:

- Any electronic device with the function of communication.
- Any paper products except for the documents required for the exam. Most likely, the AP sites will provide the blank paper.
- Anything else that may cause a problem or issue in an exam-taking process.

What Else Do I Need to Know About the AP Chinese Language and Culture Exam?

The following information is important for your preparation for the exam and your performance on it:

- The AP Chinese exam is computer based, and you will type Chinese for your writing answers.
- The exam involves test-taking procedures with a relatively complicated tech setup. Therefore, it is a good idea to practice and get used to the procedure before the actual exam.

- For the listening selections, you are not given the questions and answer choices until you finish listening to the specific selection. That means you should practice note-taking skills. In the listening section you cannot go back and change answers after a question is done.
- In the reading comprehension section of the test, you can check questions on the computer that you want to come back to later if you have time. In this section you can go back and change answers within the 60-minute time limit.
- All Chinese text displayed on the screen allows students to switch between traditional characters or simplified characters.

CHAPTER 2

How to Plan Your Time

IN THIS CHAPTER

Summary: Choose the right preparation plan for you depending on your study habits and the amount of time you have before the exam.

Key Ideas

✪ Analyze your learning habits and profile.
✪ Choose a study plan that is right for you.

Tips for Creating Your Test Preparation Plan

Before you begin your test preparation, you need a plan. A good plan will help you to pace yourself and make efficient use of your time. Here are some proven strategies to help you develop your plan:

- Give yourself specific goals or objectives. This will help you monitor your progress.
- Constantly expand your pool of vocabulary words.
- Practice your note-taking skills for the listening selections on the exam. This is especially important because, most likely, you have not done this in Chinese.
- Spend more time on your weakness. Frequently analyze and evaluate what you have learned and what you still need to learn.
- Practice using the free-response questions from past exams. You can find the released questions from previous exams on the College Board's AP website for students. Go to http://apstudent.collegeboard.org. Click on "Taking the Exam" and then on

"Preparing for the Exam." Choose "AP Chinese Language and Culture," and you will find the actual free-response questions used on the exam going back to the 2007 test.

Three Approaches to Preparing for the AP Chinese Exam

Where do I start my AP Chinese exam preparation? Analyze your study habits and calculate the time you can afford for the exam. No one knows your study habits, likes, and dislikes better than you do, so you are the only one who can decide which approach you want and/or need to adopt. This chapter presents three sample study plans, labeled A, B, and C. You can choose one to follow or adapt it to your own needs.

Overview of the Three Study Plans

MONTH	PLAN A: FULL SCHOOL YEAR	PLAN B: ONE SEMESTER	PLAN C: SIX WEEKS
September	Diagnostic Exam: Chapter 3 Appendix: Functional Grammar Appendix: Vocabulary (10 new vocabulary words daily)		
October	Exam Strategies: Chapter 4 Presentational Writing: Chapter 8 Appendix: Vocabulary (10 new vocabulary words daily)		
November	Interpersonal Writing: Chapter 9 Listening Rejoinders: Chapter 5 Appendix: Vocabulary (10 new vocabulary words daily)		
December	Listening Selections: Chapter 6 Interpersonal Speaking: Chapter 10 Appendix: Vocabulary (10 new vocabulary words daily)		

MONTH	PLAN A: FULL SCHOOL YEAR	PLAN B: ONE SEMESTER	PLAN C: SIX WEEKS
January	Reading Selections: Chapter 7 Presentational Speaking: Chapter 11 Appendix: Expressions (5 new expressions daily)	Diagnostic Exam: Chapter 3 Appendix: Functional Grammar Exam Strategies: Chapter 4 Presentational Writing: Chapter 8 Appendix: Vocabulary (20 new vocabulary words daily)	
February	Review: Chapters 3, 4, 5, 6 Appendix: Expressions (5 new expressions daily)	Interpersonal Writing: Chapter 9 Listening Rejoinders: Chapter 5 Listening Selections: Chapter 6 Interpersonal Speaking: Chapter 10 Appendix: Vocabulary (20 new vocabulary words daily)	
March	Practice Exam 1 Review: Chapters 7, 8, 10 Practice: Free-response questions from previous exams 2007–2010	Reading Selections: Chapter 7 Presentational Speaking: Chapter 11 Review: Chapters 5, 6, 7, 8, 9, 10, 11 Appendix: Expressions (10 new expressions daily)	**Week 1** Diagnostic Exam: Chapter 3 Appendix: Functional Grammar Exam Strategies: Chapter 4 Appendix: Vocabulary (20 new vocabulary words daily) **Week 2** Listening Rejoinders: Chapter 5 Listening Selections: Chapter 6 Presentational Writing: Chapter 8 Appendix: Vocabulary (20 new vocabulary words daily)

(Continued)

MONTH	PLAN A: FULL SCHOOL YEAR	PLAN B: ONE SEMESTER	PLAN C: SIX WEEKS
April	Practice Exam 2 Review: Chapters 9, 11 Practice: Free-response questions from previous exams 2011–present Final review: Any content you highlighted in this book or marked on the following checklist	Practice Exam 1 Practice: Free-response questions from previous exams 2007–present Practice Exam 2 Final Review: Any content you highlighted in this book or marked on the following checklist	**Week 3** Interpersonal Writing: Chapter 9 Interpersonal Speaking: Chapter 10 Presentational Speaking: Chapter 11 Appendix: Vocabulary (20 new vocabulary words daily) **Week 4** Reading Selections: Chapter 7 Review: Chapters 5, 6, 7 Appendix: Expressions (10 new expressions daily) **Week 5** Practice Exam 1 Review: Chapters 8, 9, 10, 11 Practice: Free-response questions from previous exams 2007–2010 **Week 6** Practice Exam 2 Practice: Free-response questions from previous exams 2011–present Final Review: Any content you highlighted in this book or marked on the following checklist

Calendar with a Checklist for Each Plan

Using a checklist is a very effective and efficient way to carry out your study plan and identify your weaknesses for future review. On the following checklists mark if you successfully reach the goal and whether you feel that you need further review. You can use different numbers of marks to differentiate the degree of difficulty or the amount of time you will need to succeed. On the checklists you can also note the page number and then highlight any specific paragraphs you want to go over.

Plan A: Full Year

MONTH	GOAL	GOAL CHECKLIST	CHECK OFF
September	Learn 10 vocabulary words per day **Week 1** Diagnostic exam: Chapter 3 **Week 2** Analyze and evaluate your performance to identify your weaknesses **Week 3** Learn functional grammar **Week 4** Write a story using functional grammar Review vocabulary	Can you identify your weakness using the self-evaluation worksheets in Chapter 4 to evaluate your performance on the diagnostic test? What are your weaknesses? Can you freely use 9 different functions for complex sentences? Did you practice 200 new vocabulary words (use the fourth week to review the vocabulary)?	
October	Learn 10 vocabulary words per day **Week 1** Learn exam strategies: Chapter 4—listening and reading **Week 2** Learn exam strategies: Chapter 4—writing and speaking **Week 3** Learn to narrate a story: Chapter 8 **Week 4** Do the exercises on story narration: Chapter 8 Review vocabulary	Did you gain an understanding of how AP Chinese is tested? Can you remember the basic strategies for the 7 types of questions? What are the 3 steps of story-narration writing? Can you successfully narrate a story based on 4 pictures in 15 minutes? If not, why? Did you practice 200 new vocabulary words (use the fourth week to review the vocabulary)?	

(Continued)

MONTH	GOAL	GOAL CHECKLIST	CHECK OFF
November	Learn 10 vocabulary words per day **Week 1** Learn to write an e-mail and start to build templates: Chapter 9 **Week 2** Do the exercises on the e-mail response and refine your templates: Chapter 9 **Week 3** Learn the strategies for listening rejoinders: Chapter 5 **Week 4** Do the exercises on listening rejoinders: Chapter 5 Review vocabulary	What are the 3 steps of writing an e-mail response?	
		Can you successfully finish an e-mail response task in 15 minutes? If not, why?	
		Did you build a template for the e-mail response with a reasonable amount of content? At least 100 characters?	
		What are the strategies for rejoinders?	
		Did you mark and review the set phrases and social formulas you have trouble with?	
		Did you practice 200 new vocabulary words (use the fourth week to review the vocabulary)?	
December	Learn 10 vocabulary words per day **Week 1** Learn the strategies for the listening selections: Chapter 6 **Week 2** Do the exercises on the listening selections: Chapter 6 **Week 3** Learn the strategies for conversation: Chapter 10 **Week 4** Do the exercises on conversation: Chapter 10 Review vocabulary	What are the strategies for each type of listening selection?	
		Analyze your performance on the exercises of Chapter 6. What type of selections do you need to practice more? How?	
		What are the strategies for the conversation responses?	
		Record your answers for the questions. Try to identify your weaknesses in answering conversation prompts.	
		Did you learn all the vocabulary and expressions listed in Chapter 6?	

MONTH	GOAL	GOAL CHECKLIST	CHECK OFF
January	Learn 5 expressions per day **Week 1** Learn the strategies for the reading selections: Chapter 7 **Week 2** Do the exercises on the reading selections: Chapter 7 **Week 3** Learn the strategies for the cultural presentation: Chapter 11 **Week 4** Do the exercises on the cultural presentation: Chapter 11 Review expressions	What are the strategies for each type of question in reading comprehension?	
		Analyze your performance on the exercises of Chapter 7. What type of selections do you need to practice more? How?	
		What are the strategies for the cultural presentation?	
		Did you record good answers for the exercises involving native Chinese speakers?	
		Did you build on your template of culture presentation with a reasonable amount of content? 1–2 minutes?	
		Did you understand all the vocabulary in these sections? If not, did you note which words need further review?	
February	Learn 5 expressions per day **Week 1** Review: Chapter 3 **Week 2** Review Chapter 4 **Week 3** Review Chapter 5 **Week 4** Review Chapter 6 Review expressions	What did you find in this round of review that you did not pay attention to before?	
		What do you need to continue working on regarding listening?	
		Did you practice all the expressions in the appendix?	

(Continued)

MONTH	GOAL	GOAL CHECKLIST	CHECK OFF
March	Practice the free-response questions of previous years: 2007–2010. **Week 1** Review Chapter 7 **Week 2** Review: Chapter 8 **Week 3** Review Chapter 10 **Week 4** Practice Exam 1 Review all your notes	Analyze your answers to the questions from previous exams based on the scoring guidelines of the College Board. What do you need to improve?	
		What did you find by this round of review that you did not pay attention to before?	
		What do you need to continue working on regarding reading, story narration, and conversation?	
		What do you need to improve on in Practice Exam 1? What weaknesses can you identify?	
		Did you review all your notes?	
April	Practice free-response questions of previous years: 2011–present. **Week 1** Review Chapter 9 **Week 2** Review Chapter 11 **Week 3** Practice Exam 2 **Week 4** Final review: Any content you highlighted in this book or marked on this checklist Memorize all the required templates.	Analyze your answers to the questions from previous exams based on the scoring guidelines of the College Board. What do you need to improve?	
		What did you find in this round of review that you did not pay attention to before?	
		What do you need to continue working on regarding the e-mail response and the cultural conversation? Did you memorize your templates thoroughly?	
		Where did you show the greatest improvement in Practice Exam 2? Are there still any weaknesses you need to work on?	
		Did you review all the difficult items you marked or highlighted before?	

Plan B: One Semester

MONTH	GOAL	GOAL CHECKLIST	CHECK OFF
January	Learn 20 vocabulary words per day **Week 1** Diagnostic exam and reflection: Chapter 3 **Week 2** Write a story with functional grammar: Appendix **Week 3** Learn exam strategies: Chapter 4 **Week 4** Learn exam strategies: Chapter 8 Review vocabulary	Can you identify your weakness using the self-evaluation worksheets in Chapter 4 to evaluate your performance on the diagnostic test? What are your weaknesses?	
		Can you freely use 9 different functions for complex sentences?	
		Can you recite the basic strategies for the 7 types of questions?	
		What are the three steps of writing a story narration? Can you successfully narrate a story based on four pictures in 15 minutes?	
		Did you practice 200 new vocabulary words (use the fourth week to review the vocabulary)?	
February	Learn 20 vocabulary words per day **Week 1** Learn exam strategies: Chapter 9 **Week 2** Learn exam strategies: Chapter 5 **Week 3** Learn exam strategies: Chapter 6 **Week 4** Learn exam strategies: Chapter 10	What are the three steps of writing an e-mail response? Can you successfully finish the e-mail-response task in 15 minutes?	
		Did you build a template for the e-mail response with reasonable amount of content? At least 100 characters?	
		What are the strategies for the rejoinders? Did you mark and review the set phrases/social formula you have trouble with?	
		Did you practice 200 new vocabulary words (use the fourth week to review the vocabulary)?	

(Continued)

MONTH	GOAL	GOAL CHECKLIST	CHECK OFF
March	Learn 20 vocabulary words per day **Week 1** Learn exam strategies: Chapter 7 **Week 2** Learn exam strategies: Chapter 11 **Week 3** Review exam strategies: Chapters 5, 6, 7 **Week 4** Review exam strategies: Chapters 8, 9, 10, 11	What are the strategies for the reading comprehension? What type of reading selection do you need to continue working on?	
		What are the strategies for the cultural presentation?	
		Did you record good answers for the cultural presentation topics? Did you do this in 1–2 minutes?	
		What did you find in this round of review that you did not pay attention to before?	
		Did you practice expressions from the appendix and review them?	
April	**Week 1** Practice Exam 1 Free-response questions: 2007–2010 **Week 2** Memorize templates for e-mail response and cultural presentation **Week 3** Practice Exam 2 Free-response questions: 2011–present **Week 4** Final review: Any content you highlighted in this book or marked on this checklist	Analyze your answers to the questions from previous exams based on the scoring guidelines of the College Board. What do you need to improve?	
		Where did you show improvement on Practice Exam 2 from Practice Exam 1? What areas are still weaknesses for you?	
		Can you do the e-mail response and the cultural presentation without difficulty in the real exam?	
		Did you finish your final review of everything you had trouble with and marked before?	

Plan C: Six Weeks

MONTH	GOAL	GOAL CHECKLIST	CHECK OFF
Week 1	Learn 20 vocabulary words per day Chapters 3, 4 Appendix: Functional Grammar	Can you identify your weakness using the self-evaluation worksheets in Chapter 4 to evaluate your performance on the diagnostic test? What are your weaknesses?	
		Can you freely use 9 different functions for complex sentences?	
		Do you know all the vocabulary in Chapters 3 and 4?	
Week 2	Learn 20 vocabulary words per day Listening Rejoinders: Chapter 5 Listening Selections: Chapter 6 Presentational Writing: Chapter 8	What are the detailed strategies for listening and story narration?	
		Do you know all the vocabulary in Chapters 5, 6, 8?	
		Did you mark down anything you need to review further?	
Week 3	Learn 20 vocabulary words per day Interpersonal Writing: Chapter 9 Interpersonal Speaking: Chapter 10 Presentational Speaking: Chapter 11	What are the detailed strategies for e-mail response, conversation, and cultural presentation?	
		Do you know all the vocabulary in Chapters 9, 10, 11?	
		Did you mark down anything you need to review further?	
Week 4	Learn frequently used expressions: Appendix Reading Selections: Chapter 7 Review: Chapters 5, 6, 7	What are the detailed strategies for reading?	
		Do you know all the vocabulary in Chapters 5, 6, 7 and the frequently used expressions in the appendix?	
		Did you mark down anything you need to review further?	

(Continued)

MONTH	GOAL	GOAL CHECKLIST	CHECK OFF
Week 5	Free-response questions: 2007–2010 Practice Exam 1 Review: Chapters 8, 9, 10, 11	Analyze your answers to the questions from previous exams based on the scoring guidelines of the College Board. What do you need to improve?	
		Can you identify any weaknesses from your performance on Practice Exam 1? What do you need to improve?	
		Did you memorize the templates for e-mail response and cultural presentation?	
Week 6	Free-response questions: 2011–present Practice Exam 2 Final review: Any content you highlighted in this book or marked on this checklist	Where did you show improvement on Practice Exam 2 from Practice Exam 1? What areas are still weaknesses for you?	
		Did you finish a final review with everything you had trouble with and marked before?	

STEP **2**

Determine Your
Test Readiness

CHAPTER **3**   Take a Diagnostic Exam

CHAPTER 3

Take a Diagnostic Exam

IN THIS CHAPTER

Summary: This chapter contains a simulated AP Chinese Language and Culture Exam, which will familiarize you with the format of the actual exam. The content is carefully designed to cover the materials and topics frequently tested on the real exam. Use the results of this exam to determine your strengths and weaknesses. Then adapt your test prep plan to focus on the weaknesses you have identified.

KEY IDEA

Key Ideas

✪ Prepare for two hours to take the exam without interruption.
✪ Answer questions within the required time limits in each section.
✪ Check your work with the given answers of multiple-choice questions.
✪ Analyze your answers for free-response questions.
✪ Convert your score to a rough AP score.

Using the Diagnostic Exam

Before you start your test preparation plan, it is important to know what you are preparing for. The diagnostic exam in this chapter will introduce you to the test and show you what you will have to do on test day. Once you are done with the exam, carefully check your responses against the correct answers that follow the test. Explanations are provided for all questions so you can learn from any mistakes you make. Analyze your performance on the test to determine what your weakest areas are and then adapt your test prep plan (Chapter 2) to focus on the knowledge and skills you identified. At the end of the chapter you will find a scoring guide that will allow you to convert your score to a rough AP score.

How to Take the Exam

To get the most out of this diagnostic exam, you should try to simulate actual test-taking conditions as much as possible. Here are some tips that will help you:

- Plan to take the two-hour exam without interruption.
- Answer the questions within the required time limits in each section.
- For the multiple-choice questions on the actual test, you will click the letter (A, B, C, or D) for the correct answer. For this diagnostic test, simply circle the letter (A, B, C, or D) for the correct answer.

After the Test

When you are done with the test, you will need to spend some time reviewing the correct answers and the explanations. Then ask yourself what areas of the test were the most difficult for you. Try to analyze your performance to determine what your weaknesses are and focus on these in your test prep plan. Here are some tips that will help you:

- Check your work against the correct answers provided for the multiple-choice questions. Read the explanations, not only for the questions you missed, but for all of those you were not sure what the correct answer was.
- Read the explanations for all the free-response questions and compare your answers to the sample ones. Try to determine how you did and what areas you need to work on.
- Convert your score on this diagnostic test to a rough AP score. This will give you a rough idea of how you might do on the test if you took it today.

ANSWER SHEET

Part A: Listening

1 Ⓐ Ⓑ Ⓒ Ⓓ   13 Ⓐ Ⓑ Ⓒ Ⓓ   25 Ⓐ Ⓑ Ⓒ Ⓓ
2 Ⓐ Ⓑ Ⓒ Ⓓ   14 Ⓐ Ⓑ Ⓒ Ⓓ   26 Ⓐ Ⓑ Ⓒ Ⓓ
3 Ⓐ Ⓑ Ⓒ Ⓓ   15 Ⓐ Ⓑ Ⓒ Ⓓ   27 Ⓐ Ⓑ Ⓒ Ⓓ
4 Ⓐ Ⓑ Ⓒ Ⓓ   16 Ⓐ Ⓑ Ⓒ Ⓓ   28 Ⓐ Ⓑ Ⓒ Ⓓ
5 Ⓐ Ⓑ Ⓒ Ⓓ   17 Ⓐ Ⓑ Ⓒ Ⓓ   29 Ⓐ Ⓑ Ⓒ Ⓓ
6 Ⓐ Ⓑ Ⓒ Ⓓ   18 Ⓐ Ⓑ Ⓒ Ⓓ   30 Ⓐ Ⓑ Ⓒ Ⓓ
7 Ⓐ Ⓑ Ⓒ Ⓓ   19 Ⓐ Ⓑ Ⓒ Ⓓ   31 Ⓐ Ⓑ Ⓒ Ⓓ
8 Ⓐ Ⓑ Ⓒ Ⓓ   20 Ⓐ Ⓑ Ⓒ Ⓓ   32 Ⓐ Ⓑ Ⓒ Ⓓ
9 Ⓐ Ⓑ Ⓒ Ⓓ   21 Ⓐ Ⓑ Ⓒ Ⓓ   33 Ⓐ Ⓑ Ⓒ Ⓓ
10 Ⓐ Ⓑ Ⓒ Ⓓ   22 Ⓐ Ⓑ Ⓒ Ⓓ   34 Ⓐ Ⓑ Ⓒ Ⓓ
11 Ⓐ Ⓑ Ⓒ Ⓓ   23 Ⓐ Ⓑ Ⓒ Ⓓ   35 Ⓐ Ⓑ Ⓒ Ⓓ
12 Ⓐ Ⓑ Ⓒ Ⓓ   24 Ⓐ Ⓑ Ⓒ Ⓓ

Part B: Reading

1 Ⓐ Ⓑ Ⓒ Ⓓ   13 Ⓐ Ⓑ Ⓒ Ⓓ   25 Ⓐ Ⓑ Ⓒ Ⓓ
2 Ⓐ Ⓑ Ⓒ Ⓓ   14 Ⓐ Ⓑ Ⓒ Ⓓ   26 Ⓐ Ⓑ Ⓒ Ⓓ
3 Ⓐ Ⓑ Ⓒ Ⓓ   15 Ⓐ Ⓑ Ⓒ Ⓓ   27 Ⓐ Ⓑ Ⓒ Ⓓ
4 Ⓐ Ⓑ Ⓒ Ⓓ   16 Ⓐ Ⓑ Ⓒ Ⓓ   28 Ⓐ Ⓑ Ⓒ Ⓓ
5 Ⓐ Ⓑ Ⓒ Ⓓ   17 Ⓐ Ⓑ Ⓒ Ⓓ   29 Ⓐ Ⓑ Ⓒ Ⓓ
6 Ⓐ Ⓑ Ⓒ Ⓓ   18 Ⓐ Ⓑ Ⓒ Ⓓ   30 Ⓐ Ⓑ Ⓒ Ⓓ
7 Ⓐ Ⓑ Ⓒ Ⓓ   19 Ⓐ Ⓑ Ⓒ Ⓓ   31 Ⓐ Ⓑ Ⓒ Ⓓ
8 Ⓐ Ⓑ Ⓒ Ⓓ   20 Ⓐ Ⓑ Ⓒ Ⓓ   32 Ⓐ Ⓑ Ⓒ Ⓓ
9 Ⓐ Ⓑ Ⓒ Ⓓ   21 Ⓐ Ⓑ Ⓒ Ⓓ   33 Ⓐ Ⓑ Ⓒ Ⓓ
10 Ⓐ Ⓑ Ⓒ Ⓓ   22 Ⓐ Ⓑ Ⓒ Ⓓ   34 Ⓐ Ⓑ Ⓒ Ⓓ
11 Ⓐ Ⓑ Ⓒ Ⓓ   23 Ⓐ Ⓑ Ⓒ Ⓓ   35 Ⓐ Ⓑ Ⓒ Ⓓ
12 Ⓐ Ⓑ Ⓒ Ⓓ   24 Ⓐ Ⓑ Ⓒ Ⓓ

Diagnostic Exam: AP Chinese Language and Culture

Section I: Multiple-Choice Questions

Section I, Part A: Listening (20–25 minutes)

Rejoinders (Weight in Final Score: 10%)

In this part of the exam, you will finish 10 to 15 questions within 10 minutes. You will hear several short or incomplete conversations. The answer choices will be read to you instead of appearing on your computer screen. After listening to the conversation and its four possible continuations, you will choose the response that is the most logical and culturally appropriate to complete the conversation. You have five seconds to choose the answer, and you cannot go back to check or change it.

The listening selections for the questions are provided on the disc accompanying this book. Play the track number that is indicated. Then mark your answers on your answer sheet provided. After you complete the test you can refer to the scripts for the conversations and answer choices, which can be found starting on page 42. On the actual test, no written script will be provided for the conversations and answer choices you will hear.

Now let us get started with the listening part of the test.

Track 1

Rejoinders
1. (A) (B) (C) (D)
2. (A) (B) (C) (D)
3. (A) (B) (C) (D)
4. (A) (B) (C) (D)
5. (A) (B) (C) (D)
6. (A) (B) (C) (D)
7. (A) (B) (C) (D)
8. (A) (B) (C) (D)
9. (A) (B) (C) (D)
10. (A) (B) (C) (D)
11. (A) (B) (C) (D)
12. (A) (B) (C) (D)
13. (A) (B) (C) (D)
14. (A) (B) (C) (D)
15. (A) (B) (C) (D)

Listening Selections (Weight in Final Score: 15%)

You will hear some audio selections in Chinese. For each selection, you will be told if it will play once or twice. You will not be able to see the questions until the audio selection is completed. Therefore, note taking is crucial in this part of the exam. You will have 12 seconds to choose the response that best answers each question. You cannot go back to check or change your answer after the 12 seconds are up. Mark the letter of your answer choice on the answer sheet.

The listening tracks for the audio selections are provided on the CD-ROM accompanying this book. Circle the letter that corresponds to the correct answer. (On the actual test you will mark your answers on a separate answer sheet.) After you have taken the test, you can look at the scripts for the passages and questions; these can be found starting on page 49. On the actual test, no written script will be provided for the listening selections.

Let us start listening selections. **Remember, you are not allowed to look at the questions and the answer choices until each audio selection is finished.** Get your pencil and paper ready to take some notes.

Weather Report (Selection plays one time.)
Do not read the following questions until the audio selection has been completed.

16. What is the weather like this afternoon?

    (A) Cloudy to sunny
    (B) Windy
    (C) Rainy to cloudy
    (D) Snowy

17. When will it rain in some areas?

    (A) Daytime today
    (B) Nighttime today
    (C) Daytime tomorrow
    (D) No rain during the next two days

18. Which day is hotter, today or tomorrow?

    (A) Almost the same
    (B) Today is hotter
    (C) Tomorrow is hotter
    (D) Did not mention

Public Announcement (Selection plays twice.)
Do not read the following questions until the listening passage has been completed.

19. Where would the announcement be heard?

    (A) On a tour bus
    (B) In the rail station
    (C) On a subway train
    (D) In an airport

20. This announcement informs the passengers about

    (A) a delayed landing.
    (B) a delayed take off.
    (C) returning to their seats.
    (D) moving to another gate.

21. What are the passengers asked to do?

    (A) Go to another gate for free food
    (B) Go to another gate to buy food
    (C) Go to the lounge for free food
    (D) Go to the lounge to buy food

Voice Message (Selection plays one time.)
Do not read the following questions until the audio selection has been completed.

22. What was the speaker's original plan for the dinner tomorrow?

    (A) Treat her friends with Chongqing Hot Pot
    (B) Go to Little Tokyo Restaurant
    (C) Eat Chongqing Hot Pot first, then go to Little Tokyo
    (D) Pick up Wang Xiaoyu

23. What caused the change of the speaker's original plan?

    (A) She cannot find Wang Xiaoyu.
    (B) Her friends will not come to meet.
    (C) She does not know how to get to the restaurant.
    (D) One of her friends booked another restaurant.

24. What will the speaker possibly do tomorrow?

    (A) She will go to Chongqing Hot Pot.
    (B) She will wait for her friends at home.
    (C) She will pick up one friend and meet the other at the restaurant.
    (D) She will pick up both of her friends.

School Conversation (Selection plays one time.)
Do not read the following questions until the audio selection has been completed.

25. What is the topic of the conversation?

    (A) Playing a music instrument
    (B) Preparing an art gallery exhibit
    (C) Cooking Chinese food
    (D) Planning culture events

26. What does the man plan to do on Wednesday?

    (A) Practice Chinese painting arts
    (B) Enjoy Chinese traditional music
    (C) Introduce Chinese traditional holidays
    (D) Cook Chinese food

27. What does the woman suggest to do on Friday?

    (A) Enjoy Chinese traditional music
    (B) Watch a Chinese movie
    (C) Cook Chinese food
    (D) Introduce Chinese traditional holidays

28. According to the passage, what will *not* be included in the cultural activities?

    (A) Learn Chinese martial arts
    (B) Watch a Chinese movie
    (C) Enjoy Chinese music
    (D) Introduce Chinese traditional holidays

Track 4

Track 5

Track 6

Instructions (Selection plays twice.)

Do not read the following questions until the audio selection has been completed.

29. What is the purpose of this instruction?

   (A)   How to make noodles
   (B)   How to cook noodles
   (C)   How to make dumplings
   (D)   How to cook dumplings

30. What is the second step in the instruction?

   (A)   Cook pork, beef, and chicken with vegetables.
   (B)   Make the stuffing.
   (C)   Boil the water.
   (D)   Fry the food.

31. What is *not* mentioned to cook the food?

   (A)   Steam cook
   (B)   Boil with water
   (C)   Fry
   (D)   Bake

32. Which statement is true according to this instruction?

   (A)   The skin of the food should be thicker in the middle.
   (B)   Seafood could not be used to make the fillings.
   (C)   The food normally does not have vegetables inside.
   (D)   The food looks like noodles.

Track 7

Radio Report (Selection plays one time.)

Do not read the following questions until the audio selection has been completed.

33. The report announces the event that is presenting what type of work?

   (A)   Sculpture
   (B)   Peking opera
   (C)   Painting
   (D)   Folk dance

34. What is the highest possible number of artists involved?

   (A)   20
   (B)   25
   (C)   30
   (D)   31

35. Which city is *not* mentioned in this passage?

   (A)   Shanghai
   (B)   Beijing
   (C)   Guangzhou
   (D)   Hong Kong

Section I, Part B: Reading (60 minutes)

Reading Selections (Weight in Final Score: 25%)

Read each passage and then choose the answer choice that best answers each question. You can switch between simplified Chinese and traditional Chinese. You are allowed to note down the key words and move back and forth between questions to check or change your answers. There is no time limit for each question, but you will need to finish all the questions within 60 minutes. On the actual test a clock on the computer screen will show how much time remains. For this test, you will need to time yourself.

Read this letter:

Simplified Chinese
发件人：李雷
收件人：周天林
邮件主题：租房
发件时间：2013年6月17日
周天林，
你好。我下个月十一号起会到北京学习两个月，想早一点在学校附近找到房子租住。我在网上看到华苑公寓有三间房出租，离你家也不太远，你能帮我去看一下吗？我的要求不高，只要屋子干净，有阳台，有冰箱和空调就行。如果你知道还有其他合适的房子，也请尽快告诉我。谢谢你！
李雷

Traditional Chinese
發件人：李雷
收件人：周天林
郵件主題：租房
發件時間：2013年6月17日
周天林，
你好。我下個月十一號起會到北京學習兩個月，想早一點在學校附近找到房子租住。我在網上看到華苑公寓有三間房出租，離你家也不太遠，你能幫我去看一下嗎？我的要求不高，只要屋子乾淨，有陽台，有冰箱和空調就行。如果你知道還有其他合適的房子，也請盡快告訴我。謝謝你！
李雷

1. The purpose of the note is to ask the recipient to

   (A) meet.
   (B) take a look at some rentals.
   (C) rent a place for the sender.
   (D) go to Beijing.

2. Where does the sender want to live when he is in Beijing?

   (A) An apartment near his school
   (B) His friend's house
   (C) A hotel
   (D) The school dormitory

3. Which factor is *not* listed as the sender's preferences of the rental?

(A) The place is clean.
(B) The place has Wi-Fi.
(C) The place has an air conditioner.
(D) The place has a balcony.

4. What do we learn from this e-mail about the recipient?

(A) The recipient likes living near the school.
(B) The recipient lives in Beijing.
(C) The recipient will rent a place for the sender.
(D) The recipient will go to China.

Read this e-mail:

Simplified Chinese
发件人：陈晨
收件人：钟雪华
邮件主题：向你问个好
发件时间：2013年11月28日
钟雪华，
你好。好久没和你联系了，你的大学申请提交了吗？我这个学期特别忙，连感恩节放假时我都没有出去玩。我学中文已经四年了，汉字学习问题不大，中文的语法却有一点儿难。我打算参加明年的全美高中生"汉语桥"演讲大赛，我的中文老师说我应该多练练口语，你有什么好的方法可以推荐一下吗？你说过春节那几天想来美国玩，千万别忘了过来看我啊！
陈晨

Traditional Chinese
發件人：陳晨
收件人：鐘雪華
郵件主題：向你問個好
發件時間：2013年11月28日
鐘雪華，
你好。好久沒和你聯繫了，你的大學申請提交了嗎？我這個學期特別忙，連感恩節放假時我都沒有出去玩。我學中文已經四年了，漢字學習問題不大，中文的語法卻有一點兒難。我打算參加明年的全美高中生"漢語橋"演講大賽，我的中文老師說我應該多練練口語，你有甚麼好的方法可以推薦一下嗎？你說過春節那幾天想來美國玩，千萬別忘了過來看我啊！
陳晨

5. The sender and recipient of the e-mail are

(A) coworkers.
(B) college students.
(C) a teacher and a student.
(D) high school students.

6. What does the sender think about learning Chinese?

(A) The characters are difficult.
(B) You need a lot of speaking practice.
(C) The grammar is a bit difficult.
(D) The grammar is not difficult.

7. What statement is *not* true about the sender according to this e-mail?

(A) The sender is going to participate in a speech contest next year.
(B) The recipient will come to the United States for the spring festival.
(C) The sender asks the recipient for some advice in practicing speaking.
(D) The sender played a lot on his Thanksgiving holiday.

Read this sign:

Simplified Chinese
电梯因故障停运，正在维修，请原谅。

Traditional Chinese
電梯因故障停運，正在維修，請原諒。

8. The purpose of the sign is to

(A) allow access for visitors.
(B) post the penalty of using a facility.
(C) stop people from using a facility.
(D) provide instruction for people with disabilities.

9. The sign's message is most likely directed to

(A) drivers on a road.
(B) visitors in a building.
(C) passengers on a train.
(D) pedestrians in a park.

Read this regulation:

Simplified Chinese
明雅博物馆参观须知
各位游客，为维护本馆的参观秩序和良好的参观环境，请您仔细阅读本须知。
1. 本馆每日限额接待1000人，观众请凭门票入馆。
2. 身高1.2米以下的儿童须由家长陪同参观，行动不便的老年人须由亲友陪同参观。
3. 保持馆内清洁，请勿在馆内吸烟或乱扔果皮纸屑。
4. 馆内允许拍照或摄像，但请勿使用闪光灯。
5. 请勿将易燃易爆物品、管制器具、液状物体等危险品及宠物带入馆内。
6. 爱护馆内公共设施，请勿触摸展品。
明雅博物馆

Traditional Chinese

明雅博物館參觀須知

各位遊客，為維護本館的參觀秩序和良好的參觀環境，請您仔細閱讀本須知。

1. 本館每日限額接待1000人，觀眾請憑門票入館。
2. 身高1.2米以下的兒童須由家長陪同參觀，行動不便的老年人須由親友陪同參觀。
3. 保持館內清潔，請勿在館內吸煙或亂扔果皮紙屑。
4. 館內允許拍照或攝像，但請勿使用閃光燈。
5. 請勿將易燃易爆物品、管制器具、液狀物體等危險品及寵物帶入館內。
6. 愛護館內公共設施，請勿觸摸展品。

明雅博物館

10. The regulations are mostly likely seen

   (A) in a museum.
   (B) in a gym.
   (C) in a classroom.
   (D) in a library.

11. What is required to enter the place?

   (A) Pets
   (B) Seniors
   (C) Cameras
   (D) Tickets

12. According to the regulation, what are you not allowed to bring in?

   (A) Camera
   (B) Video recorder
   (C) Pet
   (D) Food

13. According to the regulation, what is *not* prohibited in the museum?

   (A) Bringing in a liquid
   (B) Taking a photo
   (C) Smoking
   (D) Touching the display items

14. According to the regulation, which statement is *not* true?

   (A) Children not accompanied by an adult are not allowed to enter the museum.
   (B) No littering is permitted in the museum.
   (C) The maximum number of visitors is one thousand daily.
   (D) Turn off the flash when you are taking a photo.

Read this advertisement:

Simplified Chinese
浏阳电视台
诚聘暑期工作人员
要求热情细心、吃苦耐劳
在校学生和会说英语者优先
详情请联系：8362–0372 罗女士

Traditional Chinese
瀏陽電視台
誠聘暑期工作人員
要求熱情細心、吃苦耐勞
在校學生和會說英語者優先
詳情請聯繫：8362–0372 羅女士

15. The advertisement is placed by

    (A) a training center.
    (B) a school.
    (C) a TV station.
    (D) a company.

16. The purpose of the advertisement is to recruit

    (A) a native Chinese speaker.
    (B) a student tutor for summer.
    (C) a temporary worker for summer.
    (D) an experienced manager for summer.

17. According to the statement, which quality is *not* mandatory?

    (A) Being warm-hearted
    (B) The ability to speak English
    (C) Being detail-oriented
    (D) Being a hard worker

18. The priority will be given to the candidates who

    (A) are well experienced.
    (B) are students and detail oriented.
    (C) are teachers and work hard.
    (D) are students and can speak English.

Read this announcement on a poster:

Simplified Chinese

签证

非中国公民赴华旅游必须申请中国签证。请提供以下材料：
护照正本：有效期为六个月以上，有不少于两页的空白签证页

签证申请表：请完整填写，并附上彩色护照照片一张
邀请函：可为传真件、复印件或打印件
往返机票：接受电子机票
签证费为一百三十美元。可使用现金、现金支票或信用卡支付，不接受个人支票。

Traditional Chinese

簽證

非中國公民赴華旅遊必須申請中國簽證。請提供以下材料：
護照正本：有效期為六個月以上，有不少於兩頁的空白簽證頁
簽證申請表：請完整填寫，並附上彩色護照照片一張
邀請函：可為傳真件、復印件或打印件
往返機票：接受電子機票
簽證費為一百三十美元。可使用現金、現金支票或信用卡支付，不接受個人支票。

19. The purpose of this sign is to

    (A) provide instructions for applying for a passport.
    (B) ask people to buy the round-trip tickets.
    (C) allow immigrants to enter China.
    (D) direct people to apply for a visa.

20. What is *not* a requirement regarding the passport?

    (A) It has to be issued from the United States.
    (B) It has to be an original copy.
    (C) It has to be valid no less than six months.
    (D) It has to have at least two blank visa pages.

21. According to the announcement, what kind of payment is *not* accepted?

    (A) Cash
    (B) Credit card
    (C) Personal check
    (D) Cashier's check

22. What statement is true according to the announcement?

    (A) Only a color photo is accepted for the visa application.
    (B) The invitation letter cannot be a faxed copy.
    (C) The fee for the passport is $130.
    (D) E-tickets are not accepted.

Read this notice:

Simplified Chinese

第二中学文理分科通知

各位同学：
欢迎进入第二中学高中部学习。

我们的学习方向将分为文科和理科。除了语、数、外，文科学生主修历史、政治和地理，大学报考的专业一般与所学课程有关。理科生主修化学、物理和生物，大学报考的一般为理学和工学两方面的专业。文理兼收的专业包括经济学类、法学类、工商管理类等。请同学们认真查看细则，对自己未来的学习方向做出慎重选择。

第二中学高中部

五月七日

Traditional Chinese

第二中學文理分科通知

各位同學：

歡迎進入第二中學高中部學習。

我們的學習方向將分為文科和理科。除了語、數、外，文科學生主修歷史、政治和地理，大學報考的專業一般與所學課程有關。理科生主修化學、物理和生物，大學報考的一般為理學和工學兩方面的專業。文理兼收的專業包括經濟學類、法學類、工商管理類等。請同學們認真查看細則，對自己未來的學習方向做出慎重選擇。

第二中學高中部

五月七日

23. The announcement on a poster is primarily to

    (A) introduce course expectations.
    (B) provide information on courses for different majors.
    (C) give notice to students to write a college application.
    (D) provide a syllabus.

24. According to the notice, which course is *not* required for the students following the path of science?

    (A) Foreign language
    (B) Chinese language arts
    (C) Politics
    (D) Physics

25. Which college major will accept any student regardless of what path he or she follows?

    (A) Biology
    (B) History
    (C) Chemistry
    (D) Economics

Read this news article:

Simplified Chinese

中国年轻人社交的主流：ＱＱ

ＱＱ近年来成为中国年轻人广泛使用的沟通平台，并形成了独特的青年ＱＱ群文化。要是有人在ＱＱ上赞美你"可爱"，千万不要太激动，这个词的意思其实是"可怜没人爱"；如果有人发三个数字"520"给你，代表的意思是"我爱你”。类似的ＱＱ语言难倒了无数父母：现在的孩子们啊，到底在交流些什么呢？太可怕了！要不要禁止他们使用ＱＱ呢？

其实ＱＱ远没有想象中的那么可怕。在中国，ＱＱ不仅是一种类似网上聊天室的娱乐工具，而且在人们的学习、生活甚至工作中也发挥着越来越显著的重要作用。使用ＱＱ可以和任何人成为好友，也可以随时阻止任何人和你交流；可以加入你感兴趣的群落，也可以自己组织有共同爱好的朋友一起群聊，有许多公司也倾向于把ＱＱ作为员工内部交流的工具。

ＱＱ在中国的地位和“脸书”(Facebook)在美国的地位相当，与其兼容的视频聊天、游戏、商城、微信等功能又打开了更为广阔的市场。它满足了年轻人在理想、社交和情感等方面的各种需求，其作用也越来越多样化。

Traditional Chinese

中國年輕人社交的主流：ＱＱ

ＱＱ近年來成為中國年輕人廣泛使用的溝通平台，並形成了獨特的青年ＱＱ群文化。要是有人在ＱＱ上讚美你“可愛”，千萬不要太激動，這個詞的意思其實是“可憐沒人愛”；如果有人發三個數字“520”給你，代表的意思是“我愛你”。類似的ＱＱ語言難倒了無數父母：現在的孩子們啊，到底在交流些甚麼呢？太可怕了！要不要禁止他們使用ＱＱ呢？

其實ＱＱ遠沒有想象中的那麼可怕。在中國，ＱＱ不僅是一種類似網上聊天室的娛樂工具，而且在人們的學習、生活甚至工作中也發揮著越來越顯著的重要作用。使用ＱＱ可以和任何人成為好友，也可以隨時阻止任何人和你交流；可以加入你感興趣的群落，也可以自己組織有共同愛好的朋友一起群聊，有許多公司也傾向於把ＱＱ作為員工內部交流的工具。

ＱＱ在中國的地位和“臉書”(Facebook)在美國的地位相當，與其兼容的視頻聊天、遊戲、商城、微信等功能又打開了更為廣闊的市場。它滿足了年輕人在理想、社交和情感等方面的各種需求，其作用也越來越多樣化。

26. Which of the following best describes the primary function of QQ?

 (A) QQ provides a platform for the parents to communicate with their children.
 (B) QQ provides a chat room for youth.
 (C) QQ provides a platform for communication that is widely used by the youth in China.
 (D) QQ provides a conference room for business.

27. What does 520 mean in the QQ language?

 (A) I love you.
 (B) Very cute.
 (C) Without love.
 (D) The number 520.

28. The article listed QQ's various functions *except* for

 (A) providing an alarm clock.
 (B) group chatting.
 (C) playing games.
 (D) video chatting.

29. What statement is *not* true according to the article?

    (A)   QQ is quite scary to some parents.

    (B)   QQ cannot block the people you do not want to communicate with.

    (C)   QQ is used by some companies for their employees to communicate.

    (D)   Facebook has some functions similar to QQ.

Read this short story:

Simplified Chinese

夸父穿过一座座高山，跨过一条条河流，越跑越快，经过九天九夜，在太阳落山的地方，夸父终于追上了它。他想把太阳捉住，可是太阳太热了，夸父觉得又渴又累，转身跑到黄河边，没几口就把黄河的水喝干了。他跑到渭河边，一口气又把渭河的水喝干了。夸父还是很口渴，再往北方跑，越跑越慢，终于倒下去渴死了，化成了一座雄伟的大山。临死前，夸父觉得没有捉住太阳很遗憾。他牵挂着大地上的人们，于是将手中的木杖扔了出去。不一会儿，这木杖就化成了一大片绿色的桃林。这片桃林每年都要结出又多又大的桃子，要是路人口渴了，摘一颗尝尝又鲜又甜。

Traditional Chinese

夸父穿過一座座高山，跨過一條條河流，越跑越快，經過九天九夜，在太陽落山的地方，夸父終於追上了它。他想把太陽捉住，可是太陽太熱了，夸父覺得又渴又累，轉身跑到黃河邊，沒幾口就把黃河的水喝乾了。他跑到渭河邊，一口氣又把渭河的水喝乾了。夸父還是很口渴，再往北方跑，越跑越慢，終於倒下去渴死了，化成了一座雄偉的大山。臨死前，夸父覺得沒有捉住太陽很遺憾。他牽掛著大地上的人們，於是將手中的木杖扔了出去。不一會兒，這木杖就化成了一大片綠色的桃林。這片桃林每年都要結出又多又大的桃子，要是路人口渴了，摘一顆嚐嚐又鮮又甜。

30. The story begins with a description of the

    (A)   tree.

    (B)   sun.

    (C)   hero.

    (D)   bird.

31. Which statement is *not* true about the hero?

    (A)   He can fly like a bird.

    (B)   He is tall and huge.

    (C)   He runs fast.

    (D)   He is a good-hearted man.

32. Why did the hero decide to chase the sun?

    (A)   He likes the sun.

    (B)   He does not like sunlight.

    (C)   He wanted to leave the forest.

    (D)   He wanted the sun to stay in the sky all the time.

33. Which of the following lasted for nine days and nine nights?

(A) The time he lived in the forest
(B) The time he spent drinking the water of the rivers
(C) The time he spent chasing the sun
(D) The hero's lifetime

34. How did the hero die?

(A) The sun burned him.
(B) He died of thirst.
(C) He ran too fast and fell down.
(D) He was too disappointed with the sun.

35. What statement is true according to the story?

(A) His body was transformed into peach trees.
(B) His wood stick was transformed into peach trees.
(C) At the end, the sun was caught by the hero.
(D) The hero was very happy before he died.

Section II: Free-Response Questions

Section II, Part A: Writing (30 minutes)

Story Narration (Weight in Final Score: 15%)

You will have 15 minutes to finish the task of story narration. On the real test there will be a clock on your screen telling you how much time is left. For this practice test, you will need to time yourself.

Based on the four pictures provided, you need to write a coherent story with a beginning, a middle, and an ending. On the test you will need to type your answer using either the preset input of Microsoft IME or Microsoft New Phonetic IME system to type Chinese characters. You can switch between simplified Chinese and traditional Chinese.

The following four pictures present a story. Imagine you are telling the story to a friend. Write a complete story as suggested by the pictures. Give your story a beginning, a middle, and an ending.

E-Mail Response (Weight in Final Score: 10%)

You will have 15 minutes to read an e-mail message from a specific person and type a response. On the real test there will be a clock on your screen telling you how much time is left. For this practice test, you will need to time yourself.

On the test you will need to type your response using the preset input of Microsoft IME or Microsoft New Phonetic IME system to type Chinese characters. You can switch between simplified Chinese and traditional Chinese.

Read this e-mail from a friend and then type a response.

Simplified Chinese
发件人：周立友
邮件主题：中国旅游
小新，
你好！我暑假会去中国玩一个星期。我希望可以到香港看一看我的朋友，也可以去北京爬一下长城。我只有时间去三个城市，你觉得最后一个选西安好还是选上海好呢？还有，你对于在中国旅游的安全问题有什么建议吗？希望早点收到你的回信。

Traditional Chinese
發件人：周立友
郵件主題：中國旅遊
小新，
你好！我暑假會去中國玩一個星期。我希望可以到香港看一看我的朋友，也可以去北京爬一下長城。我只有時間去三個城市，你覺得最後一個選西安好還是選上海好呢？還有，你對於在中國旅遊的安全問題有甚麼建議嗎？希望早點收到你的回信。

Section II, Part B: Speaking

Track 8

Conversation (Weight in Final Score: 10%)

In this part of the exam, you will participate in a simulated conversation by responding to questions you will hear. The questions are based on a particular topic in a conversation with a particular person. There will be six 20-second pauses in the conversation during which you need to speak a response to the question(s) you have been asked. On the actual test, your 20-second response will be recorded and graded later.

Now you will have a conversation with Chen Ming, a friend from China, about your school life in the United States.

The listening track for conversation is provided on the CD accompanying this book. After you are done with the test, you may refer to the written script for the questions, which can be found starting on page 51. On the actual test, no script is provided for the conversation.

Cultural Presentation (Weight in Final Score: 15%)

In this part of the exam, you will make a presentation on a cultural topic you are given. You will have four minutes to prepare and then two minutes to make your oral presentation. On the actual test, your two-minute presentation will be recorded and then graded later. There will be a clock on your computer screen telling you how much time is left on the real test. For this practice test, you will need to time yourself.

Choose one famous Chinese person (e.g., a movie star, sports star, leader, author, musician, artist). In your presentation, describe the person in detail and explain his or her significance.

END OF DIAGNOSTIC TEST

Scripts for the Audio Portions of the Test

Scripts for Section I, Part A: Listening Rejoinders

Track 1

Question #1

Simplified Chinese

Woman: 请问，这里是湖景大厦E座吗？
Man: 不，这里是湖景大厦A座。从这往前走，左边第三个入口处是E座。
Woman:

(A) 湖景大厦E座在哪？
(B) 我喜欢逛商店。
(C) 谢谢，左边第三个入口，我记住了。
(D) 我们到湖景大厦以后做什么呢？

Traditional Chinese

Woman: 請問，這裡是湖景大廈E座嗎？
Man: 不，這裡是湖景大廈A座。從這往前走，左邊第三個入口處是E座。
Woman:

(A) 湖景大廈E座在哪？
(B) 我喜歡逛商店。
(C) 謝謝，左邊第三個入口，我記住了。
(D) 我們到湖景大廈以後做甚麼呢？

Question #2

Simplified Chinese

Woman: 你的头怎么这么烫？你烧得太厉害了，赶快去看大夫吧！
Man:

(A) 我很喜欢看大夫。
(B) 我刚刚看过大夫了，他给我打完针以后还开了很多药。
(C) 我得帮你买药。
(D) 你休息几天就好了。

Traditional Chinese

Woman: 你的頭怎麼這麼燙？你燒得太厲害了，趕快去看大夫吧！
Man:

(A) 我很喜歡看大夫。
(B) 我剛剛看過大夫了，他給我打完針以後還開了很多藥。
(C) 我得幫你買藥。
(D) 你休息幾天就好了。

Question #3

Simplified Chinese

Woman: 文英，你难道不知道怎么做鱼吗？看看，鱼都烧焦了！
Man: 啊，书上不是说要焖二十分钟吗？
Woman:

(A) 我不喜欢读书。
(B) 这条鱼真小。
(C) 书上说焖鱼要用小火，而且你都弄了快半个小时了！
(D) 你当然知道怎么做鱼。

Traditional Chinese

Woman: 文英，你難道不知道怎麼做魚嗎？看看，魚都燒焦了！
Man: 啊，書上不是說要燜二十分鐘嗎？
Woman:

(A) 我不喜歡讀書。
(B) 這條魚真小。
(C) 書上說燜魚要用小火，而且你都弄了快半個小時了！
(D) 你當然知道怎麼做魚。

Question #4

Simplified Chinese

Man: 我真后悔没去买古典音乐会的票，听说这次的表演特别精彩。
Woman: 你运气好，我刚好有两张星期五的票。
Man:

(A) 我们星期五去表演吧。
(B) 我也喜欢爵士乐。
(C) 我的运气一点也不好。
(D) 太棒了！我星期五可以来接你。

Traditional Chinese

Man: 我真後悔沒去買古典音樂會的票，聽說這次的表演特別精彩。
Woman: 你運氣好，我剛好有兩張星期五的票。
Man:

(A) 我們星期五去表演吧。
(B) 我也喜歡爵士樂。
(C) 我的運氣一點也不好。
(D) 太棒了！我星期五可以來接你。

Question #5

Simplified Chinese
Man: 你这件衣服挺漂亮的，在哪儿买的？
Woman:

(A) 这件衣服是很漂亮。
(B) 我买的衣服比你买的便宜多了。
(C) 这次逛商店真不容易，走了好几个钟头。
(D) 当然是在淘宝网上买的。

Traditional Chinese
Man: 你這件衣服挺漂亮的，在哪兒買的？
Woman:

(A) 這件衣服是很漂亮。
(B) 我買的衣服比你買的便宜多了。
(C) 這次逛商店真不容易，走了好幾個鐘頭。
(D) 當然是在淘寶網上買的。

Question #6

Simplified Chinese
Woman: 春节快到了，你打算出去旅游吗？
Man:

(A) 人太多了，我还是呆在家里更好。
(B) 去年春节我去中国玩了。
(C) 你们那儿过春节吃饺子吗？
(D) 你什么时候去旅游？

Traditional Chinese
Woman: 春節快到了，你打算出去旅遊嗎？
Man:

(A) 人太多了，我還是呆在家裡更好。
(B) 去年春節我去中國玩了。
(C) 你們那兒過春節吃餃子嗎？
(D) 你甚麼時候去旅遊？

Question #7

Simplified Chinese
Man: 昨天给你打了好多个电话都没人接，可把我吓了一跳。
Woman: 哦，我的手机掉在出租车上了，今天才找回来。
Man:

(A) 出租车上也可以打电话吗？
(B) 你用的手机是什么牌子的？
(C) 手机的信号有时候是不太好，收不到。
(D) 原来是这样啊，以后你可得小心点，别再丢三落四了。

Traditional Chinese

Man: 昨天給你打了好多個電話都沒人接，可把我嚇了一跳。

Woman: 哦，我的手機掉在出租車上了，今天才找回來。

Man:

(A) 出租車上也可以打電話嗎？
(B) 你用的手機是甚麼牌子的？
(C) 手機的信號有時候是不太好，收不到。
(D) 原來是這樣啊，以後你可得小心點，別再丟三落四了。

Question #8

Simplified Chinese

Woman: 好久没见到你了，是不是天天都在家里学习啊？

Man: 没有，我搬到学校宿舍去了。我妈说我每天坐公共汽车来回去学校，花的时间太长了，她怕影响我学习。

Woman:

(A) 你妈每天坐公共汽车其实很辛苦。
(B) 那你觉得在家住好还是在学校住比较好呢？
(C) 我们学校的宿舍很好。
(D) 你天天在家呆的时间太长了，应该出来玩玩。

Traditional Chinese

Woman: 好久沒見到你了，是不是天天都在家裡學習啊？

Man: 沒有，我搬到學校宿捨去了。我媽説我每天坐公共汽車來回去學校，花的時間太長了，她怕影響我學習。

Woman:

(A) 你媽每天坐公共汽車其實很辛苦。
(B) 那你覺得在家住好還是在學校住比較好呢？
(C) 我們學校的宿舍很好。
(D) 你天天在家呆的時間太長了，應該出來玩玩。

Question #9

Simplified Chinese

Woman: 听说我们的中文老师病了，所以她今天没来上课。

Man:

(A) 那你得赶快吃药啊！
(B) 干脆我们去上历史课吧。
(C) 原来学中文这么有意思！
(D) 难怪李明说我们今天不用上中文课。

Traditional Chinese

Woman: 聽說我們的中文老師病了，所以她今天沒來上課。

Man:

(A) 那你得趕快吃藥啊！
(B) 乾脆我們去上歷史課吧。
(C) 原來學中文這麼有意思！
(D) 難怪李明說我們今天不用上中文課。

Question #10

Simplified Chinese

Man: 气死人了！排了那么长时间的队，结果轮到我的时候红烧排骨已经卖完了！

Woman:

(A) 我喜欢吃麻婆豆腐。
(B) 我也很讨厌吃红烧排骨。
(C) 没关系，我晚上请你吃红烧排骨！
(D) 你一点也不生气。

Traditional Chinese

Man: 氣死人了！排了那麼長時間的隊，結果輪到我的時候紅燒排骨已經賣完了！

Woman:

(A) 我喜歡吃麻婆豆腐。
(B) 我也很討厭吃紅燒排骨。
(C) 沒關係，我晚上請你吃紅燒排骨！
(D) 你一點也不生氣。

Question #11

Simplified Chinese

Woman: 上次你说找了份周末的兼职，做得怎么样？

Man: 我觉得还挺不错的，从早上九点到下午五点，挣的钱刚好可以让我交学钢琴的学费。

Woman:

(A) 弹钢琴这份工作累不累？
(B) 我也想找份周末的兼职工作，不过我只有晚上有时间。
(C) 好吧，我们周末一起去学钢琴吧。
(D) 周末做做义工还是挺开心挺充实的。

Traditional Chinese

Woman: 上次你說找了份週末的兼職，做得怎麼樣？

Man: 我覺得還挺不錯的，從早上九點到下午五點，掙的錢剛好可以讓我交學鋼琴的學費。

Woman:

(A) 彈鋼琴這份工作累不累？

(B) 我也想找份週末的兼職工作，不過我只有晚上有時間。

(C) 好吧，我們週末一起去學鋼琴吧。

(D) 週末做做義工還是挺開心挺充實的。

Question #12

Simplified Chinese

Man: 你的化学作业做完了吗？

Woman: 正头疼呢，写到一半电脑就死机了，重新启动也启动不了。

Man:

(A) 我的电脑是新的。

(B) 头疼得看医生吃药啊。

(C) 化学作业实在是太多了。

(D) 大概是有病毒吧，你可以先用一下图书馆的电脑。

Traditional Chinese

Man: 你的化學作業做完了嗎？

Woman: 正頭疼呢，寫到一半電腦就死機了，重新啓動也啓動不了。

Man:

(A) 我的電腦是新的。

(B) 頭疼得看醫生吃藥啊。

(C) 化學作業實在是太多了。

(D) 大概是有病毒吧，你可以先用一下圖書館的電腦。

Question #13

Simplified Chinese

Man: 晓真，从洛杉矶飞到上海，坐了挺长时间吧？要不要先休息一下？

Woman:

(A) 我喜欢假期到中国旅游。

(B) 洛杉矶比上海凉快一些，所以我不热。

(C) 我在飞机上睡了一觉，所以并不太累。我们先吃饭吧。

(D) 我回到洛杉矶一定给你打电话。

Traditional Chinese

Man: 曉真，從洛杉磯飛到上海，坐了挺長時間吧？要不要先休息一下？

Woman:

(A) 我喜歡假期到中國旅遊。
(B) 洛杉磯比上海涼快一些，所以我不熱。
(C) 我在飛機上睡了一覺，所以並不太累。我們先吃飯吧。
(D) 我回到洛杉磯一定給你打電話。

Question #14

Simplified Chinese

Woman: 你得快点把书还给我呀！我在图书馆借的书，明天就到期了。

Man:

(A) 倒也是，我们一起去借书吧。
(B) 没事，你什么时候还都可以。
(C) 糟糕，图书馆关门了，我怎么还书啊！
(D) 我知道，所以我今天把书给你带来了。谢谢你啊。

Traditional Chinese

Woman: 你得快點把書還給我呀！我在圖書館借的書，明天就到期了。

Man:

(A) 倒也是，我們一起去借書吧。
(B) 沒事，你甚麼時候還都可以。
(C) 糟糕，圖書館關門了，我怎麼還書啊！
(D) 我知道，所以我今天把書給你帶來了。謝謝你啊。

Question #15

Simplified Chinese

Woman: 看你满头大汗的，跑那么快干什么？

Man: 我把手提电脑忘在教室里了！我得赶快去找，还不知道能不能找到呢！

Woman:

(A) 啊？手提电脑掉了？我帮你一起找吧。
(B) 没想到，你的手提电脑和我的一样。
(C) 每天跑到教室去上课累不累啊？
(D) 幸好你带了手提电脑。

Traditional Chinese

Woman: 看你滿頭大汗的，跑那麼快幹甚麼？

Man: 我把手提電腦忘在教室裡了！我得趕快去找，還不知道能不能找到呢！

Woman:

(A) 啊？手提電腦掉了？我幫你一起找吧。
(B) 沒想到，你的手提電腦和我的一樣。
(C) 每天跑到教室去上課累不累啊？
(D) 幸好你帶了手提電腦。

Scripts for Section I, Part A: Listening Selections

Track 2

Weather Report
Narrator: Now you will listen to a weather report. This selection will be played twice.

Simplified Chinese
Man: 根据市气象台预报，今天白天我市天气为晴转多云，最高气温25℃左右，最低气温13℃，北风4—5级。今晚气温下降，多云转阴，局部有阵雨，最高气温21℃左右，最低气温11℃，北风1级。明后两天阴转晴，气温将在14℃～31℃，北风3—4级。

Traditional Chinese
Man: 根據市氣象台預報，今天白天我市天氣為晴轉多雲，最高氣溫25℃左右，最低氣溫13℃，北風4—5級。今晚氣溫下降，多雲轉陰，局部有陣雨，最高氣溫21℃左右，最低氣溫11℃，北風1級。明後兩天陰轉晴，氣溫將在14℃～31℃，北風3—4級。

Narrator: Now listen again.
Narrator: Now answer the questions for this selection.

Track 3

Public Announcement
Narrator: Now you will listen to a public announcement. This selection will be played twice.

Simplified Chinese
Woman: 各位旅客请注意，中国国际航空公司很抱歉地通知您，由于北京国际机场上空的天气原因，飞往北京的CA907次航班将延迟起飞，预计起飞时间为22点40分。请旅客们到候机室餐饮部免费享用本航空公司提供的点心。

Traditional Chinese
Woman: 各位旅客請注意，中國國際航空公司很抱歉地通知您，由於北京國際機場上空的天氣原因，飛往北京的CA907次航班將延遲起飛，預計起飛時間為22點40分。請旅客們到候機室餐飲部免費享用本航空公司提供的點心。

Narrator: Now listen again.
Narrator: Now answer the questions for this selection.

Track 4

Voice Message
Narrator: Now you will listen to a voice message. This selection will be played only once.

Simplified Chinese
Woman: 王晓雨，你好。我打了好几次电话你都不在，你去哪儿了？我想确认一下明天到底是在哪一家餐馆吃饭。我打算请你们去吃重庆火锅，可小丽说她先订了小东京餐馆。我在网上查过，上海有两个小东京，不清楚你们订的是哪一家。我先去接小丽，然后在餐馆门口和你见面，你觉得怎么样？我现在在学校，你打我的手机吧。

Traditional Chinese

Woman: 王曉雨，你好。我打了好幾次電話你都不在，你去哪兒了？我想確認一下明天到底是在哪一家餐館吃飯。我打算請你們去吃重慶火鍋，可小麗說她先訂了小東京餐館。我在網上查過，上海有兩個小東京，不清楚你們訂的是哪一家。我先去接小麗，然後在餐館門口和你見面，你覺得怎麼樣？我現在在學校，你打我的手機吧。

Narrator: Now answer the questions for this selection.

Track 5

School Conversation

Narrator: Now you will listen to a conversation between two students. This selection will be played only once.

Simplified Chinese

Woman: 李中，你们下个星期的文化周活动都准备好了吗？

Man: 都准备得差不多了。星期一展示中国的艺术，包括制作京剧脸谱啊、画国画啊、练书法啊什么的。第二天欣赏中国传统音乐表演，星期三介绍中国的传统节日，星期四品尝一下亲手做的中国菜，星期五的活动我们还没计划好。你有什么建议吗？

Woman: 我觉得你已经准备得很全面了，不如第五天就放几部中国电影吧，肯定很有意思。

Traditional Chinese

Woman: 李中，你們下個星期的文化周活動都準備好了嗎？

Man: 都準備得差不多了。星期一展示中國的藝術，包括製作京劇臉譜啊、畫國畫啊、練書法啊甚麼的。第二天欣賞中國傳統音樂表演，星期三介紹中國的傳統節日，星期四品嘗一下親手做的中國菜，星期五的活動我們還沒計劃好。你有甚麼建議嗎？

Woman: 我覺得你們已經準備得很全面了，不如第五天就放幾部中國電影吧，肯定很有意思。

Narrator: Now answer the questions for this selection.

Track 6

Instructions

Narrator: Now you will listen to someone giving instructions. This selection will be played twice.

Simplified Chinese

Man: 说到中国的食物，很多人都会想到美味的饺子。怎样做出来的饺子才好吃呢？第一步和面要均匀；第二步就是做饺子馅了，通常用的是猪肉、牛肉、鸡肉加蔬菜，也有喜欢海鲜的；第三步是擀饺子皮，要擀得中间厚边上薄一些；第四步是包饺子。包出来的饺子可以用水煮，可以蒸着吃，也可以煎得黄黄的，怎么做都好吃。

Traditional Chinese

Man: 說到中國的食物，很多人都會想到美味的餃子。怎樣做出來的餃子才好吃呢？第一步和面要均勻；第二步就是做餃子餡了，通常用的是豬肉、牛肉、雞肉加蔬菜，也有喜歡海鮮的；第三步是擀餃子皮，要擀得中間厚邊上薄一些；第四步是包餃子。包出來的餃子可以用水煮，可以蒸著吃，也可以煎得黃黃的，怎麼做都好吃。

Narrator: Now listen again.

Narrator: Now answer the questions for this selection.

Radio Report
Narrator: Now you will listen to a radio report. This selection will be played only once.

Track 7

Simplified Chinese
Man: 文化新闻大家关注。各位听众，今天的文化焦点是广州市文化局举办的"中国红"京剧表演。来自全国各地的三十多位京剧表演艺术家为我们带来了精彩的传统京剧和现代京剧，赢得了在场观众的阵阵掌声。该京剧艺术团还将到北京、西安和香港等地继续表演。

Traditional Chinese
Man: 文化新聞大家關注。各位聽眾，今天的文化焦點是廣州市文化局舉辦的"中國紅"京劇表演。來自全國各地的三十多位京劇表演藝術家為我們帶來了精彩的傳統京劇和現代京劇，贏得了在場觀眾的陣陣掌聲。該京劇藝術團還將到北京、西安和香港等地繼續表演。

Narrator: Now answer the questions for this selection.

Scripts for Section II, Part B: Speaking

Question Type A: Conversation
Narrator: You will have a conversation with Chen Ming, a friend from China, about your school life in the United States.

Track 8

Simplified Chinese
1. 你在美国哪个学校上学？你们那儿的天气怎么样？
2. 你在学校每个学期要选哪些课？你最喜欢哪门课？
3. 你们每天上课的时间长吗？请介绍一下你在学校每天的时间安排，好吗？
4. 听说美国的中学生经常会做义工，做义工会影响学习吗？请谈一谈你的看法。
5. 除了上学以外，美国的中学生还会参加什么样的社会活动？
6. 我下个学期会作为交换生来美国学习，你觉得我在学习方面需要注意哪些问题？

Traditional Chinese
1. 你在美國哪個學校上學？你們那兒的天氣怎麼樣？
2. 你在學校每個學期要選哪些課？你最喜歡哪門課？
3. 你們每天上課的時間長嗎？請介紹一下你在學校每天的時間安排，好嗎？
4. 聽說美國的中學生經常會做義工，做義工會影響學習嗎？請談一談你的看法。
5. 除了上學以外，美國的中學生還會參加甚麼樣的社會活動？
6. 我下個學期會作為交換生來美國學習，你覺得我在學習方面需要注意哪些問題？

Answers and Explanations for Section I (Multiple-Choice Questions)

In this section you will find the answers to the multiple-choice questions as well as complete explanations for all the answers. In the next chapter you will learn helpful strategies to approach each type of question on the exam. You will find more practice with the multiple-choice questions in Chapters 5 through 7 that will help you achieve a high score.

Answers and Explanations for the Listening Rejoinders

Answers

1. C	6. A	11. B
2. B	7. D	12. D
3. C	8. B	13. C
4. D	9. D	14. D
5. D	10. C	15. A

Explanations

1. (C) The woman asks for Building E in a community. The man provided the answer and the directions to get there. Choice (C) rephrases the directions and states that she remembered, which is a good continuation. Choice (A), "Where is Building E?" is a rephrasing of the woman's question instead of continuing the dialogue. "I like shopping" (B) is not related to the dialogue. Choice (D), "What do we do after entering the community?" does not make logical sense here.

2. (B) The woman states that the man has a fever and asks him to see the doctor. Both the words of 大夫 and 医生（醫生）mean "the doctor." The man answers that he just saw the doctor. The doctor gave him a shot and prescriptions for medicine. Choice (A) "I love seeing the doctor" does not follow the dialogue. "I have to get some medicine to you" (C) could be a great answer if it was from the woman, but it is the man who is sick. Choice (D) "You will be fine after a couple days' rest" could be something the doctor would say, but he is not in the conversation.

3. (C) The woman uses a set phrase 难道不（難道不）, which is commonly used in Chinese to demonstrate disagreement: do not, are not. She said "don't you know how to cook fish? Look, it is burned." The man answers in another popular structure of 不是说……吗（不是説……嗎）, which means "Isn't it true that…" which is used to clarify or confirm. The answer should be either to explain no or yes. "I don't like reading books" (A) and "This fish is really small" (B) have no relation to the dialogue. Choice (D) "Of course you know how to cook" has the opposite meaning of the woman's statement.

4. (D) The man states that he is "really regretting" not buying the tickets, while the woman states that she has two tickets. Most likely the man will want to use the tickets with the woman. "Great. I can pick you up on Friday" is correct. The phrase 你运气好（你運氣好）means "You are lucky." Choice (A), "Let's go to perform on Friday," changes the original action. "I like Jazz music also" (B) does not logically continue the topic. "I do not have good luck" (C) is incorrect. The woman said "You are lucky. I have two tickets for Friday." The man's answer should be happy and positive.

5. (D) The man asks "Where did you buy it?" "Of course, I bought it from Taobao" is a good answer. Taobao is a popular Chinese online shopping platform similar to Amazon. Choice C, "Shopping in the stores this time is really not easy. I have walked for hours," is an opinion from the woman but not an answer to the question. The answer should be related to the location; neither (A) nor (D) are.

6. (A) The woman asks whether the man wants to travel during spring festival. The man answers that he prefers staying at home since there will be too many people. Choice (B) "I went to China last year," Choice (C) "Do you eat dumplings…," and Choice (D) "When will you go traveling?" don't answer the woman's question.

7. (D) The man mentions that he was worried since he had made a lot of calls to the woman but nobody answered yesterday. The woman explains that she lost her cell phone in the taxi. She had not had the phone until today. The answer should be related to the incident of losing her phone. "I see. You should be more careful from now on. Do not be absent-minded again!" continues the dialogue logically. Choice (A) "Can you make phone calls in the taxi?" does not make sense. "Which brand of cell phone are you using?" (B) is not related to the dialogue. Choice (C) "The cell phone signal doesn't work sometimes. You can't receive the calls," does not continue the logic of the conversation.

8. (B) The woman has not seen the man for a while and asks whether he stays at home and studies every day. The man answers that he moved to the school dormitory. His mom said that it took a long time for him to take the bus and it probably would affect his study. "Which way makes you feel better, living at home or in school dormitory?" continues the dialogue logically. Choice (A) "It's actually very hard for your mom to take the bus everyday" is incorrect because his mom did not take the bus. Choice (C), "Our school dormitory is great," could be a correct answer if spoken by the man instead of the woman. Choice (D) is "You spent too much time at home. You should go out and play." Actually the man does not spend too much time at home. He just moved to the dormitory.

9. (D) The woman heard that the Chinese teacher was sick so that the teacher is absent today. The man should answer something related to this incident. "No wonder Li Ming says we do not need to go to Chinese class today" continues the conversation. "No wonder" 难 怪（難怪）is a commonly used phrase that indicates that the speaker understood what is happening. Choice (A), "Then you should take some medicine quickly," would only be correct if he were to say: "Then *the teacher* should take some medicine quickly." "Then let's go to history class" (A) and "It turned out that learning Chinese is so interesting" (C) are both off topic.

10. (C) The man demonstrates his anger about "Hong Shao Pai Gu" being sold out after waiting in a long line. X followed by 死人了 is a commonly used structure which means "really X." Thus, really angry is 气死人了（氣死人了）and really funny is 笑死人了. You may not be able to understand what "Hong Shao Pai Gu" is, but from the frequently heard word of "eat" 吃 , you can guess it is some kind of food so you can regard this as "food X." Choice (C), "Don't worry. I will treat you X tonight," directly addresses the man's emotion and provides solution. Choice (A), "I like eating Ma Po To Fu," is off topic. Choice (B), "I don't like eating X," states the woman's opinion of food X but not the feelings of the man. "You are not mad at all" (D) is a statement opposite to what the man says.

11. (B) The woman asks the man about his weekend "part-time job" 兼职（兼職）. The man answers that he thinks it is quite good. He can spend the money he earned to pay for piano classes. Choice (B), "I want to find a weekend part-time job as well, but only in the evening," follows naturally. Choice (A), "Is your job of playing the piano tiring?" is incorrect since the man does not have a job playing the piano. "OK, let's learn piano on the weekends" (C) does not make sense because the man says he works weekends. "Doing volunteer work on the weekends is quite rewarding" (D) is off topic.

12. (D) After the man's question about finishing chemistry homework, the woman states that she is having a headache because her computer froze when the homework was half done. She could not restart it. So the answer should be related to the "computer" instead of "headache" 头疼（頭疼）(B) or "homework" (C). "My computer is new" (A) does not continue the conversation. Therefore, (D) is correct: "Probably got a virus. You can use the computer in the library."

13. (C) The man asks Xiaozhen, "From LA to Shanghai was a long trip, wasn't it? Do you want to take a break?" There is a lot of information in it, which may result in confusion. Pay attention to the last part and you can get the answer of (C) if you know the meaning of "taking a break" 休息. Or, because their content is off topic, you may eliminate the incorrect answers: "Travel in China on holidays" (A), "Los Angeles is cooler than Shanghai" (B), and "I definitely will call you once I return to LA" (D).

14. (D) The woman says: "You have to return the book to me. I borrowed it from the library. Tomorrow is the due date." "Due date" 到期，最后期限（最後期限）is an important word in AP Chinese courses and you are probably familiar with it. Choice (D), "I know, therefore I brought your book today. Thank you very much," continues the conversation. Both (A) and (B) are off topic. But you need to pay attention to (C), "Oh no, the library is closed. How could I return the book?" The content is closely related to the question, but it does not accurately fit the situation.

15. (A) The woman is surprised why the man is running so fast. You can probably understand something related to "computer," "classroom," and "not sure whether I can find it or not" in the man's response You may guess the meaning even if you do not know 忘 means "forget." The answer most likely will be related to "looking for," which fits Choice (A). Choice (B), "I didn't know your laptop is the same as mine" and Choice (C), "Are you tired running to the classroom everyday?" are both off topic. "Lucky that you brought your laptop" (D) does not fit the situation.

Answers and Explanations for the Listening Selections

Answers

16. A	21. C	26. C	31. D
17. B	22. A	27. B	32. A
18. C	23. D	28. A	33. B
19. D	24. C	29. C	34. D
20. B	25. D	30. B	35. A

Explanations

Remember: You will need to take notes when listening, because you will not see the questions until the aural part is finished.

16. (A) The key word leading to the corresponding sentence for the answer is "this afternoon" 今天下午. You will not hear this word, but the first phrase of the weather report is 晴转多云（晴轉多雲）"sunny to cloudy," which is Choice (A).

17. (B) The key word leading to the answer is "rain" 雨. That word is in the sentence with "tonight" 今晚，which is Choice (B).

18. (C) You will need the notes to answer this question. Because numbers are often key words you want to remember, write them down in your notes. Your notes might read: Today 25, 13; tomorrow and the day after tomorrow, 14, 31. Therefore, tomorrow will be hotter than today.

19. (D) You may not know the words for "air" 航空 or "passengers" 旅客（旅客），but you definitely will know that "airport" means 机场（機場）or "take off" means 起飞（起飛）.

20. (B) (A) and (B) share the same structure and they are the choices most likely to be the answer. We know it is "take off" 起飞（起飛）from the previous question. You should become familiar with these words: landing 降落; get earlier 提早; and postpone 推迟/延误（推遲/延誤）.

21. (C) From the four choices of this question, you need to make sure about two things: the gate or the lounge, free or not. You heard "free" 免费（免費）and "到XX室". 到 means "go," 室 means "room," so the passengers are being told they can go to the lounge for free food.

22. (A) Voice messages often talk about plans or a change in plans. The vocabulary normally used are "plan to do" 打算 and "originally" 本来（本來）. The message is trying to confirm the location of a restaurant. The message states that "I planned to treat you Chong Qing Hot Pot, but…Tokyo restaurant." Therefore, the caller is asking the person to go to Little Tokyo Restaurant.

23. (D) The voice message says "…but Xiao Li said that she booked the Tokyo restaurant." Therefore, is seems, one of her friends booked another restaurant, which is Choice D.

24. (C) Since they are going to eat in Tokyo restaurant, they will probably meet somewhere near the restaurant. The voice states "meet at the door of the restaurant"—an option included only in Choice (C).

25. (D) The answer for questions that ask for the topic of a conversation is normally located at the beginning or the end of the selection. "Culture" 文化 is a word you are familiar with. Also, the whole conversation mentions a lot of things related to Chinese culture, which indicates the answer is (D).

26. (C) The key word to locate the answer is "Wednesday" 星期三. The man states that on Wednesday he is introducing Chinese cultural holidays, making Choice (C) the correct one.

27. (B) At the end of the conversation, the woman suggests a Chinese movie for Friday.

28. (A) This is a relatively easy question, if you have good notes. The one activity not mentioned is "martial arts" 武术（武術）.

29. (C) This selection is very structured. You heard "dumplings" 饺子（餃子）a lot of times, and therefore you can deduce the answer is (C) or (D). All of the instructions are about making dumplings, not only cooking them, which would be the fourth step.

30. (B) The second step is to make the stuffing 饺子馅（餃子餡）. You may not understand 馅（餡）, but you understand pork, beef, chicken, and vegetables. What are those things for? They are used to make the stuffing.

31. (D) Baking is not mentioned. Review the vocabulary: steam cook 蒸；boil with water 煮；fry 煎，炒；and bake 烤.

32. (A) Even if you do not have good note-taking skills, this question can be done by common sense. You probably know enough about dumplings to know that (B), (C), and (D) are all incorrect.

33. (B) "Peking Opera" 京剧（京劇）is repeated many times. Review the words: sculpture 雕像，painting 画（畫），and folk dance 民间舞（民間舞）.

34. (D) Numbers are often key information that should be part of your note taking. 三十多 means "more than thirty" instead of just "thirty," so (D) is correct.

35. (A) Shanghai is the only answer choice not mentioned in this selection.

Answers and Explanations for Reading Comprehension

Answers

1. B	8. C	15. C	22. A	29. B
2. A	9. B	16. C	23. B	30. C
3. B	10. A	17. B	24. C	31. A
4. B	11. D	18. D	25. D	32. D
5. D	12. C	19. D	26. C	33. C
6. C	13. B	20. A	27. A	34. B
7. D	14. A	21. C	28. A	35. B

Explanations

1. (B) The frequently made mistake is to choose (C), because both (B) and (C) are related to rentals. However, in the e-mail message, there is a sentence stating "Can you help me to take a look…" 你能帮我去看一下吗（你能幫我去看一下嗎？）.

2. (A) 在学校附近（在學校附近）means "near the school."

3. (B) Take a look at the sentence 只要屋子干净，有阳台，有冰箱和空调就行 (只要屋子乾淨，有陽台，有冰箱和空調就行). It lists Choices (A), (C), and (D). Choice (B) is not specifically listed because "Wi-Fi" means 无线上网（無線上網）.

4. (B) Normally you should check the four choices before deciding your answer. Choices (A) and (D) are incorrect because they refer to the sender instead of the recipient. Choice (C) is also incorrect—refer to Question #1. Because the sender states that he is going to Beijing and asks the recipient for help, (B) is correct.

5. (D) Some students may choose (B) due to the word 大学（大學）. However, the whole phrase is "college application" 大学申请（大學申請）, which indicates that the writer is not a college student. Because he is going to participate in something of 高中生, he is a high school student.

6. (C) Choices (C) and (D) share the same structure but one is negative and the other positive. Often this is a clue that one of these two choices is the right one. Find the word "grammar" in the context. It states that the grammar is a "little difficult" 有一点儿难（有一點兒難）. Therefore, Choice (C) is the correct one.

7. (D) At the beginning, the e-mail states that "I am very busy this semester, I didn't even go out to play on Thanksgiving day." 连感恩节放假时我都没有出去玩（連感恩節放假時我都沒有出去玩）. Even…still… 连……都（連……都）. Choice (D) is definitely not true, and thus it is the correct answer.

8. (C) "停" is a commonly used word that you will see everywhere in China as the stop sign. Thus, Choice (C) is correct.

9. (B) The word of 电梯（電梯） can be translated as "electric/electronic stairs," which means elevators. We normally see elevators in a building instead of a house, a train, or a park. The sign is most likely directed to visitors in a building.

10. (A) From the character "馆（館）" in the title, we know the answer is between (A) or (D). If it is in a library, the regulations should be related to the word of book "书". There is nothing related to books, so even if you do not know 博物馆（博物館） means museum, you can get the correct answer.

11. (D) Rule number one clearly states that the "ticket" 票 is required. Other popular required documents we need to know are the "ID card" 身份证（身份證） and the "passport" 护照（護照）.

12. (C) 请勿（請勿） means "please don't," which is often used in public signs containing regulations. The word "pet" 宠物（寵物） is located in the sentence starting with 请勿（請勿）; therefore, (C) is the correct answer. Other negative words frequently used on signs include 以免, 禁止, 别, 不许（不許）, 防止, and 严禁（嚴禁）.

13. (B) There are different strategies you can use to get the answer. The easiest strategy is similar to how you found the right answer to the last question. 拍照 means "taking a picture," and it is not in a sentence starting with negative words.

14. (A) For those questions asking which statement is true or not true, it is best to check all the choices one by one before you select. You can find the corresponding sentence for the answer (A). However, there is a description of 1.2 米以下的儿（兒）童, which indicates that it is not for all children. Therefore, (A) is incorrect.

15. (C) 电视台（電視台） means "TV station."

16. (C) 聘 is the key word, which means "recruitment." Similar indications for job advertisements are 招, 招聘, 招工, 需要.

17. (B) For job advertisements, the quality of "not mandatory" is normally the "priorities" which is listed by the structure of …优先（優先）. For this selection, students and those who can speak English are given the priority.

18. (D) Refer to the explanation for Question 17.

19. (D) The title 签证（簽證） means "visa." If you do not understand this word, you still can guess from the first sentence. 非中国公民赴华旅游（非中國公民赴華旅遊） means non-Chinese citizen travel to China. What do they need to apply for? Of course, a visa.

20. (A) From the second and third lines, you can locate the information for the requirements: Choice (B) 护照正本（護照正本）, Choice (C) 有效期为（為）六个 （個）月以上, and Choice (D), no less than two blank visa pages. However, Choice (A) is not required.

21. (C) From the four choices for the answer, Choice (C), a personal check, is normally the one that cannot be accepted using our common sense. Check the answers with the passage, you can find the list of cash 现金（現金）, credit card 信用卡, and cashier's check 现金（現金）支票 listed together, which means none of them could be the answer. Then, in the last sentence, the announcement states clearly that a personal check is not accepted.

22. (A) This kind of question can be answered correctly by checking all four choices with the passage. The phrase 彩色护（護）照照片 means "colored passport photo"; therefore, only a colored photo is accepted.

23. (B) The answer of main-idea questions is generally located at the beginning or the end. The first sentence is a welcome greeting. The following sentence states that "our study is separated into two directions: science and arts." Then the courses of arts and science are introduced separately. Therefore, Choice (B) is correct. In China, students choose their major between science and arts in high school, while students in the United States decide their path in college.

24. (C) We can eliminate Choice (D) first because physics belongs to science. Then Choice (A) foreign language, and Choice (B) Chinese-language arts and math because these courses are required for all students. Politics 政治 is for students in arts, so Choice (C) is not required for science students.

25. (D) The passage states that the college majors who accept both paths (文理兼收) include economics, law, and business management, and so on.

26. (C) The answer is probably either (A) or (C) because these two choices share a similar structure and vocabulary: "platform" 平台 and "communicate/communication" 沟通（溝通）, 交流. Choice (A) is communication between the parents and their children, while Choice (C) is communication among the youth. The first sentence of this passage states that it is for "youth" 年轻人（年輕人）.

27. (A) Use the number "520" to locate the sentence for the answer. It represents "I love you" 我爱你（我愛你）.

28. (A) The third paragraph mentions "video chatting" 视频聊天（視頻聊天） and "playing games" 游戏（遊戲）. Therefore, you can eliminate (B) and (C). Choice (D) is "group chatting" 群聊, which is mentioned at the end of Paragraph 2. Alarm clock is not mentioned, so Choice (A) is correct.

29. (B) Locate the four choices one by one. Choice (A) is mentioned at the end of Paragraph 1; (C) is mentioned at the end of Paragraph 2; and (D) is mentioned at the beginning of Paragraph 3. The topic of Choice (B) is mentioned but its phrasing is opposite to the information in the passage: 也可以随时阻止任何人和你交流（也可以隨時阻止任何人和你交流） in the middle of Paragraph 2. Therefore, Choice (B) is not true.

30. (C) From the information of the second sentence, we know "his name is XX." There is no word of tree, sun, and bird in the first sentence; therefore, Choice (C) is the answer.

31. (A) The third sentence states that he is big, tall, and runs fast. He can "run faster than a bird" 跑起来连最快的鸟儿也追不上他（跑起來連最快的鳥兒也追不上他）, but not "he can fly like a bird." Therefore, Choice (A) is correct.

32. (D) Locate the answer in the passage by finding the word "sun" 太阳（太陽）. 太阳一到晚上就没有了……让太阳时时刻刻都给人们带来光明，世间再也没有了黑夜（太陽一到晚上就没有了……讓太陽時時刻刻都給人們帶來光明，世再也沒有了黑夜）。"The sun disappears at night"… "Let the sun shine all the time and there is no dark night." Therefore, he wanted the sun to stay in the sky all the time.

33. (C) Use "nine days and nine nights" to locate the answer. 经过九天九夜，在太阳落山的地方，夸父终于追上了它（經過九天九夜，在太陽落山的地方，誇父終於追上了它）。"Chase" 追 is what he did during this time.

34. (B) From the repeated words of "thirsty" 渴, "drink water" 喝水, we know the answer is (B).

35. (B) Choices (A) and (B) share a similar structure, so check these two choices first. Locate the choices in the end of the passage: 这木杖就化成了一大片绿色的桃林（這木杖就化成了一大片綠色的桃林）。The stick grew into a group of peach trees, which is the answer (B).

Answers and Explanations for Section II (Free-Response Questions)

For the free-response questions, it is not hard to get a score of 4 as long as you answer each question and complete each task. In this section you will find sample answers for all the free-response questions at a level of 5 or above. These are followed by an English translation of the sample answer and a thorough explanation of the answer. You will also find scoring guidelines for each section.

You will learn the basic strategies for the free-response questions in the next chapter and do more practice with the free-response questions in Chapters 8 through 11 to help you achieve a high score.

Answer and Explanation for the Story Narration

Sample Answer

Simplified Chinese
小王和小张在球场踢足球。小王飞起一脚把球踢了出去。糟糕！球打中了一个女孩的头，把她撞到了地上。小王和小张吓得飞快地跑过来。小王把女孩轻轻地扶起来，小张着急地盯着女孩的膝盖，问道："你怎么样？"女孩于是站起来，试着向前走了两步，回答说："不要紧，没受伤。下次你们小心点啊！"小王和小张不好意思地笑了，向她挥手说再见。(Level 6)

Traditional Chinese
小王和小張在球場踢足球。小王飛起一腳把球踢了出去。糟糕！球打中了一個女孩的頭，把她撞到了地上。小王和小張嚇得飛快地跑過來。小王把女孩輕輕地扶起來，小張著急地盯著女孩的膝蓋，問道：「你怎麼樣？」女孩於是站起來，試著向前走了兩步，回答說：「不要緊，沒受傷。下次你們小心點啊！」小王和小張不好意思地笑了，向她揮手說再見。

English translation for the answer:
Xiao Wang and Xiao Zhang are playing soccer in a field. Xiao Wang kicked the ball. Oops, the ball hit a girl's head and knocked her to the ground. This surprised Xiao Wang and Xiao Zhang and they ran to the girl. When Xiao Wang was helping the girl to sit up gently, Xiao Zhang stared at her knee and asked: "How do you feel?" The girl stood up, tried to walk a couple of steps, and then answered: "Don't worry, I wasn't hurt. You guys should be more careful next time." Xiao Wang and Xiao Zhang smiled, embarrassed, then waved to her and said goodbye.

Explanation and Scoring Guidelines

1. Did you write a basic story?
Yes. Your score may be 3 and above even if you miss one picture. Otherwise your score may be 2 or below 2. If you write a complete story, congratulations, your score may reach 4.

2. Was your story complete and understandable to the reader or listener?
Yes. Your score may be 4 and above, even if your answer lacks detail or elaboration, or includes minor inconsistencies in its logical progression. That means, translating the storyline into Chinese can get you a 4. Remember, you need transitional elements for logic flow.

3. Was your answer well structured, with rich language usage and only minor errors?
Yes. Your score may be 5 and above. A rich usage of vocabulary and grammar is essential and crucial to get to this level. There are a lot of factors to stop you from scoring 6, most of which are missing one detail or having too many grammar errors or typos. The details you could miss are as follows:

- For picture 2, you did not mention that the girl fell down.
- For picture 3, you did not write about the two boys' different actions.
- For picture 4, you did not describe that the boys are waving goodbye.

Answer and Explanation for the E-mail Response

Sample Answer

Simplified Chinese
周立，
你好！好久没和你联系了，收到你的电子邮件很开心。欢迎来中国玩！
　　你问我关于去西安好还是去上海好的问题，我认为你应该去西安。首先，西安有全世界著名的名胜古迹，那里的兵马俑是中国第一个皇帝制作的。如果你选西安的话，你就能够看到真正代表中国历史和文化的东西(global)。其次，从我个人经验来看(personal)，上海比西安更国际化和现代化，给人的感觉和香港比较相似，既然你会去香港，这次就可以不去上海。还有啊，要是你去西安，你还可以像我一样买到很便宜的纪念品，带回美国做为礼物相当合适。

你提到在中国旅游的安全问题，除了旅游的基本安全常识(global)以外，我建议(personal)你要特别小心中国的小偷骗子。你一定要把自己的东西保管好，不要轻信陌生人的话。

其实在中国旅游还是很安全的，祝你玩得开心！

小新

Traditional Chinese

周立，

你好！好久没和你联系了，收到你的电子邮件很开心。欢迎来中国玩！

你问我关于去西安好还是去上海好的问题，我认为你应该去西安。首先，西安有全世界著名的名胜古迹，那里的兵马俑是中国第一个皇帝制作的。如果你选西安的话，你就能够看到真正代表中国历史和文化的东西(global)。其次，从我个人经验来看(personal)，上海比西安更国际化和现代化，给人的感觉和香港比较相似，既然你会去香港，这次就可以不去上海。还有啊，要是你去西安，你还可以像我一样买到很便宜的纪念品，带回美国做为礼物相当合适。

你提到在中国旅游的安全问题，除了旅游的基本安全常识(global)以外，我建议(personal)你要特别小心中国的小偷骗子。你一定要把自己的东西保管好，不要轻信陌生人的话。

其实在中国旅游还是很安全的，祝你玩得开心！

小新

English translation for the answer:

Zhou Li,

How are you? It's been a long time since we communicated so I was very happy to receive your e-mail. Welcome to China!

As to the question about going to Xi'an or Shanghai, I think you should go to Xi'an. First of all, Xi'an is a historical site famous all over the world, where the terracotta army was built by the first emperor of China. If you choose Xi'an, you will be able to see the things that really represent the history and the culture of China. Secondly, from my personal experience, Shanghai is more international and modern than Xi'an. It provides an experience similar to Hong Kong. Since you will go to Hong Kong, you might as well skip Shanghai this time. Furthermore, if you go to Xi'an, you can buy very cheap souvenirs like I did. It is a great idea to bring some things back to the United States as gifts.

You mentioned Chinese tourism security issues. I suggest that you should pay special attention to pickpockets in China, in addition to the general safety common sense of traveling. Be sure to take good care of your belongings and do not believe the words of a stranger. Traveling in China is actually very safe. I hope you have fun!

Xiao Xin

Explanation and Scoring Guidelines

In order to respond to the e-mail, you need to understand the e-mail. This e-mail message is about "Travel in China" as the subject states. The sender is going to travel in China. He wishes to visit his friends in Hong Kong, and Climb the Great Wall in Beijing. However, he does not have much time, so he writes to ask for the opinions of choosing between Xi'an and Shanghai. The sender also asked for suggestions regarding the issue of safety while traveling in China.

1. Did your answer cover both questions?

Yes. Your score may be 3 and above even if you did not address all the issues raised in the e-mail. Otherwise your score may be 2 or below 2.

2. Was your response complete and understandable to the reader or listener?

Yes. Your score may be 4 and above, even if your answer lacks detail or elaboration, has only loosely connected sentences, or includes errors that are not serious enough to generally obscure meaning. That means you have to write something about suggestions of selecting a city between Xi'an and Shanghai and travel safety in China.

3. Was your response well structured, with rich language usage and minor errors?

Yes. Your score may be 5 and above. A rich usage of vocabulary and grammar is essential and crucial to get this level. There are a lot of factors that could stop you from scoring 6; the most common of these are sporadic grammar errors and occasional lapses of register to the situation.

Answers and Explanations for the Conversation

In this part of the exam, you are required to answer six questions about school life in the United States in a conversation with your friend from China. A rather detailed set of answers is provided for your reference. On the actual exam, an answer scored 5 or 6 generally consists of four to six short sentences.

Sample Answers

1. 你在美国哪个学校上学？你们那儿的天气怎么样？
你在美國哪個學校上學？你們那兒的天氣怎麼樣？

Which school do you study at in the United States? How is the weather there?

我在美国ＸＸ中学上学，我们这儿位于南加州，就在海边不远，气候真的很好，冬天不太冷，夏天也不太热……温度一般在华氏五十到七十度之间，就是有点太干了，很少下雨。
（我在美國ＸＸ中學上學，我們這兒位於南加州，就在海邊不遠，氣候真的很好，冬天不太冷，夏天也不太熱……溫度一般在華氏五十到七十度之間，就是有點太乾了，很少下雨。）

This response is a Level 6 response. The answer directly addresses the prompts. It describes in detail the weather in the area of the school (Southern California). Among the ideas conveyed are that it is not far from the ocean and has really good weather in both winter and summer. Both temperature and humidity are discussed.

2. 你在学校每个学期要选哪些课？你最喜欢哪门课？
你在學校每個學期要選哪些課？你最喜歡哪門課？

Which courses do you take each semester? What is your favorite course?

我在学校要选很多课，很多课，我是说，有英语、历史、数学、外语、科学、音乐、美术等。有的同学还会上网选其他课程。我最喜欢的课是历史。
（我在學校要選很多課，很多課，我是說，有英語、歷史、數學、外語、科學、音樂、美術等。有的同學還會上網選其他課程。我最喜歡的課是歷史。）

This response is a Level 5 response. The answer is concise with good use of language and delivery. It has a little detail but not enough. If the sentences were connected more smoothly and more elaboration added, it could reach level 6.

我在学校要选很多课，每个学期都不太一样。主要有英语、历史、政治、数学、外语，科学方面包括物理、生物、化学等，还有体育、美术和音乐方面的课。有的同学还会选一些大学预科的课程和网络计算机方面课程。我最喜欢的课是历史，因为从中学到的东西对我现在的生活和学习都有帮助。

（我在學校要選很多課，每個學期都不太一樣。主要有英語、歷史、政治、數學、外語，科學方面包括物理、生物、化學等，還有體育、美術和音樂方面的課。有的同學還會選一些大學預科的課程和網絡計算機方面課程。我最喜歡的課是歷史，因為從中學到的東西對我現在的生活和學習都有幫助。）

This response is a Level 6 response. The answer provides a very thorough and appropriate response with smooth sentence connections. There is a wide range of grammatical structures. It states that there are a lot of courses to take and that the courses are different each semester. Included are the major courses and special courses some students will take as well as an explanation of what is included in science. For the question of "favorite course," the answers provided reasons behind the choice.

3. 你们每天上课的时间长吗？请介绍一下你在学校每天的时间安排，好吗？
你們每天上課的時間長嗎？請介紹一下你在學校每天的時間安排，好嗎？

Are your daily school hours very long? Please introduce your daily schedule in school.

我们每天上课的时间比较长，从早上八点到下午四点都在学校。我们上午有四节课，每节一个小时左右；午饭时间为十二点到下午一点，和同学们边吃边聊聊天；下午的课一般是音乐、体育和美术方面的。我喜欢摄影，所以四点以后会参加摄影俱乐部的活动，五点才回家。

（我們每天上課的時間比較長，從早上八點到下午四點都在學校。我們上午有四節課，每節一個小時左右；午飯時間為十二點到下午一點，和同學們邊吃邊聊聊天；下午的課一般是音樂、體育和美術方面的。我喜歡攝影，所以四點以後會參加攝影俱樂部的活動，五點才回家。）

This response is a Level 6 response. The answer is comprehensive and well structured with minimum hesitation or repetition. The first sentence is a summary of the questions, which are then answered in detail. Included are courses in the morning, lunch activities, courses in the afternoon, club activities, and so on.

4. 听说美国的中学生经常会做义工，做义工会影响学习吗？请谈一谈你的看法。
聽說美國的中學生經常會做義工，做義工會影響學習嗎？請談一談你的看法。

It is said that high school students in the United States often participate in volunteer service. Will doing volunteer work influence your study? Please share your opinion.

是的，美国的中学生经常会做义工，而且觉得做义工帮助其他人非常光荣。其实做义工不影响学习，因为一般是在周末或者节假日做。更重要的是，做义工参加社会实践也是一种学习和交流的方式，我们有的老师还要求大家根据做义工的经历来完成作业呢。

（是的，美國的中學生經常會做義工，而且覺得做義工幫助其他人非常光榮。其實做義工不影響學習，因為一般是在週末或者節假日做。更重要的是，做義工參加社會實踐也是一種學習和交流的方式，我們有的老師還要求大家根據做義工的經歷來完成作業呢。）

This response is a Level 6 response. Rich vocabulary and a wide range of grammatical structures are the highlights of this answer. It states that the high school students in the United

States often do volunteer work. What is more, they regard volunteering to help others as an honor. Actually doing volunteer work will not influence study, because normally it is done on the weekend or on holidays. More importantly, volunteer work in the society is a learning and communication experience. Some teachers even assign homework based on volunteer experience.

5. 除了上学以外，美国的中学生还会参加什么样的社会活动？
除了上學以外，美國的中學生還會參加甚麼樣的社會活動？

What kinds of social activities do US high school students attend besides studying in school?

除了上学以外，我的学校特别重视社会实践活动，有很多活动，学生都可以参加。我们学校经常组织社区服务活动，为需要帮助的人提供服务时间啊，全校募捐啊，栽树啊，参观各种地方啊，什么的。有时还和其他学校的学生一起做义工。
（除了上學以外，我的學校特別重視社會實踐活動，有很多活動，學生都可以參加。我們學校經常組織社區服務活動，為需要幫助的人提供服務時間啊，全校募捐啊，栽樹啊，參觀各種地方啊，甚麼的。有時還和其他學校的學生一起做義工。）

This response is a Level 5 response. The answer only discusses "my school" and says "sometimes students do volunteer work with other schools." The question asks for "students in the United States" instead of just your school. Luckily the answer mentioned at the end that "sometimes students do volunteer work with other schools," so it reaches Level 5. Refer to the earlier checklist.

除了上学以外，美国的中学生还会参加各种各样的(all kinds of)社会活动。每个学校每个地区(each school and each region)可能会有些不同，但是都会组织社区服务活动，包括(include) 在医院做义工、做环境保护宣传、募捐帮助需要帮助的人等。有些中学生还是(also)当地各种非盈利性团体的成员，参加各团体的服务活动。
（除了上學以外，美國的中學生還會參加各種各樣的(all kinds of)社會活動。每個學校每個地區(each school and each region)可能會有些不同，但是都會組織社區服務活動，包括(include) 在醫院做義工、做環境保護宣傳、募捐幫助需要幫助的人等。有些中學生還是(also)當地各種非盈利性團體的成員，參加各團體的服務活動。）

This response is a Level 6 response. In addition to studying in school, US high school students participate in all kinds of social activities. There might be differences among different schools and different regions. However, social community services are organized everywhere, including volunteering in the hospitals, advocating environmental protection, fundraising for people who need help, and so on. Some students are members of local non-profit organizations and participate in the activities and services of the organizations. Refer to the earlier checklist. This answer includes all the elements.

6. 我下个学期会作为交换生来美国学习，你觉得我在学习方面需要注意哪些问题？
我下個學期會作為交換生來美國學習，你覺得我在學習方面需要注意哪些問題？

I am going to study in the United States as an exchange student next semester. In your opinion, what do I need to pay attention to academically?

欢迎你来美国学习！我觉得你作为交换生，刚来的时候在学习上(academically)首先会遇到语言问题。你应该(should)把英语学好，多和同学多和老师交流，上课也要多发言，不要担心别人听不懂。同时(meanwhile)，美国学校很注重个人能力的培养，很多作业都是没有固定答案的，你如果大胆创新，一定会学得很好。

（歡迎你來美國學習！我覺得你作為交換生，剛來的時候在學習上(academically)首先會遇到語言問題。你應該(should)把英語學好，多和同學多和老師交流，上課也要多發言，不要擔心別人聽不懂。同時(meanwhile)，美國學校很注重個人能力的培養，很多作業都是沒有固定答案的，你如果大膽創新，一定會學得很好。）

This response is a Level 6 response. Welcome to study in the United States. From my point of view, you may encounter language issues as an exchange student. It is a good idea that you learn English well, communicate with your classmates and teachers, and answer questions in class. Do not worry about others not understanding you. U.S. schools stress individual working skills. There is no fixed answer to a lot of assignments. If you are creative and innovative, you will do a great job.

Scoring Guidelines

From reading the explanations, you are probably capable of making a scoring checklist for this question. Your answer needs to have all the elements in the following checklist:

- Did you address the questions thoroughly with details?
- Do you have smooth sentence connections?
- Do your answers have a natural pace with a minimum of repetitions/hesitations?
- Did you use correct pronunciation and register?
- Do your answers show good vocabulary usage with minimal grammatical errors?

Answer and Explanation for the Cultural Presentation

Sample Answer

Simplified Chinese
我今天想介绍一位中国的名人，他的名字叫姚明。我想和大家谈谈姚明这个人为什么出名，有什么样的影响力，为什么重要。

姚明是美国ＮＢＡ和世界篮球巨星。他是上海人，从九岁就开始打篮球，后来去了休斯顿火箭队打中锋。他身高2米26，又叫小巨人、移动长城，是中国最具影响力的人物之一。首先，姚明是中国第一位以状元身份进入NBA的球员；其次，他八次入选全明星队，还被美国时代周刊列入"世界最具影响力的100人"之中；还有，姚明六次被福布斯评为中国名人榜第一名；获奥委会、篮球协会等颁发的各种奖项……姚明是中国体育界的象征性人物，无数华人都是他的球迷。

姚明有句名言："努力不一定成功，放弃却一定失败。"姚明就永远不放弃，受了伤也继续努力。我特别喜欢他，遗憾的是我从来没有见到过姚明本人。如果有机会，我一定会给他一个大拥抱！

现在你明白为什么姚明是中国的骄傲了吧？他的故事讲述了一个中国人努力奋斗的成功史，他是我们所有年轻人的榜样。

Traditional Chinese
我今天想介紹一位中國的名人，他的名字叫姚明。我想和大家談談姚明這個人為甚麼出名，有甚麼樣的影響力，為甚麼重要。

姚明是美國ＮＢＡ和世界籃球巨星。他是上海人，從九歲就開始打籃球，後來去了休斯頓火箭隊打中鋒。他身高2米26，又叫小巨人、移動長城，是中國最具影響力的人物之一。首先，姚明是中國第一位以狀元身份進入NBA的球員；其次，他八次入選全明星隊，還被美國時代週刊列入"世界最具影響力的100人"之中；還有，姚明六次被福布斯評為中國名人榜第一名；獲奧委會、籃球協會等頒發的各種獎項⋯⋯姚明是中國體育界的象徵性人物，無數華人都是他的球迷。

姚明有句名言："努力不一定成功，放棄卻一定失敗。"姚明就永遠不放棄，受了傷也繼續努力。我特別喜歡他，遺憾的是我從來沒有見到過姚明本人。如果有機會，我一定會給他一個大擁抱！

現在你明白為甚麼姚明是中國的驕傲了吧？他的故事講述了一個中國人努力奮鬥的成功史，他是我們所有年輕人的榜樣。

English translation for the answer:

I am going to introduce a famous Chinese person. His name is Yao Ming. I would like to talk about why he is famous, how he influences China, and why this is significant.

Yao Ming is a star both in the NBA in the United States and in world basketball in general. He was born in Shanghai and has played basketball since age nine. He was selected to play for the Houston Rockets. Yao Ming was called the "little giant" and the "walking great wall" with the height of 2.26 m. He is one of the most popular celebrities in China. First, Yao Ming is the first Chinese player in the NBA. Second, Yao Ming won the designation of All Star eight times, and he was listed in *Time* as one of the 100 most influential people. He tops the *Forbes* list as the most famous Chinese person and has won various awards from the Olympics and basketball associations. Yao Ming represents a milestone in sports in China and has a lot of Chinese fans.

As Yao Ming says, "Making efforts may not result in success, but giving up definitely leads to failure." Yao Ming is a person who never gives up and keeps trying even after getting wounded. I really love him! It's a pity that I never got a chance to meet him in person. I will give him a big hug once I meet him!

Now you understand why Yao Ming is the pride of China. His experience represents a story of how a Chinese person became successful through hard work. He is our role model.

Explanation

The task assigned for the cultural presentation requires you to introduce a famous Chinese person and discuss his or her significance. Yao Ming, being both famous and Chinese, is definitely a good pick.

This answer addresses all aspects of the question with thoroughness and detail. The introduction is well organized with a clear progression of ideas and transitional elements. The information is accurate and detailed and rich, and appropriate language and grammatical structures are applied. With a good delivery, this kind of answer scores a 6.

Scoring and Interpreting Your Results

For multiple-choice questions, the simple number of your correct answers can be used to convert to your AP score.

For free-response questions, it is not as easy for you to figure out what exactly your score could be. Here is a simple checklist to give you a general idea about how you did on the free-response questions so you can score yourself.

Scoring Checklist

1. Did you answer all the basic questions?
   Yes. Your score may be 3 and above. Otherwise your score may be 2 or below 2.
2. Was your answer understandable and logical to the reader or listener?
   Yes. Your score may be 4 and above.
3. Was your answer well structured, with rich language usage and minor errors?
   Yes. Your score may be 5 and above.

To see what you might have done if this had been the actual AP exam, you may convert your answers to a rough AP score using the following worksheet. This is a method for estimating your score, and the results do not guarantee that you will do similarly on the actual AP exam.

Section I: Multiple Choice

Rejoinders: (number correct) ÷15 × 0.10 = _____
Listening Selections: (number correct) ÷ (total number) × 0.15 = _____
Reading: (number correct) ÷ (total number) × 0.25 = _____

Section II: Free Response

Story Narration: (score yourself on a scale of 1 to 6) ÷ 6 × 0.15 = _____
E-mail Response: (score yourself on a scale of 1 to 6) ÷ 6 × 0.10 = _____
Conversation: (score yourself on a scale of 1 to 6) ÷ 36 × 0.10 = _____
Cultural Presentation: (score yourself on a scale of 1 to 6) ÷ 6 × 0.15 = _____
Total Score for Sections I and II = _____
Total Points for Sections I and II = _____ × 120 = _____

STEP 3

Develop Strategies for Success

CHAPTER 4   Strategies for Taking the Exam

CHAPTER 4

Strategies for Taking the Exam

IN THIS CHAPTER

Summary: This chapter provides strategies to attack the questions—strategies that will help you raise your AP score. You will find strategies explained for both the multiple-choice and free-response sections. Using these strategies will help you make the best use of time during the test and assure that you get the best score you are capable of getting. After learning and practicing the strategies, analyze and evaluate your performance on the diagnostic test to identify your weaknesses in answering each type of question. Use the worksheets in this chapter to identify problem areas or weaknesses. Then adjust your test-prep study plan so that you focus on the things you most need to work on.

Key Ideas

Multiple-Choice Questions

○ For the listening rejoinders, click the answer as quickly as possible. You cannot afford to spend a lot of time on these. Always keep in mind that you are looking for an answer continuing the dialogue logically instead of rephrasing the dialogue.

○ For the listening selections, listen to the instructions carefully, noting if the selection is played once or twice. Take notes for the key information. Skip anything you have trouble understanding.

○ For the reading selections, read the question, write down the key words on scratch paper, and find the corresponding sentence or key words in the context first. Do not spend too much time on one question.

Free-Response Questions

✪ Make sure that you understand the question and that your answer covers all the tasks.

✪ Write structured outlines as detailed as possible for the writing tasks and the cultural presentation.

✪ For speaking tasks, speak as fast and fluently as possible for the familiar parts. Rephrase the question if your mind goes blank.

✪ For writing tasks, stick to the prompts and leave some time to check for coherence and grammar, if possible.

Analyzing Your Performance

✪ Do a thorough analysis of the mistakes you made in the diagnostic exam using the self-assessment sheets provided.

✪ Use the diagnostic tools and worksheets provided in this book to determine what you most need to focus on.

Getting Started

Based on your performance on the diagnostic exam, you should now have a basic understanding about what the AP Chinese Language and Culture exam looks like and what your proficiency level would be regarding the four skills—listening, reading, writing, and speaking—tested on the AP Chinese Language and Culture exam.

This chapter provides basic exam-taking strategies for each type of question found on the AP Chinese exam. It is a good idea to learn these well and practice them. You will do more exercises in the later chapters to sharpen these strategies and practice answering the types of questions you will encounter on the exam.

After learning the exam-taking strategies that will help you get a good score, you will find strategies to help you analyze and identify the weaknesses on which you should focus your test preparation activities. This chapter provides self-assessment worksheets to identify weaknesses based on your performance on the diagnostic test in Chapter 3.

Strategies for Multiple-Choice Questions

Listening Rejoinders

The listening rejoinders are the first type of question you will encounter on the actual exam. After listening to the conversation, you will be given four possible responses that continue the conversation. You need to choose the response that is the most logical and culturally appropriate to complete the conversation. You have only five seconds to choose.

For the listening rejoinders, keep the following important strategies in mind:

1. Respond in five seconds. That means, click the answer at your first thought. You may change it in five seconds if needed. Even Chinese native speakers find the speed of listening rejoinders very quick. Pay all of your attention to the current one. Do not even bother to think back on your previous question. You *cannot* go back and forth in rejoinders. For the questions you really have no idea about, click the answer (C).

2. Continue the dialogue. Always remember, the answer is to continue the dialogue instead of rephrasing it. We tend to understand the dialogue and interpret it, but a rejoinder means a reply.

3. Use set phrases and social formulae. Did you know that the rejoinders test your knowledge and skill of "using set phrases and social formulae, communicating opinion, attitude, intent"? You can always guess and predicate the speaker's reaction. Those phrases and formulae should be one of your highest priorities in listening.

Listening Selections

You will hear several selections. The multiple-choice questions that follow will test your understanding of what you have heard. However, you will **not** be able to see the questions and answer choices until the selection is completed. There are 12 seconds allotted for each question.

You should keep the following key strategies in mind when working with the listening selections:

1. Pay attention to the instructions. Instructions tell you which type of selections you will hear and and how many times it will be played. This information can be very important for you in listening and taking notes.

2. Take notes. Write down the key information while listening. That means you should write down at least who, when, where, what happened, and of course, numbers. You are encouraged to use symbols or shorthand if you can. Just skip any vocabulary you do not know and do not worry about it, because gaining the main idea is more important than understanding each word. For better understanding, your notes can be structured differently depending on the type of selection. In Chapter 6 you will find more details about the listening selections and have the opportunity to practice answering questions based on several listening selections on the CD accompanying this book.

3. Analyze the answer choices. You have years of experience in answering multiple-choice questions. Make the best usage of your experience to quickly identify the differences between the choices, eliminate incorrect options, and select the correct answer. Sometimes you can get the correct answer just by analyzing the four answer choices.

Reading Selections

You will be given approximately nine passages to read. Following each reading are questions that test your understanding of what you have read. You will need to finish the reading and 35 to 40 questions about the readings within 60 minutes. You should pace yourself so you have enough time to finish and ideally leave some time to go back to difficult questions you highlighted earlier.

Here are strategies that can help you get a higher score.

1. Read the questions before you read the passage. This will help you know what you are looking for in the passage. It should give you a general idea of what the passage is about and help with understanding the structure of the passage. Pay attention to the notional words (mostly nouns and verbs here) including numbers and difficult words, which usually indicate the key information you need to locate in the passages. Also briefly contrast the four choices, which are normally not too long in the AP Chinese exam. Try to remember the differences between them, but do not spend more than one minute.

2. Locate the sentence(s) for the answer. Scanning and skimming skills are essential in this task. You need to quickly find the corresponding sentences you need for the answers in the passage. However, for the questions of "which is not mentioned" or "which statement is not true," you may need to locate each answer choice of the question and analyze it.

3. Analyze the answer choices. Similar to the listening sections, you should use your experience to contrast the differences, eliminate the incorrect options, and, if you need to, make a good guess. Sometimes you can get the answer just by analyzing the answer choices. Do not spend too much time on one question. If you are not sure about your answer, choose your best guess, check the question, and come back later if you have time.

Strategies for the Free-Response Questions

Story Narration

The four pictures present a story. Narrate a complete story as suggested by the pictures. Give your story a beginning, a middle, and an end. You have only 15 minutes to type.

Keep the following key strategies in mind as you take on the story narration task:

1. Complete the task. First, create a brief story in your mind and write down every action in the four pictures. This can be your outline for your narration. You will need to write about all four pictures so budget your time carefully. In your narrative story, be sure to fully address all the actions shown in the pictures. However, there is no need to add unnecessary information not shown in the pictures.

2. Pay attention to language usage and delivery. Sticking to the pictures does not mean you cannot elaborate. You can add adjectives to describe the objects and adverbs to describe the actions. You can add details describing the facial expressions, the weather, or the environment in which the story takes place. Using advanced language such as Chinese idioms, metaphors, proverbs, and so on, is a great add-in.

3. Check your work. Try to give yourself time to check your story narration using the strategies discussed in Chapter 8. Focus on the transitional elements for logic and on a culturally appropriate delivery for the situation. Check for typos and grammatical errors. Use your familiar conjunctions to make correct complex sentences.

E-Mail Response

In this section, you will read an e-mail and respond with the answers to the questions in that e-mail. You have only 15 minutes to type your delivery. Your response should be culturally appropriate to the situation.

You should keep the following key strategies in mind as you write your response to the e-mail:

1. Complete the task. Several steps are needed to complete the e-mail response. First, carefully read the e-mail message that you need to respond to. Make sure that you understand all the questions it asks. Normally, you will need to address three aspects for two questions. You are not able to predict the prompt in the actual exam, but you can always use a model response that provides a structure to compare, persuade, and suggest.

2. Pay attention to language usage and delivery. Sticking to the questions does not mean you cannot elaborate. The e-mail response requires you to provide reasons for your suggestions. Writing a statement sentence and giving a more detailed explanation is good enough. Here, too, using advanced language such as Chinese idioms, metaphors, proverbs, and so on, is a great add-in.

3. Start with a structure (template) prepared in advance. To read an e-mail and respond in 15 minutes, there may not be time left for you to check your work like you did in story narration. You can make the best use of your limited time by doing fill-in-the-blank writing instead of starting from zero in the actual exam. A prepared, well-organized structure or template with perfect grammar and the use of rich language thought out before the exam really help you to better succeed in this task. Adapt the prepared structure to the questions you are asked to respond to.

Conversation

You will participate in a simulated conversation by answering six questions with twenty seconds for each answer. You will hear the conversation prompts, and your spoken answers will be recorded. The questions are based on a particular topic and a particular person.

Keep the following key strategies in mind as you approach this task:

1. Listen carefully. Understanding the question is as important as answering it. First, listen to the English introduction carefully as it often provides you exact information about the major topic of the 6 questions, and helps you to predict the possible focuses. Then, listen to the prompt extremely carefully. In a lot of cases, there are two questions in one prompt, and you need to answer both of them. Repeat them in your mind.

2. Complete the task. Answer the questions directly first and then provide elaboration. Speak as much as possible for the 20 seconds you are given. If you did not get the question or missed some information you think is important, do not give up. Try to repeat the words you know, and then share your opinions and explain your reasoning. Most prompts involve questions about opinions and the reasons behind them.

3. Pay attention to language usage and delivery. Do not worry too much about your grammar. If your mind goes blank, start out with a phrase you know such as "As far as I know…" or "What I would like to say…." Speak as fast and fluently as possible for the familiar parts. Give examples, rephrase your answers, and use language that is culturally appropriate to the situation to demonstrate your ability for good language usage and delivery. Do not blurt out English when frustrated.

Cultural Presentation

You will give an oral presentation on a specific cultural topic and its significance. The time limit for the task is approximately seven minutes. You will have a minute to read the prompt (question), and then you will have four minutes to prepare before your two-minute presentation.

For the cultural presentation, keep the following key strategies in mind:

1. Use your four minutes for careful preparation. You can do a lot of constructive preparation in the four minutes. First, carefully read the task you are assigned (the prompt). Make sure that you understand what cultural practice or product you need to discuss. Sometimes there is a specific condition (usually adjectives such as famous, traditional, regional, etc.) added to the topic. Your preparation should be based on the condition and include some complete sentences.

2. Complete the task. Start with your main idea as the first sentence. If you are going to talk about a cultural topic and its significance, then state it. Second, describe the features and share the significance. Speak as fast and fluently as possible for the familiar parts. Give examples, rephrase your previous sentences, and explain the cultural significance appropriate to the situation. If you have time, plan a beautiful closing sentence that wows.

3. Start with a structure (template) prepared in advance. Similar to the e-mail response, you can prepare a structured outline before the exam because most topics involve a cultural practice and its significance. Thus, you can do fill-in-the-blank speaking instead of starting from zero in the actual exam. Preparing a well-organized structure with perfect grammar and the using rich language before the exam can really help you to succeed in this task.

Analyzing Your Performance on the Diagnostic Test

You have been introduced to the basic strategies in taking the exam. In the next seven chapters, you will use these strategies to practice with exam-like questions. But before we move on, there is one more strategy to discuss: focusing your preparation time on your weaknesses. This is a strategy for exam preparation, rather than for exam-taking like the previous ones.

Of course, before you can focus your preparation on your weaknesses, you will need to identify them. The following worksheets list the major reasons for mistakes—the ones frequently made by students—on each part of the exam. The lists may not reflect all your weaknesses. You are encouraged to add things to the list to reflect your own weaknesses based on your own analysis. Adjust your study plan as needed.

Now analyze your errors thoroughly and identify possible problem areas in which you want to work for improvement. Read the suggestions for each problem and think about them. Do not worry if you are not able to grasp everything totally at this point. We will review the knowledge and sharpen the strategies in the later chapters.

Analyzing Your Performance on the Listening Rejoinders

Self-Evaluation for the Listening Rejoinders

FREQUENT REASONS FOR ERRORS	WHICH QUESTION?	NUMBER OF ERRORS
1. I did not pay attention to the repeated and/or stressed key words.		
2. I did not pay attention to the numbers.		
3. My answer rephrased the dialogue instead of continuing the logic.		
4. The speaker's speed on this question was too fast.		
5. I knew that word was important but I just did not understand it.		
6. Oops. I just missed the important part.		
Think: What kinds of errors did I make the most? Why did I not find the correct answers? What could I do to improve?		

Suggestions for the Listening Rejoinders

FREQUENT REASONS FOR ERRORS	SUGGESTIONS
1. I did not pay attention to the repeated and/or stressed key words.	The key words causing the error are normally negation words; you will find a lot of practice with this in Chapter 6.
2. I did not pay attention to the numbers.	Repeat the number in your mind a couple of times.
3. My answer rephrased the dialogue instead of continuing the logic.	Change your thinking model. Pay attention to the latest content. Practice answering questions in daily study.
4. The speaker's speed on this question was too fast.	Get intensive listening practice before the exam. Tips are provided in Chapter 5.
5. I knew that word was important but I just did not understand it.	Skip it. Or guess it based on the main idea if you can.
6. Oops. I just missed the important part.	There are only five seconds. Click Choice (C) as a guess and wait for the next question.
Think: What kind of errors did I make the most? Why did I not find the correct answers? What could I do to improve?	See the study tips in Chapter 5.

Analyzing Your Performance on the Listening Selections

Self-Evaluation for the Listening Selections

FREQUENT REASONS FOR ERRORS	WHICH QUESTION?	NUMBER OF ERRORS
1. I did not pay attention to the repeated key words.		
2. I did not pay attention to the numbers.		
3. My notes did not cover the key information for the question.		
4. I did not have time to take notes about the important information.		
5. The speaker's speed of this selection was too fast.		
6. I knew that word was important but I did not understand it.		
7. Oops. I just missed it again…too fast.		
Think: What kinds of errors did I make the most? Why did I not find the correct answers? What could I do to improve?		

Suggestions for Listening Selections

FREQUENT REASONS FOR ERRORS	SUGGESTIONS
1. I did not pay attention to the repeated/stressed key words.	Pay attention to them. Key words are normally verbs, numbers, locations, and so on. Remember that the basic sentence structure of Chinese is: Subject + Time + Location + Verb, quite different from English.
2. I did not pay attention to the numbers.	Repeat in your mind and take notes.
3. My notes did not cover the key information for the question.	Take note of the main idea, numbers, and stressed or repeated vocabulary.
4. I did not have time to take notes about the important information.	Use symbols to save time. Write Pinyin down since you do not have time to interpret the information into English.
5. The speaker's speed on this selection was too fast.	Get intensive listening practice before the exam. Tips are provided in Chapter 6.
6. I knew that word was important but I did not understand it.	Write Pinyin down. Sometimes you can figure it out when reading the questions and the four answer choices.
7. Oops. I just missed it again…too fast.	Follow the flow. Do not linger at one question or one word.
Think: What kinds of errors did I make the most? Why did I not find the correct answers? What could I do to improve?	See the study tips in Chapter 6.

Analyzing Your Performance on Reading Selections

Self-Evaluation for the Reading Selections

FREQUENT REASONS FOR ERRORS	WHICH QUESTION?	NUMBER OF ERRORS
1. I did not even understand the question.		
2. The question asked for A, but I thought it was asking for B.		
3. I just could not find the sentence in the context related to the question.		
4. Too many words I do not know.		
5. The sentences for the answer are too long and complicated to understand.		
6. I thought I knew the answer, but I did not know that word means "no."		
7. Oops. I do not have enough time to finish.		
Think: What kinds of errors did I make the most? Why did I not find the correct answers? What could I do to improve?		

Suggestions for the Reading Selections

FREQUENT REASONS FOR ERRORS	SUGGESTIONS
1. I did not even understand the question.	S + V + O, skip other information. Note the key words to locate the sentences.
2. The question asked for A, but I thought it was asking for B.	Read the question thoroughly.
3. I just could not find the sentence in the context related to the question.	Look for the key words: numbers, longer phrases, and words you do not know.
4. There were too many words I do not know.	Guess by using radicals or the context. Build your vocabulary in daily study.
5. The sentences for the answer were too long and complicated to understand.	Look for "subject, verb, and object" first. The main idea helps you to figure out the details later. Review "Functional Grammar" in the appendix.
6. I thought I knew the answer, but I did not know that word means "no."	Review negation vocabulary and build your own negation vocabulary pool.
7. Oops. I do not have enough time to finish.	Choose your best guess or just mark (C). Mark the questions you do not know and come back later.
Think: What kinds of errors did I make the most? Why did I not find the correct answers? What could I do to improve?	See the study tips in Chapter 7.

Now redo the multiple-choice questions you got wrong the first time. If most of the errors come this time from not knowing vocabulary, congratulations. You have gained the basic strategies of the multiple-choice exam machine. You will find more practice to increase your knowledge and refine your strategies starting with Chapter 5.

Analyzing Your Performance on the Story Narration

FREQUENT REASONS FOR ERRORS	SUGGESTIONS
1. I did not have time to finish the task.	Use the three steps described in Chapter 8. You can finish the task within the time limit.
2. I missed some actions.	This normally happens when there are two parties acting differently in one picture. Remember to write both actions.
3. I forgot how to write the important words.	Normally the words you will have difficulty with are verbs because the nouns are easier in story narration. If you do not know how to write a word, try to describe the action in greater detail using other words or replace the word you do not know with one that is close in meaning.
4. I wrote the English words for some words I do not know.	Never use English words because the AP grader will skip them. It shows that you are not serious about taking the exam.
5. I really did not have enough to write because the four pictures are so simple.	Elaboration is required in the rubrics. Try adding adjectives and adverbs, facial expressions, and even describe the environment.
6. My grammar is so bad that I can only write simple sentences correctly.	Making a list instead of using complete sentences may give a score of 2. Using conjunctions for complex sentences win you points in language usage and delivery. Practice the "Functional Grammar" in the appendix.
7. My typing speed was too slow.	Practice makes perfect. Try to use Microsoft Pinyin IME or Microsoft New Phonetic IME, which is used by the AP Chinese exam.
Think: What kinds of errors did I make the most? Why did I not find the correct answers? What could I do to improve?	See the study tips in Chapter 8.

Analyzing Your Performance on the E-mail Response

FREQUENT REASONS FOR ERRORS	SUGGESTIONS
1. I did not have time to finish the task.	Use the three steps described in Chapter 9. Prepare your template in advance.
2. I did not answer all the questions. I did not finish all of the questions.	Keep in mind that you need to answer two major questions (three parts) and address a couple of small aspects of stimulus. a. Identify which one is better between A and B or what is the best solution for a prompt. b. Provide the evidence/reasons to support. c. Provide suggestions/comments related to the topic.
3. I forgot how to write the important words.	Normally the words you will have difficulty with are verbs because the nouns are easier in story narration. If you do not know how to write a word, try to describe the action in greater detail using other words or replace the word you do not know with one that is close in meaning.
4. I just wrote the English for some words I do not know.	Never use English words because the AP grader will skip them. It shows that you are not serious about taking the exam.
5. I really did not have much to say. I could not find more to write.	Elaboration is required in the rubrics. Practice providing comparisons and persuasion.
6. My grammar is so bad that I can only write simple sentences correctly.	You should develop a template for the e-mail response and remember it. Pay attention to two functions of sentences: comparison and persuasion.
7. My typing speed was too slow.	Practice makes perfect. Try to use Microsoft Pinyin IME or Microsoft New Phonetic IME, which is used for the AP exam.
Think: What kinds of errors did I make the most? Why did I not find the correct answers? What could I do to improve?	See the study tips in Chapter 9.

Analyzing Your Performance on Conversation

FREQUENT REASONS FOR ERRORS	SUGGESTIONS
1. I did not even understand the question.	Actually, there may be two questions together. Listen to the prompt very carefully. Repeat it in your mind.
2. I did not understand some words in the prompt.	Skip them. You can get the main idea and provide a great answer without knowing some of the words.
3. I knew that word was important, but I just did not understand it.	The speaking speed of the prompt is always fast for a nervous exam taker. Repeat the words you know and try to talk about them. It is risky, but a score of 3 is better than nothing.
4. I answered the question, but there was still time left and I did not have anything more to say.	Do not stop talking. There are so many ways to elaborate your answers: give examples, share your opinions, or even just rephrase what you said.
5. My mind went blank.	But your tongue did not. Frame your response with phrases you know such as "I mean," or "to my best knowledge." This will win you a few seconds to organize your answer.
6. My grammar is bad.	Never worry about grammar in conversation. Just blurt it out.
7. My pronunciation is bad.	Practice makes perfect. Also, watch Chinese movies and repeat the scripts of your favorite roles in daily study.
Think: What kinds of errors did I make the most? Why did I not find the correct answers? What could I do to improve?	See the study tips in Chapter 10.

Analyzing Your Performance on Cultural Presentation

FREQUENT REASONS FOR ERRORS	SUGGESTIONS
1. I did not know what to talk about because I am not familiar with this cultural practice or product.	Each prompt lists some detailed samples, and this will help you to think about something you know that is related to the cultural topic.
2. The prompt was supposed to be on a specific topic but I ended up with a general one.	Sometimes there is a specific "adjective" for the cultural practice or product. Pay attention to it, for example, ancient invention, regional food, famous person, classical art form, and so on.
3. I did not have much to write down in the four minutes given for preparing.	You have four minutes to write down your notes and prepare. You can use a structure or a template you have prepared and practiced with in advance.
4. I answered the question, but there is still time left and I did not have more to say.	Look back at the suggestion for #3. Now you know what to do. You need to prepare a detailed structure or template. You will learn how to do this in Chapter 11.
5. My mind went blank.	But your tongue did not. Frame your response with phrases you know such as "I mean," or "to my best knowledge." This will win you a few seconds to organize your answer.
6. My grammar is bad.	Go back to the suggestion for #3 again. You should prepare a template with perfect grammar before the exam.
7. My pronunciation is bad.	Practice makes perfect. Ask Chinese native speakers to give two-minute cultural presentations. Record them. Imitate this in your daily study.
Think: What kinds of errors did I make the most? Why did I not find the correct answers? What could I do to improve?	See the study tips in Chapter 11.

It is better not to redo the free-response questions of the diagnostic exam right now. You should practice the strategies for multiple-choice questions in Chapters 5 through 7 and gain a more solid foundation of vocabulary and grammar. Then you can review the writing and speaking tasks following the steps described in detail in Chapters 8 through 11. In the long run, you will find that achieving success on the free-response questions will be easier after you have completed more review.

STEP 4

Review the Knowledge You Need to Score High

CHAPTER 5

Listening Rejoinders

IN THIS CHAPTER

Summary: This chapter provides practice for the listening rejoinder section of the AP Chinese Language and Culture exam. You will start with warm-up exercises and then review the strategies that will help you attack the types of questions you will find on this part of the exam. Next are exercises designed to help you learn to avoid the most frequently made errors on the listening rejoinders. Finally you will practice with a set of test-like rejoinder exercises that reflect what are on the real exam. At the end is a worksheet that will help you to do a thorough evaluation of your performance and adjust your study plan accordingly.

Key Strategies/Ideas

✪ Mark the answer at your first thought since you have only five seconds for a question. You may change it if needed in this five seconds.

✪ Do not bother to think back on the previous question. Pay all attention to the current one.

✪ The correct answer continues the dialogue instead of rephrasing it.

✪ Practice your reaction to Chinese aurally by fast and loud reading.

✪ Practice 20 new vocabulary words/phrases daily using the appendix, "Frequently Used Vocabulary in Reading and Listening."

In this part of the exam (Section I, Part A: Rejoinders), you will finish 10 to 15 multiple-choice questions in 10 minutes. You will hear several short, incomplete conversations. The answers will be read to you instead of appearing on your screen. After listening to the conversation and its four possible continuations, you will choose the response that is the most logical and culturally appropriate to complete the conversation. You have five seconds to choose the answer, and you *cannot* get back to check or change your answer after the five seconds are over.

The listening tracks for the questions are provided on the CD accompanying this book. The scripts for the selections you hear are provided in this chapter for your reference. Do not look at these until after you complete the practice questions; the scripts will help you understand any mistakes you make.

You are sitting in front of the computer to take the AP Chinese Language and Culture exam, and you might be exhausted, having already taken another long and intense AP exam earlier in the same day. You are trying to focus. However, before you know what has hit you, a bunch of fast Chinese jumps into your brain.

That is right. Most AP Chinese exam takers are shocked how fast the speed of listening rejoinders is. The frustration caused by rejoinders in the first three minutes may ruin their performance of the whole exam. Take a deep breath, stay focused, and be prepared to miss a couple of questions. But do not worry; you can still do well on the exam.

Warm-Up Exercises

Practice Questions 1 through 5 are designed to get you started. The listening track for these questions is provided on the CD accompanying this book. Listen to the conversations without referring to the printed scripts. Answer the multiple-choice questions you will hear on the CD. Later, after you have completed the five questions, you can refer to the printed script located at the end of this section to see the conversations and questions you heard.

Track 9

Answer Sheet
1. Ⓐ Ⓑ Ⓒ Ⓓ
2. Ⓐ Ⓑ Ⓒ Ⓓ
3. Ⓐ Ⓑ Ⓒ Ⓓ
4. Ⓐ Ⓑ Ⓒ Ⓓ
5. Ⓐ Ⓑ Ⓒ Ⓓ

Script for Track 9

Question #1

Simplified Chinese
Woman: 我们的历史作业是关于欧洲十八世纪的，我正在找资料。你有什么建议吗？
Man:

(A) 我们的作业太多了。
(B) 我有一些关于这方面的资料，等明天给你吧。
(C) 我打算到欧洲学习。
(D) 你这么快就找到资料了？

Traditional Chinese

Woman: 我們的歷史作業是關於歐洲十八世紀的，我正在找資料。你有甚麼建議嗎？

Man:

(A) 我們的作業太多了。

(B) 我有一些關於這方面的資料，等明天給你吧。

(C) 我打算到歐洲學習。

(D) 你這麼快就找到資料了？

Question #2

Simplified Chinese

Woman: 你怎么八点才来参加考试？不是说好了七点半笔试吗？

Man: 七点半？明明通知上写的是九点，我还提前了一个小时呢！

Woman:

(A) 九点是正式面试的时间，我们七点半先要参加笔试！

(B) 我也不喜欢考试。

(C) 面试和笔试，你想参加哪一个？

(D) 幸好你带了通知过来。

Traditional Chinese

Woman: 你怎麼八點才來參加考試？不是說好了七點半筆試嗎？

Man: 七點半？明明通知上寫的是九點，我還提前了一個小時呢！

Woman:

(A) 九點是正式面試的時間，我們七點半先要參加筆試！

(B) 我也不喜歡考試。

(C) 面試和筆試，你想參加哪一個？

(D) 幸好你帶了通知過來。

Question #3

Simplified Chinese

Man: 你上次说想报名参加中文演讲大赛，结果怎么样？

Woman: 我报上了，我们中文老师说让我下星期五开始练习。

Man:

(A) 我们星期五去演讲吧。

(B) 对不起，演讲大赛报名已截止，不招人了。

(C) 别难过，明年去参加就行了。

(D) 你应该好好练习，争取赛出好成绩！

Traditional Chinese

Man: 你上次說想報名參加中文演講大賽，結果怎麼樣？

Woman: 我報上了，我們中文老師說讓我下星期五開始練習。

Man:

(A) 我們星期五去演講吧。
(B) 對不起，演講大賽報名已截止，不招人了。
(C) 別難過，明年去參加就行了。
(D) 你應該好好練習，爭取賽出好成績！

Question #4

Simplified Chinese
Woman: 你今年选了三门AP课啊？我怎么一点也不知道？
Man: 我本来只选了两门AP课的，可是我爸爸叫我再加一门数学。
Woman:

(A) 太可惜了，你AP考试没有考好。
(B) 难怪你爸爸喜欢数学。
(C) 我理解，我爸妈也要我今年多参加几门AP考试。
(D) 你真的从来没有考过AP吗？

Traditional Chinese
Woman: 你今年選了三門AP課啊？我怎麼一點也不知道？
Man: 我本來只選了兩門AP課的，可是我爸爸叫我再加一門數學。
Woman:

(A) 太可惜了，你AP考試沒有考好。
(B) 難怪你爸爸喜歡數學。
(C) 我理解，我爸媽也要我今年多參加幾門AP考試。
(D) 你真的從來沒有考過AP嗎？

Question #5

Simplified Chinese
Man: 你不是去中国旅游了吗？什么时候回来的？
Woman: 谁说的？尽管我想去，可是没赚够钱。
Man:

(A) 难道我赚钱就是为了去旅游吗？
(B) 没事，我没说。
(C) 要不然，我就去中国了。
(D) 看你说的，可以先赚够钱，明年再去嘛。

Traditional Chinese
Man: 你不是去中國旅遊了嗎？甚麼時候回來的？
Woman: 誰説的？儘管我想去，可是沒賺夠錢。
Man:

(A) 難道我賺錢就是為了去旅遊嗎？
(B) 沒事，我沒説。
(C) 要不然，我就去中國了。
(D) 看你説的，可以先賺夠錢，明年再去嘛。

Answers and Explanations

1. (B) Choice B is: "I have some resources for this. Wait until tomorrow and I will give them to you." The woman asks for suggestion about finding the resources for her history homework. The key words are "resources" 资料（資料）and "suggestion" 建议（建議）. Pay attention to the stressed or repeated words that can help you to identify the correct answer. Choice (A), "We have too much homework," does not logically continue the conversation. Choice (C), "I plan to study in Europe," is not related to the resources and suggestion. Choice (D) "You found the resources so quickly?" talks about "resources" like the correct answer, but this answer does not logically continue the conversation.

2. (A) "The time for the formal interview is at 9. We should have taken the written test first at 7:30." For questions that contain content with numbers, the answer normally will be related to the numbers. The woman is unhappy that the man was late and states there were different times scheduled for different things. Choice (B), "I don't like the test either," does not logically continue the conversation. Choice (C), "Which one do you want to take, the interview or the written test?" continues the conversation, but this does not make sense. Choice (D), "Luckily you brought the notice," does not make any sense here.

3. (D) "You should practice a lot and try to succeed!" is the correct answer. The most common incorrect answer would be (B), which repeats the word "speech contest" 演讲大赛（演講大賽）, but does not take into account the man's later mention of "practice on Friday." The answer should continue the dialogue about practice, which Choice (D) does. Choice (A), "Let's go to the speech on Friday," is not connected to the speech contest or the practice. Choice (C), "Don't be sad. Participate next year." would only be said if the man did not register successfully, but it is not true because he said he "registered" 我报上了（我報上了）instead of 没报上（沒報上）.

4. (C) The best answer is: "I understand. My parents want me to take more AP courses as well." Choice (B) states it is "no wonder" 难怪（難怪）his dad likes math, which does not continue the dialogue logically. Choices (A) and (C) talk about taking AP exams, which is off the topic of choosing AP courses.

5. (D) "Come on. You could make enough money and go there next year" is the best continuation of the conversation. Note that there are two sentence structures in this dialogue that may cause confusion: 不是……吗(嗎) actually means "yes." The man thought the woman went to China and asks her when she got back. The woman answers "who said so" 谁说的（誰說的）which does not mean she really wanted to know who said it. The meaning is "No, not true." Choice (A), "Are you saying that I make money only to travel?" does not make sense here. Choice (B), "Nothing, I didn't say it" is incorrect. Selecting this answer results from the misunderstanding of the real meaning of the phrase 谁说的(誰說的). Finally, Choice (C), "Otherwise I will go to China," does not logically continue the dialogue for the man.

Strategies for the Listening Rejoinders

You have probably had a lot of practice and learned a lot of strategies answering multiple-choice questions on all kinds of standardized tests in the past. But the rejoinders of the AP Chinese exam are different from the multiple-choice questions you have encountered before—you have only five seconds in which to respond.

You learned the basic strategies for the rejoinders in Chapter 4. Now you need to put them into action. Embed the following five strategies in your mind and make them your habit, because there will not be time to think about them. Using these strategies can keep you from making unnecessary errors on the rejoinders section of the AP exam.

Strategies for the Rejoinders

1. Mark your answer in five seconds. If you do not know the answer, click Choice C and move on.
2. Pay attention to the repeated and/or stressed key words. The later they appear in the dialogue, the more important they are.
3. Always keep in mind that your answer must continue the conversation.
4. Pay attention to the numbers as there may be a trap in the question.
5. Understand the social formulae. This is the most important tip. You need to spend time learning the tips of how Chinese communicate their opinions, attitudes, and intents.

Negation Phrases

Similar to English, there is a system of "modality" or "tone" in the Chinese language to demonstrate the mood or intention of the speakers. Most vocabulary/phrases/expressions causing confusion on the AP Chinese exam are those that indicate the opposite meaning of what happened. Let us call them "negation phrases"; most of them are adverbs. For example:

English: Although he likes playing video games, he has to finish homework first.
Chinese: 尽管他喜欢玩电子游戏，可是他得先做完作业。
儘管他喜歡玩電子遊戲，可是他得先做完作業。

"Although" 尽管 is a negation phrase. This sentence indicates that he could not play video games now although he likes playing them.

Here is a list of sample negation phrases. Add your own as you do rejoinder exercises.

Negation Phrases

谁说的？/哪儿的话？/说什么呀	
（誰説的？/哪兒的話？/説甚麼呀）	Who said so—It's not true.
尽管 …… 可是……	
（儘管……可是……）	Although, even though
即使…… 也……	
（即使…… 也……）	Even... still...
就算…… 也……	
（就算…… 也……）	Even if... still

无论……都/也……	
(無論……都/也……)	No matter what…
以免 / 免得	
(以免 / 免得)	In case
要是…… 就好了	
(要是…… 就好了)	What if…
要不然	
(要不然)	Otherwise
除非	
(除非)	Unless
只是	
(只是)	It's just that…
难道，莫非	
(難道，莫非)	Are you saying that…
只有……才……	
(只有……才……)	Only if… then…
怎么这么 ……	
(怎麼這麼)	Why like this…
太……了	
(太……了)	too…
……才怪！	
(……才怪！)	Won't/It is too strange that…
可惜	
(可惜)	It's a pity that…
竟然/居然	
(竟然/居然)	Surprisingly, to my surprise

Study Tips for Rejoinders

If you find the rejoinders difficult, follow these study tips to prepare for the exam.

Vocabulary Building: Practice 20 new vocabulary/phrases daily using the appendix "Frequently Used Vocabulary in Reading and Listening."

Extensive Listening: Watch Chinese movies and TV programs without subtitles. Listen to Chinese audio materials whenever you have time.

Intensive Listening: Make good usage of scripts in this book or other similar resources.

Listen to the track on the CD and answer the questions.

Read the scripts as loud as possible and as fast as possible.

Do not think about the meaning of each word when reading. In other words, do not make your listening comprehension practice into reading comprehension.

Listen again to the track on the CD and answer the questions again.

Add the important vocabulary words and phrases to your own vocabulary.

Skill-Building Exercises: Set Phrases

The exercises in this section focus on the set phrases and social formulas you may have trouble with. Without looking at the scripts, you should listen to Track 10 on the CD, or ask your classmates to read the following sentences at a very fast speed. Then look at the scripts and use our tips for Intensive Listening to review if you find it difficult. Try to continue the sentence(s) with your own idea and make your own sentences using the phrases underlined.

Track 10

The Script and Translations for Listening Rejoinders: Track 10

1. <u>谁说</u>小明不知道作业是什么？
（誰說小明不知道作業是什麼？）
Who said that Xiao Ming does not know what the homework is?

2. 易多多<u>不是</u>去机场接你了<u>吗</u>？你怎么没见到她啊？
（易多多不是去機場接你了嗎？你怎麼沒見到她啊？）
Didn't Yi Duoduo go to the airport to pick you up? Why didn't you see her?

3. 你得早点订机票，<u>免得</u>太晚了价钱就涨上去了。
（你得早點訂機票，免得太晚了價錢就漲上去了。）
You'd better book the flight ticket as early as possible, in case it becomes too late and the price goes up.

4. 花了那么多时间准备这次面试，<u>要是</u>我能得到这份工作<u>就好了</u>！
（花了那麼多時間準備這次面試，要是我能得到這份工作就好了！）
I have spent so much time to prepare for this interview, what if I could get this job?

5. 你学习也太不用功了！只有努力再努力才行，<u>要不然</u>就考不上好大学了。
（你學習也太不用功了！只有努力再努力才行，要不然就考不上好大學了。）
You were too lazy in your study. Only hard work works, otherwise you could not get into a good college.

6. 这么贵的房子，这么差的条件，他要真租了<u>才怪</u>！
（這麼貴的房子，這麼差的條件，他要真租了才怪！）
With such an expensive price and the bad condition it is in, he would never really rent this place.

7. 昨天的摇滚音乐会实在是太棒了！<u>可惜</u>我只有一张票，所以没有叫上你。
（昨天的搖滾音樂會實在是太棒了！可惜我只有一張票，所以沒有叫上你。）
The Rock and Roll concert yesterday was super great! It is a pity that I only had one ticket so I could not ask you to go.

8. 我没想到你<u>居然</u>这么会弹钢琴！
（我沒想到你居然這麼會彈鋼琴！）
I did not know that you are so good at playing the piano.

9. <u>说什么</u>你不想来烧烤，结果你<u>不还是</u>来了！
（說甚麼你不想來燒烤，結果你不還是來了！）
You said that you did not want to come for the BBQ, but you came anyway.

10. 无论我有多忙，我每天都会给你打个电话！

（無論我有多忙，我每天都會給你打個電話！）

No matter how busy I am, I will give you a call every day.

11. 你真的认为这样做能行吗？

（你真的認為這樣做能行嗎？）

Do you really think this will work?

12. 原来你在洗手间啊！难怪我按门铃这么多次都没有人来开门！

（原來你在洗手間啊！難怪我按門鈴這麼多次都沒有人來開門！）

Oh, you were in the bathroom! No wonder no one answered the door after I pushed the doorbell many times.

13. 我忘了带钥匙！幸亏你来了。

（我忘了帶鑰匙！幸虧你來了。）

I forgot my key. Lucky you came here.

14. 我要是去了，你可千万记得给我打电话啊！

（我要是去了，你可千萬記得給我打電話啊！）

If I go, you should keep in mind that you will call me.

15. 你不做作业怎么还是考得那么好？未免太过份了！

（你不做作業怎麼還是考得那麼好？未免太過份了！）

You still can do well on the test, even if you do not finish homework. That is too unfair!

16. 我才不在乎你请不请我呢。大不了我下次一个人去。

（我才不在乎你請不請我呢。大不了我下次一個人去。）

I do not care that you do not treat me. What is the big deal? I can go by myself next time.

17. 我就说吧，如果这游戏不好玩，能有那么多人买吗？

（我就說吧，如果這遊戲不好玩，能有那麼多人買嗎？）

As I said, if this game is not good, how can it get so many people to buy it?

18. 做了错事还不承认，你觉得你很聪明吗？

（做了錯事還不承認，你覺得你很聰明嗎？）

You did the wrong thing but did not admit it. Do you think you are smart?

19. 你就别说没时间了。得了吧，我还不知道你吗？

（你就別說沒時間了。得了吧，我還不知道你嗎？）

Just do not say that you do not have time. Come on, don't I know you well?

20. 都十二点了，你到底去不去看电影？

（都十二點了，你到底去不去看電影？）

It is already 12 o'clock? Are you going to the movie or not?

Listening Rejoinders Practice Test (Exam Section I, Part A)

The 15 rejoinder exercises in this section create an experience very similar to what you will encounter on the actual exam. Listen to the conversations on Track 11 of the CD accompanying this book. Answer the multiple-choice questions by choosing the best response. Do not use the printed script.

Finish the test-like experience first. Then see how many you got wrong. If you missed any, look at the script of what you heard and the explanations for the answers to find out where or how you went wrong. Note that you should understand the meanings not only of the correct answer, but also of the incorrect choices.

Finally, do a thorough analysis of where and why you made any errors. Use the self-evaluation sheet provided. Then look at the suggestions for each kind of mistake you made. Refer to "Study Tips for Rejoinders" earlier in this chapter if you feel you need more practice.

The Practice Questions

The audio track for the questions can be found on the CD accompanying this book. Listen to the conversations and the answer choices. On the following answer sheet, mark the letter that corresponds to the correct answer choice. You will have only five seconds to select your answer. After the five-second limit, you may not go back and change your answer. A script for the conversations you will hear is provided for your reference; do not look at it until after you have answered all the questions.

Track 11

1. (A) (B) (C) (D)
2. (A) (B) (C) (D)
3. (A) (B) (C) (D)
4. (A) (B) (C) (D)
5. (A) (B) (C) (D)
6. (A) (B) (C) (D)
7. (A) (B) (C) (D)
8. (A) (B) (C) (D)
9. (A) (B) (C) (D)
10. (A) (B) (C) (D)
11. (A) (B) (C) (D)
12. (A) (B) (C) (D)
13. (A) (B) (C) (D)
14. (A) (B) (C) (D)
15. (A) (B) (C) (D)

The Script for Listening Rejoinders: Track 11

Question #1

Simplified Chinese

Man: 我看过你在文化周晚会上的表演了，你的歌唱得真好！
Woman:

(A) 那还用说，我练了很多年了。
(B) 唱歌和跳舞都是很好的爱好。
(C) 难怪你也喜欢唱歌。
(D) 可惜，就是没时间去参加文化周的晚会。

Traditional Chinese

Man: 我看過你在文化周晚會上的表演了，你的歌唱得真好！
Woman:

(A) 那還用説，我練了很多年了。
(B) 唱歌和跳舞都是很好的愛好。
(C) 難怪你也喜歡唱歌。
(D) 可惜，就是沒時間去參加文化周的晚會。

Question #2

Simplified Chinese

Man: 你昨天不是给自己买了一套名牌衣服吗？今天又上街了？
Woman: 那套衣服质量不怎么样，我不打算穿，今天买的裙子才会穿。
Man:

(A) 你买的鞋子好漂亮啊。
(B) 好在我也喜欢上街。
(C) 天天花那么多钱，买了又不穿，还不如不买。
(D) 难怪你喜欢名牌，可是我不在乎什么名牌不名牌的。

Traditional Chinese

Man: 你昨天不是給自己買了一套名牌衣服嗎？今天又上街了？
Woman: 那套衣服質量不怎麼樣，我不打算穿，今天買的裙子才會穿。
Man:

(A) 你買的鞋子好漂亮啊。
(B) 好在我也喜歡上街。
(C) 天天花那麼多錢，買了又不穿，還不如不買。
(D) 難怪你喜歡名牌，可是我不在乎甚麼名牌不名牌的。

Question #3

Simplified Chinese

Woman: 我做梦也没想到，小容居然喜欢小靖！小靖平时不爱说话，小容一开口就没完没了的，这两个人在一起怎么会那么开心呢？

Man:

    (A) 萝卜白菜，各有所爱。人家自己喜欢就行了！
    (B) 幸好小容不喜欢说话。
    (C) 喜欢不了。小容和小靖性格不一样。
    (D) 没有小容，小靖当然开心。

Traditional Chinese

Woman: 我做夢也沒想到，小容居然喜歡小靖！小靖平時不愛説話，小容一開口就沒完沒了的，這兩個人在一起怎麼會那麼開心呢？

Man:

    (A) 蘿蔔白菜，各有所愛。人家自己喜歡就行了！
    (B) 幸好小容不喜歡説話。
    (C) 喜歡不了。小容和小靖性格不一樣。
    (D) 沒有小容，小靖當然開心。

Question #4

Simplified Chinese

Woman: 我正急得不得了，你倒好，还这么慢腾腾的！
Man: 我哪里慢了？反正我们会开车去，还有一个多小时呢！
Woman:

    (A) 你开车开得很快。
    (B) 我一向不急的，你慢慢来。
    (C) 你就不能等等我吗？我马上就好了。
    (D) 万一塞车，一个小时根本到不了。

Traditional Chinese

Woman: 我正急得不得了，你倒好，還這麼慢騰騰的！
Man: 我哪裡慢了？反正我們會開車去，還有一個多小時呢！
Woman:

    (A) 你開車開得很快。
    (B) 我一向不急的，你慢慢來。
    (C) 你就不能等等我嗎？我馬上就好了。
    (D) 萬一塞車，一個小時根本到不了。

Question #5

Simplified Chinese

Woman: 你怎么还在这儿磨蹭？八点半的飞机，再晚就来不及了！
Man:

    (A) 今天是多少号啊？你怎么不记得，飞机改到后天了。
    (B) 我不喜欢坐飞机。
    (C) 我们后天坐飞机去重庆好不好？
    (D) 飞机到了我就去机场接你，来得及的。

Traditional Chinese

Woman: 你怎麼還在這兒磨蹭？八點半的飛機，再晚就來不及了！

Man:

    (A) 今天是多少號啊？你怎麼不記得，飛機改到後天了。

    (B) 我不喜歡坐飛機。

    (C) 我們後天坐飛機去重慶好不好？

    (D) 飛機到了我就去機場接你，來得及的。

Question #6

Simplified Chinese

Man: 这是咱们准备送的春节礼物，你看还缺点儿什么？

Woman: 还挺不错的。怎么没有红包呢？我妈妈家兄弟多，孩子也多！

Man:

    (A) 没想到你也要收红包。

    (B) 对啊，怎么把要送的红包给忘了！

    (C) 我家亲戚的孩子也很多。

    (D) 春节我们哪儿也不去。

Traditional Chinese

Man: 這是咱們準備送的春節禮物，你看還缺點兒甚麼？

Woman: 還挺不錯的。怎麼沒有紅包呢？我媽媽家兄弟多，孩子也多！

Man:

    (A) 沒想到你也要收紅包。

    (B) 對啊，怎麼把要送的紅包給忘了！

    (C) 我家親戚的孩子也很多。

    (D) 春節我們哪兒也不去。

Question #7

Simplified Chinese

Woman: 我收拾好了，咱们可以走了。

Man: 这个箱子只怕太重了。航空公司规定每件托运行李不能超过50磅，否则就要多收钱。

Woman:

    (A) 超重行李50块一磅，有没有搞错啊？

    (B) 我这件行李不托运，随身带上飞机。

    (C) 哦，那咱们最好把东西分成两个箱子，免得浪费钱。

    (D) 你提不了这个箱子我们就不去了。

Traditional Chinese

Woman: 我收拾好了，咱們可以走了。

Man: 這個箱子只怕太重了。航空公司規定每件托運行李不能超過50磅，否則就要多收錢。

Woman:

    (A) 超重行李50塊一磅，有沒有搞錯啊？
    (B) 我這件行李不托運，隨身帶上飛機。
    (C) 哦，那咱們最好把東西分成兩個箱子，免得浪費錢。
    (D) 你提不了這個箱子我們就不去了。

Question #8

Simplified Chinese

Man: 你看了昨晚的春节联欢晚会吗？我觉得比去年的好看一点，相声和小品都不错，不过歌舞就次了点。
Woman:

    (A) 我也比较喜欢相声和小品，笑死人了。
    (B) 是啊，昨晚的歌舞挺好看的。
    (C) 你也参加了昨晚的联欢啊，怎么没见到你？
    (D) 唉，相声和小品的确是一年比一年差。

Traditional Chinese

Man: 你看了昨晚的春節聯歡晚會嗎？我覺得比去年的好看一點，相聲和小品都不錯，不過歌舞就次了點。
Woman:

    (A) 我也比較喜歡相聲和小品，笑死人了。
    (B) 是啊，昨晚的歌舞挺好看的。
    (C) 你也參加了昨晚的聯歡啊，怎麼沒見到你？
    (D) 唉，相聲和小品的確是一年比一年差。

Question #9

Simplified Chinese

Woman: 今天可把我气坏了！丽丽又迟到了，害得我们几个没看上电影。
Man:

    (A) 什么坏了？修一下吧，花不了几个钱。
    (B) 你们看了什么电影啊？
    (C) 什么，你怎么又迟到了呢？
    (D) 她就那性格，何必跟她生气。

Traditional Chinese

Woman: 今天可把我氣壞了！麗麗又遲到了，害得我們幾個沒看上電影。
Man:

    (A) 甚麼壞了？修一下吧，花不了幾個錢。
    (B) 你們看了甚麼電影啊？
    (C) 甚麼，你怎麼又遲到了呢？
    (D) 她就那性格，何必跟她生氣。

Question #10

Simplified Chinese

Man: 请问你们宾馆还有空房吗？价格怎么样？

Woman: 我们还有标准双人间，678元，豪华海景单间，558元。请问您想住几天？

Man:

    (A) 就我一个人住，你有信用卡吗？

    (B) 住不住都无所谓，你先来看看房间吧。

    (C) 我选单间，住三天。你们收信用卡吗？

    (D) 怎么单人间比双人间还贵？

Traditional Chinese

Man: 請問你們賓館還有空房嗎？價格怎麼樣？

Woman: 我們還有標準雙人間，678元，豪華海景單間，558元。請問您想住幾天？

Man:

    (A) 就我一個人住，你有信用卡嗎？

    (B) 住不住都無所謂，你先來看看房間吧。

    (C) 我選單間，住三天。你們收信用卡嗎？

    (D) 怎麼單人間比雙人間還貴？

Question #11

Simplified Chinese

Woman: 本来和小王约好明天下午去打网球，可是他突然说不能去，够扫兴的。

Man: 你竟然和小王去打网球？你不知道他从来不打网球吗？

Woman:

    (A) 他要是不喜欢打网球，为什么还答应我呢？

    (B) 我不想和小王打网球。

    (C) 你难道不喜欢打网球吗？

    (D) 和小王约好了的，你为什么不去？

Traditional Chinese

Woman: 本來和小王約好明天下午去打網球，可是他突然說不能去了，夠掃興的。

Man: 你竟然和小王去打網球？你不知道他從來不打網球嗎？

Woman:

    (A) 他要是不喜歡打網球，為甚麼還答應我呢？

    (B) 我不想和小王打網球。

    (C) 你難道不喜歡打網球嗎？

    (D) 和小王約好了的，你為甚麼不去？

Question #12

Simplified Chinese

Woman: 你再把这几个问题练习一下，争取明天面试通过。
Man: 没必要吧，反正只是一份暑期工。
Woman:

(A) 我也喜欢暑期打工，可以锻炼自己的能力。
(B) 是啊，我得多练习练习。
(C) 暑期工怎么啦？你不准备一下还不一定能得到这份工作。
(D) 倒也是，多准备一下才好。

Traditional Chinese

Woman: 你再把這幾個問題練習一下，爭取明天面試通過。
Man: 沒必要吧，反正只是一份暑期工。
Woman:

(A) 我也喜歡暑期打工，可以鍛煉自己的能力。
(B) 是啊，我得多練習練習。
(C) 暑期工怎麼啦？你不準備一下還不一定能得到這份工作。
(D) 倒也是，多準備一下才好。

Question #13

Simplified Chinese

Man: 我打算下个星期找搬家公司搬家。新家很漂亮，也很宽敞。
Woman: 恭喜你了！你家具少，搬起来一定很方便。
Man:

(A) 你下个星期搬到哪？
(B) 东西挺多的，要不为什么找搬家公司呢。
(C) 你总得给我找个新家啊。
(D) 你明天就要搬啊？太快了吧？

Traditional Chinese

Man: 我打算下個星期找搬家公司搬家。新家很漂亮，也很寬敞。
Woman: 恭喜你了！你家具少，搬起來一定很方便。
Man:

(A) 你下個星期搬到哪？
(B) 東西挺多的，要不為甚麼找搬家公司呢。
(C) 你總得給我找個新家啊。
(D) 你明天就要搬啊？太快了吧？

Question #14

Simplified Chinese

Man: 妈妈，我去美国读高中，从九年级一直到十二年级要读四年，我得迟一年才能毕业。

Woman: 哪儿的话。中国的初三正是美国的九年级，你已经读完初三了。

Man:

    (A) 那不还是要上四年？

    (B) 哦，那我就迟一年毕业好了。

    (C) 哦，我明年是高一，在美国是十年级。

    (D) 在美国读高中是比在中国难。

Traditional Chinese

Man: 媽媽，我去美國讀高中，從九年級一直到十二年級要讀四年，我得遲一年才能畢業。

Woman: 哪兒的話。中國的初三正是美國的九年級，你已經讀完初三了。

Man:

    (A) 那不還是要上四年？

    (B) 哦，那我就遲一年畢業好了。

    (C) 哦，我明年是高一，在美國是十年級。

    (D) 在美國讀高中是比在中國難。

Question #15

Simplified Chinese

Woman: 喂，您好，叔叔，请问您儿子出门了吗？比赛就要开始了！

Man: 什么比赛？我怎么不知道？我儿子还不会走路呢！

Woman:

    (A) 啊？糟糕！对不起，打错了！

    (B) 请让他有空给我回电话。

    (C) 已经在路上了？好，太好了！

    (D) 不走路就开车来，总之要赶快！

Traditional Chinese

Woman: 喂，您好，叔叔，請問您兒子出門了嗎？比賽就要開始了！

Man: 甚麼比賽？我怎麼不知道？我兒子還不會走路呢！

Woman:

    (A) 啊？糟糕！對不起，打錯了！

    (B) 請讓他有空給我回電話。

    (C) 已經在路上了？好，太好了！

    (D) 不走路就開車來，總之要趕快！

Answers

1.	A	**9.**	D
2.	C	**10.**	C
3.	A	**11.**	A
4.	D	**12.**	C
5.	A	**13.**	B
6.	B	**14.**	C
7.	C	**15.**	A
8.	A		

Explanations

1. (A) The man praises the woman, saying that she sang well at the cultural week party. The woman answers "of course, I have practiced many years." 那还用说（那還用説）means "do not need to mention, sure." Choice (B), "Both singing and dancing are good hobbies," does not relate to the topic. Choice (C), "No wonder you like singing also," does not logically continue the conversation. Choice (D), "What a pity. I just do not have time to attend the cultural week party," does not make sense here.

2. (C) The man is surprised that the woman went shopping again. The woman states that she does not want to wear the clothes she bought yesterday due to their quality. She wants to wear the dress she bought today. In Choice (C) the man complains that the woman "spent so much money every day. It's better not to buy if she doesn't wear." 不如 is a frequently used phrase that means "would rather." Choice (A), "The shoes you bought are beautiful," is not a good response because the conversation is about the clothes instead of the shoes. Choice (B), "Lucky that I like to go shopping, too" and Choice (D), "No wonder you like brand names, but I don't care whether it is a famous brand," do not logically continue the conversation.

3. (A) The woman is surprised that Xiao Rong likes Xiao Jing. The man tries to explain. Choice (B), "It's lucky that Xiao Rong is not talkative," is incorrect because it is actually Xiao Jing who is not talkative. Choice (C), "They don't like each other. They have different personalities," does not logically continue the conversation. Choice (D), "Of course Xiao Jing is happy without Xiao Rong," does not make sense here.

4. (D) The woman complains that the man is too slow. The man says that he is not slow. "Anyway we will drive there. We have more than one hour left." Choice (D) is "What if the traffic is horrible? We cannot arrive in an hour." Pay attention to three phrases: 不得了 "extremely," 反正 "anyway," and 万（萬）一 "what if, just in case." Choice (A), "You always drive fast," and Choice (B), "I usually am not in a hurry. Take your time," do not logically continue the dialogue. Choice (C), "Can't you wait for me a little bit? I will be all set soon," would fit the conversation, but it would have to be stated by the man instead of the woman.

5. (A) The woman reminds the man to hurry up for the plane at 8:30. 再⋯⋯就 is a commonly used phrase that indicates disagreement on something. 再晚就来（來）不及了 means "There will be no time if you are late again." Choice (A), "What is the date today? Don't you remember the flight was changed to the day after tomorrow?" 今天是多少号（號）啊 is not a question sentence. It is a negative statement: "Today is not the date you are thinking about." For example:

你今年要学六门AP课，还要参加那么多活动，你有多少时间啊？

你今年要學六門AP課，還要參加那麼多活動，你有多少時間啊？

"How much time do you (really) have" means you do not have enough time. Choice (B), "I don't like taking the airplane," and Choice (D), "I will go to pick you up once the plane arrives. There will be time," do not make sense here. Choice (C), "Let's fly to Chongqing the day after tomorrow, how is that?" does not continue the logic.

6. (B) The conversation is about what is missed as the spring festival gifts. The woman mentioned that "where there is no red pockets?" since she has "a lot of brothers and children in her family." (A). "I didn't know that you need to get the pocket, too" changed the subject to who will get the red pockets. (C). "My relatives have a lot of children, too" does not continue the logic. (D). "We won't go anywhere during spring festival" does not make sense here. (B). "Correct! How could I forgot the red pockets" is correct.

7. (C) The conversation is about luggage. The man states the regulation is that a bag must be less than 50 pounds otherwise you have to pay more. The woman's answer should be based on this topic, probably a solution. Choice C, "Oh, then it's better for us to separate the things into two cases so we don't waste money," is correct. 只怕 means "I am afraid," 否则（则） means "otherwise," and 免得 is "just in case." Choice (A) contains wrong information about $50 per pound. Choice (B), "So I will make it a carry-on" does not make sense because a carry-on should be even lighter. Choice (D), "We won't go if you do not carry this case," does not logically continue the conversation.

8. (A) The speakers are sharing comments about the spring festival party. The man states that "overall it is better than last year, with better talk shows and plays, though the singing and dancing were not as good as last year." (B). "Yeah, the singing and dancing performance are great." This is wrong information, opposite to the reality. (C). "You also participated in the party? Why didn't I see you?" This does not make sense because it is a show instead of real-life participation.

9. (D) The girl is really mad that Lili was late again, which stopped them from watching the movie. The answer (B) asks what movie they watched, which does not make sense. (C) "Why you are late again" changed the subject; therefore, it is incorrect. (A) "What was broken? Fix it. It's cheap." This answer comes from the phrase of 气坏了（氣壞了），which means "extremely angry, being angry until causing damages." The original meaning of 坏（壞） was "bad, broken," but here means extremely in the structure. (D) That is how she is. There is no need to be mad. 何必 means "no need to be."

10. (C) This is a conversation about booking a hotel room. (C). The woman introduces the prices and asks how long, the man answers that he books a single room, three nights, and asks whether they take credit cards. (A). The man asking the woman about the credit card does not make sense. (B). Similar to (A), the choice should be spoken from the woman instead of the man. Choice (D) makes sense but does not continue the conversation of "how long do you want to stay?"

11. (A) The woman says that she planned to play tennis with Xiao Wang but suddenly he said he could not go. The man is surprised because he knows that Xiao Wang never plays tennis. Choice A, "If he (Xiao Wang) doesn't like playing tennis, why did he agree to play with me?" is the correct response. "Frustrating" is 扫兴（掃興） and "surprisingly" is 竟然. Choice (B), "I don't want to play tennis with Xiao Wang," is opposite to the reality. Choice (C), "Don't you like playing tennis?" does not continue the conversation logically. Finally, Choice (D), "Why didn't you go since you had an appointment with Xiao Wang" does not make sense because the man did not make an appointment with Xiao Wang.

12. (C) The woman asks the man to review questions for the interview the coming day, but the man thinks it is unnecessary. The woman's reaction should be, normally, either a "Yeah, you are right" or "No, of course it is important." (A) "I also like a summer job, which can train your ability" does not continue the logic; (B) "Yes I should practice more" could be correct if it is said by the man; both (C) and (D) are related to the preparation.

13. (B) The man is going to move to a new place that is beautiful and big. The woman says that he does not have much furniture, so it will be easy for him to move. Choice (B), "Actually there are a lot of things to move. Otherwise I don't need to find a moving company," continues the conversation logically. Choices (A) and (D) are incorrect because the one who is moving is the man instead of the woman. Choice (C), "Anyway you have to find a new place for me," does not make logical sense here. "Otherwise" is 要不，要不然 and "anyway you have to" is 总得（總得）.

14. (C) The man states that there will be four years of high school if he studies in the United States. The woman, his mom, answers that it is not true, because the third year of middle school in China is the ninth grade in high school in the United States. 哪儿的话（哪兒的話） means "where do the words come out?" which indicates "it's nonsense." Choice (C), "I will be in the first year of high school (in China), which is the tenth grade in the United States," is correct. Choice (A), "Then I still need to study for four years," and Choice (B), "OK, then I will graduate one year later," are both incorrect because he already finished the corresponding ninth grade in China. Choice (D), "It's more difficult to study in the high school in the United States than in China," does not logically continue the conversation.

15. (A) The woman asks the man whether his son went out, because the competition will start soon. The man is surprised that he has no idea. He says, "My son doesn't even know how to walk." Therefore, it was a wrong number that the woman called. Choice (A) is correct.

Self-Evaluation

It is important to learn from your mistakes. Evaluate your performance on this practice test to try to understand the reason you missed each question you did. Use the following worksheet. Then look at the suggestions that follow for how to deal with each reason for missing a question.

Self-Evaluation Worksheet for the Listening Rejoinders

FREQUENT REASONS FOR ERRORS	WHICH QUESTION?	NUMBERS OF ERRORS
1. I did not pay attention to the repeated and/or stressed key words.		
2. I did not pay attention to the numbers.		
3. My answer rephrased the dialogue instead of continuing the logic.		
4. The speaker's speed on this question was too fast.		
5. I knew that word is important, but I just did not understand it.		
6. Oops. I just missed the important part.		
Think: What kinds of errors did I make the most? Why did I not find the correct answers? What could I do to improve?		

Suggestions in Response to Errors in the Listening Rejoinders

FREQUENT REASONS FOR ERRORS	SUGGESTIONS
1. I did not pay attention to the repeated and/or stressed key words.	The key words causing the error are normally negation words; see "Negation Phrases" earlier in this chapter.
2. I did not pay attention to the numbers.	Repeat the number in your mind a couple of times.
3. My answer rephrased the dialogue instead of continuing the logic.	Change your thinking model. Pay attention to the latest content. Practice answering questions in daily study.
4. The speaker's speed on this question was too fast.	Get intensive listening practice before the exam. Tips are provided earlier in this chapter.
5. I knew that word was important, but I just did not understand it.	Skip it. Or guess it based on the main idea if you can.
6. Oops. I just missed the important part.	There are only five seconds. Click Choice (C) as a guess and wait for the next question.
Think: What kinds of errors did I make the most? Why did I not find the correct answers? What could I do to improve?	See the general study tips provided earlier in this chapter.

CHAPTER 6

Listening Selections

IN THIS CHAPTER

Summary: This chapter provides practice for the listening selections of the AP Chinese Language and Culture exam. You'll start with warm-up exercises and then review the strategies that will help you attack the types of questions you'll find on this part of the exam. Next is practice with the vocabulary words frequently found in the listening selections on the test. Finally, you'll practice with a set of test-like listening selections and questions that reflect what you will find on the real exam. At the end is a worksheet that will help you to do a thorough evaluation of your performance and adjust your study plan accordingly.

Key Strategies/Ideas

✪ Building good note-taking skills is a key to success on the listening selections. Create your own note-taking system by symbols or shorthand.

✪ Ignore the unimportant information and skip over the unfamiliar words or phrases.

✪ Always listen carefully to the English instructions. They contain information on which type of selection it is and whether it plays once or twice.

✪ Learn the strategies of analyzing the questions and four answer choices to improve your chance of guessing the right answers when you aren't sure.

✪ Improve your reaction to hearing Chinese by fast and loud reading.

✪ Practice 20 vocabulary words/phrases daily by using "Frequently Used Vocabulary and Phrases" in the appendix.

In this part of the exam (Section I, Part A: Listening Selections), you will have 15 minutes to answer 15 to 20 questions based on listening selections you will hear. You will hear several selections. For each selection, you will be told if it will play once or twice. You cannot see the questions and answer options until the listening selection has been completed. Then you will have 12 seconds per question to choose the response that is the best answer. You *cannot* go back to check or change an answer.

The listening tracks for the questions are provided on the CD accompanying this book. The scripts for the selections you hear are provided in this chapter for your reference. Do not look at these until after you complete the practice questions; the scripts will help you understand any mistakes you make.

Warm-Up Exercises

There are two skills/strategies that are vital to doing well on the listening selections in the exam: taking notes and analyzing the answer choices. Get some blank paper and a pen. Practice these skills on the following warm-up exercises. **Remember:** You need to listen to the selections first and take notes. Only after you've heard the selection should you look at the questions and the choices to choose from.

The Public Announcement

Track 12

Questions on the Public Announcement
Look at the following questions *after* you've heard the public announcement. Give yourself 12 seconds per question. Do the questions in the order given; you can't go back to a question later to make a change.

1. The announcement is directed primarily to
   (A) passengers on a train.
   (B) passengers on a bus to the airport.
   (C) passengers in the airport.
   (D) passengers in a subway.

2. How long does it take for the transportation to go to the airport?
   (A) 30 minutes
   (B) One hour
   (C) Two hours
   (D) Didn't mention

3. This announcement asks passengers to
   (A) get off the transportation.
   (B) get off the airplane.
   (C) keep the transportation clean.
   (D) wait for pregnant women.

Tips for the Public Announcement

Common sense is very helpful to understanding the public announcement you will hear. It may be a notice of transportation information, a reminder for visitors or tourists, or instructions regarding behavior in public. Your notes should at least include the content of what it is about, where, when, what happened, what people are being asked to do, and specific information regarding the numbers and repeated/stressed words, if possible. If there is a change of plan, you should pay attention to the reason for the change and the words of "change to an earlier date" 提前, "delay" 晚点（晚點）, "postpone" 推迟（推遲）, "cancel" 取消, and "change"更改.

Do your notes from the listening selection you heard on Track #12 include the following information?
Changsha airport / No1. No2 buildings / 30 min. / luggage L. (location) / old, young, sick…seat / clean/ 2 h. ◄(before) take off.

Another tip for answering the questions regarding the public announcement is to learn vocabulary words often used in public announcements. A public announcement generally contains the words related to the location of the announcement (airport, train station, etc.). Make a list of vocabulary words in the public announcements in this chapter and the practice tests in this book and build your own vocabulary accordingly.

Answers and Explanations for the Public Announcement

1. (B) If you can browse the questions of this selection quickly, you may find the word "airport" in question 2. The answer (D) is not correct because it is a transportation 前往 X X 机场（機場）, which means that it is to "go to XX airport." Therefore, it is not (A) on a "train" 火车（火車）nor (C) "subway" 地铁（地鐵）.

2. (A) Numbers are always important in taking notes. We have two pieces of information related to the numbers: 30 minutes and two hours. Your notes said "2 h. ° take off," so (C) is not correct. Also, normally it would not take two hours for "an airport express bus" 机场快线（機場快線）.

3. (C) There is a word of clean 清洁（清潔）in your notes. Or you can skip A and B first since there is no clear information about these two answers. By common sense or your notes, the answer (D) should be associated with the seats, but it doesn't so (D) is incorrect also.

Script for Track 12

Narrator: Now you will listen to a public announcement. This selection will be played twice.

Simplified Chinese
Woman: 欢迎乘坐长沙市机场快线前往黄花国际机场。本快线分别途经一号、二号航站楼，行车时间全程大约是三十分钟。请自觉遵守《乘客须知》，按线候车，先下后上，并主动为老、幼、病、残、孕乘客让座。上车后请爱护车内设施，保持清洁卫生，共创文明乘车环境。请在飞机起飞前两小时出发去机场。祝您旅途愉快！

Traditional Chinese
Woman: 歡迎乘坐長沙市機場快線前往黃花國際機場。本快線分別途經一號、二號航站樓，行車時間全程大約是三十分鐘。請自覺遵守《乘客須知》，按線候車，先下後上，並主動為老、幼、病、殘、孕乘客讓座。上車後請愛護車內設施，保持清潔衛生，共創文明乘車環境。請在飛機起飛前兩小時出發去機場。祝您旅途愉快!

Narrator: Now listen again.
Narrator: Now answer the questions for this selection.

Conversation

LISTEN

Track 13

Questions on the Conversation

Look at the following questions *after* you've heard the conversation. Give yourself 12 seconds per question. Do the questions in the order given; you can't go back to a question later to make a change.

4. Where does the conversation take place?

(A) Jie Fang Road
(B) Fu Xing Road
(C) Man's home
(D) Woman's home

5. Why does the conversation take place?

(A) The woman needs the directions to Yi Jia store.
(B) The man wants to drive at night.
(C) The man needs directions to Yi Jia store.
(D) The man just got his driver's license.

6. What is the man most likely going to do?

(A) Drive to the Yi Jia store.
(B) Take a public bus to the store.
(C) Pick up the woman.
(D) Park his car and walk to the store.

TIP

Tips for the Conversation

The vocabulary of the conversation selection might be relatively easy because conversations are normally related to daily life, but the scope of content is too broad to guess. Keep in mind that the conversation may only play once. Your notes should at least include the content of what it is about, when and where it takes place, the main ideas of the woman's and the man's dialogue, any conflict or disagreement, and specific information regarding the numbers and repeated/stressed words, if possible.

Do your notes include the following information? Using symbols saves you a lot of time.

M: Fu xing road?
W: Jie fang. Fu xing 2nd + (+ means the crossing)
M: Yi jia store (or shang chang if you do not know the meaning). got ID, night, convenient safe
W: + →(crossing, right turn). parking X. Here. Walk.
M: Transportation heavy, night.

Answers and Explanations for the Conversation

4. (A) This is an easy question, the woman said "Jie Fang Lu."

5. (C) Of the four choices, (B), (C), and (D) are all about the man and (A) and (C) have similar content, so the answer could be (C). This is a strategy to guess the correct answer just by browsing the answers: Repeated information is probably important. From your notes, you confirm that you guessed it right.

6. (D) First, the correct answer should be either (A) or (D) since there is no information indicating (B) and (C). Choose (D) because both the woman and man mentioned it's better to "park" 停车（停車） here. Furthermore, parking is always a nightmare when shopping in China. In most cases, walking to a store is actually quicker.

Script for Track 13
Narrator: Now you will listen to a conversation. This selection will be played once only.

Simplified Chinese
Man: 这里是复兴路吗？

Woman: 不，这里是解放路。复兴路就在前面第二个路口。你要去哪？

Man: 我想去宜家商场。我刚刚领到驾照，正想趁着晚上人少点的时候开车去，这样比较方便和安全，没想到转来转去就找不到地方了。

Woman: 你先别急，其实宜家商场离这儿挺近的，在路口右拐就到了。不过那里停车比较难，如果你买的东西不多，还不如在这边找个地方停车，自己走过去。

Man: 太谢谢了。我也觉得晚上的交通很挤，其实还是在这儿停车好。

Traditional Chinese
Man: 這裡是復興路嗎？

Woman: 不，這裡是解放路。復興路就在前面第二個路口。你要去哪？

Man: 我想去宜家商場。我剛剛領到駕照，正想趁著晚上人少點的時候開車去，這樣比較方便和安全，沒想到轉來轉去就找不到地方了。

Woman: 你先別急，其實宜家商場離這兒挺近的，在路口右拐就到了。不過那裡停車比較難，如果你買的東西不多，還不如在這邊找個地方停車，自己走過去。

Man: 太謝謝了。我也覺得晚上的交通很擠，其實還是在這兒停車好。

Narrator: Now answer the questions for this selection.

Voice Message

Questions on the Voice Message
Look at the following questions *after* you've heard the voice message. Give yourself 12 seconds per question. Do the questions in the order given; you can't go back to a question later to make a change.

Track 14

7. What was originally planned for the day after tomorrow?

   (A) Buying tickets at the stadium.
   (B) Watching the semifinal of the Super Bowl at the stadium.
   (C) Watching the final of the Super Bowl at the stadium.
   (D) Watching TV at home.

8. What is *not* an advantage of watching the semifinal instead of the final?

(A) The tickets for the semifinal are not sold out.
(B) The semifinal is more exciting.
(C) They do not need to go to the stadium one hour earlier.
(D) The cost of the tickets for the semifinal is cheaper.

9. What does the man prefer?

(A) Canceling the activity
(B) Watching the semifinal at home
(C) Trying their luck for a ticket at the gate of the stadium
(D) Watching the semifinal at the stadium

Tips for the Voice Message

Voice message is relatively structured, and you may predict what is happening. Your notes should at least include the content of when and/or where to call, why to call, any change of plan, solution (when/where to meet next time and do what), as well as specific information regarding the numbers, repeated/stressed words if possible.

Do your notes include the following information?

Final: ticket X, wait at the gate, 1h earlier, not sure,
Semi: ok, cheaper, watch, then home final.

Answers and Explanations for the Voice Message

7. (C) Looking for similarities, you find that the only difference between choices (C) and (B) is the "final" 决赛（決賽）and the "semifinal" 半决赛（半決賽）. According to your notes, (C) is correct.

8. (B) According to your notes or common sense, (B) would be correct. A very interesting group of venders in China is the "Yellow Bull" 黄牛，who get tickets earlier and sell them at a higher price for sports games, concerts, and even popular movies. Watch out: You may get ripped off by buying fake tickets in China.

9. (D) The man listed a lot of advantages of watching the semifinal at the stadium and mentioned that they could watch the final on TV at home.

Script for Track 14

Narrator: Now you will listen to a conversation. This selection will be played twice.

Simplified Chinese
Man: 丽丽，我是陈文。你想去看的超级杯决赛已经没有票了，不过半决赛的票还有，要是你愿意，我马上就买。如果你坚持要看决赛，我们得去体育场门口等退票。这样的话，我们后天要提前一小时去体育场，还不一定买得到。你觉得怎么样更好？其实明天的半决赛也挺好看的，价格也便宜很多，大不了我们先看半决赛，再呆在家里看决赛的电视直播。请你早点定下再给我来电话。

Traditional Chinese
Man: 麗麗，我是陳文。你想去看的超級杯決賽已經沒有票了，不過半決賽的票還有，要是你願意，我馬上就買。如果你堅持要看決賽，我們得去體育場門口等退票。這樣的話，我們後天要提前一小時去體育場，還不一定買得到。你覺得怎麼樣更好？其實明天的半決賽也挺好看的，價格也便宜很多，大不了我們先看半決賽，再呆在家裡看決賽的電視直播。請你早點定下再給我來電話。

Narrator: Now listen again.
Narrator: Now answer the questions for this selection.

Instructions

Questions on the Instructions

Look at the following questions *after* you've heard the instructions. Give yourself 12 seconds per question.

10. When will these instructions mostly be heard?

    (A)   Around Spring Festival
    (B)   Around Mid-Autumn festival
    (C)   Around Dragon-Boat Day
    (D)   Around Memorial Day

11. What is the next step if you get the answer of one riddle?

    (A)   Go to another riddle.
    (B)   Go to get the awards.
    (C)   Go to tell the staff member.
    (D)   Take the lantern down.

12. What is *not* true according to this instruction?

    (A)   You should tell the staff member both the answer and the number of the riddle.
    (B)   The staff members take all the awards at the end.
    (C)   The more tickets you get, the better the awards you can exchange them for.
    (D)   The staff will change the riddles if someone provides the correct answer.

Tips for the Instructions

The audio selections with instructions may contain quite a bit of vocabulary you do not understand, but the questions are normally easy because most of them are for the main idea or major procedures. If you know the words "riddle" 谜语（謎語）, "answer to the riddle" 谜底（謎底）, and "ticket for awards" 兑奖券（兌獎券）, things become easy. If not, try a strategy of using Pinyin for the repeated words you do not know in taking notes. Reading the questions and answers later may help you to figure out the unfamiliar words.

Do your notes include the following information?
Cai Deng Mi, lantern festival, spring festival.

1. each Mi Yu. Dui Jiang Chu, staff. Number+Mi Di answer.
2. Mi Di for one award ticket.
3. staff new Mi Yu.
4. Awards a lot, tickets a lot.

Answers and Explanations for the Instructions

10. (A) You may miss a lot of information in this difficult selection, but you should hear something familiar: "lantern festival" 元宵节（元宵節）and "spring festival" 春节（春節）, both of which are around Chinese new year time. Choice (B) is 中秋节（中秋節）, (C) is 端午节（端午節）, and (D) is 清明节（清明節）. These festivals were not mentioned in the selection, so they are not answers.

11. (C) Procedures are important in instructions. The question asks for the next step after getting the answer of the riddle; by common sense, you should make sure your answer is correct by checking with someone who knows the answer. There is a word "answer" at step 1 in your notes, so read your notes for step 2: one awards ticket. Watch out: It's the ticket instead of the award. So choice (B) is not correct. Choices (A) and (D) were not mentioned in the instructions, so that leaves (C) as the correct answer.

12. (B) The questions of "which one is true/not true/not mentioned" are relatively difficult to answer. Understanding the main idea helps you to guess. Choice (A) is true according to your step 1 notes; (C) is true according to your step 4 notes; and (D) is true according to your step 3 notes. The more difficult the questions are, the more important your notes will be. Keep in mind that this kind of question decides whether or not your score will reach level 5 in listening selections.

Script for Track 15
Narrator: Now you will listen to someone giving instructions. This selection will be played once only.

Simplified Chinese
Woman: 我们的猜灯谜活动马上就要开始了。元宵节猜灯谜又叫"射虎"，是中国人春节期间非常喜欢的传统文化活动。现在宣布活动规则和注意事项：
一、每盏灯下有一个谜语，每个谜语对应一个号码。猜出谜底的同学请去兑奖处，向工作人员提供谜语的号码和谜底。
二、如果谜底正确，你将能够领取一张兑奖券。
三、工作人员会立即换上新的谜语，你可以继续猜谜。
我们的奖品种类繁多，所需要的兑奖券数目也有不同。你收集的兑奖券越多，奖品就越丰厚哦！

Traditional Chinese
Woman: 我們的猜燈謎活動馬上就要開始了。元宵節猜燈謎又叫"射虎"，是中國人春節期間非常喜歡的傳統文化活動。現在宣佈活動規則和注意事項：
一、每盞燈下有一個謎語，每個謎語對應一個號碼。猜出謎底的同學請去兌獎處，向工作人員提供謎語的號碼和謎底。
二、如果謎底正確，你將能夠領取一張兌獎券。
三、工作人員會立即換上新的謎語，你可以繼續猜謎。
我們的獎品種類繁多，所需要的獎獎券數目也有不同。你收集的兌獎券越獎多，獎品就越豐厚哦！

Narrator: Now answer the questions for this selection.

Report

Track 16

Questions on the Report
Look at the following questions *after* you've listened to the report. Give yourself 12 seconds per question. Do the questions in the order given; you can't go back to a question later to make a change.

13. The main idea of this report is that more and more Chinese

    (A)   celebrate spring festival in their hometown with their parents.
    (B)   celebrate holidays in their hometown with their parents.
    (C)   do not celebrate spring festival in their hometown with their parents.
    (D)   do not celebrate holidays in their hometown with their parents.

14. Which fact is listed as a reason for the change of the tradition?

    (A) People want to sleep more during the holiday.

    (B) People no longer want to celebrate spring festival.

    (C) They have more free time.

    (D) The traffic during spring festival is horribly heavy.

15. What percentage most likely describes how many people who won't go back home for the spring festival in Shenzhen?

    (A) 39%

    (B) 43%

    (C) 11%

    (D) 8%

16. What percentage most likely describes how many people don't have any plan to attend spring festival in Shenzhen?

    (A) 24%

    (B) 43%

    (C) 11%

    (D) 8%

Tips for the Report

The report can cover different topics and the vocabulary is relatively difficult. Short news reports, weather forecasts, and brief summaries of a practice or product in daily life are often the content of this selection.

Focus on the beginning, the end, and the conjunctions if possible while skipping over the unknown information. This won't affect your general understanding of the important information.

Your notes should cover at least the following information:

Spring festival/work traffic/not home/40+ not home/11.3 phone. Shi pin/7.8 travel/23.4 sleep/

Answers and Explanations for the Report

13. (C) Looking at the answer choices, you can quickly see this question is based on two issues: spring festival or all holidays, and whether or not they go back to their hometown.

From your notes, you should be able to tell it is not about spring festival and not back to their hometowns, so (C) is correct.

14. (D) Only (D) traffic is mentioned in your notes related to "not go home."

15. (B) The most popular incorrect answer would be (A) 39%, because you heard 40% and 39% is the closest answer. However, since the report mentioned that it is "over 40%" 超过（超過）, the likely answer has to be above 40%, which can only be (B) 43%.

16. (A) The percentage of people without any plans wasn't given. But those who just said "sleep" obviously have no special plans. This is 23.9%, therefore (A) is correct. Choice (B) 43% is the percentage of the people who won't go back home. Choice (C) 11% corresponds to the 11.3% of the people who call or video-chat with their parents. Choice (D) 8% corresponds to the 7.8% of the people who travel.

Script for Track 16

Narrator: Now you will listen to someone giving instructions. This selection will be played once only.

Simplified Chinese

Man: 春节的时候回到父母身边合家团圆，千百年来都是中国人不变的传统。然而，近年来由于工作繁忙或春运期间交通紧张等原因，越来越多的人选择不回家过年，而是用其他方式庆祝这个中国人一年中最重要的节日。最近的调查报告表明，深圳有超过40％的人今年不回家过年，11.3％的人用电话或视频和父母交流，7.8％的人一家人出去旅游，23.9％的人索性呆在家里睡大觉。

Traditional Chinese

Man: 春節的時候回到父母身邊合家團圓，千百年來都是中國人不變的傳統。然而，近年來由於工作繁忙或春運期間交通緊張等原因，越來越多的人選擇不回家過年，而是用其他方式慶祝這個中國人一年中最重要的節日。最近的調查報告表明，深圳有超過40％的人今年不回家過年，11.3％的人用電話或視頻和父母交流，7.8％的人一家人出去旅遊，23.9％的人索性呆在家裡睡大覺。

Narrator: Now answer the questions for this selection.

Strategies for the Listening Selections

You learned the basic strategies in Chapter 4. Now put them into action. Embed the following five strategies in your mind and make them your habit so you don't have to waste trying to remember them. Using these strategies can keep you from making unnecessary errors on the listening selections of the AP exam.

Strategies for the Listening Selections

1. Listen to the English instructions carefully. Adapt your structure of note taking according to different types of selections you'll hear.
2. Skim through the question as quickly as possible. Pay attention to the longer words, which may be nouns, verbs, important key phrases, etc.
3. Use symbols/shorthand to take notes. This saves time and helps you to focus on understanding the content.
4. Pay attention to the numbers as there may be a trap in the related question.
5. If you're not sure of the answer, make a good guess using common sense and comparing the answer choices (excluding any you know are wrong).

Study Tips for Listening Selections

The study tips for the listening selections are similar, but not the same as the ones for listening rejoinders. For the listening selections, you need to have powerful note-taking skills, be able to skim the questions and answers quickly, and have some cultural knowledge corresponding to the questions to do well. Follow these study tips to prepare for the listening selections on the exam.

Vocabulary Building: Practice the vocabulary organized into topics in the vocabulary-building exercises in the next section of this chapter or build your own vocabulary list if you find some topics difficult.

Extensive Listening: Watch Chinese movies and TV programs without subtitles. Listen to Chinese audio materials whenever you have time. Focus on practicing note-taking skills. Choose specific topics such as voice messages, radio reports, instructions, and public announcements when you do extensive listening practice.

Intensive Listening: Make good use of the audio tracks on the CD and the scripts printed in this book.

Listen to the audio tracks again and answer the questions. Practice taking notes to gradually develop your own system for note taking.

Listen another time and refine your notes. Listen to the questions again.

Rephrase the content in your own words. It benefits your speaking as well.

Build your vocabulary study list by adding the important words and phrases from the listening selections.

Skill-Building Exercises: Vocabulary

Look at the following vocabulary words. You probably know or you can guess the meaning of most of them. However, when you listen without looking at the printed word, how much do you really understand?

These words are frequently used in listening selections. You can listen to the words on the CD or ask your classmates to read the vocabulary at a very fast speed. Then look at the printed script and read the words aloud by yourself as fast as you can. Third, listen without looking at them again. After only three rounds, you will gain a better listening comprehension of the words. Add your own vocabulary words (or entire category) when you meet difficulties in any listening practice in this book or elsewhere.

Track 17

Simplified Chinese

School Life: 教学楼、教室、艺术楼、图书馆、电脑室、宿舍、餐厅、科学楼、体育馆、操场/体育场/运动场、校车、学期、考试、研究报告、成绩、学分、毕业、申请、奖学金、商学院、工学院、俱乐部、课外活动、义工、社区服务、英语、数学、物理、生物、地理、历史、政治、化学、音乐、戏剧、美术、摄影、法律、工程、图书管理员、阅览室、借书、还书、过期、续借、罚款、参考资料

Home: 大门、车库、公寓、楼房、客厅、卧室、饭厅、厨房、厕所/洗手间、阳台、书桌、椅子、衣柜、冰箱、空调、茶几、沙发、窗户

Entertainment: 古典音乐、摇滚乐、交响乐、民族音乐、流行音乐、明星、追星族/粉丝、舞蹈、钢琴、小提琴、吉它、球赛、决赛、半决赛、冠军、亚军、球迷、输、赢、胜利、失败、电影、电视、节目、新闻、记者、天气预报、音像、游乐场、乐园、半票、入场券、多才多艺

Social Communication: 看医生、大夫、牙医、急诊室、生病、感冒、休息、打针、吃药、处方、头疼、发烧、咳嗽、嗓子疼、拉肚子、不舒服、锻炼、健康、银行、帐单、交费、挂失、开卡、存钱、取钱、信用卡透支、邮局、包裹、信封、邮票、明信片、快递、寄信、挂号信、邮费、喧哗、排队、身份证、驾照、面试、打工、暑期工、招聘、解雇、辞职、加薪、退休

Food: 饭店、饭馆、订座、位子、中餐、西餐、服务员、菜单、点菜、上菜、饮料、酒水、素菜/蔬菜、荤菜、汤、辣、甜、酸、咸、苦、买单、结帐、小费

Shopping: 百货商场、大排档、小卖部、购物中心、商店、售货员、顾客、大号、中号、小号、换、肥、紧、长、短、颜色、合适、质量、贵、便宜、打折、大减价、跳楼价、买一送一、讨价还价、退货、保质期、保修期、不好不要钱、物美价廉、包换、值这个价、多少钱、付款、找钱、有零的、现金、信用卡、支票、刷卡

Traveling: 护照、签证、地铁、一号线、红/黄线、公交车/公共汽车、交通拥挤、车祸、车站、售票口、凭票入站、月台/站台、行李架、乘客、乘务人员/列车员、机场、机场快线、登机口、航班、航班号、托运、携带、超重、直达、转机、晚点、取消、推迟、清洁卫生、保护环境、景区、名胜古迹、导游、订房间、前台、登记入住、五星级酒店、单人房、双人房、退房

Chinese Culture: 京剧、脸谱、生旦净丑、相声、剪纸、麻将、风筝、瓷器、书法、笔墨纸砚、琴棋书画、武术、太极拳、风俗、兵马俑、紫禁城、故宫、长城、园林建筑、胡同、四合院、春节、舞龙舞狮、元宵节、汤圆、端午节、粽子、中秋节、月饼、重阳节、火药、印刷术、造纸、指南针、少数民族、旗袍、菜系、民以食为天、筷子、茶馆、十二生肖、属什么

Traditional Chinese

School Life: 教學樓、教室、藝術樓、圖書館、電腦室、宿舍、餐廳、科學樓、體育館、操場/體育場/運動場、校車、學期、考試、研究報告、成績、學分、畢業、申請、獎學金、商學院、工學院、俱樂部、課外活動、義工、社區服務、英語、數學、物理、生物、地理、歷史、政治、化學、音樂、戲劇、美術、攝影、法律、工程、圖書管理員、閱覽室、借書、還書、過期、續借、罰款、參考資料

Home: 大門、車庫、公寓、樓房、客廳、臥室、飯廳、廚房、廁所/洗手間、陽台、書桌、椅子、衣櫃、冰箱、空調、茶几、沙發、窗戶

Entertainment: 古典音樂、搖滾樂、交響樂、民族音樂、流行音樂、明星、追星族/粉絲、舞蹈、鋼琴、小提琴、吉它、球賽、決賽、半決賽、冠軍、亞軍、球迷、輸、贏、勝利、失敗、電影、電視、節目、新聞、記者、天氣預報、音像、遊樂場、樂園、半票、入場券、多才多藝

Social Communication: 看醫生、大夫、牙醫、急診室、生病、感冒、休息、打針、吃藥、處方、頭疼、發燒、咳嗽、嗓子疼、拉肚子、不舒服、鍛煉、健康、銀行、帳單、交費、掛失、開卡、存錢、取錢、信用卡透支、郵局、包裹、信封、郵票、明信片、快遞、寄信、掛號信、郵費、喧嘩、排隊、身份證、駕照、面試、打工、暑期工、招聘、解雇、辭職、加薪、退休

Food: 飯店、飯館、訂座、位子、中餐、西餐、服務員、菜單、點菜、上菜、飲料、酒水、素菜/蔬菜、葷菜、湯、辣、甜、酸、咸、苦、買單、結帳、小費

Shopping: 百貨商場、大排檔、小賣部、購物中心、商店、售貨員、顧客、大號、中號、小號、換、肥、緊、長、短、顏色、合適、質量、貴、便宜、打折、大減價、跳樓價、買一送一、討價還價、退貨、保質期、保修期、不好不要錢、物美價廉、包換、值這個價、多少錢、付款、找錢、有零的、現金、信用卡、支票、刷卡

Traveling: 護照、簽證、地鐵、一號線、紅/黃線、公交車/公共汽車、交通擁擠、車禍、車站、售票口、憑票入站、月台/站台、行李架、乘客、乘務人員/列車員、機場、機場快線、登機口、航班、航班號、托運、攜帶、超重、直達、轉機、晚點、取消、推遲、清潔衛生、保護環境、景區、名勝古蹟、導遊、訂房間、前台、登記入住、五星級酒店、單人房、雙人房、退房

Chinese Culture: 京劇、臉譜、生旦淨醜、相聲、剪紙、麻將、風箏、瓷器、書法、筆墨紙硯、琴棋書畫、武術、太極拳、風俗、兵馬俑、紫禁城、故宮、長城、園林建築、胡同、四合院、春節、舞龍舞獅、元宵節、湯圓、端午節、粽子、中秋節、月餅、重陽節、火藥、印刷術、造紙、指南針、少數民族、旗袍、菜系、民以食為天、筷子、茶館、十二生肖、屬甚麼

Listening Selections Practice Test (Exam Section I, Part A)

The listening selections and the questions about them in this section create an experience similar to what you'll encounter on the actual exam. Listen to the selections on the CD accompanying this book. Answer the multiple-choice questions by circling the best response. Don't use the printed script.

Finish the test-like experience first. Then see how many you got wrong. For any you missed, look at the script of what you heard and the explanations for the answers to find out where/how you went wrong. Note that you should understand the meanings not only of the correct answer, but also of the incorrect choices.

Finally, do a thorough analysis of where and why you made any errors. Use the self-evaluation sheet provided. Then look at the suggestions for each kind of mistake you made. Refer to the suggestion sheet and the "Study Tips for the Listening Selections" earlier in this chapter, if you feel you need more practice.

Questions

The audio tracks for the listening selections can be found on the CD accompanying this book. Listen to each selection and take notes; you will listen to *some* of the selections twice. Then, only after you've heard the listening selection, read and answer the questions about the selection. Circle the best answer choice for each question. A script for the listening selections on the CD is provided for your reference, but don't look at it until after you've answered all the questions. Time yourself, giving 12 seconds to read and answer each question. After the 12-second limit, you may not go back to the question or change your answer.

Track 18

1. The announcement is directed primarily to

    (A) parents.
    (B) teachers.
    (C) visitors.
    (D) students.

2. How long does the Moon Festival celebration take?

    (A) One hour
    (B) One and a half hours
    (C) Two and a half hours
    (D) Four hours

3. The primary purpose of this announcement is to inform the audience that

    (A) they need to prepare for the rain.
    (B) they need to go to another location.
    (C) they need to watch a movie.
    (D) they need to have fun.

4. What was the primary reason for leaving the voice message?

   (A) There is a change for picking up time.
   (B) Dulei's brother didn't go to the airport.
   (C) Ailing's flight was delayed.
   (D) Remind Ailing to take the flight.

5. What happened to change the original plan?

   (A) Ailing's brother was late.
   (B) The weather situation caused delay.
   (C) Ailing didn't pick up the phone.
   (D) Dulei had her own things to do.

6. What will most likely happen?

   (A) Dulei will drive to the airport right away.
   (B) Ailing will wait in the airport.
   (C) Ailing will take her brother home.
   (D) Dulei will give Ailing a call when he is boarding.

7. What does the father want to know about his daughter?

   (A) Her college major
   (B) Where she will go for college
   (C) Job opportunities in her field
   (D) How she is washing clothes

8. What does the woman want to do next?

   (A) Wash her own clothes
   (B) Look for a job in China
   (C) Study in China
   (D) Apply to a college in China

9. What is most likely the father's attitude toward his daughter's choice?

   (A) Happy
   (B) Sad
   (C) Mad
   (D) Shocked

10. These instructions are mostly heard when

    (A) sitting on an airplane.
    (B) nobody picks up the phone when it is ringing.
    (C) visiting some places.
    (D) emergency help is needed.

11. What will the caller do if he wants to leave a message?

    (A) Make a "Ding" sound.
    (B) Press "1."
    (C) Press "2."
    (D) Press "3."

12. What is the topic of the conversation?

    (A) Learning to drive in China
    (B) Renting a car traveling in China
    (C) Transportation in China
    (D) Historic sites in China

13. What means of transportation does the woman recommend for traveling in Beijing?

    (A) Rental car
    (B) Taxi
    (C) Subway
    (D) Motorcycle

14. What does the woman recommend when traveling in smaller cities?

    (A) Ride motorcycles
    (B) Join a tour group
    (C) Rent a car
    (D) Take a taxi

15. How does the woman say she feels about riding motorcycles as a taxi in China?

    (A) They are prohibited in China.
    (B) It's difficult to find parking.
    (C) They are more expensive but more convenient.
    (D) They are cheaper but more dangerous.

16. What kind of competition does this news report talk about?

    (A) Public service poster
    (B) Hometown music
    (C) Sports
    (D) TV program

17. Where did the ceremony take place?

    (A) A TV station
    (B) The municipal publicity department
    (C) The municipal stadium
    (D) A senior citizen's home

18. How many artists won the awards?

    (A) 15
    (B) 37
    (C) 50
    (D) 1

19. What is the attitude of municipal publicity department toward this competition?

    (A) It supports the competition.
    (B) It's against the competition.
    (C) I have doubts about it.
    (D) The report didn't mention this.

20. Which of the following is *not* true according to the news report?

(A) There were more than 600 works that were entered in the competition.
(B) The theme of the competition was "My Beautiful Hometown."
(C) The competition lasted three months.
(D) The competition is not readily accepted by the people.

Scripts for the Listening Selections

Track 18

Narrator: Now you will listen to a public announcement. This selection will be played twice.

Simplified Chinese
各位同学请注意，欢迎参加中文俱乐部举办的中秋节联欢会。由于学校操场施工建设的原因，我们的联欢活动将改在室内举行，地点定在学校大礼堂，时间为下午一点半到四点。届时各班组队进入礼堂，活动之后同学们将回各自教室看电影。请相互通知。希望大家玩得高兴！

Traditional Chinese
各位同學請注意，歡迎參加中文俱樂部舉辦的中秋節聯歡會。由於學校操場施工建設的原因，我們的聯歡活動將改在室內舉行，地點定在學校大禮堂，時間為下午一點半到四點。屆時各班組隊進入禮堂，活動之後同學們將回各自教室看電影。請相互通知。希望大家玩得高興！

Narrator: Now listen again.
Narrator: Now answer the questions for this selection.
Narrator: Now you will listen to a voice message. This selection will be played twice.

Simplified Chinese
喂，陈爱玲，我是杜雷。你弟弟还没出发去机场吧？请告诉他一下，我们这边下大雪，所有的飞机都晚点了，我们十一点到不了。刚听说我们搭乘的班机要推迟一个半小时才起飞，不过还没有最后确定。你们先忙自己的事吧，不要担心我，我登机时会再给你来一个电话。你们家离机场不远，到那时出发来接我们也不会太晚。麻烦你了，爱玲。

Traditional Chinese
喂，陳愛玲，我是杜雷。你弟弟還沒出發去機場吧？請告訴他一下，我們這邊下大雪，所有的飛機都晚點了，我們十一點到不了。剛聽說我們搭乘的班機要推遲一個半小時才起飛，不過還沒有最後確定。你們先忙自己的事吧，不要擔心我，我登機時會再給你來一個電話。你們家離機場不遠，到那時出發來接我們也不會太晚。麻煩你了，愛玲。

Narrator: Now listen again.
Narrator: Now answer the questions for this selection.
Narrator: Now you will listen to a conversation between a father and a daughter. This selection will be played once only.

Simplified Chinese
Man: 思思啊，你想好大学报哪个专业了吗？
Woman: 爸，我喜欢的专业太多了！想来想去，我还是觉得去中国读大学比较好。我中文学得不错，而且毕业后在中国工作的机会也会特别多。

Man: 去中国上大学？你连衣服都要妈妈帮你洗，在中国能过得好吗？你最好再想想。

Woman: 不用想了！其实我早就申请了中国的一所大学，而且拿到了录取通知书，是商学院。

Man: 什么？你这孩子，这么大的事，不和爸爸商量一下，爸爸又不会不理解。

Traditional Chinese

Man: 思思啊，你想好大學報哪個專業了嗎？

Woman: 爸，我喜歡的專業太多了！想來想去，我還是覺得去中國讀大學比較好。我中文學得不錯，而且畢業後在中國工作的機會也會特別多。

Man: 去中國上大學？你連衣服都要媽媽幫你洗，在中國能過得好嗎？你最好再想想。

Woman: 不用想了！其實我早就申請了中國的一所大學，而且拿到了錄取通知書，是商學院。

Man: 甚麼？你這孩子，這麼大的事，不和爸爸商量一下，爸爸又不會不理解。

Narrator: Now answer the questions for this selection.

Narrator: Now you will listen to the phone instruction. This selection will be played once only.

Simplified Chinese

您好，您所拨打的用户暂时无人接听，如需秘书台服务，请在嘀声后按键选择。附本机号码请按1，语音留言请按2，人工服务请按3，退出请挂机。

Traditional Chinese

您好，您所撥打的用戶暫時無人接聽，如需秘書台服務，請在嘀聲後按鍵選擇。附本機號碼請按1，語音留言請按2，人工服務請按3，退出請掛機。

Narrator: Now answer the questions for this selection.

Narrator: Now you will listen to a phone conversation. This selection will be played once only.

Simplified Chinese

Man: 王婷，我下个星期就去中国呆两个月，想自己租车，可能比较方便，你觉得怎么样？

Woman: 你有中国驾照吗？美国驾照要先换成中国的才行。

Man: 我可以先换。

Woman: 其实像北京、上海这样的大城市，公交车、地铁都很方便，而且车辆太多，自己租车的话停车困难。当然，最好还是打的！

Man: 我还想去一些小城市旅游。

Woman: 那就更没必要了。你人生地不熟的，为了安全还是跟旅游团走比较好。

Man: 我看到在中国有人坐在摩托车的后面。

Woman: 那个叫"摩的"，比出租车便宜，不过很危险，在很多城市禁止使用，你最好不要坐。

Traditional Chinese

Man: 王婷，我下個星期就去中國呆兩個月，想自己租車，可能比較方便，你覺得怎麼樣？

Woman: 你有中國駕照嗎？美國駕照要先換成中國的才行。

Man: 我可以先換。

Woman: 其實像北京、上海這樣的大城市，公交車、地鐵都很方便，而且車輛太多，自己租車的話停車困難。當然，最好還是打的！

Man: 我還想去一些小城市旅遊。

Woman: 那就更沒必要了。你人生地不熟的，為了安全還是跟旅遊團走比較好。

Man: 我看到在中國有人坐在摩托車的後面。

Woman: 那個叫"摩的"，比出租車便宜，不過很危險，在很多城市禁止使用，你最好不要坐。

Narrator: Now answer the questions for this selection.

Narrator: Now you will listen to a radio report. This selection will be played once only.

Simplified Chinese

Woman: 4月26日下午，由市宣传部举办的"我的美丽家乡"电视公益广告大赛颁奖仪式在市体育馆举行。本次大赛历时三个月，征集作品600多幅。评审专家们共评选出37位艺术家的50幅获奖作品，其中包括公益奖1名、一等奖1名、二等奖3名、三等奖15名、优秀奖30名。宣传部负责人表示，公益广告传播的主题更容易为广大老百姓所接受，应该多举办这种形式的活动为社会服务。

Traditional Chinese

Woman: 4月26日下午，由市宣傳部舉辦的"我的美麗家鄉"電視公益廣告大賽頒獎儀式在市體育館舉行。本次大賽歷時三個月，徵集作品600多幅。評審專家們共評選出37位藝術家的50幅獲獎作品，其中包括公益獎1名、獎一等獎1名、二等獎3名、三等獎15名、優秀獎30名。宣傳部負責人表示，公益廣告傳播的主題更容易為廣大老百姓所接受，應該多舉辦這種形式的活動為社會服務。

Narrator: Now answer the questions for this selection.

Answers

1. D	11. C
2. C	12. C
3. B	13. B
4. A	14. B
5. B	15. D
6. D	16. A
7. A	17. C
8. C	18. B
9. D	19. A
10. B	20. D

Explanations

Announcement

Your notes should at least include the content of what the announcement is about, what happened and where and when it happened, what is being requested, and specific information regarding the numbers and repeated/stressed words, if possible. If there is a change of plan, you should pay attention to the reason for the change and the words of "change to an earlier date" 提前，"delay" 晚点（晚點），"postpone" 推迟（推遲），"cancel" 取消，and "change"更改. A lot of students may have trouble with 施工建设（施工建設），which means "construction." However, this won't keep you from providing correct answers.

1. (D) The first sentence states that "all classmates pay attention" 各位同学请注意（各位同學請注意）.

2. (C) Your notes should include the numbers/time 1:30 to 4:00. The event lasts for two and a half hours.

3. (B) The primary purpose of this announcement is for a change "更改." It states that due to possible rain, the location will be changed. You notes may include the location information, and common sense would help here as well. Choice (D) is not correct because "watching a movie" is one event instead of the primary purpose.

Voice Message

The voice message is relatively structured and you may predict what is happening. Your notes should at least include the content of when and/or where to call, why to call, any change of plan, any solution (when/where to meet and to do what), as well as specific information regarding the numbers and repeated/stressed words, if possible.

4. (A) Your notes should cover the main idea of the plan changes and the solution. "Delay" 晚点（晚點）and "postpone" 推迟（推遲）indicate that it is a change of the plan. "Pick up" is 接.

5. (B) Big snow is "下大雪." There are normally three kinds of reasons for a delay of a flight: weather, scheduling (busy is 繁忙), or maintenance (technical difficulties are 技术故障（技術故障）). You just need to pay attention to find out which one.

6. (D) The narrator said "I will give you a call when boarding." 我登机时会再给你来一个电话（我登機時會再給你來一個電話）.

Conversation

Keep in mind that the conversation may only play once. Your notes should at least include the content of what it is about, where and when it takes place, the main ideas of the woman's and man's talk, the conflict (if any), and specific information regarding the numbers and repeated/stressed words if possible.

7. (A) University is 大学（大學）；major is 专业（專業）. The father wants to know her major.

8. (C) The woman said that she "feels that it is better to study in China." The conversation repeats "China" and "Chinese" several times.

9. (D) The father was shocked first and said, "What?" 什么（甚麼）。Then he asked his daughter to think about it again. Therefore, we can eliminate the choice (A). At the end, he said he won't "not understand," which means he will understand. He is not mad or sad, so the answer is (D).

Instructions

The instruction selections may contain quite a bit of vocabulary that you do not understand, but the questions are normally easy since most ask for the main idea or major procedures. There's a good chance that the instructions will contain numbers for the steps or categories.

10. (B) "Nobody pick up the phone" is 无人接听（無人接聽）. If you didn't catch this one, you will hear "Press 2 if you want to leave a voice message" 语音留言请按 2（語音留言請按2）, which also indicates that (B) is correct.

11. (C) You can get the answer from question #10. There may be a lot of unfamiliar vocabulary but keep in mind that if the information is too difficult, most likely it is not related to the answer.

Conversation

12. (C) Choice (B) may be your first choice since you heard about "rent a car" 租车（租車）. However, the whole conversation mentions all kinds of transportation; therefore, (C) is correct.

13. (B) Your notes should include Beijing and take a taxi, since it says "the best way is taking a taxi" 最好是打的. Anything indicating the "best" or "most important" in a comparison is important to pay attention to. "Take a taxi" is 打的，坐出租车（車）.

14. (B) The phrase of "small cities" is the key for you to locate the answer. Your answer should include the information "better to be with a tour group": 还是跟旅游团走比较好（還是跟旅遊團走比較好）. Look back at question #13. Now you can see that you should pay attention to any information related to comparisons.

15. (D) Even if you do not know the word "dangerous" 危险（危險）, you should know the word of "cheap" 便宜. Therefore, (D) is correct.

Report

Focus on the beginning, the end, and the conjunctions if possible while skipping over the unknown information. This won't affect your general understanding of the important information. Pay special attention to the first sentence, which usually provides the main idea and helps you to decide what to note when listening.

16. (A) To answer this question correctly, you should know the word "public service" 公益. If you don't know it, you can get the main idea from some easily understood phrases, such as "normal people" 老百姓, and "serve the society" 为社会服务（為社會服務）.

17. (C) "Municipal stadium" is 市体育馆（市體育館）.

18. (B) A number is always important to be noted. You should have the information of "37 artists."

19. (A) The news report clearly states that "there should be more" 应该多举办（應該多舉辦）.

20. (D) There may not be much time for you to consider these since the choices are so long. However, if you understand well or take good notes, this won't be a problem. If that doesn't apply to you, first, you should pay attention to (C) and (D) because they have a similar sentence structure. The news report clearly states that it is well accepted by the public. And the answer to the question 19, that there should be more, also validates choice D.

Self-Evaluation

It's important to learn from your mistakes. Evaluate your performance on this practice test to try to understand the reason you missed each question you did. Use the following worksheet. Then look at the suggestions that follow for how to deal with each reason for missing a question.

Self-Evaluation Worksheet for the Listening Selections

FREQUENT REASONS FOR ERRORS	WHICH QUESTION?	NUMBER OF ERRORS
1. I didn't pay attention to the repeated key words.		
2. I didn't pay attention to the numbers.		
3. My notes didn't cover the key information for the question.		
4. I didn't have time to take notes about the important information.		
5. The speaker's speed of this selection was too fast.		
6. I knew that word was important but I didn't understand it!		
7. Oops. I just missed it again…too fast!		
Think: What kinds of errors did I make the most? Why didn't I find the correct answers? What could I do to improve?		

Suggestions in Response to Errors in the Listening Selections

FREQUENT REASONS FOR ERRORS	SUGGESTIONS
1. I didn't pay attention to the repeated/stressed key words.	Pay attention to them! Key words are normally verbs, numbers, locations, etc. Remember: The basic sentence structure of Chinese is: Subject + Time + Location + Verb, quite different from English!
2. I didn't pay attention to the numbers.	Repeat in your mind and take notes.
3. My notes didn't cover the key information for the question.	Take note of the main idea, numbers, and stressed or repeated vocabulary.
4. I didn't have time to take notes about the important information.	Use symbols to save time. Write Pinyin down since you don't have time to interpret the information into English.
5. The speaker's speed on this selection was too fast.	Get intensive listening practice before the exam. See tips provided earlier in this chapter.
6. I knew that word was important but I didn't understand it!	Write Pinyin down. Sometimes you can figure it out when reading the questions and the four answer choices.
7. Oops. I just missed it again…too fast!	Follow the flow. Do not linger at one question or one word.
Think: What kinds of errors did I make the most? Why didn't I find the correct answers? What could I do to improve?	See the general study tips presented earlier in this chapter.

CHAPTER 7

Reading Comprehension

IN THIS CHAPTER

Summary: This chapter provides practice for the reading comprehension section of the AP Chinese Language and Culture Exam. You'll start with warm-up exercises and then review the strategies that will help you attack the types of questions you'll find on this part of the exam. Next are exercises designed to help you learn to avoid the frequently made errors on the reading selections. Finally, you'll practice with a set of test-like reading selections and questions that reflect those on the real exam. At the end is a worksheet that will help you to do a thorough evaluation of your performance and adjust your study plan accordingly.

Key Strategies/Ideas

- ✪ Find the main idea: Browse all the questions first to find the main idea of the selection before you read the passage.
- ✪ Locate the question: Mark the key words in each question and its four answer choices. This will help you to locate the sentences related to the answers in the passage.
- ✪ Find the answer: Read the questions again after you've skimmed the reading selection. Analyze how the sentences are related and choose your answer.
- ✪ Mark the questions you are not sure about. You can come back to these later.
- ✪ Practice scanning and skimming skills and learn to spot the subject, verb, and object of longer sentences in one second.

❂ Practice 20 new vocabulary words/phrases daily using "Frequently Used Vocabulary and Phrases" in the appendix. Add additional notes you need to review to your notebook.

❂ Review "Functional Grammar" in the appendix.

In this part of the exam (Section I, Part B), you will have 60 minutes to answer 35 to 40 questions based on about nine written passages. After each passage, there will be a series of multiple-choice questions in English. Choose the answer that is the best match to the question. There is no time limit for each question though you will have to finish all the questions within 60 minutes. You can switch between simplified Chinese and traditional Chinese. In this section of the test you can move back and forth between questions to check or change your answers.

Warm-Up Exercises

The passages in this section have been carefully selected to cover all types of questions in the reading comprehension section of the AP exam. As you work through the passages and questions, you'll discover different strategies should be applied in responding to different types of passages. However, for all passages, read the questions to get the main idea before you start to read the passage. Note key words in the questions and answer choices. Pay special attention to the sentences in the reading selection that have these words in them. Finally, read the questions and the four choices again and choose your answer.

Signs and Regulations

Reading Selection and Questions

Simplified Chinese
员工通道，游客止步

Traditional Chinese
（員工通道，遊客止步）

1. The purpose of the sign is to

   (A) post the penalty of using a facility.
   (B) stop people from using a facility.
   (C) allow access for visitors.
   (D) provide instruction for people with disabilities.

2. The sign's message is directed most likely to

   (A) drivers.
   (B) employees.
   (C) tourists.
   (D) pedestrians.

Tips for Reading Signs and Regulations

Reading signs and regulations is a skill required for AP exam takers. The signs are normally short and simple, but the vocabulary may be difficult especially if you are not familiar with the structures used. Regulations are normally more detailed; this makes it harder to find the sentences related to the questions and answer choices. Therefore, the focus when reading signs should be in understanding the vocabulary. When reading regulations focus on scanning or skimming for key words.

The frequently used structures for signs typically include the following vocabulary:

- To stop people from an action: 莫、禁、免、止
- To give the penalty of an action: 罚（罰）、惩(懲)
- To remind people of an action：请（請）、小心、注意
- To inform people of a regulation: 遵守、规则 (規則)、守则 (守則)、禁止, etc.

Explanations

1. **(B)** 止步 means "stop walking"; therefore, (B) is the correct answer.

2. **(C)** There are two answers (B) "employees" 员工（員工） and (C) "tourists" 游客（遊客） that you can find in the passage. The purpose of this sign is to stop people from taking an action. 游客（遊客）止步 literally means "tourists stop walking/access"; therefore, the answer is (C). 员工通道（員工通道） means "employee path."

Advertisements and Brochures

Reading Selection and Questions

Simplified Chinese

本文化中心今年继续举办"中国梦"暑期夏令营活动，16岁以上、身体健康、有无中文学习经验的中学生（含毕业生）均可申请参加。
夏令营时间：7月3日至 7月31日
夏令营地点：云南大学
夏令营活动内容：
汉语强化半月班：7月5日至20日
中国文化之旅：7月21日至30日
观看少数民族歌舞表演，品尝各地风味小吃，领略少数民族风土人情，并组织学生参加北京、西安、上海等地的"八日游"活动。
申请时间：5月31日截止
有意者请本人亲自到报名处索取申请表格，填好后交到报名处。本中心将于6月中旬统一申请签证，具体时间另行通知。
名额有限，欲报从速。

Traditional Chinese

本文化中心今年繼續舉辦"中國夢"暑期夏令營活動，16歲以上、身體健康、有無中文學習經驗的中學生（含畢業生）均可申請參加。
夏令營時間：7月3日至 7月31日
夏令營地點：雲南大學
夏令營活動內容：

漢語強化半月班：7月5日至20日
中國文化之旅：7月21日至30日
觀看少數民族歌舞表演，品嘗各地風味小吃，領略少數民族風土人情，並組織學生參加北京、西安、上海等地的"八日游"活動。
申請時間：5月31日截止
有意者請本人親自到報名處索取申請表格，填好後交到報名處。本中心將於6月中旬統一申請簽證，具體時間另行通知。
名額有限，欲報從速。

3. What is *not* required to participate in this summer camp?

(A)   Being 16 years old and above
(B)   Being a student
(C)   Being healthy
(D)   Having experience in Chinese learning.

4. How long does the summer camp last?

(A)   Two weeks
(B)   Three weeks
(C)   Four weeks
(D)   Five weeks

5. According to the brochure, what activity is *not* included in the summer camp?

(A)   Cultural performances by minority peoples
(B)   Traveling in other cities for 8 days
(C)   Learning Chinese calligraphy
(D)   Tasting different types of food

6. What method is specified for requesting an application to register?

(A)   In person
(B)   E-mail
(C)   Fax
(D)   Regular mail

7. Priority will be given to applicants who

(A)   are members of minorities.
(B)   apply earlier.
(C)   are high school students.
(D)   have a valid passport.

Tips for Reading Advertisements and Brochures

Just like a regulation can be an elaborated version of a sign, a brochure is often an elaborated version of the advertisement. Spending a couple of hours practicing reading the classified advertisements in the newspaper can help you succeed in this type of reading selection. The topics could be anything: a training center recruiting students, a person seeking a job, somebody renting his or her place, and so on. Just type "classified advertisements" 分类广告（分類廣告） and Google it.

Explanations

3. (D) For the questions of "not required" or "not true," checking the answer choices is the quickest way to find the right answer. You can locate the choices of (A) 16岁以上（16歲

以上），(B) 中学生（中學生）, and (C) 身体健康（身體健康） in the passage. Also, the passage states that "with or without" 有无（有無） Chinese experience is fine, which makes choice (D) an incorrect statement. Therefore, the answer is (D). Pay attention to the character 均, which means "all" and is frequently used in advertisements.

4. (C) There are three places where the duration of the time is mentioned. The question asks for the "summer camp" 夏令营（夏令營）. This key word 夏令营（夏令營） helps you to locate the answer in the passage: 7月3日至7月31日. That is 28 days or four weeks.

5. (C) This question is similar to question #3, and we can use the similar strategies. You can locate the choices of (A) 少数（數）民族歌舞表演, (B) 等地 "八日游", and (D) 品尝各地风味小吃（品嘗各地風味小吃）, but there is nothing regarding choice (C); therefore, the answer is (C).

6. (A) 请本人亲自（請本人親自） means "by somebody himself/herself," which is choice (A). There is no information regarding choices (B), (C), and (D).

7. (B) This question tests your common sense and comprehension skills. There is no key word of "priority," which normally is translated as 优先（優先）. However, 名额有限，欲报从速（名額有限，欲報從速） means "there is limited availability and if you want to register, hurry up." It is often used in Chinese advertisements. Similar expressions are 先到先得，送完为（為）止， and so on. Therefore, priority will be given to the early birds.

E-mail Message

Reading Selection and Questions

Simplified Chinese
各位同学：
因连日下雨，原定于十一日下午举行的游览大罗山森林公园活动暂时取消，内容更改为参观南区科技博览会。我们照计划租车前往，请自带雨具，并于十二点半之前到达科学实验楼的停车场等大巴。晚餐和餐后ＫＴＶ娱乐照常进行，时间、地点不变。
祝大家玩得开心。

Traditional Chinese
各位同學：
因連日下雨，原定於十一日下午舉行的遊覽大羅山森林公園活動暫時取消，內容更改為參觀南區科技博覽會。我們照計劃租車前往，請自帶雨具，并於十二點半之前到達科學實驗樓的停車場等大巴。晚餐和餐後ＫＴＶ娛樂照常進行，時間、地點不變。
祝大家玩得開心。

8. What happened to the original plan?

(A) It was cancelled due to the rain.
(B) It was postponed due to the rain.
(C) It was cancelled due to another activity.
(D) It was postponed due to another activity.

9. The plan is to go there by

   (A) a rented car.
   (B) a rented bike.
   (C) a rented boat.
   (D) a rented bus.

10. Where will they meet?

   (A) At the Da Luo Mountain Forest Park
   (B) At the science and technology exhibition
   (C) At the parking lot of the science and lab building
   (D) Not mentioned in the e-mail

Tips for Reading the E-mail Message

This type of message is often seen in a letter, an e-mail, or an announcement. The key information covered includes what was originally planned, the reason causing the change, and what the change will be. Keep this structure in mind, and you will easily locate the answers for the questions.

Another type of e-mail or letter is to explain something or ask someone to explain something. The topics are usually related to a student's school life or social life, such as the college application, the summer holiday, study issues, and so on. A solid foundation in the vocabulary of these topics is crucial in your exam preparation.

Explanations

8. (A) "Due to" 因，因为（為），由于（於）is the key word for you to locate to find the answer. In the first of the passage, it says "due to the rain in these days" 因连（連）日下雨. Therefore, (A) is correct.

9. (D) In the passage, there is a word, 租车（車）, which is usually regarded as "rent a car." However, 等大巴 means "wait for the big bus." They will go there by a rented bus. School bus is 校车, and bus is 公交车（車）or 公共汽车（車）or 大巴.

10. (C) The fact that several of these choices can be found in the e-mail message adds difficulty to this question. You need to keep the goal (what the question asks for exactly) in mind and locate each answer to confirm. Read the sentences that contain these answer choices carefully in case you make mistakes. (A) is the location of the original plan; (B) is the location of the changed plan; (C) is the place to meet to then ride on the bus to the destination. Therefore, choice (C) is correct.

News Article

Reading Selection and Questions

Simplified Chinese

培养二十一世纪人才

近期，新浪网主持的教育论坛掀起了一场关于二十一世纪人才技能的讨论，学生的学习及思考技能，信息技术运用技能和独立生活的技能成为最热门的话题。

传统的学习方法侧重于知识的培养，很多高分学生习惯了死记硬背，连起码的提问能力都没有，更缺乏大胆创新的能力。同时，虽然信息技术日新月异，不少教师和教育机构却常常以考试成绩为目的进行教育，不能或不愿尝试新的科技。21世纪的人才竞争更生活化、社会化、合作化，独立生活能力和社会实践能力也是教育界不可忽视的重点和方向。许多发言者认为，现代的中学生不但要养成批判性思考的习惯，学习运用各种新技术，同时还应该增加自己跨国度跨文化的交流机会以及发展与各种不同背景的人相互协调、共同进步的合作能力。

实现这一理想最大的困难仍然是观念的变化。只有更多的人参与了解二十一世纪人才技能的重要性行动起来，我们的中学生才会有真正的未来。

Traditional Chinese

培養二十一世紀人才

近期，新浪網主持的教育論壇掀起了一場關於二十一世紀人才技能的討論，學生的學習及思考技能，信息技術運用技能和獨立生活的技能成為最熱門的話題。

傳統的學習方法側重於知識的培養，很多高分學生習慣了死記硬背，連起碼的提問能力都沒有，更缺乏大膽創新的能力。同時，雖然信息技術日新月異，不少教師和教育機構卻常常以考試成績為目的進行教育，不能或不願嘗試新的科技。21世紀的人才競爭更生活化、社會化、合作化，獨立生活能力和社會實踐能力也是教育界不可忽視的重點和方向。許多發言者認為，現代的中學生不但要養成批判性思考的習慣，學習運用各種新技術，同時還應該增加自己跨國度跨文化的交流機會以及發展與各種不同背景的人相互協調、共同進步的合作能力。

實現這一理想最大的困難仍然是觀念的變化。只有更多的人參與瞭解二十一世紀人才技能的重要性行動起來，我們的中學生才會有真正的未來。

11. Which of the following is mentioned as the primary source for the information in the article?

   (A) A survey of high school students
   (B) A web forum
   (C) An interview with administrators
   (D) A research report

12. According to the article, what is *not* valued as an important skill of the twenty-first century?

   (A) Critical thinking
   (B) Applying technology
   (C) Social skills
   (D) Good memory

13. Which of the following best describes the primary purpose of the author?

   (A) To complain about skill training in education in the twenty-first century
   (B) To promote technology reform
   (C) To support skill training in education in the twenty-first century
   (D) To describe the life of high school students

14. The greatest obstacle to cultivating students with good skills is expected to be

   (A) a lack of money.
   (B) undeveloped technology.
   (C) cultural diversity.
   (D) the concept itself.

Tips for Reading a News Article

Both the words "news" and "article" indicate that this is a selection that will be difficult to read in detail. The vocabulary is more complicated, the sentences are long, and the grammatical structures are more formal. The good news is that this kind of article is clearly structured and the questions normally only test your understanding of the structure. You should try scanning and skimming to spot the subject, verb, and object to get the main idea of the sentences.

Here are some tips to help understand complicated sentences. You can get used to using these tips in an hour and you can also collect your own tips. More practice with longer sentences is provided in the skill-building exercises later in this chapter.

Tips for Complicated Sentences

Conjunctions

Review "Functional Grammar" in the appendixes.

Particles

的: If you want to find the subject or object in a long sentence, look for the vocabulary after "的 ('s)." If the subject or object is very long, the last several characters contain the actual subject or object of the sentence.

和: If you see "和 (and)," there are two or more than two things listed. Synonyms: 与（與）、及、并、且、或 (or).

了、于（於）、着（著）、到、为（為）: The word before any of these characters: 了 (past tense, similar to –ed)、于 (at, after the verb)、or 着（著）(present tense, similar to –ing) is most likely a verb.

地: The word after "地 (used as a particle)" mostly likely is a verb.

得: The word before "得 (used as a particle)" is normally a verb.

Modality Verb

要、肯、敢、必须、应该、愿意、能、可以、会（要、肯、敢、必須、應該、願意、能、可以、會）always go before the verb.

Radicals

扌、辶、⻊: Because a lot of actions are related to the "hand" 扌, the "feet" ⻊, and "movement" 辶, a lot of the characters with these radicals may be verbs.

Now apply these tips to the first paragraph. Read this part thoroughly until you really grasp how to apply the tips.

Clause 1

近期，新浪网主持的教育论坛掀起了一场关于二十一世纪人才技能的讨论，
（近期，新浪網主持的教育論壇掀起了一場關於二十一世紀人才技能的討論，）

……（的）教育论坛 ……（的）教育論壇	掀起（了）	关（于）…… 關（於）……	（的）讨论 （的）討論
Subject: educational forum	Verb: 扌 (action) and 了 (did)	A popular phrase that means "about"	Object: discussion

Main Idea: Educational forum "did" discussion about something.

Clause 2

学生<u>的</u>学习<u>及</u>思考技能，信息技术运用技能<u>和</u>独立生活<u>的</u>技能成为最热门的话题。

（學生的學習及思考技能，信息技術運用技能和獨立生活的技能成為最熱門的話題。）

（的）学习 （及）思考技能	信息技术运用 技能	（和）独立生活 （的）技能	成（为） 成（為）	（的）话题
（的）學習 （及）思考技能	信息技術運用 技能	（和）獨立生活 （的）技能		（的）話題
Subject 1: study (and) think skills	Subject 2: tech skills	Subject 3: (and) independent living skills	Verb: become	Object: topic

Main Idea: Skill A(A1 + A2) , skill B, and skill C become a topic.

Explanations

11. (B) Using the analysis described earlier to apply the tips to the first paragraph, you know it is from a web forum.

12. (D) Using the analysis described previously to apply the tips to the first paragraph, you know there are three skills mentioned. You can skip the choices (A), critical thinking, and (B), technology, as they are the two subjects in clause 2. Choice (C), social skills, is closer in meaning to the third subject "independent living skills" than choice (D), good memory. Therefore, you can guess that (D) is the correct choice. Read the second paragraph to confirm:

（很多高分）学生 (subject) 习惯了(verb) 死记硬背 (object)，连起码的提问能力 (subject/object) 都没有 (verb)，更缺乏（verb after 更）大胆创新的能力 (object)。

（很多高分）學生 (subject) 習慣了(verb) 死記硬背 (object)，連起碼的提問能力 (subject/object) 都沒有 (verb)，更缺乏（verb after 更）大膽創新的能力 (object)。

The main idea could be: "Students get used to mechanic memorization, without （连（連）……都没（沒）有） questioning skills; (they) lack creative skills."

Therefore, choice (D) is correct.

13. (C) From questions 11 and 12, you can guess that the answer here is (C), to support training in skills. The second strategy would be to compare (A) and (C), since they share the same structure with the opposite meaning. Of course, the author supports skill training instead of complaining about it.

14. (D) Read the following explanation for this question and spend a little time to think it through. It's somewhat complicated but it covers a lot of tips for answering difficult questions.

a. The word "greatest" means you need to find a character for "the most" 最. Locate it from the end of the paragraph since this is the last question. "The greatest obstacle,"

最大的困难（最大的困難），is 观念的变化（觀念的變化）. So 观念的变化（觀念的變化） is the Chinese version of the answer.

b. "Change" 变化（變化） is a commonly used phrase. But all the answers seem unrelated to 变化（變化）. And you probably do not know the Chinese word for (D) "concept."

c. Do not panic. Try the following different ways:

Option 1: The vocabulary of (A) lack of money 钱（錢）, (B) technology 技术（術），科技 and (C) cultural 文化的 are relatively easy and you should already know them. They are most likely incorrect since these words do not appear. The answer has a word 观念（觀念） you don't know. You can guess that that word is probably concept (D). Did you get the logic?

Option 2: Learn to figure out the meaning of 观念（觀念）. 观（觀） has the radical of "见（見），" which means "look, see, view." 念 has the radical of "心" which means "thought, think." Some view, some thoughts, isn't that the meaning of "concept" (D)?

Short Story

Reading Selection and Questions

Simplified Chinese

我们今天要讲的是一个神话故事。相传在上古时代，有一片美丽的大地，花草树木、鸟兽虫鱼在一起快乐地生活了很久。后来出现了一位人首蛇身的女神，她的名字叫女娲。有一天她来到水边，看着水面上自己的倒影，突然发现整个世界只有她自己一个人，实在是太孤单了。所以她决定按照自己的样子创造人类。女娲心灵手巧，用泥土捏成了一个个的小人，还给他们配上了两条腿。她用嘴一吹，泥土就变成了一个个活生生的人，这就是我们人类的起源。

一天夜里，不知道什么原因，宇宙发生了巨大的变动，天空忽然塌下了一大块，露出一个黑漆漆的大洞，天火把山林都烧着了。大地也被震裂，出现了一道道裂缝，洪水从裂缝中涌出来，吞没了田野。野兽四处出没，凶狠的黑龙也冒出来害人，成千上万的人不断死去。女娲看到自己创造的人类生活在水深火热之中，焦急万分。她先用五彩石补天，花了九天九夜把天上的大洞补好，然后又从东海找来一只巨龟，把它的四只脚砍下来，立在大地的四个角上，终于把天空撑了起来。紧接着，女娲又填平了大地的裂缝，堵住了洪水，杀死了黑龙，赶走了野兽，这样人们才再次过上了幸福的生活。人们对女娲充满感激，都尊敬地称她"女娲娘娘"。

Traditional Chinese

我們今天要講的是一個神話故事。相傳在上古時代，有一片美麗的大地，花草樹木、鳥獸蟲魚在一起快樂地生活了很久。後來出現了一位人首蛇身的女神，她的名字叫女媧。有一天她來到水邊，看著水面上自己的倒影，突然發現整個世界只有她自己一個人，實在是太孤單了。所以她決定按照自己的樣子創造人類。女媧心靈手巧，用泥土捏成了一個個的小人，還給他們配上了兩條腿。她用嘴一吹，泥土就變成了一個個活生生的人，這就是我們人類的起源。

一天夜裡，不知道甚麼原因，宇宙發生了巨大的變動，天空忽然塌下了一大塊，露出一個黑漆漆的大洞，天火把山林都燒著了。大地也被震裂，出現了一道道裂縫，洪水從裂縫中湧出來，吞沒了田野。野獸四處出沒，凶狠的黑龍也冒出來害人，成千上萬的人不斷死去。女媧看到自己創造的人類生活在水深火熱之中，焦急萬分。她先用五彩石補天，花了九天九夜把天上的大洞補好，然後又從東海找來一隻巨龜，把它的四隻腳砍下來，立在大地的四個角上，終於把天空撐了起來。緊接著，女媧又填平了大地的裂縫，堵住了洪水，殺死了黑龍，趕走了野獸，這樣人們才再次過上了幸福的生活。人們對女媧充滿感激，都尊敬地稱她"女媧娘娘"。

15. The story begins with a description of

    (A)   the earth.
    (B)   trees.
    (C)   the goddess Nu Wa.
    (D)   animals.

16. Why did Nu Wa create human beings?

    (A)   She wanted two legs.
    (B)   She liked human beings.
    (C)   She felt lonely.
    (D)   She went to the river.

17. What did Nu Wa use to make human beings?

    (A)   Plants
    (B)   Mud
    (C)   Animals
    (D)   Air

18. Which of the following was *not* mentioned in the description of disaster?

    (A)   The wild beasts attacked people.
    (B)   The flood took the fields.
    (C)   The people were dying.
    (D)   The black dragon hurt Nu Wa.

19. Which of the following lasted for nine days and nine nights?

    (A)   The creation of human beings
    (B)   The fire caused by the broken sky
    (C)   The time spent to repair the sky
    (D)   Nu Wa's life time

20. Why did Nu Wa find a turtle from the east sea?

    (A)   To hold the sky from the earth
    (B)   To kill the black dragon
    (C)   To stop the flood
    (D)   To repair the sky

Tips for Familiarizing Yourself with Important Chinese Stories

The actual exam is likely to include a legend, a fairy tale, and/or a story that is famous in Chinese culture. This kind of passage is long and probably contains a lot of vocabulary you are not familiar with. However, the sentence structures in these kinds of stories are relatively simple and easy to understand, since it is a narration instead of an essay or an article. The questions will test your understanding of what happens in the story. Therefore, knowing some of these types of stories ahead of time will improve your performance in answering the questions, even if the version in the exam is a little different from what you know.

Here is a list of famous stories in Chinese culture that you should Google and get to know. Feel free to search the English version by typing their Pinyin. To be honest, cultural knowledge is probably more important than actually being able to read the language in this case.

Stories/Legends Important in Chinese Culture	
Simplified Chinese:	**Traditional Chinese:**
天仙配	天仙配
白蛇传	白蛇傳
后羿射日	后羿射日
嫦娥奔月	嫦娥奔月
精卫填海	精衛填海
大禹治水	大禹治水
愚公移山	愚公移山
塞翁失马	塞翁失馬
孟姜女哭长城	孟姜女哭長城
梁山伯与祝英台	梁山伯與祝英台

Explanations

15. (A) Read the first couple of sentences. Look for the choices of (A) 大地, (B) （樹）木, (C) 女娲（媧）, and (D) 鸟兽（鳥獸）, and you will find that 大地 is mentioned first.

16. (C) Use "create human beings" 创造人类（創造人類） to locate your answers in the texts. The sentence with that phrase starts with "therefore" 所以, which means the reason is in the sentence before. That sentence can be translated as "Suddenly found out that she was the only one in this world, and it is too lonely." 突然发现整个世界只有她自己一个人，实在是太孤单了（突然發現整個世界只有她自己一個人，實在是太孤單了）。If you don't know that 孤单（單） means "lonely," you still can get the correct answer from 只有她自己 "only herself."

17. (B) 用 means "use." The passage clearly states that 用泥土捏成了一个个的小人（用泥土捏成了一個個的小人）.

18. (D) Locate the choices by looking for 野兽（獸） "wild beasts," 洪水 "flood," 死 "dying," and 黑龙（龍） "black dragon." The black dragon hurt people but nothing was mentioned about it hurting Nu Wa.

19. (C) Use 九天九夜 "nine days and nine nights" to locate the answer in the text. 花了九天九夜把天上的大洞补（補）好 means "spent nine days and nine nights to repair the hole."

20. (A) Even if you don't remember the Chinese character for "turtle," you can locate the answer by 东（東）海 "the east sea." Or use the measure word "只," which is used to describe small animals. In the sentence with "turtle" and "east sea," there is no mention of (B) dragon or (C) flood, but (D) sky 天空 is mentioned. Choices (A) and (D) both have 天空, but the turtle comes into the story after Nu Wa has fixed the sky. Therefore, turtle was used to "hold" 撑（撐） the sky.

Strategies for Reading Comprehension

You can apply all the strategies in answering multiple-choice questions that you've learned from all kinds of standardized tests and exams. Chapter 4 introduced the basic strategies for the multiple-choice questions of the reading comprehension part of the AP Chinese Language and Culture exam. Now you should put them into action. Embed the following five strategies in your mind and make them your habit so you don't even have to waste time thinking about them when you take the exam. Using these strategies can keep you from making unnecessary errors in on the reading comprehension section of the AP exam.

Strategies for the Reading Selections

1. Browse the questions and answer choices first to gain a main idea of the selection before you read the passages. (The questions are in English while the reading passages are in Chinese.) Then note the key words in the questions and in the four answer choices for each question. Use these key words to help you to locate the sentences in the passage that answer the questions.
2. For any question, read the whole question and then analyze the sentences in the passage related to the question. Scan or skim for the subject, verb, and object. Sometimes you need to locate all four answer choices in the passage to pick the correct answer choice.
3. Do not spend too much time on the difficult questions. Try to quickly choose the most likely answer and flag this question on the computer. You can come back to it later.
4. Pay attention to the numbers as there may be a trap in the question related to these numbers. Also, use the numbers to help you locate information quickly.
5. When you're unsure, guess the answer using good common sense and comparing the four choices.

Study Tips for the Reading Selections

Daily practice for reading comprehension can be more fun than you thought. Read about your favorite topics and choose use your favorite methods to improve your reading comprehension. You learned the exam-taking strategies, and now here are study tips on how best to prepare for the reading comprehension section of the exam.

Vocabulary Building: Take note of any new vocabulary you encounter. Work on them for a while; making flashcards can be helpful. Sort them by themes, by radicals, by sounds, by meanings, by logic stories—whatever helps you to memorize.

Extensive Reading: Browse www.wenxuecity.com or www.sohu.com, or Google the topics you like. Read the titles and guess the content. Talk about what you read with your classmates. You can do this in English if you prefer; however, read the materials in Chinese! Read a lot of Chinese "classified advertisements" 分类广告（分類廣告）. They provide a good tool for learning basic vocabulary and expressions. The more you read, the easier finding key words and understanding the content will be on the readings you encounter on the exam.

Intensive Reading: Make good use of this book. The appendixes provide vocabulary words and expressions as well as grammatical materials appropriate for the AP exam. Try to understand each word or structure. The amount of material in this book is not overwhelming, but it is all essential. You not only need to understand these words, phrases, and structures in the reading passages, but you will also be able to use them in speaking, listening, and writing.

Skill-Building Exercises

Vocabulary Building

After you have refined your strategies for the different types of reading selections, your biggest challenge is building your vocabulary. Always keep in mind that you may not know all the characters, but that shouldn't be a barrier to understanding the phrase as a whole or the main idea.

Do not immediately look words up in the dictionary. Guess first and try to figure it out without the dictionary. Learn the meanings of the key vocabulary words listed in this book to clarify your guessing. And, of course, do not forget to refer to the radicals, which may help you out as well.

In the end, check the meaning of words using www.nciku.com or the iPhone. They both provide handwritten functions for you to check the meaning of the characters without Pinyin provided. To see how this works on the iPhone go to www.youtube.com/watch?v=Ed4XiGRinO4. It takes more time to input, but you will memorize the new characters much more efficiently this way.

1. 节目单（節目單）

Simplified Chinese
今日电视
08:30 天天美食
09:10 动物传奇
09:45 电视剧：新包大人
11:30 卡通动画：中国小飞龙
12:00 午间新闻
12:30 实况录像：2013 年第十五届世界游泳锦标赛
14:00 电视连续剧：西游记
16:00 正爱电影剧场：北京遇上西雅图
18:00 儿童乐园
19:00 新闻联播
20:00 电视剧：寻唐记
21:30 超级文艺
22:20 世界旅游快递
23:00 电视系列剧：终极生化（第5季）

Traditional Chinese
今日電視
08:30 天天美食
09:10 動物傳奇
09:45 電視劇：新包大人
11:30 卡通動畫：中國小飛龍
12:00 午間新聞
12:30 實況錄像：2013 年第十五屆世界游泳錦標賽
14:00 電視連續劇：西遊記
16:00 正愛電影劇場：北京遇上西雅圖
18:00 兒童樂園
19:00 新聞聯播
20:00 電視劇：尋唐記
21:30 超級文藝
22:20 世界旅遊快遞
23:00 電視系列劇：終極生化（第5季）

2. 网站栏目（網站欄目）

Simplified Chinese
滚动新闻
时事点评
生活频道
法律顾问
股市财经
投资理财
职场生涯
创业论坛
科技世界
数码沙龙
旅游天地
影视八卦
娱乐百态
流行时尚
奇闻怪录
摄影沙龙
音乐速递
健康养生
教育咨询
体育看台
原创文学
军事之窗
人到中年
老年之家
购物指南
环境资源

Traditional Chinese

滾動新聞
時事點評
生活頻道
法律顧問
股市財經
投資理財
職場生涯
創業論壇
科技世界
數碼沙龍
旅遊天地
影視八卦
娛樂百態
流行時尚
奇聞怪錄
攝影沙龍
音樂速遞
健康養生
教育咨詢
體育看台
原創文學
軍事之窗
人到中年
老年之家
購物指南
環境資源

3. 华人黄页（華人黃頁）

Simplified Chinese

居住类：房屋装修、水电管道、家具、房地产租赁、清洁公司、钟点工、搬家服务、家政服务、家用电器、二手买卖

医药保健类：卫生局、家庭医生、中医、针灸理疗、中药店、盲人按摩、健身房

文教类：托儿所、幼儿园、培训中心、补习班、家教、大专院校、特长班、图书馆、书店、报摊、平面设计、出版印刷、广告策划、求职招聘

饮食类：中餐馆、西餐馆、日本餐馆、韩国餐馆、麦当劳、肯德基、咖啡屋、茶楼、酒吧、大排档、酒楼、糕饼店、夜宵、零售店

交通类：车行、汽车修理、驾驶培训、租车服务、机场接送、机票代理、快递公司、客运、货运

娱乐类：卡拉OK厅、歌舞厅、影院、服饰、婚纱影楼、游乐场、美容美发、乐器店、麻将馆、玩具城

电脑通信类：硬件、软件、配件、网络、电脑维修、电信营业厅、电话和电话卡

法律类：家庭纠纷、交通违章、翻译与公证、移民签证

投資理財类：股票、期货、金融、人寿保险、房屋保险、健康保险、汽车保险、银行、贷款、外汇兑换、会计师
宗教社团类：教堂、慈善机构、校友会、各种协会

Traditional Chinese
居住類：房屋裝修、水電管道、傢具、房地產租賃、清潔公司、鐘點工、搬家服務、家政服務、家用電器、二手買賣
醫藥保健類：衛生局、家庭醫生、中醫、針灸理療、中藥店、盲人按摩、健身房
文教類：托兒所、幼兒園、培訓中心、補習班、家教、大專院校、特長班、圖書館、書店、報攤、平面設計、出版印刷、廣告策劃、求職招聘
飲食類：中餐館、西餐館、日本餐館、韓國餐館、麥當勞、肯德基、咖啡屋、茶樓、酒吧、大排檔、酒樓、糕餅店、夜宵、零售店
交通類：車行、汽車修理、駕駛培訓、租車服務、機場接送、機票代理、快遞公司、客運、貨運
娛樂類：卡拉ＯＫ廳、歌舞廳、影院、服飾、婚紗影樓、遊樂場、美容美髮、樂器店、麻將館、玩具城
電腦通信類：硬件、軟件、配件、網絡、電腦維修、電信營業廳、電話和電話卡
法律類：家庭糾紛、交通違章、翻譯與公證、移民簽證
投資理財類：股票、期貨、金融、人壽保險、房屋保險、健康保險、汽車保險、銀行、貸款、外匯兌換、會計師
宗教社團類：教堂、慈善機構、校友會、各種協會

Practice with Longer Sentences

What kinds of challenges do you find in reading comprehension besides the unfamiliar vocabulary? Of course, the long, long, long sentences. How can you understand long sentences with a lot of unknown vocabulary? Earlier in this chapter you learned strategies to spot the subject, verb, and object. Now let's try to do that in order to understand the following passages with long sentences. Do not get frustrated by the limited vocabulary you have. In a lot of cases, you can skip all of the words you don't know and still get the basic meaning.

Passage 1

Simplified Chinese
近日，随着各地持续高温天气，许多人都出现了各种各样的"上火"症状。记者采访了中医药大学康复科的金教授。他指出，上火是人体阴阳失衡，体内热毒渗出的表现。所以大家首先要保持情绪良好，睡眠充足，不要过份劳累；其次要注意饮食，多吃清火的蔬菜水果；同时，如果出现不适反應，应该及时就医，根据医生的诊断用药。

Traditional Chinese
（近日，隨著各地持續高溫天氣，許多人都出現了各種各樣的"上火"症狀。記者採訪了中醫藥大學康復科的金教授。他指出，上火是人體陰陽失衡，體內熱毒滲出的表現。所以大家首先要保持情緒良好，睡眠充足，不要過份勞累；其次要注意飲食，多吃清火的蔬菜水果；同時，如果出現不適反應，應該及時就醫，根據醫生的診斷用藥。）

Explanation for Passage 1

近日，随着各地持续高温天气 (weather)，许多人 (subject, 人 is people) 都出现 (verb, before 了) 了各种各样的"上火"症状 (object, after 的)。

近日，隨著各地持續高溫天氣 (weather)，許多人 (subject, 人 is people) 都出現 (verb, before 了) 了各種各樣的"上火"症狀 (object, after 的)。

记者 (subject, 者 means people) 采访 (verb, before 了) 了中医药大学康复科的金教授 (object, after 的)。

記者 (subject, 者 means people) 採訪 (verb, before 了) 了中醫藥大學康復科的金教授 (object, after 的)。

他指出 (verb, points out, states)，上火是 (verb, am/is/are) 人体阴阳失衡，体内热毒渗出的表现 (object, after 的, 现 means "show up, now")。

他指出 (verb, points out, states)，上火是 (verb, am/is/are) 人體陰陽失衡，體內熱毒渗出的表現 (object, after 的, 現 means "show up, now")。

所以 (conjunctions, therefore) 大家 (subject) 首先 (conjunctions, firstly) 要保持 (verb, after modality verb 要) 情绪良好，睡眠充足，不要过份劳累 (verb, after modality verb 不要)；其次 (conjunctions, secondly) 要注意 (verb, after modality verb 要) 饮食，多吃清火的蔬菜水果；

所以 (conjunctions, therefore) 大家 (subject) 首先 (conjunctions, firstly) 要保持 (verb, after modality verb 要) 情緒良好，睡眠充足，不要過份勞累 (verb, after modality verb 不要)；其次 (conjunctions, secondly) 要注意 (verb, after modality verb 要) 飲食，多吃清火的蔬菜水果；

同时 (conjunctions, at the same time)，如果 (conjunctions, if) 出现不适反应，应该及时就医 (verb, after modality verb 应该)，根据医生的诊断 (object due to the verb 根据) 用药。

同時 (conjunctions, at the same time)，如果 (conjunctions, if) 出現不適反應，應該及時就醫 (verb, after modality verb 應該)，根據醫生的診斷 (object due to the verb 根據) 用藥。

The main structure:

天气，许多人出现了"上火"症状 (any character with the radical "疒" is related to disease, sickness, or illness)。记者采访 (any character with the radical "讠" is related to speak, or language) 了金教授。他指出，上火是……表现。所以大家首先要……，不要……，其次要……，同时；如果……，应该……。

天氣，許多人出現了"上火"症狀 (any character with the radical "疒" is related to disease, sickness, or illness)。記者採訪 (any character with the radical "言" is related to speak, or language) 了金教授。他指出，上火是……表現。所以大家首先要……，不要……，其次要……，同時；如果……，應該……。

　　You can easily get the main idea from the small amount of vocabulary and radicals you probably already knew in the first year of Chinese learning. Here's what you know:
Due to the weather, many people have the illness of "上火." Someone interviewed Professor 金 (related to medicine，中医药大学（中醫藥大學） Chinese Medicine University). He pointed out, the illness of "上火" was the show of…… Therefore, everybody should first sleep（睡眠）, not tired（累）, then eat vegetables and fruits（菜，水果）… Meanwhile, if something bad（不, no）happens, they should see the doctor（医生，药，（醫生，藥））.

Passage 2

Simplified Chinese

我国人口的男女比例严重失调，据2011年人口普查统计，大陆人口中男性占51.27%，而女性则占48.73%。但是，在各高校招生中，这个比例却反了过来，大学的新生中女生比男生多。为改变这种现象，一些高校在录取时设置了性别比例，导致了分数线"女高男低"的奇怪现象。例如，海南省考试局2012年公布的提前批院校面试最低分数线就对男女有不同的要求。特别是报考国际关系学院，女生需要715分才能达到提档线，而男生只要668分，差距竟有47分之多！

Traditional Chinese

我國人口的男女比例嚴重失調，據2011年人口普查統計，大陸人口中男性佔51.27%，而女性則佔48.73%。但是，在各高校招生中，這個比例卻反了過來，大學的新生中女生比男生多。為改變這種現象，一些高校在錄取時設置了性別比例，導致了分數線"女高男低"的奇怪現象。例如，海南省考試局2012年公佈的提前批院校面試最低分數線就對男女有不同的要求。特別是報考國際關係學院，女生需要715分才能達到提檔線，而男生只要668分，差距竟有47分之多！

Explanation for Passage 2

（我国的）男女人口比例（严重失调），（据2011年人口普查统计，大陆人口中）男（性占）51.27%，（而）女（性则占）48.73%。 <u>但是</u>，（在各高校招生中，这个）比例<u>却</u>反了（过来），（大学的）新生中女生比男生多。

（我國的）男女人口比例（嚴重失調），（據2011年人口普查統計，大陸人口中）男（性佔）51.27%，（而）女（性則佔）48.73%。 但是，（在各高校招生中，這個）比例卻反了（<u>過來</u>），（大學的）新生中女生比男生多。

（为改变这种现象，一些）高校（在录取时）设置了(verb)性别比例，导致了(verb)（分数线）"女高男低 (quotes are important to keep)"（的）奇怪现象。

（為改變這種現象，一些）高校（在錄取時）設置了(verb)性別比例，導致了(verb)（分數線）"女高男低 (quotes are important to keep)"（的）奇怪現象。

例如，（海南省考试局2012年公布的）（提前批院校面试 subject is too long, so take the last part）最低分数线（就对男女）<u>有</u>（不同）的要求。（特别）是（报考国际关系）学院，女生需要715分（才能达到提档线），（而）男生只要668分，差距竟有47分（之多)！

例如，（海南省考試局2012年公佈的）（提前批院校面試 subject is too long, so take the last part）最低分數線（就對男女）<u>有</u>（不同）的要求。（特別）是（報考國際關係）學院，女生需要715分（才能達到提檔線），（而）男生只要668分，差距竟有47分（之多） ！

Main structure without the detailed description or difficult vocabulary:

男女人口比例 /男51.27%，女48.73%。 <u>但是</u>，（高校 universities ）比例却反了，新生中女生比男生多。高校（设置）了性别比例，导致了(girl higher boy lower) 奇怪现象。例如，最低<u>有</u>要求。是 (one kind of) 专业，女生需要715分，男生只要668分，有47分！

男女人口比例 /男51.27%，女48.73%。 但是，（高校 universities ）比例卻反了，新生中女生比男生多。高校（設置）了性別比例，導致了(girl higher boy lower) 奇怪現象。例如，最低有要求。是 (one kind of) 專業，女生需要715分，男生只要668分，有47分！

Here's the main idea from the limited vocabulary you totally understand:

China's population boy/male is 51.25% and girl/female is 48.73%. However, universities are opposite ("however" indicates opposite). For new students, female is more than the male. Universities "did" (you may not know the meaning of the verb, so regard it as "did") male/female ratio/comparison（比）, "girl higher boy lower." For example, some place has different（不同）lowest line (bottom line). One major, female needs to score 715, while 668 for male. That's a 47-point difference (715 − 668 = 47).

Therefore, the complicated report you read is just describing that girls need a higher score than the boys for some universities.

Practice with Riddles

Although the types of reading selections used in the AP exam are specific, you can read anything to improve your comprehension skills. The most important thing is to find something you think is interesting. For example, you can practice with the following riddles. Search by 脑筋急转弯（腦筋急轉彎）on the Internet to enjoy more of these if you find this fun.

Riddles

Simplified Chinese
1. 你能做，我能做，大家都能做。一个人能做，两个人不能做。请问是什么？
2. 这东西是假的，人们却心甘情愿去买，为什么？
3. 小张今天考试，他昨天已经把中文课上学到的东西复习好了，结果还是不及格，为什么？
4. 阿发用蓝色的笔写出了红字，他是怎么写的？
5. 公共汽车来了，一位先生投了两元钱，司机让他上车；一位美丽的女孩没有投钱，司机也让她上车。司机这样做对吗？
6. 文文拿着鸡蛋扔石头，鸡蛋居然没有破。文文是魔术师吗？
7. 有四个人打网球，警察来了，却抓了五个人，为什么？
8. 太平洋的中间是什么？
9. 有种水果，没吃的时候是绿的，吃的时候是红的，吐出来的却是黑的，这是什么水果？
10. 小李明明知道考试的答案，可是考试时仍然一直看着其他同学，为什么？

Traditional Chinese
1. 你能做，我能做，大家都能做。一個人能做，兩個人不能做。請問是甚麼？
2. 這東西是假的，人們卻心甘情願去買，為甚麼？
3. 小張今天考試，他昨天已經把中文課上學到的東西復習好了，結果還是不及格，為甚麼？
4. 阿發用藍色的筆寫出了紅字，他是怎麼寫的？
5. 公共汽車來了，一位先生投了兩元錢，司機讓他上車；一位美麗的女孩沒有投錢，司機也讓她上車。司機這樣做對嗎？
6. 文文拿著雞蛋扔石頭，雞蛋居然沒有破。文文是魔術師嗎？
7. 有四個人打網球，警察來了，卻抓了五個人，為甚麼？
8. 太平洋的中間是甚麼？
9. 有種水果，沒吃的時候是綠的，吃的時候是紅的，吐出來的卻是黑的，這是甚麼水果？
10. 小李明明知道考試的答案，可是考試時仍然一直看著其他同學，為甚麼？

Answers to the Riddles

Simplified Chinese
1. 做梦。
2. 假牙/假发。
3. 考的不是中文。
4. 蓝色的笔写了一个"红"。
5. 没什么不对，那个女孩用了月票。
6. 文文左手拿鸡蛋，右手把一块石头扔出去，鸡蛋当然不会破。
7. 总共有五个人，其中一个人的名字叫"网球"。
8. 平。
9. 西瓜。
10. 小李是老师。

Traditional Chinese
1. 做夢。
2. 假牙/假髮。
3. 考的不是中文。
4. 藍色的筆寫了一個"紅"。
5. 沒甚麼不對，那個女孩用了月票。
6. 文文左手拿雞蛋，右手把一塊石頭扔出去，雞蛋當然不會破。
7. 總共有五個人，其中一個人的名字叫"網球"。
8. 平。
9. 西瓜。
10. 小李是老師。

Reading Comprehension Practice Test (Exam Section I, Part B)

The reading selections and the questions that follow them in this section create an experience similar to what you'll encounter on the actual exam. Finish the test-like experience first. Then see how many you got wrong. For any questions you missed, look at the explanations to find out where/how you went wrong. Note that you should understand the meanings not only of the correct answer, but also of the incorrect choices.

Finally, do a thorough analysis of where and why you made any errors. Use the self-evaluation sheet provided. Then look at the suggestions for each kind of mistake you made. Refer to the suggestion sheet and the "Study Tips for the Reading Selections" earlier in this chapter, if you feel you need more practice.

The Practice Questions

Give yourself 60 minutes to complete this practice test. You can mark any questions you want to come back to later if you have time within the 60-minute time limit.

Read this advertisement:

Simplified Chinese
"天路" 宽带大优惠 698元套餐
1. 宽带一年使用费
2. 价值218元的有线数字电视基本收视费一年
3. 价值398元的有线数字电视付费节目收视费一年
4. 免费安装
电话：3981-4677

Traditional Chinese
"天路" 寬帶大優惠 698元套餐
1. 寬帶一年使用費
2. 價值218元的有線數字電視基本收視費一年
3. 價值398元的有線數字電視付費節目收視費一年
4. 免費安裝
電話：3981-4677

1. The purpose of this advertisement is to promote

   (A) digital TV programs.
   (B) broadband cable service.
   (C) tech set-up service.
   (D) road service.

2. The promotion doesn't include

   (A) one-year usage of broadband cable.
   (B) one-year usage of premium TV channels.
   (C) free usage of basic TV channels.
   (D) free installation.

3. How much is the charge for the premium channels?

   (A) 398 Yuan yearly
   (B) 218 Yuan yearly
   (C) Free of charge
   (D) 698 Yuan yearly

Read this advertisement:

Simplified Chinese
高薪诚聘客户服务人员两名，非暑期生，有印刷业务经验者优先
薪资组成：底薪＋提成＋全勤奖
只要你足够优秀，薪金不是问题！
有意者请致电：13823498008 谢绝中介。

Traditional Chinese
高薪誠聘客戶服務人員兩名，非暑期生，有印刷業務經驗者優先
薪资组成：底薪＋提成＋全勤獎
只要你足夠優秀，薪金不是問題！
有意者請致電：13823498008 謝絕中介。

4. What type of job is being offered?

(A) Printing
(B) Administration
(C) Accounting
(D) Customer service

5. According to the advertisement, what is not provided in the salary?

(A) Basic salary
(B) Full attendance bonus
(C) Printing work
(D) Commission

6. The purpose of the advertisement is primarily to get two employees who

(A) are searching for a summer job.
(B) don't think money is a problem.
(C) are recommended by head hunters.
(D) have experience in the printing industry.

Read this poster:

Simplified Chinese
人民中路双门面超市，地理位置好，交通方便，独立厨卫，客源稳定。因本人要出国发展，现带货转让，证件齐全，接手即可营业。

Traditional Chinese
人民中路雙門面超市，地理位置好，交通方便，獨立廚衛，客源穩定。因本人要出國發展，現帶貨轉讓，證件齊全，接手即可營業。

7. The purpose of this poster is to get

(A) a business rental.
(B) a business sale.
(C) an apartment rental.
(D) an apartment sale.

8. The place this poster described is a

(A) supermarket.
(B) restaurant.
(C) condo.
(D) house.

9. What is *not* mentioned regarding the place?

(A) Workers
(B) Goods included
(C) Returning customers
(D) Convenient transportation

10. Which of the following is *not* true according to the poster?

(A) The owner is going abroad.
(B) The place is located on Renmin Road.
(C) There is no kitchen or bathroom.
(D) The documents of license and certificates are provided.

Read this sign:

Simplified Chinese
友情提示：请保管好随身携带物品，以防被盗。

Traditional Chinese
友情提示：請保管好隨身攜帶物品，以防被盜。

11. The sign's message is most likely directed to

    (A) subway passengers.
    (B) schoolchildren.
    (C) bus drivers.
    (D) police officers.

12. The purpose of the sign is to

    (A) post a penalty for violating a regulation.
    (B) provide instructions for luggage.
    (C) protect people from theft.
    (D) direct friends to a location.

Read this e-mail:

Simplified Chinese
发件人：杨修
收件人：刘备
邮件主题：吃药
发件时间：2014年7月28日
刘备，
我寄过来的药你收到了吗？虽然你的胃病不严重，但身体的事可不能马虎。这是两个疗程的用量，记住啊，每天吃三次，饭前服用，每次两片。只要你能按时吃药，注意休息，一般一个月左右就能感觉到效果。以后你可得按时吃饭，多吃蔬菜多喝汤，不要吃刺激性的食物，也不能吃太硬的，不能像从前一样，饱一顿饿一顿的。要不然，万一弄出个胃穿孔，再住院就来不及了！
祝早日康复！

Traditional Chinese
發件人：楊修
收件人：劉備
郵件主題：吃藥
發件時間：2014年7月28日
劉備，
我寄過來的藥你收到了嗎？雖然你的胃病不嚴重，但身體的事可不能馬虎。這是兩個療程的用量，記住啊，每天吃三次，飯前服用，每次兩片。只要你能按時吃藥，注意休息，一般一個月左右就能感覺到效果。以後你可得按時吃飯，多吃蔬菜多喝湯，不要吃刺激性的食物，也不能吃太硬的，不能像從前一樣，飽一頓餓一頓的。要不然，萬一弄出個胃穿孔，再住院就來不及了！
祝早日康復！

13. What does the sender say about the receiver's condition?

    (A) It's a serious problem.
    (B) It requires exercises.
    (C) It requires a doctor's opinion.
    (D) It requires attention to his body.

14. How is the prescribed medicine to be taken?

    (A) Twice per day, three tablets each time, before food
    (B) Three times per day, two tablets each time, before food
    (C) Twice per day, two tablets each time, after food
    (D) Three times per day, two tablets each time, after food

15. What is not recommended for the receiver's diet?

    (A) Hard food
    (B) Soup
    (C) Vegetables
    (D) Regular dining hours

Read this letter:

Simplified Chinese

麦克，

你好。

上次邮件中，你问过去中国朋友家吃饭要注意什么，我觉得最重要的是要记得带上礼物，用来表示对他们的感谢和尊重。中国人很讲究送礼的，这里边的窍门可多呢，你得学着点，千万不能犯了人家的忌讳。不送钟，不送伞。如果人家有小孩子，带些玩具巧克力什么的最合适不过了，蜡烛也不能送，就怕不吉利。你要记得穿干净袜子，因为在很多中国人家里要脱鞋的，而且你也要准时，提前五分钟最好，别让其他人等你一个，也最好不要第一个走。我记得你一直没用过筷子，早点告诉主人比较好，免得人家没有准备。中国人吃菜都是共享的，如果不是自助餐，一般不会分开来吃，看起来不是很卫生，不过你最好入乡随俗。

祝玩得开心！

林真

Traditional Chinese

麥克，

你好。

上次郵件中，你問過去中國朋友家吃飯要注意甚麼，我覺得最重要的是要記得帶上禮物，用來表示對他們的感謝和尊重。中國人很講究送禮的，這裡邊的竅門可多呢，你得學著點，千萬不能犯了人家的忌諱。不送鐘，不送傘。如果人家有小孩子，帶些玩具巧克力甚麼的最合適不過了，蠟燭也不能送，就怕不吉利。你要記得穿乾淨襪子，因為在很多中國人家裡要脫鞋的，而且你也要準時，提前五分鐘最好，別讓其他人等你一個，也最好不要第一個走。我記得你一直沒用過筷子，早點告訴主人比較好，免得人家沒有準備。中國人吃菜都是共享的，如果不是自助餐，一般不會分開來吃，看起來不是很衛生，不過你最好入鄉隨俗。

祝玩得開心！

林真

16. According to the letter, what is most important for a guest in China?

(A) To be punctual
(B) To bring some presents
(C) To use chopsticks
(D) To be nice to the host's children

17. Which of the following is appropriate as a gift when going to visit a Chinese family?

(A) Clock
(B) Umbrella
(C) Chocolate
(D) Candle

18. The letter states that the best time to arrive for a dinner is

(A) to be the first one there.
(B) to be on time.
(C) to be five minutes late.
(D) to be five minutes early.

19. What is true in the letter about Chinese customs in regard to being a guest?

(A) You don't have to take off your shoes.
(B) You eat separately from others.
(C) You need to be the last one to leave to show your respect.
(D) You let the host know earlier if you are not good at using chopsticks.

Read this brochure:

Simplified Chinese
天龙山森林公园入园须知
一、票价为50元，一人一票，当天有效，一经售出，概不退票。十岁以下儿童免票。
二、敬请遵守护林防火规定，严禁野外用火及吸烟，违者罚款一千元。
三、园内允许拍照，但不准损坏花草、树木、景点设施及各类公共设施。严禁狩猎，一经发现，按《森林公园管理条例》进行处罚。
四、游览过程中，请注意人身安全及财产安全。当受到侵害时请拨110，当您需要医疗服务时请拨120，火警请拨119。
森林公园管理处

Traditional Chinese
天龍山森林公園入園須知
一、票價為50元，一人一票，當天有效，一經售出，概不退票。十歲以下兒童免票。
二、敬請遵守護林防火規定，嚴禁野外用火及吸煙，違者罰款一千元。
三、園內允許拍照，但不准損壞花草、樹木、景點設施及各類公共設施。嚴禁狩獵，一經發現，按《森林公園管理條例》進行處罰。
四、遊覽過程中，請注意人身安全及財產安全。當受到侵害時請撥110，當您需要醫療服務時請撥120，火警請撥119。
森林公園管理處

20. How long is an admission ticket valid?

    (A) One day
    (B) One week
    (C) One month
    (D) One year

21. Who is admitted free of charge?

    (A) Children
    (B) Children with adults
    (C) Children under 10
    (D) Senior citizens

22. What is required for using fire in the park?

    (A) You must ask for permission to smoke.
    (B) No fires are allowed.
    (C) Fire is allowed for hunters.
    (D) Use fire only in case of emergency.

23. Which of the following is true according to the brochure?

    (A) Damaging the facility carries a penalty of 1,000 Yuan.
    (B) The ticket is nonrefundable.
    (C) No personal belongings are allowed in the park.
    (D) No photo taking is allowed in the park.

24. If someone needs medical care, the visitors should call

    (A) 110.
    (B) 120.
    (C) 119.
    (D) the park office.

Read this news article:

Simplified Chinese

记者采访国家旅游局监管司负责人时得知，旅游和观光本来是一件轻松愉悦的事，可由于一些商家和旅行社受利益驱使，为了赚更多的钱，往往会使用一些不正当手段侵犯消费者权益。网上疯传的"五十大旅游陷阱"也许有些夸张，但对消费者也是一个警示。

据了解，一般消费者被"宰"的地方很多。第一要注意的是吃的方面。到一个地方旅游就希望能品尝当地的特色美食，黑心导游可能带你去以次充好或漫天要价的地方，所以点餐前一定要问明价格再做决定。第二是住的方面。要确认宾馆的星级和配套设施并在合同中注明，有不符合之处果断换房。第三是玩的方面。换路线、拼团、景点缩水都有可能发生，要坚决拒绝，不要随便拍照或参加所谓的文化活动。

选择信誉良好的正规旅行社，签定明确的合同及意外险，更能防止纠纷发生。同时，消费者在旅游途中应当理智购物，一定要索取发票。而当自身权益受到侵害时，不要消极对待，应及时向政府部门投诉。

Traditional Chinese

記者採訪國家旅遊局監管司負責人時得知，旅遊和觀光本來是一件輕鬆愉悦的事，可由於一些商家和旅行社受利益驅使，為了賺更多的錢，往往會使用一些不正當手段侵犯消費者權益。網上瘋傳的"五十大旅遊陷阱"也許有些誇張，但對消費者也是一個警示。

據瞭解，一般消費者被"宰"的地方很多。第一要注意的是吃的方面。到一個地方旅遊就希望能品嘗當地的特色美食，黑心導遊可能帶你去以次充好或漫天要價的地方，所以點餐前一定要問明價格再做決定。第二是住的方面。要確認賓館的星級和配套設施並在合同中注明，有不符合之處果斷換房。第三是玩的方面。換路線、拼團、景點縮水都有可能發生，要堅決拒絕，不要隨便拍照或參加所謂的文化活動。

選擇信譽良好的正規旅行社，簽定明確的合同及意外險，更能防止糾紛發生。同時，消費者在旅遊途中應當理智購物，一定要索取發票。而當自身權益受到侵害時，不要消極對待，應及時向政府部門投訴。

25. Which of the following is mentioned as the primary source for the information in the article?

    (A) School administrators
    (B) Government officials
    (C) Journalists
    (D) Questionnaire reports

26. According to the article, what causes the travel traps?

    (A) Unethical practices by some travel agencies and businesses
    (B) Internet advocates traveling improperly
    (C) Consumers' choices
    (D) Traveling is a happy experience

27. What is the best way to eat when traveling?

    (A) Bring your own food.
    (B) Eat local food recommended by the tour guide.
    (C) Make sure about the price before eating.
    (D) Do not eat local food recommended by the tour guide.

28. Which of the following is *not* recommended when traveling?

    (A) Signing a contract specifying details with the travel agency.
    (B) Buying travel insurance.
    (C) Not getting a receipt after purchase.
    (D) Refusing any change of traveling routes not written in the contract.

29. What should the consumer do as a victim of a traveling trap?

    (A) Beat the tour guide.
    (B) Call the police.
    (C) Don't travel anymore.
    (D) Make a claim to the corresponding government department.

Read this story:

Simplified Chinese

很久很久以前，有一个种田的小伙子叫牛郎，他和一头老牛相依为命。有一天，那头老牛突然开口说话了！牛郎按照老牛的指示去了河边，遇到了一位美丽的姑娘。那位姑娘本是天庭玉帝的女儿，喜欢上了牛郎，两人便结为了夫妻。牛郎每天去地里干活，织女则在家中织布做衣，日子越过越幸福，他们还生了一双可爱的儿女。那头牛也越来越老，死去的时候叮嘱牛郎要把它的皮留下来，叫牛郎一有难就披到身上去。

好景不长，织女的母亲王母娘娘发现了女儿下凡的事，勃然大怒，她把织女捉回了天上。牛郎又着急又伤心，想起老牛的话，他就用担子挑起一儿一女，披上牛皮就追。没想到那牛皮有着神奇的力量，牛郎竟然飞了起来！眼看着就可以追上织女了，王母娘娘拔下头上的金簪一划，一条天河就隔在了牛郎和织女的中间，生生拆散了一对恩爱夫妻。他们日日隔河相守，人间的喜鹊被他们的爱情所感动，每年七月初七都要飞上天去，在银河中搭鹊桥让他们相会。每年的这一天，姑娘们会在葡萄架下仰望星空，庆祝七夕，乞求自己拥有织女般心灵手巧的能力和一心一意的爱人。所以七月初七便成了中国的传统节日七夕节，又叫乞巧节或七巧节，就是中国的情人节。

Traditional Chinese

很久很久以前，有一個種田的小伙子叫牛郎，他和一頭老牛相依為命。有一天，那頭老牛突然開口說話了！牛郎按照老牛的指示去了河邊，遇到了一位美麗的姑娘。那位姑娘本是天庭玉帝的女兒，喜歡上了牛郎，兩人便結為了夫妻。牛郎每天去地裡乾活，織女則在家中織布做衣，日子越過越幸福，他們還生了一雙可愛的兒女。那頭牛也越來越老，死去的時候叮囑牛郎要把它的皮留下來，叫牛郎一有難就披到身上去。

好景不長，織女的母親王母娘娘發現了女兒下凡的事，勃然大怒，她把織女捉回了天上。牛郎又著急又傷心，想起老牛的話，他就用擔子挑起一兒一女，披上牛皮就追。沒想到那牛皮有著神奇的力量，牛郎竟然飛了起來！眼看著就可以追上織女了，王母娘娘拔下頭上的金簪一划，一條天河就隔在了牛郎和織女的中間，生生拆散了一對恩愛夫妻。他們日日隔河相守，人間的喜鵲被他們的愛情所感動，每年七月初七都要飛上天去，在銀河中搭鵲橋讓他們相會。每年的這一天，姑娘們會在葡萄架下仰望星空，慶祝七夕，乞求自己擁有織女般心靈手巧的能力和一心一意的愛人。所以七月初七便成了中國的傳統節日七夕節，又叫乞巧節或七巧節，就是中國的情人節。

30. What is unusual about the ox?

    (A) It is immortal.
    (B) It likes Zhi Nu.
    (C) It is Niu Lang's best friend.
    (D) It can talk.

31. What was unusual about the girl Zhi Nu?

    (A) She was the daughter of the Jade Emperor.
    (B) She weaved at home.
    (C) She has a son and a daughter.
    (D) She is Niu Lang's wife.

32. What did the ox ask Niu Lang to do?

(A) Work in the field.
(B) Take care of Zhi Nu.
(C) Keep its skin for a disaster.
(D) Stay away from Zhi Nu's parents.

33. Which of the following is true according to the story?

(A) Niu Lang and Zhi Nu lived together at the end.
(B) Zhi Nu's mother made the Milky Way between Niu Lang and Zhi Nu.
(C) Zhi Nu's mother liked Niu Lang.
(D) Zhi Nu lived with her children but not Niu Lang.

34. The girls celebrate July 7 of the Chinese lunar calendar because they

(A) like watching the milky river.
(B) want to fly to the sky.
(C) want a great lover like Niu Lang.
(D) want to be as beautiful as Zhi Nu.

35. This story tells us the origin of

(A) Chinese Valentine's Day.
(B) Chinese spring festival.
(C) Chinese moon festival.
(D) Chinese lantern festival.

Answers

1. B		19. D	
2. C		20. A	
3. A		21. C	
4. D		22. B	
5. C		23. B	
6. D		24. D	
7. B		25. B	
8. A		26. A	
9. A		27. C	
10. C		28. C	
11. A		29. D	
12. C		30. D	
13. D		31. A	
14. B		32. C	
15. A		33. B	
16. B		34. C	
17. C		35. A	
18. D			

Explanations

1. (B) The purpose is usually located at the beginning or the end. The first line states that the ad is about broadband cable service 宽带大优惠（寬帶大優惠）, which is the choice B. The most likely mistake would be to select (A), because the advertisement mentioned digital TV a couple of times. However, digital cable and digital TV programs are different concepts.

2. (C) For questions of what's not included, or not true, match the choices with the passage. Statement #1 matches (A), statement #3 matches (B), and statement #4 matches (D). To make sure that (C) is correct, double check the context. Look at statement #2, because it is the only one left. It states there is a restriction of "one year" for the free usage of basic TV channels.

3. (A) "Premium channels" will normally be translated into 付费电视频道（付費電视频道）. Statement #2 is about basic channels and statement #3 is about paid channels, which are premium channels. Statement #3 gives the price of 398, making (A) correct.

4. (D) "Customer service" is 客户服务（客戶服務）. The most likely wrong answer would be printing (A), because there is "printing" 印刷业务（印刷業務） in the context. However, 有……经验者优先（有……經驗者優先） is a structure commonly used in employment advertisements; it means "priority is given to somebody……" It doesn't mean the job is printing.

5. (C) To answer what is not included, match the four choices to the context. 底薪＋提成＋全勤奖（底薪＋提成＋全勤獎）means basic salary + commissions + full attendance bonus. Therefore, printing work (C) is not included.

6. (D) Match the four choices to the context. The context states 非暑期生, not summer job (A). 不认为钱是问题（不認為錢是問題） doesn't match 薪金不是问题 （薪金不是問題） in the context, which means "salary is not a problem," which makes (B) incorrect. The context states 谢绝中介（謝絕中介）, which means "no agents in between, contact directly," which makes (C) incorrect. The advertisements often ended with the sentence of 谢绝（謝絕）……, which means "thank you, but no" to avoid harassment.

7. (B) This is a question of choosing between "business" and "apartment," and between "rental" and "sale," There is a lot of vocabulary indicating that it is a business instead of an apartment: "supermarket" 超市, "customers" 客源, "goods" 货（貨）, "run business" 营业（營業）, and so on. Therefore, the answer is between (A) and (B). 带货转让，证件齐全（帶貨轉讓，證件齊全）means "transfer (business) with the goods, the documents of license and certificates are complete," which indicates it is a business sale instead of a rental.

8. (A) 超市 means 超级市场（超級市場）, which is "supermarket."

9. (A) Match the four choices to the context. We saw 带货（帶貨）(B), 客源稳定（客源穩定）(C), and 地理位置好 (D). However, there is nothing mentioned about the workers, so (A) is correct.

10. (C) Match the four choices to the context. We saw (A) 本人要出国发展（本人要出國發展）,(B)人民中路, and (D) 证件齐全（證件齊全）. It states that there is "independent bathroom and kitchen," so (C) is not true.

11. (A) The sign is a "friendly"（友情）"reminder" 请（請）. 保 is a character that means "take care of, protect." 防 is a commonly used character on the signs and posters, which means "no, stop, prevent from." Similar vocabulary includes: 严禁（嚴禁）、止、停、免、莫， and so on. The sign reminds people to take care of their own belongings to prevent thefts. Schoolchildren (B) and police officers (D) normally won't face this situation. Bus drivers (C) are more likely to give this reminder instead of receiving it. Therefore, the most likely audience intended for this sign is subway passengers (A).

12. (C) It's not easy to figure out the correct answer if you don't know that 盗（盜）means "steal." However, if you can guess the meaning of the sentence before by some characters you may know, such as "please" 请, "protect" 保, and "things" 物品, you can guess the meaning out as well.

13. (D) First, it is not (A) a serious problem 不严重（不嚴重）; there is no information that it requires exercises (B) or a doctor's opinion (C). Therefore, (D) is correct: 身体的事可不能马虎（身體的事可不能馬虎）.

14. (B) The passage states 每天三次，每次两片，饭前服用（每天三次，每次兩片，飯前服用）, which makes the answer (B).

15. (A) Using either common sense or the information of the passage, the answer is (A) 硬的食物. Another tip to answer this question is (C) "vegetables" and (B) "soup" are parallel, so neither of them could be the correct answer. 按时吃饭（按時吃飯）means dine regularly (D), which is also recommended.

16. (B) Use "the most important" 最重要的 to locate the answer. The second sentence states "remember to bring a present" 记得带上礼物（記得帶上禮物）; therefore, choice (B) is correct.

17. (C) (A) Clock and (B) umbrella are parallel, so neither of them can be the one correct answer. Candle (D) is not correct either based on the context: 蜡烛也不能送（蠟燭也不能送）. That leaves (C) as the correct choice.

18. (D) The best time is "5 minutes earlier" 提前五分钟（鐘）最好.

19. (D) Match the four choices to the sentences in the passage. 因为在很多中国人家里要脱鞋的（因為在很多中國人家裡要脱鞋的）relates to A; 一般不会分开来吃（一般不會分開來吃）relates to B; and 也最好不要第一个走（也最好不要第一個走）relates to C. However, the text is different from each of these three choices, so these choices are all incorrect. 如果你没用过筷子，早点告诉主人比较好（如果你没用過筷子，早點告訴主人比較好）matches choice (D), which is correct.

20. (A) 当（當）天有效 means valid for the day it was sold.

21. (C) 十岁以下儿童免票（十歲以下兒童免票）means children under 10 do not need a ticket.

22. (B) Match the four choices to the sentences in the passage. 严禁……及吸烟（嚴禁……及吸煙）strongly states that there is no permission to smoke, which makes (A) incorrect. There is no information related to choices (C) and (D). So the best answer is (B).

23. (B) Use 1,000 to locate the sentence (rule #2) for choice (A). The penalty here is for fire usage instead of facility damage, which makes (A) incorrect. The phrase of "personal belongings" (C) is normally translated to 随身携带物品（隨身攜帶物品）for the signs and posters. There is no specific information regarding whether personal belongings are allowed or not. The brochure clearly states that taking photos is permitted (rule 3), which makes (D) incorrect. "The tickets are nonrefundable" is 概（概）不退票 (rule #1), making (B) the correct choice.

24. (D) The number for "medical care" 医疗服务（醫療服務）in China is 120.

25. (B) In news articles, the first sentence normally states the primary source for the information. Here is 国家旅游局监督管理司负责人（國家旅遊局監督管理司負責人）, which means something related to the "nation" 国家（國家）, the bureau "局," the department "司." This indicates the source is government officials (B).

26. (A) Travel traps are not a happy thing to deal with according to the article, so (D) can be easily eliminated. The first long sentence clearly states that "however, because" 可由 于（於）"some business and travel agencies" 一些商家和旅行社......"in order to make more money" 为了赚更多的钱（為了賺更多的錢）. Therefore, we know (A) is correct.

27. (C) First, locate the questions in the second paragraph. Pay attention to the conjunctions. 所以 often leads to a result or a solution. 问明价格（問明價格）is easily understandable as "to make sure about the price."

28. (C) Locates the four choices in the passage. (A) and (B) is so common sense that we just don't need to pay attention to it. Paragraph 2, sentence 3 states that the unexpected change in plan should always be rejected.

29. (D) By common sense, either (B) and (D) are possible answers. Look in the last paragraph (since this is the last question). There you'll find information about claim to "government" 政府，政府部门（門）, but no information about police. Therefore, (B) is correct.

30. (D) The second sentence states that the ox suddenly（突然）starts to talk.

31. (A) The fourth sentence states that Zhi Nu is the daughter of Jade Emperor. Other choices are not necessarily incorrect, but they refer to things that do not seem that "unusual."

32. (C) At the end of the first paragraph, the ox asks Niu Lang to keep his skin.

33. (B) Locate the answer choices in the story. Niu Yang of course didn't catch Zhi Nu, which makes (A) incorrect. 眼看着（著）就可以......means "it seemed like it could." Zhi Nu's mother didn't like Niu Lang—that's why she separated them—so (C) is incorrect. In regard to choice (D), Niu Lang actually lives with their children, since at the beginning of the second paragraph, it states Zhi Nu's mom only took Zhi Nu away.

34. (C) Common sense tells us that choices (C) and (D) are possible answers, but at the end of the story, nothing about Zhi Nu being beautiful is mentioned. Furthermore, the last sentence states that the girls want lovers and therefore July 7 is Valentine's Day in China.

35. (A) The last sentence of the story states the correct answer.

Self-Evaluation

It's important to learn from your mistakes. Evaluate your performance on this practice test to try to understand the reason you missed each question you did. Use the following worksheet. Then look at the suggestions that follow for how to deal with each reason for missing a question.

Self-Evaluation Worksheet for the Reading Selections

FREQUENT REASONS FOR ERRORS	WHICH QUESTION?	NUMBER OF ERRORS
1. I didn't even understand the question!		
2. The question asked for A, but I thought it was asking for B!		
3. I just could not find the sentence in the context related to the question.		
4. Too many words I don't know!		
5. The sentences for the answer are too long and complicated to understand.		
6. I thought I knew the answer but I didn't know that word means "no."		
7. Oops. I don't have enough time to finish!		
Think: What kinds of errors did I make the most? Why didn't I find the correct answers? What could I do to improve?		

Suggestions in Response to Errors in the Reading Selections

FREQUENT REASONS FOR ERRORS	SUGGESTIONS
1. I didn't even understand the question!	S + V + O, skip other information. Note the key words to locate the sentences.
2. The question asked for A, but I thought it was asking for B!	Read the question thoroughly.
3. I just could not find the sentence in the context related to the question.	Look for the key words: numbers, longer phrases, words you do not know.
4. Too many words I don't know!	Guess by using radicals or the context. Build your vocabulary in daily study.
5. The sentences for the answer were too long and complicated to understand.	Look for "subject, verb, and object" first. The main idea helps you to figure out the details later. Review "Functional Grammar" in appendix.
6. I thought I knew the answer but I didn't know that word means "no."	Review negation vocabulary and build your own negation vocabulary pool.
7. Oops. I don't have enough time to finish!	Choose your best guess or just mark (C). Mark the questions you don't know and come back later.
Think: What kinds of errors did I make the most? Why didn't I find the correct answers? What could I do to improve?	See "Study Tips for the Reading Selections" earlier in this chapter.

CHAPTER 8

Presentational Writing: Story Narration

IN THIS CHAPTER

Summary: This chapter provides practice for the story narration part of the AP Chinese Language and Culture Exam. First, you'll learn what story narration is and how it's scored. Then you'll practice the story narration strategies and learn to use a three-step approach to writing your story. Presented next are skill-building exercises designed to help you avoid the errors students frequently make on this part of the exam. Finally, you will practice applying the strategies you've learned in two practice tests that are similar to what you'll find on the actual test. At the end, analyze and evaluate your performance on the story narration task and use the suggestions provided to adjust your study plan accordingly.

Key Strategies/Ideas

- ✪ Learn how the story narration is graded so you'll know what's expected and how you measure up.
- ✪ Practice browsing the four pictures provided to create a brief story in your mind. Start by typing the actions shown in the pictures that you need to write about.
- ✪ Learn to use the three steps for writing a complete, vivid story with minimal errors.
- ✪ Practice writing the story narration within the time limit of 15 minutes.
- ✪ To enhance your story and minimize errors, review "Functional Grammar" in the appendix.

Story Narration: What It Is and How It Is Scored

In this part of the exam—the first task of Section II, Part A (Writing)—you'll finish a task of story narration within a time limit of 15 minutes. There will be a clock on your computer screen in the real exam telling you how much time is left. Based on the four pictures that you'll be given, you will have to write a coherent story with a beginning, a middle, and an ending. You can use either the preset input of Microsoft IME or Microsoft New Phonetic IME system to type Chinese characters. You can switch between simplified Chinese and traditional Chinese.

Scoring Guidelines: Story Narration

The College Board provides grading guidelines for the story narration. You can find these on its website. At the time of publication the specific URL for these was http://media. collegeboard.com/digitalServices/pdf/ap/apcentral/ap13_chinese_scoring_guidelines.pdf.

Each student's written response is graded on a scale of 1 to 6. Stories at level 6 are considered "excellent," while those graded at level 5 are "very good." Level 4 scores competence as "good" and level 3 rates your performance as "adequate."

Your performance on the story narration part of the exam—like the scoring on all the free-response questions—is evaluated on the basis of three criteria called rubrics:

  I. Task Completion
 II. Language Usage
III. Delivery

How do you get a high score on story narration? To answer this question, you'll need to have an idea of what kinds of answers can reach a score of 5 and above. Let's start with an analysis of the scoring guidelines (rubrics). First, you need to write a complete story to score 4 or higher (task completion). Second, you need to add elaborated description to get a score of 5 or higher (language usage). At the end, you should check and minimize errors to obtain the score of 6 (delivery).

Task completion is the most important rubric and also the easiest one on which to get a high score. A common mistake many students make is to write too much at the beginning and then they don't have time for the fourth picture. However great the answers are, if you miss the fourth picture, the highest score you can get is only a 3. To score higher, you definitely need a complete story.

The following table summarizes the most important keys to differentiate levels 3, 4, 5, and 6.

Scoring Guidelines for Story Narration

	SCORE: 3	SCORE: 4	SCORE: 5	SCORE: 6
I. TASK COMPLETION				
Story Completion	Basic.	Complete. Minor inconsistency with the pictures.	Logical and complete. Consistent with pictures.	More thorough and greater detail compared to a 5.
Organization	Portions may lack organization.	Lacks detail. Inconsistent transitional elements. Loosely connected sentences.	Generally clear progression. Some transitional elements and cohesive devices.	Clear progression with detail. Appropriate use of transitional elements and cohesive devices.
II. LANGUAGE USAGE				
Vocabulary and Idioms	Limited use of vocabulary. Frequent errors.	Mostly appropriate vocabulary usage. Mistakes do not obscure meaning.	Appropriate vocabulary. Sporadic errors.	Rich and appropriate vocabulary. Minimal errors.
Grammatical Structures	Simple grammatical structures. Frequent errors.	Mostly appropriate grammatical structures. Mistakes do not obscure meaning.	Variety of grammatical structures. Sporadic errors.	Wide range of grammatical structures. Minimum errors.
III. DELIVERY				
Register	Inconsistent. Many errors.	May include several lapses.	Occasional lapses.	Consistent use. Appropriate.

Strategies for Story Narration: A Step-by-Step Approach

The basic strategies for story narration were presented in Chapter 4 and are summarized in the following sidebar. To apply these strategies, consider each of them to be one step in a step-by-step approach to story narration. Using the warm-up story narration exercise, this chapter will take you step by step through the process of applying the strategies to the actual task of writing or narrating a story. By using these strategies in a step-by-step approach, you'll be able to master story narration.

Strategies for Story Narration

1. **Complete the task.** First, create a brief story in your mind and write down each action in the four pictures. You will need to write about all four pictures so budget your time carefully. In your narrative story, be sure to fully address all of the actions shown in the pictures.

2. **Pay attention to language usage and delivery.** Sticking to the pictures doesn't mean you cannot elaborate. You can add adjectives to describe the objects and adverbs to describe the actions. You can add details describing the facial expressions, the weather, or the environment in which the story takes place. Try to use advanced language such as Chinese idioms, metaphors, proverbs, and so on.

3. **Check your work.** Try to give yourself time to check your story narration. Focus on the transitional elements for logic and on a culturally appropriate delivery for the situation. Check for typos and grammatical errors. Use familiar conjunctions to make correct complex sentences.

Warm-up Exercise

For the warm-up exercise you will have another try at the story narration task that was in the diagnostic test.

The four following pictures present a story. Imagine you are writing the story to a friend. Narrate a complete story as suggested by the pictures. Give your story a beginning, a middle, and an ending. You will have 15 minutes to complete this task.

Now, using this story narration exercise as an example, we'll walk through the three steps to create a great story in 15 minutes. Learn these three steps and make this method your habit so you don't even have to think about it on test day.

Step 1: A *Complete* Story in 7 Minutes (Task Completion)

There are three things you should do in Step 1:

1. Quickly look at the pictures and create a brief story in your mind. (30 seconds) Two boys were playing soccer in the field. One boy kicked the ball, and the ball bumped the head of a girl pedestrian. The boys ran to the girl to check and found out that she was OK.

2. After you've spent a few seconds to create a story in your mind, begin typing. List each action in the pictures; you should cover all the actions shown. (2½ minutes)

两个男孩踢足球，一个踢球，球打了女孩的头，女孩坐地上，一男扶起女孩，一男看她膝盖，两男挥手，女孩笑
（兩個男孩踢足球，一個踢球，球打了女孩的頭，女孩坐地上，一男扶起女孩，一男看她膝蓋，兩男揮手，女孩笑）

Two boys, playing soccer, one kicks the ball, the ball bumped the girl, the girl sits on the ground, one boy holds the girl, one boy checks her knee, boys waves to the girl, girl smiles.

3. Working from the actions you wrote down, you should write approximately four sentences to finish the story. (4 minutes)

1. Who, where, and what (and maybe when)?
小王和小张在球场踢足球。
（小王和小張在球場踢足球。）

2. What happened?
球打到了一个女孩子的头，她倒在了地上。小王和小张跑过来。
（球打到了一個女孩子的頭，她倒在了地上。小王和小張跑過來。）

3. What happened next?
小王扶起女孩，小张看女孩的膝盖。
（小王扶起女孩，小張看女孩的膝蓋。）

4. A happy ending.
女孩子站起来，向前走了两步，小王和小张跟她说再见。
（女孩子站起來，向前走了兩步，小王和小張跟她說再見。）

Step 2: A Complete and *Vivid* Story in Another Four Minutes (Language Usage)

There are a lot of strategies to make your narration more vivid and interesting. You can add adverbs and adjectives; describe the environment, facial expressions, or body movements; and/or add details about the action. By making your narration more vivid you'll improve you score on language usage.

1. First, ask yourself what you missed that can be added. When thinking about what should be added, consider the following:

The actions of different people
Environmental changes (location, time, weather, etc.)
Facial expressions

2. Add adjectives or adverbs to describe the environment, facial expressions, body movements, and the details of the pictures. This is shown here.

1. 小王和小张在球场踢足球。

小王和小张在球场踢足球。小王把球踢了出去。

（1. 小王和小張在球場踢足球。

小王和小張在球場踢足球。小王把球踢了出去。）

2. 球打到了一个女孩子的头，她倒在了地上。小王和小张跑过来。

球打到了一个女孩子的头，她倒在了地上。小王和小张飞快地跑过来。

（2. 球打到了一個女孩子的頭，她倒在地上。小王和小張跑過來。

球打到了一個女孩子的頭，她倒在地上。小王和小張飛快地跑過來。）

3. 小王扶起女孩，小张看女孩的膝盖。

小王把女孩轻轻地扶起来，小张紧紧地盯着女孩的膝盖，有些着急。

（3. 小王扶起女孩，小張看女孩的膝蓋。

小王把女孩輕輕地扶起來，小張緊緊地盯著女孩的膝蓋，有些著急。）

4. 女孩站起来向前走，小王和小张向她挥手。

女孩站起来，向前走了两步，小王和小张笑着向她挥手再见。

（4. 女孩站起來向前走，小王和小張向她揮手。

女孩站起來，向前走了兩步，小王和小張笑著向她揮手再見。）

Step 3: A *Coherent*, Complete, and Vivid Story *with Good Grammar* in Another Four Minutes

If your response consists of only a list of sentences about the four pictures, you will end up with a score of 2. It needs to be a coherent story. Therefore, you need some "CG" time; that is, pay attention to conjunctions and grammar. If time permits, add some idioms or richer and more accurate vocabulary and expressions. This will allow you to demonstrate your higher proficiency in both the categories of "Language Usage" and "Delivery."

Using these three steps you'll be able to enhance your story to a level 6. The changes made in step 3 to achieve that level are underlined.

小王和小张在球场踢足球。小王<u>飞起一脚</u>把球踢了出去。<u>糟糕!</u> 球<u>打中</u>了一个女孩的头，把她<u>撞到</u>了地上。小王和小张<u>吓得</u>飞快地跑来。小王把女孩轻轻地扶起来，小张着急地盯着女孩的膝盖，<u>问道："你怎么样?"</u>女孩<u>于是</u>站起来，<u>试着</u>向前走了两步，<u>回答说："不要紧，没受伤。下次你们小心点啊!"</u>小王和小张<u>不好意思地</u>笑了，向她挥手说再见。

（小王和小張在球場踢足球。小王飛起一腳把球踢了出去。糟糕!球打中了一個女孩的頭，把她撞到了地上。小王和小張嚇得飛快地跑過來。小王把女孩輕輕地扶起來，小張著急地盯著女孩的膝蓋，問道："你怎麼樣?"女孩於是站起來，試著向前走了兩步，回答說："不要緊，沒受傷。下次你們小心點啊!"小王和小張不好意思地笑了，向她揮手說再見。）

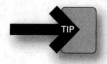

Study Tips for the Story Narration

You've learned the three-step exam-taking strategy, but do you still find story narration difficult? Here are some general study tips if you are still having trouble with story narration:

Grammatical Practice and Vocabulary Building: Focus on slowly building a flexible set of Chinese vocabulary and grammatical structures frequently used in a story. Review "Functional Grammar" in the appendix. Practice telling what happened, providing information (who/what/when/where), explaining cause/effect, and relating the resolution of the story. Learn commonly used phrases in storytelling such as "happily doing something," "suddenly what happened," "get an idea," "finally," and so on. Also learn descriptive words often used in a story such as scared, worried, excited, and embarrassed.

Extensive Writing: You should write simple stories about topics you experienced or imagined. Try messaging your friends and your teacher or text-chatting in the online community in Chinese. Collect good vocabulary, phrases, and grammatical structures to use.

Intensive Writing: Make good use of this book. Practice the questions in this book and carefully analyze the sample answers provided. Then modify your written answers to reach a level of 5 and above. Use the self-evaluation worksheet provided at the end of this chapter to analyze your errors and use the suggestions on the worksheet to address weak areas. Particularly helpful are the free-response questions from past exams that are posted on the College Board's website: http://apcentral.collegeboard.com/apc/members/exam/exam_information/157009.html. Practice story narration using these questions.

Skill-Building Exercises: Grammar

No matter what language you are using, the purpose of grammar is the same: to clarify what you are trying to express in a sentence. After reviewing "Functional Grammar" in the appendix, translate the follow sentences from English to Chinese. The sentences here are all typical sentences you will need to use in story narration. Pay particular attention to the grammatical structure of the underlined phrases often used in telling a story.

1. Ma Ke and Kai Di <u>are going</u> to have a birthday party. <u>However</u>, they forgot to order the cake.

   _____

   _____

2. <u>Because</u> there is no time for Da Wei to wait in the line, he has to park the car and start to run to the airport.

   _____

   _____

3. <u>Although</u> Xiao Ming lost his luggage, his friends all came with necessities to help him.

   _____

   _____

4. <u>Suddenly</u>, his glass fell down <u>and</u> broke into pieces.

   _____

   _____

5. "What can we do?" Lei <u>got a great idea</u>.

   _____

   _____

6. My sister likes making fish. <u>So</u> she bought a couple of fresh fish today.
   _____
   _____

7. We are happy that the problem was <u>finally solved</u>.
   _____
   _____

8. <u>When</u> Wang You was writing his homework, Adam rushed into the room and cried.
   _____
   _____

9. <u>Only if</u> you give him a call can he buy the ticket.
   _____
   _____

10. <u>Why</u> can't Ma Shan be more careful?
    _____
    _____

Answers

1. 马克和凯蒂打算办一个生日庆祝会。可是，他们忘了买蛋糕。
（馬克和凱蒂打算辦一個生日慶祝會。可是，他們忘了買蛋糕）
"Planning to do something" is often used in story narration: 打算 is a good word to replace 会（會），想。

2. 因为大伟没时间排队（等），他不得不把车泊好，开始向机场跑去。
（因為大偉沒時間排隊（等），他不得不把車泊好，開始向機場跑去。）
Because can be expressed as: 因为，由于（因為，由於）。

3. 虽然小明的托运行李掉了，他的朋友们带来了日用品帮助他（渡过难关）。
（雖然小明的托運行李掉了，他的朋友們帶來了日用品幫助他（渡過難關））。
Although can be expressed as: 虽然，尽管（雖然，儘管）。

4. 突然，他的杯子掉下来摔成了碎片。
（突然，他的杯子掉下來摔成了碎片。）
"Suddenly" is often used in telling about the second picture in the AP exam.

5. "我们该怎么办？" 蕾蕾想出了个好办法。
（"我們該怎麼辦？" 蕾蕾想出了個好辦法。）
"Got a good idea" is often used in writing about the third picture to lead to a resolution.

6. 我的姐姐喜欢做鱼吃，于是她买了两条新鲜鱼。
（我的姐姐喜歡做魚吃，於是她買了兩條新鮮魚。）
"So then" can be expressed as: 于是，所以（於是，所以）。
If you use 便, it should be after the subject. 我的姐姐喜欢做鱼吃，她<u>便</u>买了两条新鲜鱼（我的姐姐喜歡做魚吃，她<u>便</u>買了兩條新鮮魚）。

7. 问题终于解决了，我们都非常高兴。
（問題終於解決了，我們都非常高興。）

"Finally" is often used in narrating picture 4 to describe how a problem/incident was resolved.

8. 正当王友写作业的时候，亚当冲进门大哭起来。

（正當王友寫作業的時候，亞當衝進門大哭起來。）

Regarding the translation of "when," keep in mind that 正当……的时候（正當……的時候） is more authentic than 当（當）……的时候.

9. 只有你给他打电话他才会买票。

（只有你給他打電話他才會買票。）

"Only if" can be expressed as: 只有……才； as long as: 只要……就。

10. 为什么马杉不能更小心一点?

（為甚麼馬杉不能更小心一點？）

"Why (subject) cannot" can be expressed as：为什么（為甚麼） sb. 不。

Story Narration Practice Tests

In this section you'll find two picture sets like the one that will appear on the actual exam. Set a timer for 15 minutes and practice the three-step approach you learned earlier in this chapter to complete the written story for the first picture set. After you've completed this test-like experience, read the sample answer that follows. Then review the detailed explanation and analysis to help you evaluate your performance.

For more practice, go through the same process with the second picture set.

When you are done, do a thorough analysis of where and why you made any errors. Use the worksheet at the end of this chapter. Then look at the suggestions that correspond to each kind of mistake you made. Use the suggestions and the "Study Tips for the Story Narration" earlier in this chapter if you feel you need more practice.

Story Narration Practice Test #1

The four pictures present a story. Imagine you are writing the story to a classmate. Narrate a complete story as suggested by the pictures. Give your story a beginning, a middle, and an ending.

Sample Answer

Simplified Chinese
小王站在图书馆的门口，突然想起自己把手提电脑忘在图书馆的桌上了。他一拍头，说了声糟糕就往门里走。走到原来的座位上，桌上的电脑不见了，他赶忙跑到图书管理员那儿，向她说明了丢失电脑的情况。于是管理员把小王带到了失物招领箱前，指着箱子说："如果有人找到了，一般会放在这里面。"小王往里一看，自己的手提电脑好端端地躺在那儿。他抱起电脑，和管理员握手道谢。管理员摆摆手，说道："不客气。你以后要保管好自己的东西。" (Level 6)

Traditional Chinese
小王站在圖書館的門口，突然想起自己把手提電腦忘在圖書館的桌上了。他一拍頭，說了聲糟糕就往門裡走。走到原來的座位上，桌上的電腦不見了，他趕忙跑到圖書管理員那兒，向她說明瞭丟失電腦的情況。於是管理員把小王帶到了失物招領箱前，指著箱子說："如果有人找到了，一般會放在這裡面。"小王往裡一看，自己的手提電腦好端端地躺在那兒。他抱起電腦，和管理員握手道謝。管理員擺擺手，說道："不客氣。你以後要保管好自己的東西。" (Level 6)

English Translation for the Answer

Xiao Wang was standing at the door of the library. Suddenly he remembered that he left his laptop on a desk in the library. "Oops!" He patted his head and rushed back into the library. Xiao Wang went to the desk but the laptop was gone. He went to the librarian quickly and explained the incident. The librarian took him to the lost-and-found container, pointed at the container, and said: "If someone found your laptop, they would normally put it here." Xiao Wang took a look inside and saw his laptop. He held his laptop and shook hands with the librarian and said "Thank you!" The librarian answered: "You are welcome. You should take care of your belongings in the future."

Explanation and Scoring Analysis

Based on the four pictures, the storyline is: The boy lost his laptop in the library. He went to the librarian asking for help. The librarian took him to the lost and found. The boy found his laptop. He was grateful.

1. Did you write a basic story?

Yes. Your score may be 3 even if you miss one picture. Otherwise your score may be 2 or below. If you write a complete story covering the action in all four pictures, congratulations, your score will be higher.

2. Was your story complete and understandable to the reader or listener?

Yes. Your score may be 4 or above, even if your answer lacks detail or elaboration, or includes minor inconsistencies in its logical progression. That means, simply writing the storyline in Chinese can get you a 4. Remember, you need transitional elements for a logical flow.

3. Was your answer well structured, with rich language usage and only minor errors?

Yes. Your score may be 5 or above. A rich usage of vocabulary and grammar is essential to get this level. There are a lot of factors to stop you from scoring 6, most of which are missing an action in the storyline or having too many grammar errors or typos. Some actions in the storyline you may miss are as follows:

a. For picture #1, you didn't mention that the boy was patting his head.
b. For picture #2, you wrote that he went to the librarian, but you didn't mention that he was describing the laptop.
c. For picture #3, you didn't describe that the librarian was pointing at the lost and found or didn't write the transitional content that the librarian took him to the lost-and-found container.
d. For picture #4, you said only that the boy got his laptop back without mentioning his action of holding the laptop or shaking hands with the librarian.

Now use the self-evaluation sheet at the end of the chapter to identify your weakness and adjust your study plan.

Tips to Raise Your Score

1. If you didn't specifically mention all the steps/actions, you could add statements like: "He went to the desk but the laptop was gone," or "The librarian took him to the lost and found." This will give your answer a better, more logical flow.

2. You could add quotation marks and create a conversation to elaborate your description and make the story more vivid.

3. 糟糕 is a good word to show that something bad happens. It means "oops." 赶忙，马上，立即（趕忙，馬上，立即）could be used as the adverb for any quick action.

4. A lot of students will not know the term for "lost and found." If you don't know the specific term, you can describe it as "a place where all the things being found will be put" 一个地方，找到的东西都放在那里（一個地方，找到的東西都放在那裡）。

Story Narration Practice Test #2

The four pictures present a story. Imagine you are writing the story to a friend. Narrate a complete story as suggested by the pictures. Give your story a beginning, a middle, and an ending.

Sample Answer

Simplified Chinese

小王和小李兴高采烈地开车去玩，他们一边听音乐一边聊天。小王突然觉得车子有些问题，于是他们停了车走出车门。小王检查了一下轮胎，说："糟糕，车胎坏了！"小李拿出手机赶忙给爸爸打电话，想叫他来帮忙，可是打了很久也没人接。正当两人束手无策的时候，一位师傅把车停在旁边，问："出了什么事？"小王向他说明了情况，那位师傅便把他们俩拉到了附近的汽车修理店。小王和小李非常感激，谢过他便朝修理店走去。(Level 6)

Traditional Chinese

小王和小李興高采烈地開車去玩，他們一邊聽音樂一邊聊天。小王突然覺得車子有些問題，於是他們停了車走出車門。小王檢查了一下輪胎，説："糟糕，車胎壞了！"小李拿出手機趕忙給爸爸打電話，想叫他來幫忙，可是打了很久也沒人接。正當兩人束手無策的時候，一位老師傅把車停在旁邊，問："出了甚麼事？"小王向他説明瞭情況，那位老師傅便把他們倆拉到了附近的汽車修理店。小王和小李非常感激，謝過他便朝修理店走去。(Level 6)

English Translation for the Answer

Xiao Wang and Xiao Li were driving happily down the road. They were listening to the music and talking about their trip. Xiao Wang felt something was wrong with the car, so they stopped the car and got out. Xiao Wang checked the tire and said, "Oops, the tire is flat!" Xiao Li promptly took out her cell phone and called her father. She tried several times but no one picked up the phone. When they had no idea of what to do, a guy stopped his car beside them and asked, "What's the matter?" Xiao Wang told him what happened and the guy took them to a car repair shop nearby. Xiao Wang and Xiao Li thanked him and went into the car repair stop.

Explanation and Scoring Analysis

Based on the four pictures, the storyline is: A boy and a girl were driving on the road. They stopped because there was something wrong with the tire. The girl called for help but nobody picked up the phone. A guy stopped his car and asked what happened. Then he took them to a car repair shop.

1. Did you write a basic story?
Yes. Your score may be 3 even if you miss one picture. Otherwise your score may be 2 or below. If you write a complete story covering the action in all four pictures, congratulations, your score will be higher.

2. Was your story complete and understandable to the reader or listener?
Yes. Your score may be 4 or above, even if your answer lacks detail or elaboration, or includes minor inconsistencies in its logical progression. That means, simply writing the storyline in Chinese can get you a 4. Remember, you need transitional elements for a logical flow.

3. Was your answer well structured, with rich language usage and only minor errors?
Yes. Your score may be 5 or above. A rich usage of vocabulary and grammar is essential to get this level. There are a lot of factors to stop you from scoring 6, most of which are missing an action in the storyline or having too many grammatical errors or typos. Some actions in the storyline you may miss are:

a. For picture #1, you didn't mention that they were listening to the music.
b. For picture #2, you didn't mention that the girl called somebody but nobody answered.

c. For picture #3, you didn't describe that the man stopped his car. Instead, you stated only that a man came to help.

d. For picture #4, you said only that they went to a car repair shop and didn't specifically say that the boy and the girl got out of the man's car and then went into the shop.

Now use the self-evaluation sheet at the end of the chapter to identify your weakness and adjust your study plan.

Tips to Raise Your Score

1. If you didn't specifically mention all the steps/actions, you could add statements like: "when they had no idea what to do" and "ask for his help" as the transitional elements. This will give your answer a better, more logical flow.

2. You could add quotation marks and create a conversation to elaborate your description and make the story more vivid.

3. You can give a name to the hero in the story, although sometimes it's not easy to add a third party or stranger later. You may state their occupation or describe their identity in different ways. Here are some good words to know to refer to other people in a story narration:

very old man: 老爷爷（老爺爺）
elder man: 老师傅（老師傅），叔叔，伯伯
very old woman: 老奶奶
elder woman: 阿姨，女士
high school students/friends/boys/girls: 同学（同學），朋友们，男孩子们，女孩子们
little boy: 小男孩
little girl: 小女孩
police: 警察
manager: 经理（經理）
clerk: 服务员（服務員）
employee: 工作人员（工作人員）

Self-Evaluation Worksheet

FREQUENT REASONS FOR ERRORS	SUGGESTIONS
1. I didn't have time to finish the task!	Use the three steps described earlier in this chapter. You can finish the task within the time limit.
2. I missed some actions.	This normally happens when there are two parties acting differently in one picture. Remember to write both actions!
3. I forgot how to write the important words!	Normally the words you'll have difficulty with are verbs since the nouns are easier in story narration. If you don't know how to write a word, try to describe the action in greater detail using other words or replace the word you don't know with one that is close in meaning.
4. I wrote the English words for some words I don't know.	Never use English words since the AP grader will skip them. It shows that you are not serious about taking the exam.
5. I really did not have enough to write because the four pictures are so simple.	Elaboration is required for a high score. Try adding adjectives and adverbs, facial expressions, and even describe the environment.
6. My grammar is so bad that I can only write simple sentences correctly!	Making a list instead of using complete sentences may give a score of 2. Using conjunctions for complex sentences earns you points in language usage and delivery. Practice the "Functional Grammar" in the appendix.
7. My typing speed was too slow.	Practice makes perfect. Try to use Microsoft Pinyin IME or Microsoft New Phonetic IME, which is used for the AP Chinese exam.
Think: What kinds of errors did I make the most? Why didn't I find the correct answers? What could I do to improve?	See "Study Tips for the Story Narration" earlier in this chapter.

Interpersonal Writing: E-mail Response

IN THIS CHAPTER

Summary: This chapter provides practice for the e-mail response part of the AP Chinese Language and Culture exam. First, you'll learn what the e-mail response is and how it's scored. Then you'll practice the strategies for e-mail response and learn to use these in a three-step approach to writing your response. Presented next are skill-building exercises designed to help you avoid the errors students frequently make on this part of the exam. Finally, you will practice applying the strategies in two practice tests that are similar to what you'll find on the actual AP exam. At the end, analyze and evaluate your performance on the e-mail response and use the suggestions provided to adjust your study plan accordingly.

Key Strategies/Ideas

- ✪ Learn how the e-mail response is graded so you'll know what's expected and how you measure up.
- ✪ Read the e-mail message carefully and identify all the questions (usually two) that you need to answer.
- ✪ Learn to use the three steps for writing an e-mail response with minimal errors.
- ✪ Practice writing the e-mail response within the time limit of 15 minutes.
- ✪ Memorize useful expressions and build a template for the e-mail response before the test.

The E-mail Response: What It Is and How It Is Scored

In this part of the exam—the second task of Section II, Part A (Writing)—you will write a response to an e-mail message in 15 minutes. There will be a clock on your computer screen in the real exam telling you how much time is left. You will read an e-mail message and then write a response that answers all the questions in the e-mail. You will use the preset input of Microsoft IME or Microsoft New Phonetic IME system to type in Chinese characters. You can switch between simplified Chinese and traditional Chinese.

Scoring Guidelines: E-mail Response

The College Board provides scoring guidelines for the e-mail response. You can find these on its website. At the time of publication, the specific URL for these was http://media. collegeboard.com/digitalServices/pdf/ap/apcentral/ap13_chinese_scoring_guidelines.pdf.

Like the scoring for the story narration, each student's written response is graded on a scale of 1 to 6. E-mail responses at level 6 are considered "excellent," while those graded at level 5 are "very good." Level 4 scores competence as "good," and level 3 rates your performance as "adequate."

Your performance on the e-mail response portion of the exam—like the scoring on all the free-response questions—is evaluated on the basis of three criteria called rubrics:

I.   Task Completion
II. Language Usage
III. Delivery

The following table summarizes the most important keys to differentiate levels 3, 4, 5, and 6.

Scoring Guidelines for the E-mail Response

	SCORE: 3	SCORE: 4	SCORE: 5	SCORE: 6
I. TASK COMPLETION				
Response Completion	Response addresses the e-mail directly but doesn't answer all the questions.	Addresses all questions in the e-mail message but lacks detail.	Addresses all questions.	More thorough and detailed compared to 5.
Organization	Portions may lack organization. Disconnected sentences.	Lacks detail. Inconsistent transitional elements. Loosely connected sentences.	Generally clear progression. Some transitional elements and cohesive devices.	Clear progression with detail. Appropriate use of transitional elements and cohesive devices.
II. LANGUAGE USAGE				
Vocabulary and Idioms	Limited vocabulary. Frequent errors.	Mostly appropriate vocabulary usage. Mistakes do not obscure meaning.	Appropriate vocabulary. Sporadic errors.	Rich and appropriate vocabulary. Minimal errors.
Grammatical Structures	Simple. Frequent errors.	Mostly appropriate. Mistakes do not obscure meaning.	Variety of grammatical structures. Sporadic errors.	Wide range of grammatical structures. Minimal errors.
III. DELIVERY				
Register	Inconsistent. Many errors.	May include several lapses.	Occasional lapses.	Consistent use. Appropriate.

Strategies for the E-mail Response: A Step-by-Step Approach

The basic strategies for writing the e-mail response were presented in Chapter 4 and are summarized in the following sidebar. The strategies are similar to the strategies you learned for story narration in the previous chapter. Using the warm-up exercise, this chapter will take you step by step through the process of applying the strategies to the task of writing an e-mail message. Using these strategies in a step-by-step approach will help you get a high score on the e-mail response.

Strategies for the E-mail Response

1. **Complete the task.** First, carefully read the e-mail message that you will need to respond to. Make sure that you understand all the questions it asks (usually there are two questions). Normally, one question that the e-mail asks for is your opinion in choosing the best solution. This question needs to address two aspects of information: what the best solution is and why it is the best solution. Another question that appears often asks for suggestions. You can always use a model response that provides a structure to compare, persuade, and suggest.

2. **Pay attention to language usage and delivery.** Sticking to the questions doesn't mean you cannot elaborate. The e-mail response requires you to provide reasons for your suggestions. Writing a statement sentence and giving a more detailed explanation is good enough. Here, too, using advanced language such as Chinese idioms, metaphors, proverbs, and so on, is a great add-in.

3. **Start with a structure (template) prepared in advance.** To read an e-mail message and respond in 15 minutes, there may not be any time left for you to check your work like you did in story narration. You can make the best use of your limited time by doing fill-in-the-blank writing instead of starting from zero in the actual exam. A prepared, well-organized structure with perfect grammar and the use of rich language thought out before the exam really helps you to better succeed in this task. Adapt the prepared structure to the questions you are asked to respond to.

Warm-up Exercise

For the warm-up exercise you will have another try at the e-mail response task that was in the diagnostic test:

Read this e-mail from a friend and then type a response.

Simplified Chinese

发件人：周立
邮件主题：中国旅游
小新，
你好！我暑假会去中国玩一个星期。我希望可以去香港看一看我的朋友，也可以到北京去爬一下长城。由于时间有限，关于旅游的第三个城市你觉得是西安好还是上海好呢？还有，你对于在中国旅游的安全问题有什么建议吗？希望早点收到你的回信。

Traditional Chinese

發件人：周立
郵件主題：中國旅遊
小新，
你好！我暑假會去中國玩一個星期。我希望可以去香港看一看我的朋友，也可以到北京去爬一下長城。由於時間有限，關於旅遊的第三個城市你覺得是西安好還是上海好呢？還有，你對於在中國旅遊的安全問題有甚麼建議嗎？希望早點收到你的回信。

Now, using this exercise as an example, we'll walk through the three steps to create a high-scoring e-mail response in 15 minutes. Learn these three steps and make this method your habit so you don't even have to think about it on test day.

Step 1: What to Write?

You'll find that this task is designed to test your writing skills normally in two aspects: comparison and persuasion. You will be asked to provide your suggestions and explain the reasons to support them. Your focus should be on practicing the skills of two kinds of questions:

1. A or B, which one is better and why? Or what is the best solution and why?

2. What are your suggestions on a broader topic related to A and B?

For this topic, you can identify the two questions as:

1. Which city is better, Xi'an or Shanghai? 西安好还是上海好（西安好還是上海好）？ The word 还是（還是） helps you to identify this question.

2. What are your suggestions on travel safety in China? 有什么建议吗（有甚麼建議吗）？The words help you to identify this question in the e-mail message are normally: 觉得，认为，建议，考虑（覺得，認為，建議，考慮），etc.

Step 2: How to Respond?

Now is the time for "structured writing." You may be familiar with the style of a five-paragraph essay; however, due to the time limit this is probably *not* a good structure for this task. All you need here are four paragraphs.

Paragraph #1: Greeting
[Name],
Long time no see, how is everything?
How is your life recently?

Paragraph #2: Answer to Question #1
Regarding your question of … (repeat the question), I would say that … is the best solution. First, if it is (the best solution), you will … (common sense); second, to my best experience, (the best solution) will be able to help you …. Therefore, you can ….

Paragraph #3: Answer to Question #2
Regarding …, my personal suggestion would be ….

Paragraph #4: Closing
I hope that you ….
Sincerely yours,
[your name]

A good answer to the e-mail response is always a very structured one that compares and persuades. That means you actually can create the structure as completely as possible *before* the exam. Remember, you have only 15 minutes, including reading the e-mail, in which to respond. Creating and memorizing in advance a well-prepared structure with concise logic and good language usage will win you a lot of time in the real exam. Furthermore, collecting frequently used expressions can make your writing more beautiful and the delivery smoother.

For most prompts (the e-mail message you need to respond to), you may try the following.

Greetings

周立,

你好！好久没和你联系了，收到你的电子邮件很开心。

(周立,

你好！好久没和你聯繫了，收到你的電子郵件很開心。)

Question 1

你问我关于……的问题，我认为你应该……。首先，A……。如果你选A的话，你就能够……。其次，从我个人的经验来看，A比B……。要是你选A，你还可以……。

(你問我關於……的問題，我認為你應該……。首先，A……。如果你選A的話，你就能夠……。其次，從我個人的經驗來看，A比B……。要是你選A，你還可以……。)

Question 2

你提到……(question 2)，我觉得/的建议是……。

你提到……(question 2)，我覺得/的建議是……。)

Ending

祝你……

XX

Step 3: What to Fill In to Complete Your Response

The real creative work starts at step #3. You may feel it difficult to find reasons to support your point in just several minutes. In most cases, the best way to think about your responses for both questions consists of looking at two types of reasons: "personal reasons" and "global reasons," or to be more exact, your subjective personal experiences and the objective common sense of the world. Thinking in this way will help you to focus and more quickly come up with some reasons you can write about.

For this e-mail message, you can create a final answer for the e-mail response by filling in these words (underlined):

1. Greetings

周立,

你好！好久没和你联系了，收到你的电子邮件很开心。<u>欢迎来中国玩！</u>

(周立,

你好！好久没和你聯繫了，收到你的電子郵件很開心。<u>歡迎來中國玩！</u>)

2. Question 1

你问我关于<u>去西安好还是去上海好</u>的问题，我认为你应该<u>去西安</u>。首先，<u>西安有全世界著名的名胜古迹，那里的兵马俑是中国第一个皇帝制作的。如果你选西安的话，你就能够看到真正代表中国历史和文化的东西</u>(global)。其次，从我个人经验来看(personal)，<u>上海比西安更国际化，给人的感觉和香港比较相似，既然你会去香港，这次就可以不去上海</u>。还有啊，要是你去西安，你还可以像我一样<u>买到很便宜的纪念品，带回美国做为礼物相当合适</u>。

(你問我關於去西安好還是去上海好的問題，我認為你應該去西安。首先，西安有全世界著名的名勝古蹟，那裡的兵馬俑是中國第一個皇帝製作的。如果你選西安的話，你就能夠看到真正代表中國歷史和文化的東西(global)。其次，從我個人經驗來看(personal)，上海比西安更國際化，給人的感覺和香港比較相似，既然你會去香港，這次就可以不去上海。還有啊，要是你去西安，你還可以像我一樣買到很便宜的紀念品，帶回美國做為禮物相當合適。)

3. Question 2

你提到<u>在中国旅游的安全问题，除了旅游的基本安全常识(global)以外，我建议(personal)你要特别小心中国的小偷骗子。你一定要把自己的东西保管好，不要轻信陌生人的话</u>。

（你提到在中國旅遊的安全問題，除了旅遊的基本安全常識(global)以外，我建議(personal)你要特別小心中國的小偷騙子。你一定要把自己的東西保管好，不要輕信陌生人的話。）

4. Ending

<u>其实在中国旅游还是很安全的，祝你玩得开心！</u>
小新

（其實在中國旅遊還是很安全的，祝你玩得開心！
小新）

Study Tips for the E-mail Response

Structured writing is the key to writing an e-mail response. You've learned the three-step exam-taking strategy, but do you still find story narration difficult? Here are some general study tips if you are still having trouble writing the e-mail response:

Building Structures: Review the "Functional Grammar" in appendixes. Practice the grammatical structures specifically for the objectives of "choosing between A and B" and "giving suggestions/opinions." Then practice with the e-mail response test questions from previous years to build and apply a couple of templates for the e-mail response. Some questions may require adjustments to the templates in order to directly address the questions in the e-mail message (the prompt) you are given. Previous e-mail response prompts have been released by the College Board and can be found on its website at http://apcentral.collegeboard.com/apc/members/exam/exam_information/157009.html.

Extensive Writing: Write e-mails in Chinese. Collect good vocabulary words, phrases, and grammatical structures to use.

Intensive Writing: Make good use of this book. Use the strategies and tips provided here to practice writing e-mail responses for the prompts included in this chapter. Do the same for the questions the College Board has released from previous AP Chinese Language and Culture exams (available on its website). Modify your e-mail responses until they reach a level of 5 or above. Finally, analyze your performance using the self-evaluation worksheet at the end of this chapter and review the suggestions provided there to address each type of error you made.

Skill-Building Exercises: Comparison and Persuasion Sentences

The task of e-mail response is focused on providing solutions and suggestions, which requires tactful writing skills for comparison and persuasion. Following, you'll find sentence templates frequently used to accomplish those tasks. Learn them and select a couple of sets to memorize and use to build your own structure for the e-mail response you need to write for the AP exam. The more details you prepare in advance, the better you can apply them on the real exam. Then, practice typing your sentence templates on the computer until you can finish the structure of the e-mail response in 4 minutes.

1. Greetings

* 收到你的邮件我很开心。你有……的机会真是太棒了！
（收到你的郵件我很開心。你有……的機會真是太棒了！）

* 好久没和你联系了，我一直挺想你的。
（好久沒和你聯繫了，我一直挺想你的。）
* 原来你……我还真是羡慕你有……的生活。
（原來你……我還真是羨慕你有……的生活。）

2. Question 1
Repeat the Question
* 得知你正在为……发愁，我觉得这个问题不难解决。
（得知你正在為……發愁，我覺得這個問題不難解決。）
* 你在信中问我……，关于这个问题，我的建议是……。
（你在信中問我……，關於這個問題，我的建議是……。）
* 你想了解/确定最好的……是什么，每个人的看法都不一样。
（你想瞭解/確定最好的……是甚麼，每個人的看法都不一樣。）

Give Reasons (Global and Personal)
* 我认为你完全可以选A。首先，A是……，可以帮助你……，还可以……。
另一方面，A能……；当然，B也能……，但是总的来说，A比B更能……
(global)。我自己也有过同样的经历 (personal)，后来选了A，结果……(great result)。
（我認為你完全可以選A。首先，A是……，可以幫助你……，還可以……。
另一方面，A能……；當然，B也能……，但是總的來說，A比B更能……
(global)。我自己也有過同樣的經歷(personal)，後來選了A，結果……(great result)
。）
* A和B各有利弊。A的话，……(strength)，不过，A……(weakness)。如果选
B，B可以……但无法……(global)。当然，说起来容易做起来难，我也遇到过
同样的问题。当时我……(choose A)，后来……(solved A's weakness)，最后……
(good result)，我觉得你也可以试试(personal)。
（A和B各有利弊。A的話，……(strength)，不過，A……(weakness)。如果選
B，B可以……但無法……(global)。當然，说起來容易做起來難，我也遇到過
同樣的問題。當時我……(choose A)，後來……(solved A's weakness)，最後……
(good result)，我覺得你也可以試試(personal)。）
* 有的人喜欢……，有的人喜欢……，但无论如何，最好的……应当包括……
(the best way)。如果有……，就可以……。要是没有……，……就无法(reach the
best result)；因为……(global)。并且，我从前……，发现……，所以我个人认为，
还是……最能解决问题(personal)。
（有的人喜歡……，有的人喜歡……，但無論如何，最好的……應當包括……
(the best way)。如果有……，就可以……。要是沒有……，……就無法(reach the
best result)；因為……(global)。並且，我從前……，發現……，所以我個人認
為，還是……最能解決問題(personal)。）

Provide a Better Solution
* ……有冲突其实很正常，两全其美的方法是A时间做A，B时间做B。
（……有衝突其實很正常，兩全其美的方法是A時間做A，B時間做B。）
* ……如果你实在不能取舍，你可以先选A……(what you like or what you are good
at)，然后再……。
（……如果你實在不能取捨，你可以先選A……(what you like or what you are good
at)，然後再……。）

3. Question 2
* 说起这个 question 2，我的建议是……。你可以……，还可以……，最重要的是……。
（说起這個 question 2，我的建議是……。你可以……，還可以……，最重要的是……。）
* 你问我 question 2，我认为你首先应该注意……，还有你也不能忽视……，至于……，同样可以帮助你……。
（你問我 question 2，我認為你首先應該注意……，還有你也不能忽視……，至於……，同樣可以幫助你……。）
* 一个好的 question 2，第一可以考虑……。其次要注意的是……。另外，也不要忘了……，因为……带来的是……。
（一個好的 question 2，第一可以考慮……。其次要注意的是……。另外，也不要忘了……，因為……帶來的是……。）

4. Ending
* 希望我的看法对你有所帮助。你最后是怎样决定的，一定要记得来信告诉我。
（希望我的看法對你有所幫助。你最後是怎樣決定的，一定要記得來信告訴我。）
* 我的看法不一定对，你还可以咨询一下……（朋友、老师、父母等），听听他们的建议。
（我的看法不一定對，你還可以咨詢一下……（朋友、老師、父母等），聽聽他們的建議。）
* 祝一切顺（順）利！(an issue the receiver needs solved)
* 祝心想事成！(something difficult the receiver decides to try)
* 祝你玩得开（開）心！(happy activities the receiver wants to do)

E-mail Response Practice Tests

In this section you'll find two e-mail prompts (the e-mail messages you need to respond to). Both prompts are similar to those you'll encounter on the actual exam. Set a timer for 15 minutes and practice the three-step approach you learned earlier in this chapter to complete your e-mail response. After you've completed this test-like experience, read the sample answer that follows. Then review the detailed explanation and analysis to help you evaluate your performance.

For more practice, go through the same process with the second prompt.

When you are done, do a thorough analysis of where and why you made any errors. Use the worksheet at the end of this chapter. Then look at the suggestions that correspond to each kind of mistake you made. Use the suggestions and the "Study Tips for the E-mail Response" earlier in this chapter, if you feel you need more practice.

E-mail Response Practice Test #1

Read this e-mail from a friend and then type a response.

Simplified Chinese
发件人：方晓
邮件主题：社会实践
陈亮军，
你好！我打算暑假参加社会实践活动，现在有两个不同的机会，一个是在市游泳馆做救生员，另一个是在公共图书馆做义工。你觉得我应该参加哪一个比较好？另外我也很好奇，你从前经常做义工，你认为怎样才能在社会实践活动中更好地锻炼自己的能力呢？谢谢。

Traditional Chinese
發件人：方曉
郵件主題：社會實踐
陳亮軍，

你好！我打算暑假參加社會實踐活動，現在有兩個不同的機會，一個是在市游泳館做救生員，另一個是在公共圖書館做義工。你覺得我應該參加哪一個比較好？另外我也很好奇，你從前經常做義工，你認為怎樣才能在社會實踐活動中更好地鍛煉自己的能力呢？謝謝。

Sample Answer

Simplified Chinese
方晓，
你好。

收到你的邮件我很开心。你有这些好机会真是太棒了！

你在信中问我去游泳馆做救生员好还是在公共图书馆做义工好，关于这个问题，我的建议是去公共图书馆。首先，在公共图书馆做义工，你会得到各种各样的信息，还可以交到不同的朋友，从而获得更多的社会实践经验。其次，公共图书馆的义工种类很多，你可以根据自己的兴趣爱好和特长选最适合的，充分锻炼你的才干。另一方面，在游泳馆也能交到朋友碰到机会，但还是不如图书馆给予的选择面大。我自己也有过类似的经历，后来还是去了图书馆，每年都可以选择不同的义工种类，结果我不仅帮助了有需要的人，而且自己也非常快乐。

我认为要锻炼自己的社会实践能力，首先应该注意学会和不同的人相处；同时你也不能忽视解决问题，以此为目的，做出真正的成绩。只要你认真对待这份工作，脚踏实地，你就一定会有收获。

希望我的看法对你有所帮助。你最后是怎样决定的，一定要记得来信告诉我。

祝一切顺利。
陈亮军

Traditional Chinese
方曉，
你好。

收到你的郵件我很開心。你有這些好機會真是太棒了！

你在信中問我去游泳館做救生員好還是在公共圖書館做義工好，關於這個問題，我的建議是去公共圖書館。首先，在公共圖書館做義工，你會得到各種各樣的信息，還可以交到不同的朋友，從而獲得更多的社會實踐經驗。其次，公共圖書館的義工種類很多，你可以根據自己的興趣愛好和特長選最適合的，充分鍛煉你的才干。另一方面，在游泳館也能交到朋友碰到機會，但還是不如圖書館給予的選擇面大。我自己也有過類似的經歷，後來還是去了圖書館，每年都可以選擇不同的義工種類，結果我不僅幫助了有需要的人，而且自己也非常快樂。

我認為要鍛煉自己的社會實踐能力，首先應該注意學會和不同的人相處；同時你也不能忽視解決問題，以此為目的，做出真正的成績。只要你認真對待這份工作，腳踏實地，你就一定會有收獲。

希望我的看法對你有所幫助。你最後是怎樣決定的，一定要記得來信告訴我。
祝一切順利。
陳亮軍

English Translation of the Sample Answer

Fang Xiao,

I am so glad to hear from you. It's amazing that you have these opportunities!

You asked the question about choosing between being a lifeguard or participating in volunteer work in the public library. My suggestion is to go to the library. First, you can get all kinds of information, meet different people, and gain a lot more experience in social work by working in the library. Second, there are many types of volunteer work you can choose from. You can select volunteer work based on your interests and skills in order to practice your skills thoroughly. On the other hand, you can make friends and get opportunities working as the lifeguard as well, but there are fewer chances to practice your skills in social work. I had a similar experience to yours. I chose working in the library, and I can do a different volunteer job each year. Not only did this help the people who needed help, but I also achieved happiness doing this.

In order to practice your skills in social work, you should learn to get along with different kinds of people. At the same time, you should not neglect the goal of problem solving, and you should really make positive progress in your work. As long as you take these tasks seriously with a down-to-earth attitude, you will enjoy the harvest at the end.

I hope my opinion helps. Please remember to let me know after your final decision.

Best wishes,

Chen Liang Jun

Explanation

In order to respond to the e-mail, you need to understand the e-mail. This e-mail is about "social experience" as the subject states. The sender is asking for advice about choosing a summer job as a lifeguard or a library volunteer. The sender also asked how to gain more by participating in social work. Now use our self-evaluation sheet at the end of this chapter to identify your weakness and adjust your study plan.

Besides the two major questions to be asked, you should pay attention to one prompt: 你从前经常做义工 (你從前經常做義工), which means that your answer should be based on this specific situation: you are sharing your previous volunteering experience.

This is a relatively long answer of 395 characters and it includes 254 characters prepared before the exam. That's a very promising number. If you do a detailed review of the answer, you will find that it repeats a lot of characters from the original e-mail message, especially in the 141 characters that filled in the blanks. The totally new information you need to come up with is less than 70 characters.

As an AP grader, I have seen the level 6 answers of less than 200 characters. The better you can handle the language, the shorter your answer could be. Although, if you are not that confident in your writing, it's better for you to prepare a more established and detailed structure, so that you can select what is needed for different topics.

Let's see a successful version of this answer but with fewer characters (289 characters):

Simplified Chinese

方晓，

你好。你有这些好的社会实践机会真是太棒了！

关于你的选择，我的建议是去公共图书馆做义工。首先，你会得到各种各样的信息，还可以交到不同的朋友，从而获得更多的社会实践经验。其次，图书馆义工种类很多，你可以根据自己的兴趣爱好和特长选最适合的，充分锻炼你的才干。在游泳馆就不如图书馆给予的选择面大。我自己也有过类似的经历，后来还是去了图书馆，每年选一种义工做，真正享受了助人为乐的感觉。

我认为要锻炼自己的社会实践能力，首先应该注意学会和不同的人相处；同时你也不能忽视解决问题，以此为目的，做出真正的成绩。只要你脚踏实地地工作，你就一定会有收获。

希望我的看法对你有所帮助。

祝一切顺利。

陈亮军

Traditional Chinese

方曉，

你好。你有這些好的社會實踐機會真是太棒了！

關於你的選擇，我的建議是去公共圖書館做義工。首先，你會得到各種各樣的信息，還可以交到不同的朋友，從而獲得更多的社會實踐經驗。其次，圖書館義工種類很多，你可以根據自己的興趣愛好和特長選最適合的，充分鍛煉你的才干。在游泳館就不如圖書館給予的選擇面大。我自己也有過類似的經歷，後來還是去了圖書館，每年選一種義工做，真正享受了助人為樂的感覺。

我認為要鍛煉自己的社會實踐能力，首先應該注意學會和不同的人相處；同時你也不能忽視解決問題，以此為目的，做出真正的成績。只要你腳踏實地地工作，你就一定會有收獲。

希望我的看法對你有所幫助。

祝一切順利。

陳亮軍

Self-Evaluation and Scoring Analysis

1. Did your answer cover both questions?

Yes. Your score may be a 3 even if you didn't completely address all the questions of the e-mail message.

2. Was your response complete and understandable to the reader?

Yes. Your score may be 4 and above, even if your answer lacks detail or elaboration, has loosely connected sentences, or includes some errors that are not serious enough to not obscure the meaning. That means you have to write something about why you should choose the social work and how to be a good social worker.

3. Was your response well structured, with rich language usage and minor errors?

Yes. Your score may be 5 and above. A rich use of vocabulary and grammar is essential and crucial to get to this level. There are a lot of factors to stop you from scoring 6, most of which are sporadic grammatical errors and occasional lapses of register to the situation.

Now use the self-evaluation worksheet at the end of this chapter to identify your weakness and adjust your study plan.

Tips to Raise Your Score

1. You may use "My dear friend" 我亲爱的朋友 if you don't know the characters of the sender's name.

2. You should practice typing your prepared template as fast as you can, so that you will have time to fill in the information in the real exam.

3. This is a good topic to prepare not only for writing, but also for Interpersonal Speaking: Conversation. Try to memorize the basic structure and useful expressions of this e-mail response.

4. Highlight the important conjunctions to understand a good logical structure for writing to compare and persuade.

E-mail Response Practice Test #2

Read this e-mail from a friend and then type a response.

Simplified Chinese
发件人：刘星星
邮件主题：学习方法
你好！我最近快忙疯了！由于我今年选了四门AP课，总是觉得时间不够用。我听说你去年选了六门AP课，不但学得好，考得好，还参加了许多课外活动。你认为我怎样才能改进学习方法呢？你的理由是什么？另外，除了成绩好以外，我还应该注意哪些方面才能申请到好大学呢？盼你早日回信！

Traditional Chinese
發件人：劉星星
郵件主題：學習方法
你好！我最近快忙瘋了！由於我今年選了四門AP課，總是覺得時間不夠用。我聽說你去年選了六門AP課，不但學得好，考得好，還參加了許多課外活動。你認為我怎樣才能改進學習方法呢？你的理由是甚麼？另外，除了成績好以外，我還應該注意哪些方面才能申請到好大學呢？盼你早日回信！

Sample Answer

Simplified Chinese
星星，
你好。好久没和你联系了，我一直挺想你的。
得知你正在为学习时间不够用而发愁，我觉得这个问题不难解决。首先，你要养成做计划的习惯，合理地安排学习内容，不要总是浪费时间想我现在该干什么；其次，你可以用固定的时间完成作业，无论如何也不要变，这样就可以提高做作业的效率。同时，你可以利用一些不起眼的空闲来复习一些需要记忆的内容。虽然说起来容易做起来难，但我去年的AP历史和外语复习就几乎全是在校车上完成的，你也可以试试。
要申请一个好的大学，除了学习以外，第一就是要考虑多参加社会实践活动，不但可以帮助有需要的人，还可以锻炼自己的能力；其次要注意的是根据自己的特长选专业，如果拿过奖什么的就更好了；另外也不要忘了认真准备申请材料，因为一封好的推荐信、一篇出色的个人介绍，都可以为你带来好运气！
我的看法不一定全对，你也可以咨询一下其他老师、同学，听听他们的建议。
祝你心想事成！

Traditional Chinese
星星，
你好。好久沒和你聯繫了，我一直挺想你的。
得知你正在為學習時間不夠用而發愁，我覺得這個問題不難解決。首先，你要養成做計劃的習慣，合理地安排學習內容，不要總是浪費時間想我現在該幹甚麼；其次，你可以用固定的時間完成作業，無論如何也不要變，這樣就可以提高做作業的效率。同時，你可以利用一些不起眼的空閒來復習一些需要記憶的內容。雖然說起來容易做起來難，但我去年的AP歷史和外語復習就幾乎全是在校車上完成的，你也可以試試。

要申請一個好的大學，除了學習以外，第一就是要考慮多參加社會實踐活動，不但可以幫助有需要的人，還可以鍛煉自己的能力；其次要注意的是根據自己的特長選專業，如果拿過獎甚麼的就更好了；另外也不要忘了認真準備申請材料，因為一封好的推薦信、一篇出色的個人介紹，都可以為你帶來好運氣！

我的看法不一定全對，你也可以咨詢一下其他老師、同學，聽聽他們的建議。

祝你心想事成！

English Translation of the Sample Answer

Xing xing,

How are you? It's been a long time since I've seen you and I have been thinking about you.

I know you are worried about the lack of time to study, but I think this is not an issue. First, you should make a habit of planning, so that you can arrange your study in a reasonable way instead of wasting time figuring out what you need to do next. Second, you should set up a fixed time for homework. Do not make changes to this, no matter what happens. This will help you to improve your efficiency in finishing homework. At the same time, you should make good use of your free time to review content that requires memorization. Although it is easy to say, I almost finished reviewing all the content for AP history and foreign language last year on the school bus! You should try it.

To apply to a good university, besides studying well, the first key is to take part in more social service activities. Not only can you help others, but you can also practice your skills. Second, you should pay attention to choosing your major based on your talents. Awards based on your talents are a great bonus. In addition, do not forget to prepare your application documents carefully. A convincing recommendation letter or a wonderful personal statement will bring you good luck!

This is just my opinion. You could consult other teachers or your classmates and listen to their suggestions as well.

I hope your dream will come true!

Explanation

This prompt is a little different from the usual ones. It doesn't provide A and B for you to compare and select. Instead, it asks directly for the "best way"—good study strategies focusing on time management. The sample answer provided here is a great example of adjusting the templates you worked on in Skill-Building Exercises earlier in this chapter.

Here is a hidden prompt which you need to stick to: 听说你去年选了六门AP课 (聽說你去年選了六門AP課). When responding to the e-mail, you should identify that you are writing as someone who has taken many AP exams with a lot of experience. Do not miss that part!

Besides the templates, did you find that there is a lot of information familiar to you? Yes, some information in the first e-mail response practice test can be used in this one as well. And as you dig into more topics, you will definitely feel that you can write more easily using a lot of structures and phrases you've already practiced.

You can use the scoring analysis provided for the first e-mail response practice test to determine your score on this one. Then use the self-evaluation worksheet at the end of this chapter to identify your weakness and adjust your study plan.

Tips to Raise Your Score

1. Learn more of the frequently used phrases and be able to add these to your templates.

2. Practice typing your prepared content (template) as fast as you can, so that you will have time to fill in the information in the real exam.

3. Ask your teacher or a native Chinese speaker to help you modify your templates until the grammar is perfect.

4. Practice using your templates to answer the actual questions used on the AP Chinese Language and Culture exam in previous years. You'll find the free-response questions from the previous exam on the College Board website: http://apcentral.collegeboard. com/apc/members/exam/exam_information/157009.html.

5. Strictly follow the e-mail logic or even type the same phrases if necessary to answer questions in case you miss some hidden prompts. For example, when the e-mail asks you for your opinion about the "school policies" of community service, do not miss the "school requiring" part.

Self-Evaluation Worksheet

FREQUENT REASONS FOR ERRORS	SUGGESTIONS
1. I didn't have time to finish the task!	Practice using the three steps described earlier in this chapter. Prepare your template in advance.
2. I did not answer all the questions.	Keep in mind that you need to answer two major questions (three parts) and address a couple of small aspects of stimulus.
	a. Identify which one is better between A and B or what is the best solution for a prompt.
	b. Provide the evidence/reasons to support.
	c. Provide suggestions/comments related to the topic.
3. I forgot how to write the important words!	Normally the words you'll have difficulty with are verbs because the nouns are easier in story narration. If you don't know how to write a word, try to describe the action in greater detail using other words or replace the word you don't know with one that's close in meaning.
4. I just wrote the English for some words I don't know.	Never use English words because the AP grader will skip them. It shows that you are not serious about taking the exam.

(Continued)

Self-Evaluation Worksheet *(continued)*

FREQUENT REASONS FOR ERRORS	SUGGESTIONS
5. I really didn't have much to say. I couldn't find more to write.	Elaboration is required to get a high score. Practice providing comparisons and persuasion.
6. My grammar is so bad that I can only write simple sentences correctly.	You should develop a template for the e-mail response and remember it. Pay attention to two functions of sentences: comparison and persuasion.
7. My typing speed was too slow.	Practice makes perfect. Try to use Microsoft Pinyin IME or Microsoft New Phonetic IME, which is used for the AP exam.
Think: What kinds of errors did I make the most? Why didn't I find the correct answers? What could I do to improve?	See the study tips presented earlier in this chapter.

CHAPTER 10

Interpersonal Speaking: Conversation

IN THIS CHAPTER

Summary: This chapter provides practice for the conversation that is part of the AP Chinese Language and Culture exam. First, you'll learn what the conversation is and how it's scored. Then you'll practice the strategies for the conversation and learn to use these in a basic step-by-step approach. Presented next are skill-building exercises designed to help you avoid an error students frequently make on this part of the exam—failing to understand the questions. Finally, you will practice applying the strategies in a practice test that closely resembles what you'll find on the actual AP exam. At the end, analyze and evaluate your performance on the conversation portion of the exam and use the suggestions provided to adjust your study plan accordingly.

Key Strategies/Ideas

- ✪ Learn how the conversation is graded so you'll know what's expected and how you measure up.
- ✪ Understanding the question is as important as answering it. You will usually have to answer at least one question, and usually two questions, in the 20-second interval before the conversation continues and another question is asked.
- ✪ First, address the question directly, then elaborate in greater detail.

- ✪ Twenty seconds is not short. Speak as much as possible. If your mind goes blank, restate the question or use a familiar expression such as "As far as I know ..." or "In my opinion ..." to give yourself time to think.
- ✪ Do not worry about your Chinese grammar and do not speak English.
- ✪ Practice 20 new vocabulary/phrases daily using "Frequently Used Vocabulary Words and Phrases" in the appendix.
- ✪ Make speaking Chinese a daily habit.

The Conversation: What It Is and How It Is Scored

In this part of the exam—the first task of Section II, Part B (Speaking)—you will participate in a simulated conversation, responding to six prompts (a question or set of questions) in approximately four minutes. The questions are part of a conversation on a particular topic with a particular person. You will listen to a recording that includes the questions you need to answer. You will have 20 seconds to respond to each prompt. On the actual test, your responses will be recorded so they can be scored later.

Attention! Conversation is probably the most difficult part of the AP Chinese exam. It tests not only your speaking skills but also your abilities in listening comprehension. Twenty seconds is actually *not* a very short time; you need to speak at least five sentences.

Scoring Guidelines: Conversation

The College Board provides scoring guidelines for the simulated conversation. You can find these on its website. At the time of publication, the specific URL for these was http://media. collegeboard.com/digitalServices/pdf/ap/apcentral/ap13_chinese_scoring_guidelines.pdf.

Like the scoring for the story narration and e-mail response, each student's response is graded on a scale of 1 to 6. Conversations at level 6 are considered "excellent," while those graded at level 5 are "very good." Level 4 scores competence as "good," and level 3 rates your performance as "adequate."

Your performance on the conversation portion of the exam—like the scoring on all the free-response questions—is evaluated on the basis of three criteria called rubrics:

  I. Task Completion
 II. Language Usage
III. Delivery

The following table summarizes and explains the different scoring of levels 3, 4, 5, and 6.

Scoring Guidelines for the Conversation

	SCORE: 3	SCORE: 4	SCORE: 5	SCORE: 6
I. TASK COMPLETION				
Response	Directly addresses the questions. Basic and proper.	Directly addresses the questions with an appropriate answer.	Directly addresses the questions. Thorough, appropriate, although the responses may lack detail.	Directly addresses the questions. Thorough, appropriate, detailed with elaboration.
Organization	Disconnected.	Sentences may be loosely connected.	Connected sentences.	Smoothly connected sentences.
II. LANGUAGE USAGE				
Vocabulary and Idioms	Vocabulary limited. Frequent errors.	Mostly appropriate. Errors do not obscure meaning.	Appropriate. Sporadic errors.	Rich and appropriate. Minimal errors.
Grammatical Structures	Simple. Frequent errors.	Mostly appropriate. Errors do not obscure meaning.	Variety of grammatical structures. Sporadic errors.	Wide range of grammatical structures. Minimal errors.
III. DELIVERY				
Pace and Intonation	Inconsistent. Hesitation and repetition may interfere with comprehension.	Generally consistent. Intermittent hesitation and repetition.	Smooth. Occasional hesitation and repetition.	Natural. Minimal hesitation or repetition.
Pronunciation	Errors sometimes need an effort on the part of the listener to understand.	May have several errors that need an effort on the part of the listener to understand.	Occasional errors (tones or pronunciation).	Accurate with minimal errors.
Register	Inconsistent. Many errors.	Includes several lapses.	Occasional lapses.	Consistent use. Appropriate.

Strategies for the Conversation: A Step-by-Step Approach

The basic strategies for speaking in the conversation were presented in Chapter 4 and are summarized in the following sidebar. Using the warm-up exercise, this chapter will take you step by step through the process of applying the strategies to the task of speaking in a conversation. Learn these two steps and how to apply them to the task. Make this method your habit so you don't even have to think about it on test day. Using these strategies in a step-by-step approach will help you do your best on the conversation.

Strategies for the Conversation

1. **Listen carefully.** Understanding the question is as important as answering it. First, listen to the English introduction carefully as it often provides you exact information about the major topic of the 6 questions, and helps you to predict the possible focuses. Then, listen to the prompt very carefully. In a lot of cases, there are two questions in one prompt and you need to answer both of them. Repeat them in your mind.

2. **Complete the task.** Answer the questions directly first and then provide elaboration. Speak as much as possible for the 20 seconds you are given. If you didn't get the question or missed some information you think is important, don't give up. Try to repeat the words you know, then share your opinions and explain your reasoning. Most prompts involve questions about opinions and the reasons behind them.

3. **Pay attention to language usage and delivery.** Do not worry too much about your grammar. If your mind goes blank, start out with a phrase you know such as "As far as I know…" or "What I would like to say…." Speak as fast and fluently as possible for the familiar parts. Give examples, rephrase your answers, and use language that is culturally appropriate to the situation to demonstrate your ability for good language usage and delivery. Don't blurt out English when frustrated!

Warm-up Exercise

For the warm-up exercise you will have another try at the conversation that was in the diagnostic test. You will have 20 seconds to speak in six different places in the conversation.

You will have a conversation with Chen Ming, a friend from China, about your school life in the United States.

Script for Track 8
Now here's the written script for what you heard on Track 8:

Track 8

Simplified Chinese
1. 你在美国哪个学校上学？你们那儿的天气怎么样？
2. 你在学校每个学期要选哪些课？你最喜欢哪门课？
3. 你们每天上课的时间长吗？请介绍一下你在学校每天的时间安排，好吗？
4. 听说美国的中学生经常会做义工，做义工会影响学习吗？请谈一谈你的看法。
5. 除了上学以外，美国的中学生还会参加什么样的社会活动？
6. 我下个学期会作为交换生来美国学习，你觉得我在学习方面需要注意哪些问题？

Traditional Chinese
1. 你在美國哪個學校上學？你們那兒的天氣怎麼樣？
2. 你在學校每個學期要選哪些課？你最喜歡哪門課？
3. 你們每天上課的時間長嗎？請介紹一下你在學校每天的時間安排，好嗎？
4. 聽說美國的中學生經常會做義工，做義工會影響學習嗎？請談一談你的看法。
5. 除了上學以外，美國的中學生還會參加甚麼樣的社會活動？
6. 我下個學期會作為交換生來美國學習，你覺得我在學習方面需要注意哪些問題？

Step 1: Listen

Understanding the question is as important as you presenting your answer.

1. Listen to the questions very carefully. Try to repeat the key words or phrases in your mind as you hear them.

2. There is a good chance that at least one of the questions you have to respond to will have two parts. For example, "What is it?" and "Why?" Listen closely, and if there are two parts, you need to answer both parts of the question.

3. Do not worry about any word you don't know. Try to guess the main idea. For example, in the first prompt of the warm-up exercise:

   1. 你们每天上课的时间长吗？请介绍一下你在学校每天的时间安排，好吗？

      （你們每天上課的時間長嗎？請介紹一下你在學校每天的時間安排，好嗎？）

      You may not know the word 安排, but the question twice mentions "time" 时间; that's an easy word. You can get the main idea of "Please introduce your everyday's time 安排 in the school", so this can help you to figure out the question asks for a daily time "thing," which would probably be your daily routine or daily schedule. You guessed it right! 安排 means arrangement.

Step 2: Answer

Answer each question directly and provide as much information as possible.

1. Do not worry about grammar. Any phrase, blurt it out!

2. Repeat or rephrase the question if you are not well-prepared or don't understand the whole question. Use phrases like "As far as I know…" or "What I would like to say…" to win you some time to organize the answer. If you don't understand the whole question, talk about the words you know. It's risky but better than nothing. For example, in the sixth prompt of the warm-up exercise:

   6. 我下个学期会作为交换生来美国学习，你觉得我在学习方面需要注意哪些问题？
      （我下個學期會作為交換生來美國學習，你覺得我在學習方面需要注意哪些問題？）

      You might find half the sentence difficult due to the following vocabulary: 作为（作為）、交换生（交換生）、方面、需要、注意。But you can get the main idea "I next semester _____ will come to study in the United States. What do you think I at study _____ which questions/problems." Look only at the information you do understand and talk about study in the United States and some problems related to that. Congratulations! You hit the ball!

3. Elaborate details even if you think you already answered the question. Forget about being truthful. Feel free to create.

4. Parts of your answers in the previous questions can be used again in another question. For example, for the fourth and fifth prompts in the warm-up exercise:

   4. 听说美国的中学生经常会做义工，做义工会影响学习吗？请谈一谈你的看法。

（聽說美國的中學生經常會做義工，做義工會影響學習嗎？請談一談你的看法。）

Translation: It is said that the high school students in the United States often do volunteer work. Will volunteer work affect study? Please share your opinion.

5. 除了上学以外，美国的中学生还会参加什么样的社会活动？
（除了上學以外，美國的中學生還會參加甚麼樣的社會活動？）

Translation: What kind societal activities do the high school students in the United States do besides studying in the school?

Volunteer work is one kind of important societal activity for high school students in the United States. A lot of students will mention their volunteer work in their answers. Any details of the answer in question 4 can be used again in question 5.

Keep Practicing

Now listen to the six questions on Track 8 again. Apply the tips and strategies discussed earlier to speak, giving the best answer you can. Answer each question at least three times. In fact, continue practice responding to the question until your response would score a level of 5 or above before you move on to another one.

For a sample of a good response to each question in the conversation on Track 8, you can refer to the sample level 5 and 6 responses that are provided in Chapter 3. See pages 62–65.

After each attempt to answer a question, quickly review your performance in your mind. Try to quickly estimate your own score on that question:

a. Did you address the question thoroughly and provide details?
b. Did you include smooth sentence connections?
c. Did your response show natural pace with minimal repetitions and/or hesitations?
d. Did you use good pronunciation and register?
e. Did your answer show a rich vocabulary and various grammatical structures?

When you've practiced until your answer would probably score a 5 or a 6, congratulations! Move on to the next question.

Study Tips for the Conversation

You've practiced responding to the questions in the conversation using the strategies and previous tips, but do you still find the conversation responses difficult? Here are some general study tips if you are still having trouble with speaking good responses to the questions presented in the conversation:

Extensive Speaking: Make speaking Chinese a habit in your daily life. Speak about anything. Have conversation in Chinese and practice both listening and speaking skills.

Intensive Speaking: Make good use of this book. Practice the sample conversation questions in this book using the strategies you've learned. Modify your answers until you reach a level of 5 or above. Use the self-evaluation worksheet provided at the end of this chapter to analyze your errors, and then use the suggestions on the worksheet to address weak areas. Finally, practice with the conversation prompts from previous years' exams that are posted on the College Board's website: http://apcentral.collegeboard.com/apc/members/exam/exam_information/157009.html.

Skill-Building Exercises: Understanding Questions in a Conversation

The questions on the conversation part of the AP exam could be anything based on a specific scene. Luckily, most questions fall into the following types. It's important to understand and memorize these questions. Only when you know the question can you prepare your answers.

WHAT 什么	
你想做什么?	What are you planning to do?
你需要注意什么?	What do you need to pay attention to?
他们有什么不同?	What are the differences between them?
这有什么特色?	What are special?
解释一下是什么意思。	Explain what the meaning is.
从……到……做什么?	What do you do from (when) to (when)?
哪一个?	Which one?
哪些?	Which ones?
哪几天?	Which days?
哪方面?	Which aspect?
哪儿?	Which place?

OPINION OR SUGGESTION	
有什么认识和了解?	What to know or understand?
请谈谈你的看法。	Please share your opinion.
请你描述一下……	Please describe ….
你怎么解释?	How do you explain?
请给我提几个建议。	Please give me some suggestions.
给我介绍一下吧。	Please introduce something to me.
你觉得……怎么样?	What do you think about…?
你推荐什么?	What do you recommend?
用什么比较好?	What is relatively better to use?
你觉得什么……最有意思/最合适?	What do you think will be the most meaningful/suitable?

WHY 为什么	
为什么?	Why?
说说你的理由。	Please share your reasons.

HOW 怎么	
怎么……?	How to do?
你怎么知道……?	How do you know?
……了吧?	You are …, is that right?

A OR B 还是	
你喜欢……还是……？	What do you prefer, … or …?

Conversation Practice Test

In this section you'll take part in a simulated conversation like the one on the actual test. Practice the step-by-step approach you learned earlier in this chapter to respond to the questions you will be asked. After you've completed this test-like experience, read the sample level 6 answers for each question. Then review the detailed explanation and try to score your own performance in your mind.

When you are done, do a thorough analysis of where and why you made any errors. Use the self-evaluation worksheet at the end of this chapter. Then look at the suggestions that correspond to each kind of mistake you made. Use the suggestions provided on the worksheet and the "Study Tips for the Conversation" earlier in this chapter if you feel you need more practice.

Conversation

You will have a conversation with Tang Wei, a friend who has been to China many times, about traveling in China.

Now listen to the six questions and answer them one by one. You will have 20 seconds for each answer; on the actual test, your spoken answers will be recorded. The listening track for this conversation practice test is provided on the CD accompanying this book.

Script for Track 19

The written script for the conversation on the CD is provided for your reference. However, do not look at this until *after* you have completed this practice test. The actual AP exam will *not* include a printed script for the conversation you hear.

Simplified Chinese
1. 我听说你要去中国参加夏令营，是在哪一个城市？你为什么想去？
2. 你们的夏令营有多长时间？什么时候回美国？
3. 去中国以前，你还需要做好哪些准备？
4. 你参加的夏令营会举办哪些活动？有没有旅游方面的活动？
5. 中国的夏令营和美国的还是不同的，你觉得应该注意哪些问题？
6. 中国的东西比较便宜，你打算买些什么回来？

Traditional Chinese
1. 我聽說你要去中國參加夏令營，是在哪一個城市？你為甚麼想去？
2. 你們的夏令營有多長時間？甚麼時候回美國？
3. 去中國以前，你還需要做好哪些準備？
4. 你參加的夏令營會舉辦哪些活動？有沒有旅游方面的活動？
5. 中國的夏令營和美國的還是不同的，你覺得應該注意哪些問題？
6. 中國的東西比較便宜，你打算買些甚麼回來？

Answers and Explanations

After you read the sample answers and the explanations in this section, answer the following questions to quickly evaluate how well you did in responding to the questions you were asked in the conversation. Your performance on the conversation is scored on a scale of 1 to 6.

a. Did you address the question thoroughly and provide details?
b. Did you include smooth sentence connections?
c. Did your response show natural pace with minimal repetitions and/or hesitations?
d. Did you use good pronunciation and register?
e. Did your answer show a rich vocabulary and various grammatical structures?

A rather detailed set of answers is provided for your reference. On the actual exam, an answer scored 5 or 6 generally consists of four to six short sentences.

Question #1

你好，听说你要去中国参加夏令营，是在哪一个城市？你为什么想去？
（你好，聽說你要去中國參加夏令營，是在哪一個城市？你為甚麼想去？）

Translation: I was told that you would go to a summer camp in China. Which city? Why do you want to go?

Sample Response:
我参加的夏令营在云南昆明，不过最后几天夏令营会组织我们去桂林和张家界旅游。我想去是因为从前去过那里。昆明不是那种特别国际化的城市，有很多少数民族，可以了解真正的中国和中国人的生活。而且听说昆明风景优美，四季如春。
（我參加的夏令營在雲南昆明，不過最後幾天夏令營會組織我們去桂林和張家界旅遊。我想去是因為從前去過那裡。昆明不是那種特別國際化的城市，有很多少數民族，可以瞭解真正的中國和中國人的生活。而且聽說昆明風景優美，四季如春。）

This is a level 6 response. The answer directly addresses the questions. It describes in detail not only the city of the summer camp but also other places to travel. The reasons for picking this city are very convincing: Kun Ming is not really international and it has a lot of minorities, so it is a great place to get to know the "real" China and how Chinese live. Also, the answer mentions that Kun Ming has beautiful scenery and good weather. The response shows rich vocabulary usage and a wide range of grammatical structures.

Question #2

你们的夏令营有多长时间？什么时候回美国？
（你們的夏令營有多長時間？甚麼時候回美國？）

Translation: How long will the summer camp last? When will you come back to the United States?

Sample Response:
我们的夏令营有三个星期，八月七号会回美国。夏令营前两个星期学中文，最后一个星期去桂林和张家界旅游，那里也是少数民族特别多的地方，不是特别国际化，可以了解真正的中国和中国人的生活。
（我們的夏令營有三個星期，八月七號會回美國。夏令營前兩個星期學中文，最後一個星期去桂林和張家界旅遊，那裡也是少數民族特別多的地方，不是特別國際化，可以瞭解真正的中國和中國人的生活。）

This is a level 6 response. The answer directly addresses the questions. Although the question only requires a short, simple answer, this answer provides a very thorough and appropriate response with smooth sentence connections. Furthermore, it uses some information from the first question. This is an example of a good strategy to answer the questions in the conversation.

Question #3
去中国以前，你需要做好哪些准备？
（去中國以前，你需要做好哪些準備？）

Translation: What do you need to prepare before going to China?

Sample Response:
去中国前，首先要把护照和签证弄好。然后就是准备衣服了。听说昆明不是太热，所以我得带一两件外套，还有一些常用药。相机和手提电脑是一定要准备的，好记录下中国的美丽景色。对了，我喜欢游泳，一定要记得准备游泳衣。中国东西便宜，其他的去那儿买好了。
（去中國前，首先要把護照和簽證弄好。然後就是準備衣服了。聽說昆明不是太熱，所以我得帶一兩件外套，還有一些常用藥。相機和手提電腦是一定要準備的，好記錄下中國的美麗景色。對了，我喜歡游泳，一定要記得準備游泳衣。中國東西便宜，其他的去那兒買好了。）

This is a level 6 response. The structure of the answer is quite amazing for such a short paragraph. It states many aspects of preparation including a passport and visa, clothes, commonly used medicines, a camera and a laptop (including the reason for these), and a swimming suit (including the reason for this). It also mentions that an unprepared student can purchase these items cheaply in China.

Question #4
你参加的夏令营会举办哪些活动？有没有旅游方面的活动？
（你參加的夏令營會舉辦哪些活動？有沒有旅遊方面的活動？）

Translation: Which kinds of activities will you have in the summer camp? Is any traveling included?

Sample Response:
我们的夏令营活动特别多，也有旅游方面的活动。老师介绍过，我们会学习中文，画中国画，写毛笔字，练中国武术，还有各种各样的歌舞晚会，还会到一些少数民族居住的地方，和那里的人们交流，听说还有泼水节呢。我们最后一个星期会去桂林和张家界旅行，听说风景优美极了。
（我們的夏令營活動特別多，也有旅遊方面的活動。老師介紹過，我們會學習中文，畫中國畫，寫毛筆字，練中國武術，還有各種各樣的歌舞晚會，還會到一些少數民族居住的地方，和那裡的人們交流，聽說還有潑水節呢。我們最後一個星期會去桂林和張家界旅行，聽說風景優美極了。）

This is a level 6 response and is definitely a good answer. A lot of students may forget or have no time left to answer the second question and get a score of 2, no matter how well they answered the first question. However, this answer addressed the two questions in the first sentence, so that it could easily get a score of 4 or above even with limited elaboration.

Question #5
中国的夏令营和美国的还是不同的，你觉得应该注意哪些问题？
（中國的夏令營和美國的還是不同的，你覺得應該注意哪些問題？）

Translation: There are differences between summer camp in China and in the United States. What do you need to pay attention to?

Sample Response:
我觉得第一要注意的是身体。中国的环境和我习惯的美国环境还是有区别的，可能水土不服啊，吃不惯啊，生病啊什么的，这些都要注意。第二就是安全了。听说中国的小偷挺厉害，我得保管好自己的东西，尤其是护照，还得小心不要迷路。第三是文化差异。我会尊重他们的礼节和风俗，免得闹矛盾。
（我覺得第一要注意的是身體。中國的環境和我習慣的美國環境還是有區別的，可能水土不服啊，吃不慣啊，生病啊甚麼的，這些都要注意。第二就是安全了。聽説中國的小偷挺厲害，我得保管好自己的東西，尤其是護照，還得小心不要迷路。第三是文化差異。我會尊重他們的禮節和風俗，免得鬧矛盾。）

This is a level 6 response. The answer is comprehensive and well structured with minimal hesitation and repetition. It lists three important facts to pay attention to: health, safety, and cultural shock. The content demonstrates great cultural knowledge and a wide range of transitional elements: first, possibly, second, especially, also, have to, in case, and so on.

Question #6
中国的东西比较便宜，你打算买些什么回来？
（中國的東西比較便宜，你打算買些甚麼回來？）
Translation: The goods in China are relatively cheap. What are you going to buy and bring home?

Sample Response:
是啊，中国的东西很便宜，我打算买很多跟文化有关的小东西，什么中国结啊，剪纸啊，国画啊，瓷器啊，茶叶啊等等。我还想买一些少数民族的特产，刺绣啊，孔雀翎啊，他们的服饰啊什么的，当礼物送给朋友挺不错的。
（是啊，中國的東西很便宜，我打算買很多跟文化有關的小東西，甚麼中國結啊，剪紙啊，國畫啊，瓷器啊，茶葉啊等等。我還想買一些少數民族的特產，刺繡啊，孔雀翎啊，他們的服飾啊甚麼的，當禮物送給朋友挺不錯的。）

This is a level 6 response. A rephrase of the question is always a good start. The answer even catalogues the things to buy with "culture" and "minorities." This is a good example of reaching level 6 without using complicated sentence structure. In addition, it states that the things to be bought could be used as gifts for friends. The elaboration is closely connected with the question.

Self-Evaluation and Scoring Analysis

1. Did your answers cover all the questions of the prompts?
    Yes. Your score may be 3 or above. Otherwise your score may be 2 or below 2.

2. Was your presentation complete and understandable to the listener?
    Yes. Your score may be 4 or above, even if your answer lacks detail or elaboration, or includes minor inconsistencies in its logical progression. As long as you have good pace and intonation, intermittent hesitation and repetition are acceptable.

3. Was your answer well structured with rich language usage and only minor errors?
    Yes. Your score may be 5 or above. An ample vocabulary, accurate word usage, detailed cultural knowledge, and only minimal hesitation or repetition with accurate pronunciation and tones are crucial at this level.

4. Based on the data from College Board, students score the lowest in the conversation section. I collected the top five specific frequently made errors which you can avoid despite your Chinese proficiency:

    * Not paying attention to the English instruction, which identifies the relationship and circumstances. For example, speak as if you are in the U.S. when the questions are based on traveling in Beijing.

* Not using proper register such as 谢谢你 (謝謝你), 你好, etc.

* Forgetting to answer the "why" or "how" part if there is one in a question.

* Not providing the specific time or activities when addressing "scheduling."

* When the question asks for extra samples " 除了A 以外, except for A," only describing A without providing other samples.

Now use the self-evaluation sheet to identify your weakness and adjust your study plan.

Self-Evaluation Worksheet

FREQUENT REASONS FOR ERRORS	SUGGESTIONS
1. I didn't even understand the question.	Actually there may be two questions together. Listen to the prompt very carefully. Repeat it in your mind.
2. I didn't understand some words in the prompt.	Skip them. You can get the main idea and provide a great answer without knowing some of the words.
3. I knew that word was important but I just didn't understand it!	The speaking speed of the prompt is always fast for a nervous exam taker. Repeat the words you know and try to talk about them. It's risky but a score of 3 is better than nothing.
4. I answered the question but there was still time left and I didn't have anything more to say.	Do not stop talking! There are so many ways to elaborate your answers: give examples, share your opinions, or even just rephrase what you said.
5. My mind went blank.	But your tongue didn't! Frame your response with phrases you know such as "I mean," or "to my best knowledge." This will win you a few seconds to organize your answer.
6. My grammar is bad.	Never worry about grammar in conversation. Just blurt it out.
7. My pronunciation is bad.	Practice makes perfect. Also, watch Chinese movies and repeat the scripts of your favorite roles in daily study.
Think: What kinds of errors did I make the most? Why didn't I find the correct answers? What could I do to improve?	See the "Study Tips for the Conversation" earlier in this chapter if you feel you need more practice for the conversation.

CHAPTER 11

Presentational Speaking: Cultural Presentation

IN THIS CHAPTER

Summary: This chapter provides practice for the cultural presentation that is part of the AP Chinese Language and Culture exam. First, you'll learn what the cultural presentation is and how it's scored. Then you'll practice the strategies for the cultural presentation and learn to use these in a basic step-by-step approach. Presented next are skill-building exercises designed to help you build a template for your response and learn more about Chinese culture. Finally, you will practice applying the strategies in a practice test that closely resembles what you'll find on the actual AP exam. At the end, analyze and evaluate your performance on the cultural presentation and use the suggestions provided to adjust your study plan accordingly.

Key Strategies/Ideas

- ✪ Learn how the cultural presentation is graded so you'll know what's expected and how you measure up.
- ✪ Carefully read the prompt. Pay attention to any adjectives that specify the cultural practice or product you need to talk about.
- ✪ Make the best use of the four-minute preparation time.
- ✪ State your main idea first before elaborating. Speak fast and fluently for the familiar part. Use set phrases or rephrase the question if your mind goes blank or you are having difficulty.

- Build your structure (template) for the cultural presentation and memorize it.
- Record the description of Chinese cultural practices/products given by native speakers of Chinese and learn from these.
- Learn from the answers of the questions from previous years. Practice adapting your prepared structure to the 10 sample topics we provide.

The Cultural Presentation: What It Is and How It Is Scored

In this part of the exam—the second task of Section II, Part B (Speaking)—you will make a presentation on a specific cultural topic you are given. You will have four minutes to prepare for your two-minute presentation. Your two-minute presentation will be recorded so it can be scored later. Don't panic! It is just like any presentation your teacher asked you to do in the class, and you can take notes in the four minutes before your presentation.

Although it may sound difficult, the cultural presentation is actually the easiest part of the whole exam because you can prepare the structure and content quite well before the exam. You are given some latitude in choosing the topic you want to talk about. Choose a topic for which you know the Chinese name and can talk about its significance.

Scoring Guidelines: Cultural Presentation

The College Board provides scoring guidelines for the cultural presentation. You can find these on its website. At the time of publication, the specific URL for these was http://media.collegeboard.com/digitalServices/pdf/ap/apcentral/ap13_chinese_scoring_guidelines.pdf.

Like the scoring on all the free response questions, each student's response is graded on a scale of 1 to 6. Cultural presentations at level 6 are considered "excellent," while those graded at level 5 are "very good." Level 4 scores competence as "good," and level 3 rates your performance as "adequate."

Your performance on the cultural presentation portion of the exam—like the scoring on all the free-response questions—is evaluated on the basis of three criteria called rubrics:

  I. Task Completion
 II. Language Usage
III. Delivery

The following table summarizes and explains the differences for scoring of levels 3, 4, 5, and 6.

Scoring Guidelines for the Cultural Presentation

	SCORE: 3	SCORE: 4	SCORE: 5	SCORE: 6
I. TASK COMPLETION				
Question Completion	Directly addresses the topic but not all aspects of the topic.	Directly addresses the topic but may lack detail.	Directly addresses the topic. Thorough, appropriate, but still may lack detail.	Directly addresses the topic. Thorough, appropriate, detail with elaboration.
Organization	Portions may lack organization. Disconnected sentences.	Inconsistent transitional elements. Loosely connected sentences.	Generally clear progression. Some transitional elements and cohesive devices.	Clear progression with detail. Appropriate use of transitional elements and cohesive devices.
Cultural Information	Basically correct but with some inaccuracies.	Accurate but lacks detail.	Accurate and detailed.	Ample, accurate, and detailed.
II. LANGUAGE USAGE				
Vocabulary and Idioms	Limited vocabulary usage. Frequent errors.	Mostly appropriate vocabulary usage. Errors not serious enough to obscure meaning.	Appropriate vocabulary usage. Sporadic errors.	Rich and appropriate vocabulary. Minimal errors.
Grammatical Structures	Simple grammatical structures. Frequent errors.	Mostly appropriate grammatical structures. Errors not serious enough to obscure meaning.	Variety of grammatical structures. Sporadic errors.	Wide range of grammatical structures. Minimal errors.
III. DELIVERY				
Pronunciation	Errors sometimes need listener's efforts to understand.	May have several errors that need listener's efforts to understand.	Occasional errors (tones or pronunciation).	Accurate with minimal errors.
Pace and Intonation	Inconsistent. Hesitation and repetition may interfere with comprehension.	Generally consistent. Intermittent hesitation and repetition.	Smooth. Occasional hesitation and repetition.	Natural. Minimal hesitation or repetition.
Register	Inconsistent. Many errors.	Include several lapses.	Occasional lapses.	Consistent use. Appropriate.

Strategies for the Cultural Presentation: A Step-by-Step Approach

How do you get a high score in the cultural presentation? The basic strategies for giving the cultural presentation were presented in Chapter 4 and are summarized in the following sidebar. Using the warm-up exercise, this chapter will take you step by step through the process of applying the strategies to the task of making the cultural presentation. Using these strategies in a step-by-step approach will help you do your best on the cultural presentation.

Strategies for the Cultural Presentation

1. **Use your four minutes for careful preparation.** You can do a lot of constructive preparation in the four minutes. First, carefully read the task you are assigned (the prompt). Make sure that you understand what culture practice or product you need to discuss. Sometimes there is a specific condition (usually adjectives such as famous, traditional, regional, etc.) added to the topic. Your preparation should be based on the condition and include some complete sentences.

2. **Complete the task.** Start with your main idea as the first sentence. If you are going to talk about a cultural topic and its significance, then state it. Second, describe the features and share the significance. Speak as fast and fluently as possible for the familiar parts. If you have time, plan a beautiful closing sentence that wows.

3. **Start with a structure (template) prepared in advance.** Similar to the e-mail response, you can prepare a structured outline before the exam because the topics involve a cultural practice and its significance. Thus, you can do fill-in-the-blank writing instead of starting from zero in the actual exam. Preparing a well-organized structure with perfect grammar and the use of rich language before the exam can really help you to succeed in this task.

Warm-up Exercise

For the warm-up exercise you will have another try at the cultural presentation task that was in the diagnostic test:

Choose one famous Chinese person (e.g., movie stars, sports stars, leaders, authors, musicians, artists, etc.). In your presentation, describe the person in detail and explain his/her significance.

For a sample of a good answer for this task, see the sample answer and the English translation for it in Chapter 3. Go to page 65.

Step 1: Preparation

1. Read the instructions carefully. Normally the question involves choosing one Chinese cultural practice or product (foods, arts, customs, cities, etc.) and discussing its significance. But beware, neglecting some specific words may unexpectedly put you on the wrong track, for example: Does the music have to be traditional? Is the food required to be regional? You need to make sure that you read the instructions regarding the task specifically.

2. Develop a well-structured outline. Various structures can be used in answering this question to get a high score on the AP exam. You are encouraged to analyze your own

thinking logic and speaking style to set up a structure you feel comfortable with. If you are comfortable with the structure of "global" (objective common sense) and "personal" (subjective personal experiences) organizational structure, that you used for the e-mail response, you can try it again.

Here's a sample outline:

Part I. Introduction
State the cultural practice/product you are going to talk about and briefly state its significance.
我今天想介绍一位中国的名人，他的名字叫姚明。我想和大家谈谈姚明这个人为什么出名，有什么样的影响力，为什么重要。
（我今天想介紹一位中國的名人，他的名字叫姚明。我想和大家談談姚明這個人為甚麼出名，有甚麼樣的影響力，為甚麼重要。）

Part II. Development of Your Ideas

a. Description:
姚明是美国ＮＢＡ和世界篮球巨星，上海人，从九岁就开始打篮球，休斯顿火箭队打中锋，身高2米26，又叫小巨人、移动长城，在中国最具影响力.
（姚明是美國ＮＢＡ和世界籃球巨星，上海人，從九歲就開始打籃球，休斯頓火箭隊打中鋒，身高2米26，又叫小巨人、移動長城，在中國最具影響力。）

b. Global significance:
中国第一位以状元身份进入NBA的球员；八次入选全明星队，美国时代周刊列入"世界最具影响力的100人"之中；六次被福布斯评为中国名人榜第一名；写书《我的世界我的梦》；奥委会、篮球协会颁发的奖项；华人球迷……
（中國第一位以狀元身份進入NBA的球員；八次入選全明星隊，美國時代週刊列入"世界最具影響力的100人"之中；六次被福布斯評為中國名人榜第一名；寫書《我的世界我的夢》；奧委會、籃球協會頒發的獎項；華人球迷……）

c. Personal impression:
名言："努力不一定成功，放弃却一定失败。"遗憾的是我从来没有见到过姚明本人。
（名言："努力不一定成功，放棄卻一定失敗。"遺憾的是我從來沒有見到過姚明本人。）

Part III. Ending
Summarize and rephrase the introduction.
中国的骄傲，中国人的成功。
（中國的驕傲，中國人的成功。）

Step 2: Presentation

You need a presentation that addresses all aspects of the task with thoroughness and detail. It needs to be well organized with a clear progression of ideas and the use of transitional elements. You need to have accurate information and detail with rich and appropriate language and grammatical structures. With good delivery, this kind of answer scores 5 or above.

After you've prepared a good structure or outline and filled it with detailed information, you will have enough content to present for two minutes. Here are some tips for your presentation:

1. Speak as fast and fluently as possible for the familiar parts, such as Part I (the introduction). You can adjust your prepared introduction to any topic for a perfect start.

2. Use a set phrase if your mind goes blank or you encounter difficulties. These will get you started and win a little time for you to think. Memorize some of the following set phrases so you can easily use them:

I feel that	我觉得啊（我覺得啊）
I think	我认为（我認為）
in another way/that is	也就是说（也就是说）
how to say	怎么说呢（怎麼说呢）
from another point of view	从另一方面来看（從另一方面來看）
for example	比如说（比如说）
for instance	举个例子吧（舉個例子吧）
to be more exact	说得更确切一点（说得更確切一點）
in detail	说得更具体一点（说得更具體一點）
just like what I said	就像我刚才所说的（就像我剛才所說的）
as everybody knows	大家都知道的（大家都知道的）
as we all heard about	我们都听说过的（我們都聽说過的）

Study Tips for the Cultural Presentation

Structured speaking is the focus of the cultural presentation. Use the strategies and tips provided earlier to help build a structure and achieve a great cultural presentation. But if you find this task difficult and would like more practice, here are some general study tips for the cultural presentation:

Building a Structure: Review the "Functional Grammar" in the appendix. Set up a structure specifically for introducing a practice or a product of Chinese culture. Write down your template of the structure and memorize it.

Intensive Speaking: Practice the questions in this book following the strategies provided. Also practice with the cultural presentation questions from previous years' exams that are posted on the College Board's website: http://apcentral.collegeboard.com/apc/members/exam/exam_information/157009.html. Keep practicing your responses until you reach a level of 5 or above. Focus on developing your cultural knowledge, especially the details of a cultural product or practice. The more topics you prepare and practice before the exam, the more comprehensive and adjustable your structure and your answer will be. Finally, use the self-evaluation worksheet to analyze your errors, and use the suggestions on the worksheet to address weak areas.

Skill-Building Exercises

Building a Template

In this section you'll go through the process of building a very thorough template for the cultural presentation; this sample template is to be based on the topic of Chinese traditional arts. Learn what a good structure encompasses and start to build your basic template.

Introduction

a. What am I going to talk about?

中国是有着五千年历史和文明的国家。我今天想介绍中国一种著名的<u>艺术</u>，这种艺术就是<u>书法</u>。我想和大家谈谈ＸＸ为什么很重要，ＸＸ有什么特点，有什么样的意义。

（中國是有著五千年歷史和文明的國家。我今天想介紹中國一種著名的藝術，這種藝術就是書法。我想和大家談談ＸＸ為甚麼很重要，ＸＸ有甚麼特點，有甚麼樣的意義。）

b. State the English meaning of the topic if you are not that confident about your pronunciation.

<u>书法</u>的英文意思是 calligraphy，而对大多数中国人来说，就是他们常说的<u>毛笔字</u>。

（書法的英文意思是 calligraphy，而對大多數中國人來説，就是他們常説的毛筆字。）

Body

a. Describe in detail the features of the topic.

我特别喜欢看各种各样的<u>书法作品</u>，就像<u>黑白画</u>一样。<u>书法有不同的字体，行体啊，楷体啊，草体啊什么的。书法用的是文房四宝，即笔、墨、纸、砚。</u>

（我特別喜歡看各種各樣的書法作品，就像黑白畫一樣。書法有不同的字體，行體啊，楷體啊，草體啊甚麼的。書法用的是文房四寶，即筆、墨、紙、硯。）

b. Share the global significance of the topic.

In China:

在中国，很多人都会谈论<u>书法</u>，几乎每个城市都有<u>书法博物馆</u>。

（中國，很多人都會談論書法，幾乎每個城市都有書法博物館。）

In the United States or in the world:

我认识的<u>美国朋友</u>还收藏了很多<u>书法作品</u>，看起来<u>书法</u>不但在中国很有名，而且在美国也有不少人喜欢。

（我認識的美國朋友還收藏了很多書法作品，看起來書法不但在中國很有名，而且在美國也有不少人喜歡。）

Compare:

<u>书法</u>在中国的地位就像<u>油画</u>在美国一样，具有价值和重要意义。<u>书法</u>是中国文化不可缺少的部分。

（書法在中國的地位就像油畫在美國一樣，具有價值和重要意義。書法是中國文化不可缺少的部分。）

c. Share personal experience with the topic.

Merits:

我觉得<u>国画</u>不但好看，而且<u>画国画</u>对我们的身体和心理都很有好处。第一，画国画对身体有好处，因为是全身运动，可以锻炼全身；第二，这对我们的心理也有好处，因为我全神贯注地画，时间过得很快，什么烦恼都没有了。

（我覺得國畫不但好看，而且畫國畫對我們的身體和心理都很有好處。第一，畫國畫對身體有好處，因為是全身運動，可以鍛煉全身；第二，這對我們的心理也有好處，因為我全神貫注地畫，時間過得很快，甚麼煩惱都沒有了。）

Experience:

我从初中开始<u>练习书法</u>，参加了许多<u>书法比赛</u>，认识了许多热爱<u>书法</u>的朋友。

（我從初中開始練習書法，參加了許多書法比賽，認識了許多熱愛書法的朋友。）

Ending

a. Seeing is believing.

说实在的，我一直想再去中国旅游，找个机会亲自去<u>书法</u>博物馆看一看，欣赏一下那些传说中的<u>名家名作</u>，肯定很值得。

（說實在的，我一直想再去中國旅遊，找個機會親自去書法博物館看一看，欣賞一下那些傳說中的名家名作，肯定很值得。）

b. My goal for promoting this Chinese cultural practice or product.

我希望继续<u>练习书法</u>，将这种中国文化发扬光大。

（我希望繼續練習書法，將這種中國文化發揚光大。）

Building Your Knowledge of Chinese Culture

Learning from others is the key to success in cultural presentation. Try to discuss different cultural topics with Chinese native speakers. Record their answers and imitate. Analyze their answers and gradually add useful expressions from native speakers in order to develop your own structure or template. The more topics you practice and the more detail you prepare, the better you'll develop the required knowledge and skills to apply to your real exam.

Besides recording and imitating how native Chinese speakers talk about their culture, listen to the model presentations for the cultural presentation task in previous years' AP exams. Analyze these presentations and note their strengths in order to improve your own presentation. Here are the topics for the cultural presentation that have appeared on previous AP exams:

2007: One Chinese social custom
2008: One city in mainland China or Taiwan
2009: One Chinese art
2010: One Chinese celebrity
2011: One Chinese leisure activity
2012: One traditional Chinese concept or value
2013: One Chinese regional cuisine

You should practice these topics and analyze the model answers that the College Board has released. These are available at http://apcentral.collegeboard.com/apc/members/exam/exam_information/157009.html.

After developing your presentational skills and deepening your knowledge of Chinese culture by analyzing and imitating the model answers on the College Board's website, prepare presentations for the following topics. You should research each topic, taking notes on the cultural practice/product and its objective and subject significance. Use your template to create your cultural presentation; practice adapting the template for each topic.

1. One Chinese movie
2. One Chinese cultural sport (Tai Chi, Qi Gong, yo-yo, etc.)
3. One Chinese idiom or proverb
4. One Chinese taboo topic
5. One ancient Chinese invention
6. One famous person in ancient China
7. One traditional Chinese holiday

8. One auspicious Chinese symbol (dragon, Ba Gua, lucky cat, etc.)
9. One Chinese landmark or architectural style (Si He Yuan, bamboo house, etc.)
10. One Chinese performing art form

Remember: You should keep practicing one topic until your answer reaches level 5 or above before moving on to the next topic. Intensive speaking is much more important than extensive speaking for this type of question.

Cultural Presentation Practice Test

In this section you'll prepare and deliver a cultural presentation like the one on the actual test. Practice the step-by-step approach you learned earlier in this chapter to create an outline and make the presentation. Time yourself so you can practice pacing yourself. After you've completed this test-like experience, read the sample level-6 presentation. Then review the detailed explanation and try to score your own performance.

When you are done, do a thorough analysis of where and why you made any errors. Use the self-evaluation worksheet at the end of this chapter. Then look at the suggestions that correspond to each kind of mistake you made. If you feel you need more practice with the cultural presentation, use the suggestions provided on the worksheet and the "Study Tips for the Cultural Presentation" earlier in this chapter.

Cultural Presentation

Time limits: four minutes for the preparation period and two minutes for the presentation. On the actual test your two-minute oral presentation will be recorded.

Choose one Chinese traditional festival activity (dinner on Chinese New Year's Eve, the dragon boat competition during the Duan Wu Festival, etc.), describe this festival activity, and explain its significance.

Answer and Explanation

Sample Presentation

Simplified Chinese

中国是有着五千年历史和文明的国家。中国的传统节日一直是中国文化的象征。我今天想介绍一种和传统节日有关的活动，这种活动就是元宵节的舞龙舞狮。我想和大家谈谈中国的舞龙舞狮为什么很重要，有什么特点，有什么样的意义。

舞龙舞狮的英文意思是 dragon dance and lion dance。我特别喜欢在网上看各种各样的舞龙和舞狮。人们穿着漂亮的衣服，敲锣打鼓，非常热闹。龙和狮子都是手工做的，龙一般要七个人或九个人舞，也有十一个人的。狮子一般是两个人舞，一头一尾。不同的舞龙队和舞狮队还表演他们的技术，赢了还有奖呢。这一风俗在中国很多地方从春节开始，直到元宵节结束。在有些地方最后还会把龙和狮子烧掉，用来表示新年的开始。

在中国，没有人不知道舞龙舞狮，而在美国的中国城，这个传统也一直保留着。对于中国人来说，它有着无可比拟的重要意义，是中国文化不可缺少的部分。很多美国人都会在元宵节前后去中国城观看龙狮大赛。我听说还有世界性的舞龙舞狮比赛呢！我觉得舞龙舞狮不但好看，而且练习起来就像体育运动一样，对身体很有好处。我们老师带着我们舞过狮子，一节课下来，就像打了场球一样，又开心又累。

说实在的，我一直想再去中国旅游，找个机会亲自去中国的大街上看一看，亲眼欣赏一下那些传说中的技术竞赛，肯定很值得。我也希望有一天可以参加舞龙舞狮活动，将这种中国文化发扬光大。

Traditional Chinese

中國是有著五千年歷史和文明的國家。中國的傳統節日一直是中國文化的象徵。我今天想介紹一種和傳統節日有關的活動，這種活動就是元宵節的舞龍舞獅。我想和大家談談中國的舞龍舞獅為甚麼很重要，有甚麼特點，有甚麼樣的意義。

舞龍舞獅的英文意思是 dragon dance and lion dance。我特別喜歡在網上看各種各樣的舞龍和舞獅。人們穿著漂亮的衣服，敲鑼打鼓，非常熱鬧。龍和獅子都是手工做的，龍一般要七個人或九個人舞，也有十一個人的。獅子一般是兩個人舞，一頭一尾。不同的舞龍隊和舞獅隊還表演他們的技術，贏了還有獎呢。這一風俗在中國很多地方從春節開始，直到元宵節結束。在有些地方最後還會把龍和獅子燒掉，用來表示新年的開始。

在中國，沒有人不知道舞龍舞獅，而在美國的中國城，這個傳統也一直保留著。對於中國人來說，它有著無可比擬的重要意義，是中國文化不可缺少的部分。很多美國人都會在元宵節前後去中國城觀看龍獅大賽。我聽說還有世界性的舞龍舞獅比賽呢！我覺得舞龍舞獅不但好看，而且練習起來就像體育運動一樣，對身體很有好處。我們老師帶著我們舞過獅子，一節課下來，就像打了場球一樣，又開心又累。

說實在的，我一直想再去中國旅遊，找個機會親自去中國的大街上看一看，親眼欣賞一下那些傳說中的技術競賽，肯定很值得。我也希望有一天可以參加舞龍舞獅活動，將這種中國文化發揚光大。

English Translation

China is a country with 5,000 years of history and civilization. The Chinese traditional festivals are always the symbol of Chinese culture. I am going to introduce an activity related to the traditional festivals today: the dragon dance and lion dance on Lantern Festival. I am going to discuss about what is the dragon dance and lion dance, why it is important in Chinese cultural, what the significance will be.

Dragon Dance and Lion Dance is how we call it in English. I really like watching the dragon dance and lion dance online. Everybody got dressed, the music is loud and it is such a nice party! The dragon and lion normally are made by hand. There are normally seven people or nine people to perform the dragon dance, though sometimes could be 11 dancers. The lion dance is normally performed by two: one people plays the head, and the other one plays the tail. Sometimes different teams will have competitions together showing their skills in dancing. The winner may gain rewards. In a lot of places in China, this custom starts at Spring Festival and ends at Lantern Festival. The dragon or lion may be burned at the end in some places, demonstrating the beginning of the new year.

Dragon dance and lion dance is well-known in China. But also, this custom has always been kept in China town in the United States. To Chinese people, there is nothing comparable to the dragon dance and lion dance in celebrating the new year. It is the indispensable element in Chinese culture. Many Americans will go to China town to enjoy the dragon dance and lion dance competition around lantern festival. I was told that there are international competitions, too. I think dragon dance and lion dance is not just fun for watching, but also a great sports to practice. It is good to our health. My teacher taught us to play the lion dance. It was like finishing a basketball game after class.

To be honest, I have always thought about going to visit China again. I want to find an opportunity to enjoy the real dragon dance and lion dance competition on the street in China. It's worth seeing! I also hope I can join in a dragon dance and lion dance team, to promote this culture in the future.

Explanation

This topic is a little complicated since you need to find an activity related to a festival. Only if you write about an activity and connect it to a festival can you get a score of 4 or above. The good news is you can add information about the festival in general to elaborate your answer. Be very careful that you understand exactly what you are being asked to do. Many students got a lower score on the 2013 cultural presentation topic on the actual AP exam because it asked for "regional" cuisine—an adjective many test takers neglected.

There are various ways to finish the cultural presentation successfully. You are encouraged to do research based on "the dragon dance and lion dance" 舞龙舞狮（舞龍舞獅）in Chinese to gain ample cultural information and learn how the native Chinese introduce this activity. In creating this cultural presentation, continue using the template you created and memorized so that you can practice how to adjust your prepared structure to different topics.

Self-Evaluation and Scoring Analysis

1. Have you described the product or practice and explained its significance?
    Yes. Your score may be 3 or above. Otherwise your score may be 2 or below 2.

2. Was your presentation complete and understandable to the listener?
    Yes. Your score may be 4 or above, even if your answer lacks detail or elaboration, or includes minor inconsistencies in its logical progression. As long as you have general pace and intonation, intermittent hesitation and repetition are acceptable.

3. Was your answer well structured, with rich language usage and only minor errors?
    Yes. Your score may be 5 or above. Accurate and detailed cultural knowledge, minimal hesitation or repetition, and accurate pronunciation and tones are all crucial at this level.

Now use the self-evaluation sheet to identify your weakness and adjust your study plan.

Self-Evaluation Worksheet

FREQUENT REASONS FOR ERRORS	SUGGESTIONS
1. I didn't know what to talk about because I am not familiar with this cultural practice or product.	Each prompt lists some detailed samples and this will help you to think about something you know that is related to the cultural topic.
2. The prompt was supposed to be on a specific topic but I ended up with a general one.	Sometimes there is a specific "adjective" for the cultural practice or product. Pay attention to it. Take, for example, ancient invention, regional food, famous person, classical art form, and so on.
3. I didn't have much to write down in the four minutes given for preparing.	You have four minutes to write down your notes and prepare. You can use a structure or a template you have prepared and practiced with in advance.
4. I answered the question but there is still time left and I didn't have more to say.	Look back at the suggestion for #3. Now you know what to do. You need to prepare a detailed structure or template. You will learn how to do this in Chapter 11.
5. My mind went blank.	But your tongue didn't! Frame your response with phrases you know such as "I mean," or "to my best knowledge." This will win you a few seconds to organize your answer.
6. My grammar is bad.	Go back to the suggestion for #3 again. You should prepare a template with perfect grammar before the exam.
7. My pronunciation is bad.	Practice makes perfect. Ask Chinese native speakers to give two-minute cultural presentations. Record them. Imitate this in your daily study.
Think: What kinds of errors did I make the most? Why didn't I find the correct answers? What could I do to improve?	See the "Study Tips for the Cultural Presentation" earlier in this chapter.

STEP 5

Build Your
Test-Taking Confidence

AP Chinese Language and Cultural Practice Test 1
AP Chinese Language and Cultural Practice Test 2

AP Chinese Language and Cultural Practice Test 1

Using the Practice Test

This practice test closely resembles the actual AP Chinese Language and Culture exam. Take this test to experience what the real test will be like. This practice test is especially valuable in helping to

- Familiarize yourself with the AP exam
- Learn to pace yourself within the time limits of the exam
- Practice the strategies you've learned in this book
- Build your test-taking confidence

How to Take the Practice Test

To get the most out of this diagnostic exam, you should try to simulate actual test-taking conditions as much as possible. Here are some tips that will help you:

- Plan to take the two-hour exam without interruption.
- Answer the questions within the required time limits in each section.
- Follow the instructions carefully.
- For the listening section of the test (Section I, Part A) and the conversation (Section II, Part B), you will find the audio content on the accompanying CD-ROM.
- Tear out the answer sheet provided (see the next page). Grid-in your answers for Section I (multiple choice) on this answer sheet. Or, if you wish, write your answers on scratch paper and take this test again later.
- Practice using the strategies you've learned in this book.

You may find this practice test to be slightly harder than the actual test. This slightly greater degree of difficulty will better prepare you for the actual test.

After the Test

- Check your work against the correct answers provided for the multiple-choice questions. Read the explanations, not only for the questions you missed, but for all those for which you weren't sure what the correct answer was.
- Read the explanations for all the free-response questions and compare your answers to the sample ones. Do over the ones you had difficulty with to learn from your mistakes.
- Look up the vocabulary words you had difficulty with on the test and note down anything else you had trouble with when taking the exam.
- At the very end of the answers and explanations for this practice test, you'll find a score conversion sheet. Use this to determine a rough AP score; this will give you a rough idea of how you might do on the test if you took it today.
- Review the specific strategies if you found any section of this practice test challenging.
- You can reuse the self-evaluation worksheets at the end of Chapter 4 to analyze your performance on this practice test. Use the suggestions on these worksheets if you feel you need more practice.

AP Chinese Language and Culture Practice Test 1—Multiple Choice

ANSWER SHEET

Part A: Listening

1 Ⓐ Ⓑ Ⓒ Ⓓ	13 Ⓐ Ⓑ Ⓒ Ⓓ	25 Ⓐ Ⓑ Ⓒ Ⓓ
2 Ⓐ Ⓑ Ⓒ Ⓓ	14 Ⓐ Ⓑ Ⓒ Ⓓ	26 Ⓐ Ⓑ Ⓒ Ⓓ
3 Ⓐ Ⓑ Ⓒ Ⓓ	15 Ⓐ Ⓑ Ⓒ Ⓓ	27 Ⓐ Ⓑ Ⓒ Ⓓ
4 Ⓐ Ⓑ Ⓒ Ⓓ	16 Ⓐ Ⓑ Ⓒ Ⓓ	28 Ⓐ Ⓑ Ⓒ Ⓓ
5 Ⓐ Ⓑ Ⓒ Ⓓ	17 Ⓐ Ⓑ Ⓒ Ⓓ	29 Ⓐ Ⓑ Ⓒ Ⓓ
6 Ⓐ Ⓑ Ⓒ Ⓓ	18 Ⓐ Ⓑ Ⓒ Ⓓ	30 Ⓐ Ⓑ Ⓒ Ⓓ
7 Ⓐ Ⓑ Ⓒ Ⓓ	19 Ⓐ Ⓑ Ⓒ Ⓓ	31 Ⓐ Ⓑ Ⓒ Ⓓ
8 Ⓐ Ⓑ Ⓒ Ⓓ	20 Ⓐ Ⓑ Ⓒ Ⓓ	32 Ⓐ Ⓑ Ⓒ Ⓓ
9 Ⓐ Ⓑ Ⓒ Ⓓ	21 Ⓐ Ⓑ Ⓒ Ⓓ	33 Ⓐ Ⓑ Ⓒ Ⓓ
10 Ⓐ Ⓑ Ⓒ Ⓓ	22 Ⓐ Ⓑ Ⓒ Ⓓ	34 Ⓐ Ⓑ Ⓒ Ⓓ
11 Ⓐ Ⓑ Ⓒ Ⓓ	23 Ⓐ Ⓑ Ⓒ Ⓓ	35 Ⓐ Ⓑ Ⓒ Ⓓ
12 Ⓐ Ⓑ Ⓒ Ⓓ	24 Ⓐ Ⓑ Ⓒ Ⓓ	

Part B: Reading

1 Ⓐ Ⓑ Ⓒ Ⓓ	13 Ⓐ Ⓑ Ⓒ Ⓓ	25 Ⓐ Ⓑ Ⓒ Ⓓ
2 Ⓐ Ⓑ Ⓒ Ⓓ	14 Ⓐ Ⓑ Ⓒ Ⓓ	26 Ⓐ Ⓑ Ⓒ Ⓓ
3 Ⓐ Ⓑ Ⓒ Ⓓ	15 Ⓐ Ⓑ Ⓒ Ⓓ	27 Ⓐ Ⓑ Ⓒ Ⓓ
4 Ⓐ Ⓑ Ⓒ Ⓓ	16 Ⓐ Ⓑ Ⓒ Ⓓ	28 Ⓐ Ⓑ Ⓒ Ⓓ
5 Ⓐ Ⓑ Ⓒ Ⓓ	17 Ⓐ Ⓑ Ⓒ Ⓓ	29 Ⓐ Ⓑ Ⓒ Ⓓ
6 Ⓐ Ⓑ Ⓒ Ⓓ	18 Ⓐ Ⓑ Ⓒ Ⓓ	30 Ⓐ Ⓑ Ⓒ Ⓓ
7 Ⓐ Ⓑ Ⓒ Ⓓ	19 Ⓐ Ⓑ Ⓒ Ⓓ	31 Ⓐ Ⓑ Ⓒ Ⓓ
8 Ⓐ Ⓑ Ⓒ Ⓓ	20 Ⓐ Ⓑ Ⓒ Ⓓ	32 Ⓐ Ⓑ Ⓒ Ⓓ
9 Ⓐ Ⓑ Ⓒ Ⓓ	21 Ⓐ Ⓑ Ⓒ Ⓓ	33 Ⓐ Ⓑ Ⓒ Ⓓ
10 Ⓐ Ⓑ Ⓒ Ⓓ	22 Ⓐ Ⓑ Ⓒ Ⓓ	34 Ⓐ Ⓑ Ⓒ Ⓓ
11 Ⓐ Ⓑ Ⓒ Ⓓ	23 Ⓐ Ⓑ Ⓒ Ⓓ	35 Ⓐ Ⓑ Ⓒ Ⓓ
12 Ⓐ Ⓑ Ⓒ Ⓓ	24 Ⓐ Ⓑ Ⓒ Ⓓ	

AP Chinese Language and Culture Practice Test 1

Section I: Multiple-Choice Questions

Section I, Part A: Listening

Track 20

Rejoinders

You will hear several short or incomplete conversations in Chinese. The answer choices will be read to you instead of appearing on your computer screen. After listening to the conversation and its four possible continuations, you will choose the response that is the most logical and culturally appropriate to complete the conversation. Mark the letter of your answer choice on the answer sheet. You have **five seconds** to choose the answer, and you cannot go back to check or change it after the five seconds are up.

The listening tracks for the questions are provided on the CD-ROM accompanying this book. After you are done with the test, you may refer to the written script for the conversations and answer choices, which can be found starting on page 242. On the actual test, no script is provided.

1. (A) (B) (C) (D)
2. (A) (B) (C) (D)
3. (A) (B) (C) (D)
4. (A) (B) (C) (D)
5. (A) (B) (C) (D)
6. (A) (B) (C) (D)
7. (A) (B) (C) (D)
8. (A) (B) (C) (D)
9. (A) (B) (C) (D)
10. (A) (B) (C) (D)
11. (A) (B) (C) (D)
12. (A) (B) (C) (D)
13. (A) (B) (C) (D)
14. (A) (B) (C) (D)
15. (A) (B) (C) (D)

Track 21

Listening Selections

You will hear some audio selections in Chinese. For each selection, you will be told if it will play once or twice. You will not be able to see the questions until the audio selection is completed. Therefore, note taking is crucial in this part of the exam. You will have 12 seconds to choose the response that best answers each question. You cannot go back to check or change your answer after the 12 seconds are up. Mark the letter of your answer choice on the answer sheet.

The listening tracks for the questions are provided on the disc accompanying this book. After you are done with the test, you may refer to the written script for the listening selections, which can be found starting on page 248. On the actual test, no script is provided.

Commercial (Selection plays twice.)

Do not read the following questions until the audio selection has been completed.

16. When will Huan Zhu Ge Ge be on during the National Day holiday?

    (A) After 10 p.m.
    (B) Before 10 p.m.
    (C) After 4 p.m.
    (D) Before 4 p.m.

17. When is the best time to watch Hollywood movies?

    (A) At night
    (B) Golden time
    (C) In the morning
    (D) In the afternoon

18. Which is *not* mentioned in this TV commercial?

    (A) TV series
    (B) European movies
    (C) TV shopping
    (D) TV news

Public Announcement (Selection plays twice.)

Do not read the following questions until the audio selection has been completed.

19. This announcement is mostly likely to be heard

    (A) on a school bus.
    (B) in the rail station.
    (C) on a subway train.
    (D) in a bus station.

20. This announcement informs the passengers to

    (A) prepare to get on.
    (B) prepare to get off.
    (C) take turns getting on.
    (D) buy a ticket before getting on.

21. What information is not included in this announcement?

    (A) Take your personal belongs.
    (B) Pay attention to the gaps between the train and the platform.
    (C) Get off through the left door.
    (D) Return to your seats.

Voice Message (Selection plays one time.)

Do not read the following questions until the audio selection has been completed.

22. The speaker plans to attend

    (A) the college application lecture.
    (B) the library meeting.
    (C) the sports game in the gym.
    (D) the lab class.

23. What caused the change of the lecture?

(A) Too many colleges
(B) Too many participants
(C) Bad weather
(D) A conflict in the schedule

24. The lecture will be held

(A) in the library.
(B) in the lab building.
(C) in the gym.
(D) in the middle school.

25. When will the lecture be held?

(A) It didn't mention.
(B) 2 p.m. tomorrow
(C) Very early
(D) 3 p.m. tomorrow

School Conversation (Selection plays one time.)
Do not read the following questions until the audio selection has been completed.

26. The woman hasn't seen the man for a while because

(A) the woman was sick.
(B) the man was sick.
(C) the woman went to the gym.
(D) the man went to the gym.

27. Which of the following is *not* true according to the conversation?

(A) The weather here changes all the time.
(B) The man has been sick for two weeks.
(C) There is a gym the man can go to do exercise.
(D) The man likes sports.

28. The gym does *not* provide the activity of

(A) table tennis.
(B) dancing.
(C) video games.
(D) Tai Ji Quan.

Instructions (Selection plays twice.)
Do not read the following questions until the audio selection has been completed.

29. What is the purpose of this instruction?

(A) To tell how to make kites
(B) To tell how to draw pictures
(C) To tell how to fix a toy
(D) To tell how to make crafts

30. What is the second step in the instruction?

    (A) Tighten the bamboo sticks.
    (B) Draw pictures on the paper.
    (C) Stick the paper onto the bamboo cross.
    (D) Add a tail to the kite.

31. What is *not* mentioned about making a kite?

    (A) Use bamboo sticks.
    (B) Draw colorful pictures.
    (C) Blow the kite.
    (D) Add a tail for balance.

32. Which statement is true according to this instruction?

    (A) Flying kites is not good for elderly people.
    (B) Birds and insects are very popular for the pictures of kites.
    (C) Making kites is very difficult.
    (D) The stronger the wind blows, the better the kites will fly.

Radio Report (Selection plays one time.)
Do not read the following questions until the audio selection has been completed.

33. The main theme is concerns of

    (A) environmental pollution.
    (B) cultural traditions.
    (C) international relationships.
    (D) societal issues.

34. The pollution problems do *not* include

    (A) wasted water.
    (B) wasted gas.
    (C) wasted soil.
    (D) wasted clothing.

35. Which city or region is *not* mentioned in this report?

    (A) Beijing
    (B) Tianjin
    (C) Hong Kong
    (D) The Yangtze River Delta

Section I, Part B: Reading (60 minutes)

Read each passage and then choose the answer choice that best answers each question. You can switch between simplified Chinese and traditional Chinese. You are allowed to mark key words and move back and forth between questions to check or change your answers. There is no time limit for each question, but you will need to finish all the questions within 60 minutes. On the actual test a clock on the computer screen will show how much time remains. For this test, you will need to time yourself.

Read this e-mail:

Simplified Chinese

发件人：林路
收件人：顾文思
邮件主题：中国传统服装
发件时间：4月29日

文思，

你好！你寄来的那些关于中国传统服装的图片都很漂亮，的确比较难选。我的问题是：你参加文化节的表演时希望穿哪一种类型的中国传统服装？

我们常说的旗袍实际上来源于清朝旗人的着装，属于少数民族的服饰，主要特点是立领、斜襟、收腰，所以旗袍看起来非常高雅大方，很显身材。而中国的主要民族是汉族，汉族人的传统服饰叫汉服，又称为汉装、华服，主要特点是交领、右衽，不用扣子而是用绳带系住，所以汉服看起来非常飘逸洒脱、大气灵动。

我们对旗袍并不陌生，而汉服就非常少见了。我觉得你应该试试穿汉服表演。宽袍大袖，在舞台上一定非常好看。

祝玩得开心！

林路

Traditional Chinese

發件人：林路
收件人：顧文思
郵件主題：中國傳統服裝
發件時間：4月29日

文思，

你好！你寄來的那些關於中國傳統服裝的圖片都很漂亮，的確比較難選。我的問題是：你參加文化節的表演時希望穿哪一種類型的中國傳統服裝？

我們常說的旗袍實際上來源於清朝旗人的著裝，屬於少數民族的服飾，主要特點是立領、斜襟、收腰，所以旗袍看起來非常高雅大方，很顯身材。而中國的主要民族是漢族，漢族人的傳統服飾叫漢服，又稱為漢裝、華服，主要特點是交領、右衽，不用扣子而是用繩帶系住，所以漢服看起來非常飄逸灑脫、大氣靈動。

我們對旗袍並不陌生，而漢服就非常少見了。我覺得你應該試試穿漢服表演。寬袍大袖，在舞台上一定非常好看。

祝玩得開心！

林路

1. The purpose of the e-mail message is to

   (A) discuss selecting clothes for a cultural festival performance.
   (B) discuss selecting one kind of Qipao for a cultural festival performance.
   (C) discuss selecting one kind of Hhanfu for a cultural festival performance.
   (D) ask for suggestions about a cultural festival performance.

2. Which one of the following statements correctly describes Qipao?

   (A) Qipao is the traditional clothing of the Han majority.
   (B) Qipao was originally from minorities.
   (C) Qipao is as big as a robe.
   (D) Qipao is rarely seen nowadays.

3. Which one of the following statements correctly describes Hanfu?

  (A) Hanfu is very popular in China today.
  (B) Hanfu fits the body smoothly.
  (C) Hanfu was originally from minorities.
  (D) Hanfu uses ropes instead of buttons to tighten up.

4. What does the writer recommend according to the e-mail message?

  (A) Qipao
  (B) Hanfu
  (C) Neither of them
  (D) It didn't mention.

Read this letter:

Simplified Chinese
发信人：林建
收信人：彭丽姗
丽姗同学，
你好。能被选上去昆明参加中文夏令营，我觉得你也太幸运了！你上次去北京登过长城，游过故宫和颐和园，看过西安的兵马俑。我建议你还可以在北京看看鸟巢和水立方，那是当年中国举办奥林匹克运动会的地方。既然你从前去过四川熊猫保护基地和九寨沟，这次就选湖南的张家界吧，听说电影《Avatar》就是在那儿取的景，那儿和安徽的黄山一样美。
这个季节在中国旅游特别好。我最喜欢广西桂林了。如果能抽出一两天去桂林漓江泛舟，你就明白为什么人们说"桂林山水甲天下"了！
祝一路平安。
你的同学林建

Traditional Chinese
發信人：林建
收信人：彭麗姍
麗姍同學，
你好。能被選上去昆明參加中文夏令營，我覺得你也太幸運了！你上次去北京登過長城，游過故宮和頤和園，看過西安的兵馬俑。我建議你還可以在北京看看鳥巢和水立方，那是當年中國舉辦奧林匹克運動會的地方。既然你從前去過四川熊貓保護基地和九寨溝，這次就選湖南的張家界吧，聽說電影《Avatar》就是在那兒取的景，那兒和安徽的黃山一樣美。
這個季節在中國旅遊特別好。我最喜歡廣西桂林了。如果能抽出一兩天去桂林灘江泛舟，你就明白為甚麼人們說"桂林山水甲天下"了！
祝一路平安。
你的同學林建

5. The writer and recipient of the e-mail are

  (A) coworkers.
  (B) teachers.
  (C) a teacher and a student.
  (D) high school students.

6. To which city or province hasn't the recipient of the letter traveled before?

(A) Beijing
(B) Xi'an
(C) Hunan
(D) Sichuan

7. The writer's favorite site to visit is

(A) the Great Wall.
(B) the panda reservation.
(C) Huang Mountain in Anhui.
(D) the Guilin Lijiang River.

Read this sign:

Simplified Chinese
请遵守小区的文明秩序，爱护区内环境和公共设施。

Traditional Chinese
請遵守小區的文明秩序，愛護區內環境和公共設施。

8. The purpose of the sign is to

(A) post the penalty for using a facility.
(B) remind people to protect the environment.
(C) stop people from using a facility.
(D) provide instructions for access.

9. The sign's message is directed most likely to

(A) residents and visitors of the complex or community.
(B) residents and visitors of a house.
(C) pedestrians in a museum.
(D) pedestrians in a public park.

Read this coupon:

Simplified Chinese
三只耳火锅 优惠券使用须知
一、优惠券有效期：2014年03月20日－05月31日。
二、本券可无限量购买，可累计使用，全场菜品可通兑（酒水除外）。
三、请提前1天致电预约，直接到店消费（结账时出示本券）。
四、使用本券时不再享受店内其他优惠，不积分、不打折、不兑现、不找零、不开票、不外卖。
五、宴席、会议包席不在本券使用范围内。
六、本券加盖本店印章生效，本店拥有最终解释权。

Traditional Chinese

三隻耳火鍋　優惠券使用須知

一、優惠券有效期：２０１４年０３月２０日－０５月３１日。

二、本券可無限量購買，可累計使用，全場菜品可通兌（酒水除外）。

三、請提前１天致電預約，直接到店消費（結賬時出示本券）。

四、使用本券時不再享受店內其他優惠，不積分、不打折、不兌現、不找零、不開票、不外賣。

五、宴席、會議包席不在本券使用範圍內。

六、本券加蓋本店印章生效，本店擁有最終解釋權。

10. The coupon is mostly likely given to the customers who want to

    (A) eat in a restaurant.
    (B) shop for clothes.
    (C) place orders online.
    (D) buy groceries.

11. What restriction does the coupon have?

    (A) It's only available for drinks.
    (B) It's only available during a specific period.
    (C) It can only be used once.
    (D) It's only available for delivery service.

12. What benefit is included when using this coupon?

    (A) A receipt is provided.
    (B) It can be exchanged for cash.
    (C) The usage is cumulative.
    (D) No appointment is needed.

13. According to the coupon, which statement is *not* true?

    (A) The coupon has an expiration date.
    (B) The coupon could be used for a banquet.
    (C) The coupon cannot be used with other coupons together.
    (D) The coupon is not valid without the seal of the restaurant.

Read this advertisement:

Simplified Chinese

游泳中心招聘

暑期接待人员数名

要求喜欢孩子，有责任心和亲和力。

年龄：18－35岁，男女不限，待遇面议。

咨询热线：8477－5368 （李教练）

地址：市体育馆游泳中心

Traditional Chinese
游泳中心招聘
暑期接待人員數名
要求喜歡孩子，有責任心和親和力。
年齡：１８－３５歲，男女不限，待遇面議。
咨詢熱線：８４７７－５３６８（李教練）
地址：市體育館游泳中心

14. The advertisement was placed by

(A) a shopping center.
(B) a new store.
(C) a school.
(D) a gym.

15. The purpose of the advertisement is to recruit

(A) lifeguards for the summer.
(B) coaches for the summer.
(C) temporary workers for the summer.
(D) children learning how to swim for the summer.

16. According to the advertisement, which quality is mandatory?

(A) Love children
(B) Male
(C) Female
(D) Experienced

17. Which of the following information is *not* mentioned in this advertisement?

(A) Salary
(B) Working hours
(C) Contact information
(D) Job location

Read this poster:

Simplified Chinese
车保姆
上门洗车、汽车美容、汽车玻璃修复、凹陷修复

Traditional Chinese
車保姆
上門洗車、汽車美容、汽車玻璃修復、凹陷修復

18. The purpose of the poster is to promote

(A) a beauty salon business.
(B) a child care center.
(C) a car care business.
(D) a nanny agency.

19. The poster's message is directed most likely to

    (A) car owners.
    (B) someone seeking beauty service.
    (C) someone needing child care.
    (D) the patients.

Read this flyer:

Simplified Chinese
康尼电器城十年店庆
节能冰箱 酷暑夏日大酬宾
购买金额4000元以上，送杰西运动套装和迷你微波炉
旧冰箱换节能家电，享受500元置换补贴

Traditional Chinese
康尼電器城十年店慶
節能冰箱　酷暑夏日大酬賓
購買金額４０００元以上，送傑西運動套裝和迷你微波爐
舊冰箱換節能家電，享受５００元置換補貼

20. The purpose of this flyer is to

    (A) promote sales of sports clothes.
    (B) promote sales of an electronic appliance.
    (C) promote sales of a refrigerator.
    (D) promote sales of a microwave oven.

21. What is the requirement to get the free sports clothes?

    (A) The purchase has to be above 500 yuan.
    (B) The purchase has to be above 4,000 yuan.
    (C) The customer has to provide the old refrigerator.
    (D) The customer has to purchase the mini microwave oven.

22. The promotion is sponsored by

    (A) a supermarket.
    (B) a department store.
    (C) a clothing store.
    (D) an electronic appliance store.

Read these instructions:

Simplified Chinese
仿真模型玩具
产品型号：立体拼图
产品规格：230*370*3 mm （3大片装）
配件：磨砂纸一小张，眼镜一对
适合人群：6岁及以上
使用方法：按图拼装，无需电池
保养维护：阴凉处放置，防水防热
警告：本玩具内含细小零件，谨防吞食，应由成人陪同使用

Traditional Chinese
仿真模型玩具
產品型號： 立體拼圖
產品規格： ２３０＊３７０＊３ｍｍ （３大片裝）
配件：磨砂紙一小張，眼鏡一對
適合人群：６歲及以上
使用方法：按圖拼裝，無需電池
保養維護：陰涼處放置，防水防熱
警告：本玩具內含細小零件，謹防吞食，應由成人陪同使用

23. The instructions are primarily

   (A) to introduce the use of a toy.
   (B) to provide application information.
   (C) to teach how to draw.
   (D) for children under 6 years old.

24. According to the instruction, where is the best place to store the product?

   (A) In water
   (B) In a cool and dry place
   (C) In the kitchen
   (D) In a hot and wet place

25. Which statement is true according to the information provided?

   (A) No assembly is needed for the product.
   (B) The product is for adults.
   (C) The product requires a battery.
   (D) Children above 6 years old are allowed to use it.

Read this article:

Simplified Chinese
中国古代四大发明包括指南针、造纸、印刷术和火药。这些发明推动了人类社会的发展，为世界文明做出了突出的贡献。
指南针是一种指示方向的仪器，主要组成部分为一根可以转动的磁针。它的前身叫司南，很早就被广泛应用于航海和野外探险。指南针后被改制成罗盘，明代郑和下西洋时就使用过罗盘。火药则是中国古代的炼丹师们无意中发明的，根据古代医药学家孙思邈的记载，其最早的配方是硫磺、硝石和皂角。
除了指南针，中国还是世界上最早发明纸的国家。起初，纸的造价特别昂贵，不过自从东汉蔡伦改进了造纸术，成本大大降低，纸的应用也终于得到了推广，人们开始进行大规模的商业制造。没有印刷术之前，人们所看的书籍都是被一本一本抄出来的。后来慢慢出现了拓印和雕版技术用于印刷。宋代毕升发明了活字印刷术。活字印刷为文化和知识的传承提供了高效的途径，人类文明的进程又有了一次大飞跃。
有趣的是，世界上现在还出现了中国五大发明的说法，第五个影响力巨大的发明是算盘。

Traditional Chinese

中國古代四大發明包括指南針、造紙、印刷術和火藥。這些發明推動了人類社會的發展，為世界文明做出了突出的貢獻。

指南針是一種指示方向的儀器，主要組成部分為一根可以轉動的磁針。它的前身叫司南，很早就被廣泛應用於航海和野外探險。指南針後被改製成羅盤，明代鄭和下西洋時就使用過羅盤。火藥則是中國古代的煉丹師們無意中發明的，根據古代醫藥學家孫思邈的記載，其最早的配方是硫磺、硝石和皂角。

除了指南針，中國還是世界上最早發明紙的國家。起初，紙的造價特別昂貴，不過自從東漢蔡倫改進了造紙術，成本大大降低，紙的應用也終於得到了推廣，人們開始進行大規模的商業製造。沒有印刷術之前，人們所看的書籍都是被一本一本抄出來的。後來慢慢出現了拓印和雕版技術用於印刷。宋代畢昇發明了活字印刷術。活字印刷為文化和知識的傳承提供了高效的途徑，人類文明的進程又有了一次大飛躍。

有趣的是，世界上現在還出現了中國五大發明的說法，第五個影響力巨大的發明是算盤。

26. Which of the following is *not* included in the four inventions from ancient China?

   (A) Compass
   (B) Printing
   (C) Gunpowder
   (D) Ship

27. Which one of the following inventions was used in navigation by sea according to the article?

   (A) Compass
   (B) Paper
   (C) Gunpowder
   (D) Printing

28. According to the article, gunpowder was invented by

   (A) a doctor.
   (B) alchemists.
   (C) an emperor.
   (D) travelers.

29. What of the following statements is true according to the article?

   (A) Cai Lun invented paper.
   (B) Paper has been a very cheap product since it was invented.
   (C) The fifth famous invention from China is an abacus.
   (D) Bi Sheng invented the compass.

Read this short story:

Simplified Chinese

今天我们要讲的是大禹治水的故事。传说在五千年前，不知道什么原因，中国的黄河经常改道，引起了特别严重的洪水灾难。中国的皇帝非常着急，为了让人们能过上安定的生活，就派大禹去治理洪水。大禹很聪明，从他父亲的治水经验中发现建筑堤坝堵水不是一个好方法，他就带领大家挖渠排水，把洪水引到大海中去。

大禹一心治水，一治就是十三年。在这十三年中，大禹有三次路过了自己的家。第一次路过时，他的妻子刚刚生下儿子。听着儿子的哭声，他怕延误治水，没有进去。过了七年，大禹再次经过家门。远远地看到家门口自己的儿子高高兴兴地和小伙伴玩，他放心地走了。到第三次时，大禹的儿子已经长到十多岁了。那天下起了大雨，他到自己家的屋檐下避雨，听到屋里妻子对儿子说："你爹爹是一个了不起的人，他治好了洪水就会回家和我们团圆。"大禹非常感动，立刻又转身上路了。

大禹终于治好了洪水，让大家重新过上了幸福的生活。他"三过家门而不入"的故事也被传颂至今。

Traditional Chinese

今天我們要講的是大禹治水的故事。傳說在五千年前，不知道甚麼原因，中國的黃河經常改道，引起了特別嚴重的洪水災難。中國的皇帝非常著急，為了讓人們能過上安定的生活，就派大禹去治理洪水。大禹很聰明，從他父親的治水經驗中發現建築堤壩堵水不是一個好方法，他就帶領大家挖渠排水，把洪水引到大海中去。

大禹一心治水，一治就是十三年。在這十三年中，大禹有三次路過了自己的家。第一次路過時，他的妻子剛剛生下兒子。聽著兒子的哭聲，他怕延誤治水，沒有進去。過了七年，大禹再次經過家門。遠遠地看到家門口自己的兒子高高興興地和小夥伴玩，他放心地走了。到第三次時，大禹的兒子已經長到十多歲了。那天下起了大雨，他到自己家的屋檐下避雨，聽到屋裡妻子對兒子說："你爹爹是一個了不起的人，他治好了洪水就會回家和我們團圓。"大禹非常感動，立刻又轉身上路了。

大禹終於治好了洪水，讓大家重新過上了幸福的生活。他"三過家門而不入"的故事也被傳頌至今。

30. The story begins with a description of the

    (A)   flood of the Yellow River.
    (B)   emperor in China.
    (C)   hero named Da Yu.
    (D)   father of Da Yu.

31. What statement correctly describes the hero?

    (A)   He was a prince in China.
    (B)   He caused the flood.
    (C)   He never got married.
    (D)   He was a very smart man.

32. What method was used to stop flooding before Da Yu?

    (A)   Dig lakes to store water
    (B)   Build dams to block water
    (C)   Add rivers to the water
    (D)   It was not mentioned.

33. When Da Yu was dealing with the flood, what did he do when he passed his home?

(A) He took his wife with him.
(B) He didn't enter his own home.
(C) He took his son with him.
(D) He stayed three days with his family.

34. When was the second time Da Yu passed his home?

(A) When he got married
(B) When his father died
(C) When his son was around seven years old
(D) When his son was a teenager

35. What did Da Yu feel the third time he passed his home?

(A) He didn't have time.
(B) He was sad that his mother was not at home.
(C) He was happy that his family didn't need him.
(D) He was impressed that his family felt proud about him.

STOP. END OF SECTION I

Section II: Free-Response Questions

Section II, Part A: Writing

Story Narration

You will have 15 minutes to finish the task of story narration. On the real test there will be a clock on your screen telling you how much time is left. For this practice test, you will need to time yourself.

Based on the four pictures provided, you need to write a coherent story with a beginning, a middle, and an ending. On the test you will need to type your answer using either the preset input of Microsoft IME or Microsoft New Phonetic IME system to type Chinese characters. You can switch between simplified Chinese and traditional Chinese.

The following four pictures present a story. Imagine you are telling the story to a friend. Write a complete story as suggested by the pictures. Give your story a beginning, a middle, and an end.

E-mail Response

You will have 15 minutes to read an e-mail message from a specific person and type a response. On the real test there will be a clock on your screen in the real exam telling you how much time is left. For this practice test, you will need to time yourself.

On the test you will need to type your response using the preset input of Microsoft IME or Microsoft New Phonetic IME system to type Chinese characters. You can switch between simplified Chinese and traditional Chinese.

Read this e-mail from a friend and then type a response.

Simplified Chinese

发件人：刘静

邮件主题：大学专业

赵芸，

你好！最近申请大学的事儿让我有些心烦。我拿到了"汉语桥"的奖学金，想去中国继续学中文。可是我的父母坚决让我在美国报考商科。我知道他们所做的一切都是在为我的将来考虑，可我又不愿意放弃中文。你觉得应该怎么解决这个问题？还有，你认为大学选择专业应该注意哪些方面？非常感谢！

Traditional Chinese

發件人：劉靜

郵件主題：大學專業

趙芸，

你好！最近申請大學的事兒讓我有些心煩。我拿到了"漢語橋"的獎學金，想去中國繼續學中文。可是我的父母堅決讓我在美國報考商科。我知道他們所做的一切都是在為我的將來考慮，可我又不願意放棄中文。你覺得應該怎麼解決這個問題？還有，你認為大學選擇專業應該注意哪些方面？非常感謝！

Section II, Part B: Speaking

Conversation

In this part of the exam, you will participate in a simulated conversation by responding to questions you will hear. The questions are based on a particular topic in a conversation with a particular person. There will be six 20-second pauses in the conversation during which you need to speak a response to the question(s) you've been asked. On the actual test, your 20-second response will be recorded and graded later.

You will have a conversation with Chen Ming, a friend from China, about your school life in the United States.

The listening track for conversation is provided on the disc accompanying this book. After you are done with the test, you may refer to the written script for the questions, which can be found starting on page 251. On the actual test, no script is provided for the conversation.

Cultural Presentation

In this part of the exam, you will make a presentation on a cultural topic you are given. You will have four minutes to prepare and then two minutes to make your oral presentation. On the actual test, your two-minute presentation will be recorded and then graded later. There will be a clock on your computer screen telling you how much time is left on the real test. For this practice test, you will need to time yourself.

Choose one current social or family issue (e.g., one-child policy, aging problem, "little emperor") in China. In your presentation, describe the issue in detail and explain its significance.

STOP. END OF PRACTICE TEST 1

Scripts for the Audio Portions of the Test

Script for Section I, Part A: Listening Rejoinders

Question #1

Simplified Chinese
Woman: 我后天接你去看电影，你说好不好？
Man:

    (A) 什么？谁带你去看电影？
    (B) 对不起，我后天想看电视。
    (C) 什么时候看的？你怎么不早点告诉我呢？
    (D) 好啊，我们一起去看电视吧。

Traditional Chinese
Woman: 我後天接你去看電影，你説好不好？
Man:

    (A) 甚麼？誰帶你去看電影？
    (B) 對不起，我後天想看電視。
    (C) 甚麼時候看的？你怎麼不早點告訴我呢？
    (D) 好啊，我們一起去看電視吧。

Question #2

Simplified Chinese
Woman: 听说你上个星期六去参观天坛了，感觉怎么样？
Man: 没什么好看的，不像别人说的那么好玩。
Woman:

    (A) 真的那么好玩吗？
    (B) 长城难道不好玩吗？
    (C) 真的没什么好看的吗？
    (D) 是啊，我也觉得很好玩。

Traditional Chinese
Woman: 聽説你上個星期六去參觀天壇了，感覺怎麼樣？
Man: 沒甚麼好看的，不像別人説的那麼好玩。
Woman:

    (A) 真的那麼好玩嗎？
    (B) 長城難道不好玩嗎？
    (C) 真的沒甚麼好看的嗎？
    (D) 是啊，我也覺得很好玩。

Question #3

Simplified Chinese
Woman: 我父母希望我上完大学就工作，可是我想读研究生。
Man:

    (A) 你要劝他们同意才行。
    (B) 恭喜你考上了研究生。
    (C) 你父母希望你读什么专业？
    (D) 你打算找什么样的工作？

Traditional Chinese
Woman: 我父母希望我上完大學就工作，可是我想讀研究生。
Man:

    (A) 你要勸他們同意才行。
    (B) 恭喜你考上了研究生。
    (C) 你父母希望你讀甚麼專業？
    (D) 你打算找甚麼樣的工作？

Question #4

Simplified Chinese
Man: 今天上课时坐在你前面的那个女孩是谁啊？好像没见过。
Woman: 她是我们的新同学曾宁，就住在我们那条街上。我们放学以后和她一起回家吧。
Man:

    (A) 原来曾宁是我们的新老师啊。
    (B) 她下午会到我家来。
    (C) 放学以后你应该早点回家。
    (D) 等我们放学以后再说吧。

Traditional Chinese
Man: 今天上課時坐在你前面的那個女孩是誰啊？好像沒見過。
Woman: 她是我們的新同學曾寧，就住在我們那條街上。我們放學以後和她一起回家吧。
Man:

    (A) 原來曾寧是我們的新老師啊。
    (B) 她下午會到我家來。
    (C) 放學以後你應該早點回家。
    (D) 等我們放學以後再說吧。

Question #5

Simplified Chinese
Man: 我差点忘了，这药是一天三次，每次两片，饭前服用。
Woman:

(A) 你这人也真是，快点吃药，服完药再吃饭。
(B) 你忘了买药，怎么办呢？
(C) 你连吃饭都忘了？
(D) 你吃完饭再去看医生不是更方便吗？

Traditional Chinese
Man: 我差點忘了，這藥是一天三次，每次兩片，飯前服用。
Woman:

(A) 你這人也真是，快點吃藥，服完藥再吃飯。
(B) 你忘了買藥，怎麼辦呢？
(C) 你連吃飯都忘了？
(D) 你吃完飯再去看醫生不是更方便嗎？

Question #6

Simplified Chinese
Woman: 张志，你觉得我们明天的球赛能赢吗？
Man: 这个啊，我也说不好。我觉得对方球队还是挺棒的。你认为呢？
Woman:

(A) 我和你的看法差不多，我们肯定不会赢。
(B) 是啊，我们球队很棒，一定能赢。
(C) 我也认为这就要看谁的运气好了。
(D) 我在哪儿都喜欢看球赛。

Traditional Chinese
Woman: 張志，你覺得我們明天的球賽能贏嗎？
Man: 這個啊，我也說不好。我覺得對方球隊還是挺棒的。你認為呢？
Woman:

(A) 我和你的看法差不多，我們肯定不會贏。
(B) 是啊，我們球隊很棒，一定能贏。
(C) 我也認為這就要看誰的運氣好了。
(D) 我在哪兒都喜歡看球賽。

Question #7

Simplified Chinese
Man: 今天晚上我请客，我和你开车去中国城吃大餐！
Woman:

(A) 明天晚上你可以请我吃饭吗？
(B) 怎么又要我请你呢？
(C) 中国城那么远，我宁愿在家吃。
(D) 我也去过中国城。

Traditional Chinese
Man: 今天晚上我請客，我和你開車去中國城吃大餐！
Woman:

(A) 明天晚上你可以請我吃飯嗎？
(B) 怎麼又要我請你呢？
(C) 中國城那麼遠，我寧願在家吃。
(D) 我也去過中國城。

Question #8

Simplified Chinese
Woman: 学习中文其实很简单，只要每天和别人说中文就可以了。
Man: 那可不见得，还要会看会写的。
Woman:

(A) 为什么看不见呢？
(B) 你说得不错，光说不看是不行。
(C) 你到底在看什么呢？
(D) 我简直不敢相信自己的眼睛！

Traditional Chinese
Woman: 學習中文其實很簡單，只要每天和別人説中文就可以了。
Man: 那可不見得，還要會看會寫的。
Woman:

(A) 為甚麼看不見呢？
(B) 你説得不錯，光説不看是不行。
(C) 你到底在看甚麼呢？
(D) 我簡直不敢相信自己的眼睛！

Question #9

Simplified Chinese
Woman: 天气预报明明说今天温度特别低的啊，害得我穿了这么多衣服。
Man:

(A) 每天听天气预报挺好的。
(B) 你的衣服很好看，在哪儿买的?
(C) 今天是太冷了。
(D) 天气预报你也能相信?

Traditional Chinese
Woman: 天氣預報明明説今天溫度特別低的啊，害得我穿了這麼多衣服。
Man:

(A) 每天聽天氣預報挺好的。
(B) 你的衣服很好看，在哪兒買的？
(C) 今天是太冷了。
(D) 天氣預報你也能相信？

Question #10

Simplified Chinese
Man: 你是从哪个城市来的？
Woman: 我是从洛杉矶来的。你在那儿呆过吗？
Man:

(A) 真可惜，你不喜欢洛杉矶。
(B) 不会吧？你连洛杉矶在哪都不知道啊？
(C) 老实说，我就是那儿出生的啊。
(D) 你可不要跟我去洛杉矶那个地方。

Traditional Chinese
Man: 你是從哪個城市來的？
Woman: 我是從洛杉磯來的。你在那兒呆過嗎？
Man:

(A) 真可惜，你不喜歡洛杉磯。
(B) 不會吧？你連洛杉磯在哪都不知道啊？
(C) 老實說，我就是那兒出生的啊。
(D) 你可不要跟我去洛杉磯那個地方。

Question #11

Simplified Chinese
Woman: 我妈要我周末去上数学班，我一听就头疼：我哪有时间啊。
Man: 怎么没有时间？你少玩一点游戏就行了。
Woman:

(A) 你也不喜欢上数学班吗？
(B) 我也没怎么玩啊。
(C) 好吧，我们一起玩游戏吧。
(D) 周末上数学班时可以玩游戏。

Traditional Chinese
Woman: 我媽要我週末去上數學班，我一聽就頭疼：我哪有時間啊。
Man: 怎麼沒有時間？你少玩一點遊戲就行了。
Woman:

(A) 你也不喜歡上數學班嗎？
(B) 我也沒怎麼玩啊。
(C) 好吧，我們一起玩遊戲吧。
(D) 週末上數學班時可以玩遊戲。

Question #12

Simplified Chinese
Man: 这次的聚餐居然会在办公室举行，怎么可能？
Woman: 是不是真的你自己看着办，又不是第一次在那儿聚餐。
Man:

   (A) 哦，那我还是去吧。
   (B) 那我们等会儿餐馆见！
   (C) 是啊，办公室太小了。
   (D) 为什么要看着办公室呢？

Traditional Chinese
Man: 這次的聚餐居然會在辦公室舉行，怎麼可能？
Woman: 是不是真的你自己看著辦，又不是第一次在那兒聚餐。
Man:

   (A) 哦，那我還是去吧。
   (B) 那我們等會兒餐館見！
   (C) 是啊，辦公室太小了。
   (D) 為什麼要看著辦公室呢？

Question #13

Simplified Chinese
Man: 陈明，你打球打了这么长时间，累坏了吧？要不要先休息一下？
Woman:

   (A) 我喜欢先休息再打球，所以现在要打球了。
   (B) 因为打球打了这么长时间，所以我不累。
   (C) 我只是坐在那儿看人家打，所以并不累，我们先吃饭吧。
   (D) 我下次打球一定叫上你。

Traditional Chinese
Man: 陳明，你打球打了這麼長時間，累壞了吧？要不要先休息一下？
Woman:

   (A) 我喜歡先休息再打球，所以現在要打球了。
   (B) 因為打球打了這麼長時間，所以我不累。
   (C) 我只是坐在那兒看人家打，所以並不累，我們先吃飯吧。
   (D) 我下次打球一定叫上你。

Question #14

Simplified Chinese
Woman: 实在不好意思，没什么好菜，将就着吃吧。
Man:

   (A) 别着急，菜马上就好了。
   (B) 真可惜，招待不周。
   (C) 对不起，我也不知道做菜。
   (D) 你也太客气了，我都吃了三大碗！

Traditional Chinese

Woman: 實在不好意思，沒甚麼好菜，將就著吃吧。

Man:

(A) 別著急，菜馬上就好了。

(B) 真可惜，招待不周。

(C) 對不起，我也不知道做菜。

(D) 你也太客氣了，我都吃了三大碗!

Question #15

Simplified Chinese

Woman: 听说这次考试成绩出来了，你考得怎么样?

Man: 我终于可以痛痛快快地睡觉，开开心心地玩了。

Woman:

(A) 看来你还考得挺不错的。

(B) 考完就想睡觉啊?

(C) 考得不好不要紧，下次努力就行了。

(D) 原来你在睡觉，没去考试啊。

Traditional Chinese

Woman: 聽說這次考試成績出來了，你考得怎麼樣?

Man: 我終於可以痛痛快快地睡覺，開開心心地玩了。

Woman:

(A) 看來你還考得挺不錯的。

(B) 考完就想睡覺啊?

(C) 考得不好不要緊，下次努力就行了。

(D) 原來你在睡覺，沒去考試啊。

Script for Section I, Part A: Listening Selections

Commercial

Track 21

Narrator: Now you will listen to a commercial. This selection will be played twice.

Simplified Chinese

Man: 为答谢新老观众，滨城卫视国庆特播：黄金时段好剧连连，综艺节目应有尽有。应广大用户要求，自9月27日起，电视剧《还珠格格》晚十点后第三次重播，每晚四集；欧美获奖电影十二部均在上午播出，天天送您惊喜；电视购物新奇不断，展现生活新概念。愿您与滨城卫视共同度过难忘的国庆假期。

Traditional Chinese

Man: 為答謝新老觀眾，濱城衛視國慶特播：黃金時段好劇連連，綜藝節目應有盡有。應廣大用戶要求，自9月27日起，電視劇《還珠格格》晚十點後第三次重播，每晚四集；歐美獲獎電影十二部均在上午播出，天天送您驚喜；電視購物新奇不斷，展現生活新概念。願您與濱城衛視共同度過難忘的國慶假期。

Narrator: Now listen again.

[Repeat]

Narrator: Now answer the questions for this selection.

Public Announcement
Narrator: Now you will listen to a public announcement. This selection will be played twice.

Simplified Chinese
各位乘客，欢迎乘坐深圳地铁。列车运行前方到站是会展中心，换乘龙华线的乘客请在此下车。请提前做好准备，带好您的随身物品从左边车门下车，下车时请注意列车与站台之间的空隙。

Traditional Chinese
各位乘客，歡迎乘坐深圳地鐵。列車運行前方到站是會展中心，換乘龍華線的乘客請在此下車。請提前做好準備，帶好您的隨身物品從左邊車門下車，下車時請注意列車與站台之間的空隙。

Narrator: Now listen again.
[Repeat]
Narrator: Now answer the questions for this selection.

Voice Message
Narrator: Now you will listen to a voice message. This selection will be played only once.

Simplified Chinese
Woman: 张飞，我是孔明。明天下午的"大学申请须知"讲座，因为参加的人很多，今年的地点不再是图书馆，而是改成了初中部的体育馆。时间是下午三点，不过我们得早点去占好座位。有好几所著名的大学都派了代表过来，这个机会很难得，你可千万不要错过。我和李兰约好了两点钟在实验楼一楼门口见面，你能按时到吗？早点回电话。

Traditional Chinese
Woman: 張飛，我是孔明。明天下午的"大學申請須知"講座，因為參加的人很多，今年的地點不再是圖書館，而是改成了初中部的體育館。時間是下午三點，不過我們得早點去佔好座位。有好幾所著名的大學都派了代表過來，這個機會很難得，你可千萬不要錯過。我和李蘭約好了兩點鐘在實驗樓一樓門口見面，你能按時到嗎？早點回電話。

Narrator: Now answer the questions for this selection.

School Conversation
Narrator: Now you will listen to a conversation between two students. This selection will be played only once.

Simplified Chinese
Woman: 很长时间没见到你了，忙什么呢？
Man: 别提了，我感冒快两个星期了，又打针又吃药的，一直没有好。这儿的天气忽冷忽热的，早晚温差二十多度，刮起风来就更冷了。
Woman: 你好像经常感冒似的，应该多运动多锻炼，身体健康才不容易得病。
Man: 什么呀，天天下雨，哪有地方锻炼。
Woman: 那倒不一定，你住的地方附近就有一个二十四小时健身馆，可以打乒乓球和室内网球，听说晚上还有舞蹈班和太极拳学习班呢。
Man: 那些运动我都不喜欢。
Woman: 那就找你喜欢的。你喜欢什么？
Man: 我喜欢玩电子游戏。
Woman: 你这病啊，恐怕没得治了。

Traditional Chinese

Woman: 很長時間沒見到你了，忙甚麼呢？

Man: 別提了，我感冒快兩個星期了，又打針又吃藥的，一直沒有好。這兒的天氣忽冷忽熱的，早晚溫差二十多度，刮起風來就更冷了。

Woman: 你好像經常感冒似的，應該多運動多鍛鍊，身體健康才不容易得病。

Man: 甚麼呀，天天下雨，哪有地方鍛鍊。

Woman: 那倒不一定，你住的地方附近就有一個二十四小時健身館，可以打乒乓球和室內網球，聽說晚上還有舞蹈班和太極拳學習班呢。

Man: 那些運動我都不喜歡。

Woman: 那就找你喜歡的。你喜歡甚麼？

Man: 我喜歡玩電子遊戲。

Woman: 你這病啊，恐怕沒得治了。

Narrator: Now answer the questions for this selection.

Instructions

Narrator: Now you will listen to someone giving instructions. This selection will be played twice.

Simplified Chinese

Woman: 放风筝是一种中国传统的休闲活动，老少皆宜，深受人们的喜爱。那些漂亮精致的风筝到底是怎么做的呢？其实，它的制作工艺相当简单：首先用细细的竹签做一个十字架，绑好。然后就是在纸上画图案了。作为中国古老的民间艺术，风筝的图案大多是颜色鲜艳的鸟类和昆虫，不过你也可以根据自己的喜好，画什么都可以。接下来把画好的图案贴在十字架上，最好几个角都要固定好，以免风太大给吹跑了。最后一步是在十字架上绑风筝线。绑的时候要注意平衡，不能一边重一边轻。还有啊，最好记得贴条尾巴，这样就可以防止风筝打转了。

Traditional Chinese

Woman: 放風箏是一種中國傳統的休閒活動，老少皆宜，深受人們的喜愛。那些漂亮精緻的風箏到底是怎麼做的呢？其實，它的製作工藝相當簡單：首先用細細的竹籤做一個十字架，綁好。然後就是在紙上畫圖案了。作為中國古老的民間藝術，風箏的圖案大多是顏色鮮艷的鳥類和昆蟲，不過你也可以根據自己的喜好，畫甚麼都可以。接下來把畫好的圖案貼在十字架上，最好幾個角都要固定好，以免風太大給吹跑了。最後一步是在十字架上綁風箏線。綁的時候要注意平衡，不能一邊重一邊輕。還有啊，最好記得貼條尾巴，這樣就可以防止風箏打轉了。

Narrator: Now listen again.

[Repeat]

Narrator: Now answer the questions for this selection.

Radio Report

Narrator: Now you will listen to a radio report. This selection will be played twice.

Simplified Chinese

Man: 中国近几十年来经济的高速发展导致了中国的环境遭受了严重破坏，废水、废气、废土等污染问题正威胁着人民的生活和健康。据中国环境保护部24日的通报，以中国国务院发布的《大气污染防治计划》为指导，中国将在长江三角洲、珠江三角洲、北京、天津及周边地区等重点地区启动大气污染防治专项检查，采取各项措施控制和改善中国的空气污染状况。此次检查特别设立了有奖举报制度，鼓励民众举报各种违反环境法律法规的行为。

Traditional Chinese

Man: 中國近幾十年來經濟的高速發展導致了中國的環境遭受了嚴重破壞，廢水、廢氣、廢土等污染問題正威脅著人民的生活和健康。據中國環境保護部24日的通報，以中國國務院發佈的《大氣污染防治計劃》為指導，中國將在長江三角洲、珠江三角洲、北京、天津及周邊地區等重點地區啟動大氣污染防治專項檢查，採取各項措施控制和改善中國的空氣污染狀況。此次檢查特別設立了有獎舉報制度，鼓勵民眾舉報各種違反環境法律法規的行為。

Narrator: Now listen again.

[Repeat]

Narrator: Now answer the questions for this selection.

Track 22

Script for Section II, Part B: Conversation

Narrator: You will have a conversation with Feng Qing, a reporter from a newspaper, who is interviewing high school students about their Chinese cultural experience.

Simplified Chinese

1. 你们学校有中文俱乐部吗？如果想加入应该怎么申请？
2. 对于中文俱乐部的活动，你有什么建议？
3. 参加了中文俱乐部以后，你对中国文化有什么新的认识或了解？
4. 如果去你的中国同学家做客，你觉得要注意哪些问题？
5. 有人说虽然中国菜很好吃，但中国人的饮食习惯并不健康。请谈一谈你的看法。
6. 你希望了解哪些中国文化方面的知识？为什么？

Traditional Chinese

1. 你們學校有中文俱樂部嗎？如果想加入應該怎麼申請？
2. 對於中文俱樂部的活動，你有甚麼建議？
3. 參加了中文俱樂部以後，你對中國文化有甚麼新的認識或瞭解？
4. 如果去你的中國同學家做客，你覺得要注意哪些問題？
5. 有人說雖然中國菜很好吃，但中國人的飲食習慣並不健康。請談一談你的看法。
6. 你希望瞭解哪些中國文化方面的知識？為甚麼？

Answers and Explanations for Section I

Here are the correct answers with complete explanations. Check your answers on the practice test. Look at the explanations not only for the ones you missed but also all those that you were unsure about and could have missed.

Answers and Explanations for the Listening Rejoinders

Answers

1. B	**6.** C	**11.** B
2. C	**7.** C	**12.** A
3. A	**8.** B	**13.** C
4. D	**9.** D	**14.** D
5. A	**10.** C	**15.** A

Explanations

Look back at "Strategies for the Listening Rejoinders" in Chapter 5. Did you remember all the strategies and use them effectively?

1. (B) The woman is willing to pick up the man for a movie and asks his opinion, and the man says that he would like to watch TV. Choices (A) and (C) do not continue the logic. Choice (D) gives the man's opinion but doesn't answer the question, which should be related to the movie.

2. (C) The woman asks for the man's experience about traveling to the Temple of Heaven. The man answers that "nothing attractive, not as much fun as stated by others." Choice (B) is not related to the Temple of Heaven. Choices (A) and (D) don't logically continue the dialogue.

3. (A) The woman mentions that her parents want her to work while she herself wants to enroll in a graduate program. Choice (B) "Congratulates on attending graduate school!" (C) "What is the major your parents prefer?" and (D) "What kind of job you are seeking for?" do not continue the conversation logically.

4. (D) The man asks for one girl's name, and the woman explains that the girl lives on the same street as theirs and they will go back home together. Choice (A) is incorrect since the girl is their classmate instead of their teacher. Choices (B) and (C) are logical but don't answer the question.

5. (A) The man talks about the instruction of taking one kind of medicine. He says that he "almost forgot it" 差点忘了（差點忘了）. Both (C) and (D) provide wrong information based on the original dialogue. Choice (B) does not continue the logic.

6. (C) The woman asks whether their ball team will win in a game. The man answers that he is not sure. He states that their competitor is quite good. So he actually didn't give an affirmative answer. Choices (A) and (B) show that he is sure about the results, which is not true. Choice (D) is not related to the question. Note that "be sure" is 一定，肯定.

7. (C) The man wants to treat the woman to a meal in Chinatown. Choices (A) and (D) don't continue the logic of the dialogue. Choice (B) is not related to the invitation. (C) "I prefer to eat at home since Chinatown is far away" is the correct response.

8. (B) The woman and the man are talking about learning Chinese. The man emphasizes that reading and writing are important as well. There are several popular phrases here which are important. "It may not be true" is 不见得（不見得）, "Speaking without reading" is 光说不看（光說不看）, and "at all" is 简直（簡直）.

9. (D) The woman is not happy with the weather report about the low temperature today. The man says that the weather report is not reliable. Pay attention to these popular phrases: "obviously" 明明, "to cause or to lead something bad" 害得, and "how could you believe" 也能相信？

10. (C) The woman answers the man's question about where she is from and asks whether he has been in Los Angeles before. Therefore, the man needs to answer about his relationship to Los Angeles. Choices (A) and (B) don't include the relationship. Choice (D) "You'd better not go to Los Angeles with me" is off topic.

11. (B) The woman says that she has no time for weekend math class, which her parents asked her to attend. The man states that she will have time as long as she doesn't play games. Choice (A) "You don't like math class either?", as well as choices (C) and (D) don't make sense for this situation. (B) "I didn't really play a lot" continues the dialogue. Note these expressions: "where do I have" 哪有 and "not really do much" 没怎么（沒怎麼）.

12. (A) The woman is surprised about dining together in the office. The man states that it is not the first time. The man says "you can decide for yourself about whether it is true" 是不是真的你自己看着办（是不是真的你自己看著辦）actually shows that he believes it is true. Therefore, the correct choice is (A), that the woman says she will go.

13. (C) The man suggests a rest to the woman, since she has played ball sports for a long time. The woman says that she is not tired because she was sitting there watching instead of playing. Choice (A) "I like taking a rest first before playing the ball sports. Now I will play" doesn't continue the conversation. Choice (B) "I am not tired because I have played ball sports for such a long time" is not logical itself. Choice (D) "I will ask you to go next time I play ball sports" is off topic.

14. (D) The woman says "Sorry, there is nothing really good to eat. Just have some." This is a very common way in Chinese culture to invite others to eat, showing the humbleness of the person who is inviting others. The most appropriate answer is (D) "It's very kind of you. I have eaten three big bowls of food!" Choice (B) "It's a pity. Forgive that I am inattentive to take care of you" simply rephrases the woman's words.

15. (A) The woman asks how the man did in the test since the results came out. The man says that "finally I could happily sleep and play." This indicates that he is satisfied with his test results. Therefore, Choice (A) is correct. Choice (B) "Did you want to sleep once you finished the exam?" doesn't make sense. Choice (C) "It's ok that you didn't do well. Try harder next time," isn't logical since he did do well. Choice (D) "Actually you were sleeping instead of taking the exam," doesn't make sense.

Answers and Explanations for the Listening Selections

Look back at "Strategies for the Listening Selections" in Chapter 6. Did you remember all the strategies and use them effectively? How did you do on note taking? Remember: You will need to take notes when you listen to the selections, because you won't see the questions until the audio selection is finished.

Answers

16. A	**23.** B	**30.** B
17. C	**24.** C	**31.** C
18. D	**25.** D	**32.** B
19. C	**26.** B	**33.** A
20. B	**27.** D	**34.** D
21. D	**28.** C	**35.** C
22. A	**29.** A	

Explanations

16. (A) Based on the easily caught key word of Huan Zhu Ge Ge, your notes should include its showtime 晚十点后（晚十點後）. It's always important to note any numbers you hear.

17. (C) Hollywood movies are from the United States, and even if you missed the words "United States," you won't miss the popular word of "movie." "The movies from Europe and the United States are in the morning."

18. (D) There is nothing related to "news" 新闻（新聞） mentioned.

19. (C) The word of "subway" is 地铁（地鐵）.

20. (B) The phrase "get off" 下车（下車） was repeated many times.

21. (D) Based on "getting off," Choice (D) is the only answer choice that is not related and not logical.

22. (A) The "college application lecture" is 大学申请讲座（大學申請講座）.

23. (B) For the voice message, there is a good chance you will hear something changed from the original plan. And for any cause-and-effect situation, you will hear conjunctions such as 因为、由于、所以（因為、由於、所以）, and so on. This should alert you that what you hear next is something important.

24. (C) The change of plan in the voice message normally will be either location or time. This is a tip that you may use if you missed some related information. Since you heard two locations, the second location will be the answer. Because we normally will say: it is not the original Plan A; it is now changed to Plan B.

25. (D) In this selection, the only number you can note down is 3 p.m.

26. (B) The man mentioned a lot of vocabulary related to being sick: "flu" 感冒, "injection" 打针（打針）, and "take medicine" 吃药（吃藥）.

27. (D) The woman suggests that he should exercise more, and then the man said the weather stopped him from exercise. At the end, he said he likes playing video games.

28. (C) Your notes should include table tennis, tennis, dance, and Taiji, which are all very easily caught when listening. Did you draw simple sketching pictures to show the vocabulary? Your notes could be anything, including a sketch.

29. (A) "Kites" 风筝（風箏） was repeated many times.

30. (B) The "first of all" 首先 and "after that" 然后（然後） structure helps you catch the answer, which follows "after that."

31. (C) You may struggle between the answer choices (C) and (D) since you may not recognize the word "balance." However, if you've made a kite before—or even saw a kite before—you can get the correct answer just using common sense.

32. (B) You can use common sense for this one, too.

33. (A) is the correct answer. "Environment pollution" 环境污染（環境污染） may be an unfamiliar phrase for you. However, the other answers won't be unfamiliar. Did you hear about them? No. So the answer is (A) by the process of elimination.

34. (D) You should have heard the words "water," "air," and "soil" together, which indicates answer choices of (A), (B), and (C). Also, using common sense, you know that Choice (D) is not in the same category.

35. (C) Hong Kong is not mentioned in this selection. Keep in mind that Yangtze the River is often called the "long river" 长江（長江）.

Answers and Explanations for Reading Comprehension

Look back at "Strategies for Reading Comprehension" in Chapter 7. Did you remember all the strategies and use them effectively? Which ones do you still need to work on?

Answers

1. A	**13.** B	**25.** D
2. B	**14.** D	**26.** D
3. D	**15.** C	**27.** A
4. B	**16.** A	**28.** B
5. D	**17.** B	**29.** C
6. C	**18.** C	**30.** A
7. D	**19.** A	**31.** D
8. B	**20.** C	**32.** B
9. A	**21.** B	**33.** B
10. A	**22.** D	**34.** C
11. B	**23.** A	**35.** D
12. C	**24.** B	

Explanations

1. (A) The first paragraph clearly stated the theme. Based on the strategies we have learned, you should skim for the word in the question 哪一种（哪一種） and the word after 的, which is 中国传统服装（中國傳統服裝）. So the answer is "which kind… Chinese traditional clothes."

2. (B) The first sentence in the paragraph said Qipao came from a "minority" 少数民族（少數民族）.

3. (D) Locate the part describing 汉服（漢服）, it states that the Hanfu "doesn't use buttons, but ropes to tighten up": 不是用扣子而是用绳带系住（不是用扣子而是用繩帶系住）.

4. (B) The last paragraph clearly states that 汉服（漢服） is recommended.

5. (D) The letter addresses both the recipient and the sender as "classmate" 同学（同學）.

6. (C) Choices (A) and (B) can be eliminated since the second sentence states that "you" have been there before. Choices (C) and (D) are mentioned in one sentence: "Since you went to (C)…, this time then (D)…." Therefore, (C) is correct.

7. (D) In the last paragraph it states that the writer's "favorite" 我最喜欢（我最喜歡）is Guangxi "Guilin" 桂林. Even if you do not know the word 桂, 林 is a popular word for which you know the Pinyin "lin."

8. (B) "Environment" is 环境（環境）.

9. (A) 小区（小區）is a well-known phrase. It normally means a complex or community.

10. (A) 火锅（火鍋）means "hot pot." Furthermore, Rule 2 has several vocabulary words related to restaurant: "dishes" 菜, "wine" 酒, and "drinks" 水.

11. (B) The phrase "valid time" is 有效期.

12. (C) Based on Rule 4, Choice (A) is incorrect since it says "no receipt provided" 不开票（不開票）, and (B) is incorrect since it says "no cashing" 不兑现（不兑現）. In Rule 3, it states that booking one day earlier is required; therefore, (D) is incorrect, too.

13. (B) Locate the answer choices in the selection one by one. Rule 5 states that the coupon cannot be used for a banquet.

14. (D) The bottom of the advertisement states that it is from the swimming center of a gym.

15. (C) 暑期接待人员（暑期接待人員）is the answer. 接待 means "take care of." Choices (A), (B), and (D) are not mentioned.

16. (A) Line 3 states the answer A.

17. (B) When you browse through the choices, what caught your attention first? I hope it was "working hours," because that means you can easily locate the answer in the selection using numbers. Neither of the two sets of numbers is related to the working hours, so without digging in detail, you will get the correct answer B.

18. (C) The word of "car" 车（車）is repeated a number of times.

19. (A) Refer to the answer for Question 18.

20. (C) The word "refrigerator" 冰箱 is in the title and repeated in the context.

21. (B) The sentence with the word "sports clothes" started with "buy 4000 yuan and above" 购买4000元以上（購買4000元以上）.

22. (D) The first sentence provided the answer. 电器（電器）means "electronic appliance."

23. (A) The answer of main-idea questions is generally located at the beginning or the end of the reading selection. The first line states "toy" 玩具. Then there is a word of "use" 用 repeated in the selection.

24. (B) The answer is possibly either (B) or (D) since they share the same structure. 处（處）means "location," so the location should be "shaded" 阴（陰）and "cool" 凉（涼）. Also remember this popular word: "prevent (from)" 防.

25. (D) You can try choices with numbers first since it is easy to locate the corresponding information in the context. Yeah, it is for children above 6 years old.

26. (D) The first sentence provides the answer: "Ship" is not included.

27. (A) Do you need to read the text to know the answer? Use common sense. Of course it is "compass" 指南针（指南針）.

28. (B) Gunpowder is located in the second part of paragraph 2. You may struggle in choosing between (A) and (B), since (C) and (D) are two phrases you are familiar with and should have recognized the characters if they were mentioned. Read the sentence with gunpowder all the way through. 炼丹师们（煉丹師們）"invented" 发明了（發明了）gunpowder, the doctor only "documented" 记载了（記載了）it. It is not (A) the doctor; therefore, it is (B) the alchemists. There is another fun strategy for this specific question. 们（們）is the plural form for all nouns in Chinese; therefore, the answer has to be more than one person, which means you just need to choose between (B) and (D). 师 means someone very good at something, such as "teacher" 老师（老師）, or "lawyer" 律师（律師）. This is a hint for the answer as well.

29. (C) Do you find a number again? Yeah, "the fifth" 五. So locate the sentence by this number. The last sentence clearly states that "the fifth famous invention from China is the abacus," which is the correct answer (C).

30. (A) The story begins in the second sentence, which mentions "yellow river" 黄河 and a repeated character of "water" 水.

31. (D) If you know the characters for "smart" 聪明（聰明）, you can check (D) and go to the next question. If not, then locate the four choices one by one and read the context. You can get rid of the incorrect answers easily.

32. (B) From the question you can guess that there was another way before, which probably didn't work well. You can see the sentence of 建筑堤坝堵水（建築堤壩堵水）"is not a good idea." You probably only understand one character of 水. However, did you notice the three characters in front of 水 share the same radical of "soil, mud, ground" 土? So, what to do with so much soil? Build the dams to block water! To confirm your guess, you can look for some popular characters you know: (A) "lake" 湖 and (C) "river" 河. You cannot find these two characters; therefore, neither of them is probably the answer. Choice (D), "It was not mentioned" normally will not be a correct answer in the AP Chinese exam.

33. (B) "Didn't enter" 没有进去（沒有進去）is mentioned with his first time passing his home.

34. (C) There is a number again in the question. You cannot find "the second time," but you definitely have learned "again" 再. What number was in the sentence with 再? Seven years. Therefore, choice (C) is correct.

35. (D) 感动（感動）means "moved, touched, impressed."

Section II: Free-Response Questions

For the free-response questions, it's not hard to get a score of 4 as long as you answered each question and completed each task. In this section are sample answers at a level of 5 or above. These are followed by an English translation of the sample answer and an explanation of the answer.

Answer and Explanation for the Story Narration

Look back at "Strategies for the Story Narration" in Chapter 8. Did you remember all the strategies and use them effectively? Which ones do you still need to work on?

Sample Answer

Simplified Chinese

小王给他的三个朋友打电话，邀请他们来参加自己的生日派对。朋友们兴高采烈地来到他家，跑来跑去，大吃大喝。他们一起玩游戏、看电影，有说有笑地庆祝生日，把屋子弄得乱七八糟的。朋友们走后，小王的妈妈回来了。望着地上的盘子和满屋子的狼籍，妈妈非常生气："你怎么搞的？连墙上的镜框都可以弄坏？"小王非常不好意思，老老实实地把屋子打扫干净，摆好了镜框，妈妈终于很开心地笑了。 (Level 6)

Traditional Chinese

小王給他的三個朋友打電話，邀請他們來參加自己的生日派對。朋友們興高采烈地來到他家，跑來跑去，大吃大喝。他們一起玩遊戲、看電影，有說有笑地慶祝生日，把屋子弄得亂七八糟的。朋友們走後，小王的媽媽回來了。望著地上的盤子和滿屋子的狼籍，媽媽非常生氣："你怎麼搞的？連牆上的鏡框都可以弄壞？"小王非常不好意思，老老實實地把屋子打掃乾淨，擺好了鏡框，媽媽終於很開心地笑了。 (Level 6)

English translation

Xiao Wang called three of his friends to come over for a birthday party. His friends happily arrived. They had a great birthday celebration, talking, laughing, eating, drinking, playing games, and watching movies. Xiao Wang's mom came home after his friends had left. Looking at the plates on the floor and the mess in their home, his mother became very mad: "What did you do? You even damaged the frame on the wall." Xiao Wang was very embarrassed. He cleaned the rooms and fixed the frame. Finally, his mother smiled.

Explanation

Based on the four pictures, the storyline is: The boy called his friends. His friends came and enjoyed a great time together. They played very well, laughing, eating, running, drinking, and so on. His mom was very mad at the mess afterwards. He cleaned the house later.

For this prompt, there are a lot of factors that could keep you from scoring a 6. The most common mistakes would be missing an important action in the pictures or not providing all the transitional elements for the logic of the four pictures. Pay attention to the following details:

- For picture #2, be sure to mention as many of the activities as you can: drinking, eating, laughing, running, and so on.
- For picture #3, don't forget to mention that his friends are gone. Describe the mother's reaction of getting mad. You should also mention the falling frame on the wall.
- For picture #4, you should mention that the frame is fixed. And to conclude the logic of the story you need to say, "Finally, his mother smiled."
- You may want to mention that it is a birthday party. If you do not know how to write "party" in Chinese, skipping that would be fine as well.

Answer and Explanation for the E-mail Response

Look back at "Strategies for the E-mail Response" in Chapter 9. Did you remember all the strategies and use them effectively? Which ones do you still need to work on?

Sample Answer

Simplified Chinese

刘静,

你好。原来你今年就要毕业了啊？我还真是羡慕你拿到了奖学金。

你在信中问我学中文还是学商科，关于这个问题，我的建议是都可以学，但应该先学中文。

学中文和学商科各有利弊。学中文的话，既然有奖学金，你就花不了多少钱，还能学习和适应中国文化。不过去中国，离你爸妈很远，他们自然不希望这样。如果选商科，他们在美国可以经常去看你。但是商学院学费可贵呢！我选专业的时候也遇到过同样的问题，当时我选择了学工程，课余时间进修美术，也挺不错的。我觉得你完全可以先去中国。你都这么大了，应该学会独立。有了一些社会经验再学商科，其实更好。

一个好的大学专业，老实说，首先考虑的是费用。如果有奖学金，我会优先选择。其次要注意的是自己的兴趣，尽量选自己喜欢的，有可能是一辈子哦。另外，也不要忘了时间安排，因为如果时间安排得当，说不定两个都可以，当然问题就解决了。

我的看法不一定对，你还可以咨询一下你的老师，听听他们的建议。

祝心想事成。

赵芸

Traditional Chinese

劉靜,

你好。原來你今年就要畢業了啊？我還真是羨慕你拿到了獎學金。

你在信中問我學中文還是學商科，關於這個問題，我的建議是都可以學，但應該先學中文。

學中文和學商科各有利弊。學中文的話，既然有獎學金，你就花不了多少錢，還能學習和適應中國文化。不過去中國，離你爸媽很遠，他們自然不希望這樣。如果選商科，他們在美國可以經常去看你。但是商學院學費可貴呢！我選專業的時候也遇到過同樣的問題，當時我選擇了學工程，課余時間進修美術，也挺不錯的。我覺得你完全可以先去中國。你都這麼大了，應該學會獨立。有了一些社會經驗再學商科，其實更好。

一個好的大學專業，老實說，首先考慮的是費用。如果有獎學金，我會優先選擇。其次要注意的是自己的興趣，盡量選自己喜歡的，有可能是一輩子哦。另外，也不要忘了時間安排，因為如果時間安排得當，說不定兩個都可以，當然問題就解決了。

我的看法不一定對，你還可以咨詢一下你的老師，聽聽他們的建議。

祝心想事成。

趙芸

English translation

Liu Jing,

How are you? You are graduating this year, and I do envy that you got the scholarship.

You asked about which to choose, learning Chinese or going to business school. My suggestion is that you do both, though learn Chinese first.

There are advantages and disadvantages for both choices. If you learn Chinese, the cost is low due to your scholarship, and you can learn and adjust to their culture. However, you parents will not be happy since it is far away from them. If you go to business school, they can visit you often, though business schools are expensive. I encountered a similar problem when choosing my major. I chose engineering and took art courses in my spare time, and it worked out fine. I think you should go to China first. You are old enough, and you should learn to be independent. It's better to go to business school after gaining some social experience.

To choose a good college major, to be honest, I would consider the cost first. I would give priority to the offers with scholarships. Second, I would follow my own interests. It is probably a major for your whole life, so try to pick your favorite one. In addition, do not forget to arrange your time well, because if you can manage your time well, there is a possibility that you could take both.

This is just my personal opinion. You should consult your teachers and ask for their suggestions.

Wishing your dreams come true.

Zhao Yun

Explanation

First—what to write? The two choices to compare are obvious. Choosing from learning Chinese in China or going to business school. You are also asked for your opinion on selecting a good college major.

The second step is to apply your prepared template. The sample answer provides a thorough adaptation of a prepared template to the specific questions in this e-mail message. You do not need to write in such detail in the real exam. You can "fill in the blanks" by adding the content from the e-mail message. There are actually only two basic components of your reply:

1. The concerns of the cost and the parent's concern on the distance.
2. The solution of time management to obtain the advantages for both.

If you haven't prepared a template for the e-mail response and memorized it yet, do that right now. Review the skill-building exercises in Chapter 9 and use these to create your template. Then all you need to do in the test is adapt your template and fill in the blanks.

Answers and Explanations for the Conversation

Look back at "Strategies for the Conversation" in Chapter 10. Did you remember all the strategies and use them effectively? Which ones do you still need to work on?

Sample Answers

In this part of the exam, you are required to answer six questions about your school life in the United States in a conversation with a friend from China. A rather detailed set of answers is provided for your reference. On the actual exam, an answer scored 5 or 6 generally consists of four to six short sentences.

Simplified Chinese

1. 你们学校有中文俱乐部吗？如果想加入应该怎么申请？

Does your school have a Chinese club? What is the process of application if you want to join?

我们学校有中文俱乐部。如果想参加的话，首先可以去看看加入的要求，有些什么活动。然后要向俱乐部提出申请，填好申请表交上去。中文俱乐部在我们学校有自己的信箱，放进去就可以了。接下来就是等消息了。

2. 对于中文俱乐部的活动，你有什么建议？

What are your suggestions for the activities of a Chinese club?

对于中文俱乐部的活动，我有一些想法。我觉得第一是要与中国文化有关，可以帮助成员了解中国；第二是最好有趣一点，像看中国画画展什么的就不如让大家学画中国画。自己动手才有乐趣，而且可以吸引更多的人参加。中国人喜欢的游戏也可以加进来，还可以庆祝中国的节日。

3. 参加了中文俱乐部以后，你对中国文化有什么新的认识或了解？

What new understanding about Chinese culture have you learned from participating in the Chinese club?

参加中文俱乐部以后，我对中国文化有了很多新的认识和了解。首先我发现中国的数字是有意义的，例如8这个数字很吉利，但是数字4就不太好了，因为4听起来像"死"。我也知道了中国人不是天天都吃饺子的，南方人吃米饭比较多。还有啊，中国很大，少数民族也很多，西北边还有白种人呢！

4. 如果去你的中国同学家做客，你觉得要注意哪些问题？

What should you pay attention to if you are invited to be a guest at your Chinese classmates' house?

如果去中国同学家做客，要注意的问题很多。第一次上门的话最好要带个小礼物。人家有小弟弟小妹妹的话，玩具或书就特别好。在很多中国人家里是要把鞋脱掉的，所以最好是穿新袜子。和他们一家人吃饭的话，很可能要用筷子，先练习一下挺好的。还有啊，我觉得中国人很好客，主人会夹菜给你，一定不要往外推。

5. 有人说虽然中国菜很好吃，但中国人的饮食习惯并不健康。请谈一谈你的看法。

Some people say that Chinese food is delicious, but that the customary diet of Chinese people is not healthy. Please share your opinion.

关于中国人的饮食习惯啊，这个还不太好说。中国菜基本上都是熟的，所以还是很干净的。用的是植物油，所以比用动物油健康。没什么甜点巧克力，这样对身体好。不过，中国菜里放的盐很多，也有很多油炸的菜，这些就对健康没什么好处了。

6. 你希望了解哪些中国文化方面的知识？为什么？

What kind of knowledge do you want to obtain regarding Chinese culture? Why?

我希望了解很多关于中国文化方面的知识，尤其是关于中国教育和社会方面的。因为我觉得中国的父母对孩子的教育和美国人的不一样，像很多中国同学的数学都特别好，我实在想学一学。还有啊，听说中国的社会最注重"关系"，这个关系到底是怎么一回事，我也想知道。

Traditional Chinese

1. 你們學校有中文俱樂部嗎？如果想加入應該怎麼申請？

Does your school have a Chinese club? What is the process of application if you want to join?

我們學校有中文俱樂部。如果想參加的話，首先可以去看看加入的要求，有些甚麼活動。然後要向俱樂部提出申請，填好申請表交上去。中文俱樂部在我們學校有自己的信箱，放進去就可以了。接下來就是等消息了。

2. 對於中文俱樂部的活動，你有甚麼建議？

What are your suggestions for the activities of a Chinese club?

對於中文俱樂部的活動，我有一些想法。我覺得第一是要與中國文化有關，可以幫助成員瞭解中國；第二是最好有趣一點，像看中國畫畫展甚麼的就不如讓大家學畫中國畫。自己動手才有樂趣，而且可以吸引更多的人參加。中國人喜歡的遊戲也可以加進來，還可以慶祝中國的節日。

3. 參加了中文俱樂部以後，你對中國文化有甚麼新的認識或瞭解？

What new understanding about Chinese culture have you learned from participating in the Chinese club?

參加中文俱樂部以後，我對中國文化有了很多新的認識和瞭解。首先我發現中國的數字是有意義的，例如8這個數字很吉利，但是數字4就不太好了，因為4聽起來像"死"。我也知道了中國人不是天天都吃餃子的，南方人吃米飯比較多。還有啊，中國很大，少數民族也很多，西北邊還有白種人呢！

4. 如果去你的中國同學家做客，你覺得要注意哪些問題？

What should you pay attention to if you are invited to be a guest at your Chinese class-mates' house?

如果去中國同學家做客，要注意的問題很多。第一次上門的話最好要帶個小禮物。人家有小弟弟小妹妹的話，玩具或書就特別好。在很多中國人家裡是要把鞋脫掉的，所以最好是穿新襪子。和他們一家人吃飯的話，很可能要用筷子，先練習一下挺好的。還有啊，我覺得中國人很好客，主人會夾菜給你，一定不要往外推。

5. 有人說雖然中國菜很好吃，但中國人的飲食習慣並不健康。請談一談你的看法。

Some people say that Chinese food is delicious, but that the customary diet of Chinese people is not healthy. Please share your opinion.

關於中國人的飲食習慣啊，這個還不太好說。中國菜基本上都是熟的，所以還是很乾淨的。用的是植物油，所以比用動物油健康。沒甚麼甜點巧克力，這樣對身體好。不過，中國菜里放的鹽很多，也有很多油炸的菜，這些就對健康沒甚麼好處了。

6. 你希望瞭解哪些中國文化方面的知識？為甚麼？

What kind of knowledge do you want to obtain regarding Chinese culture? Why?

我希望瞭解很多關於中國文化方面的知識，尤其是關於中國教育和社會方面的。因為我覺得中國的父母對孩子的教育和美國人的不一樣，像很多中國同學的數學都特別好，我實在想學一學。還有啊，聽說中國的社會最注重"關係"，這個關係到底是怎麼一回事，我也想知道。

Explanation

The questions in the conversation in this practice exam are relatively difficult and the sample answers are at level 6. Did you figure out some patterns regarding these questions and answers? Here are some general characteristics of the conversation task that you should remember:

- The first sentence of your response should always directly address the question(s). Did you figure out that repeating or rephrasing the questions is a good idea? If the question asks for "several" instead of "one," you can use "a lot" 很多 or "some" 一些 to finish your first sentence.

- You will need to respond to specific questions. You are familiar with the simple vocabulary for questions, such as "what" 什么（甚麼）, "how" 怎么（怎麼）, and "why" 为什么（為甚麼）. If you have difficulty understanding what exactly the questions are getting at, review the skill-building exercises in Chapter 10.
- The answers need to be well structured with two or three supportive points. Keep in mind that you can use the following transitional elements to answer every question. These will also help you fulfill the requirement of "wide range of grammar usage." Memorize them and use them!

First	首先，第一
Second	然后，第二，也（然後，第二，也）
In addition	还有啊，而且（還有啊，而且）
Especially	特别是
However	不过，但是，可是（不過，但是，可是）
For example/such as	例如，像……
Include	包括
You'd better	最好，最好是
It was said	听说（聽説）
Relatively	比较（比較）
I think	我觉得，我认为（我覺得，我認為）
Not easy to say	不太好说，不太好回答（不太好説，不太好回答）

Scoring Guidelines

Review in your mind your answers to each of the six questions. To get a high score, your answers need to meet the following characteristics:

- Did you address the questions thoroughly with details?
- Did you have smooth sentence connections?
- Did your answers have a natural pace with a minimum of repetitions/hesitations?
- Did you use correct pronunciation and register?
- Did your answers show good vocabulary usage with minimal grammatical errors?

Answer and Explanation for the Cultural Presentation

Look back at "Strategies for the Cultural Presentation" in Chapter 11. Did you remember all the strategies and use them effectively? Which ones do you still need to work on?

Sample Answer

Simplified Chinese

中国是有着五千年历史和文明的国家。中国的社会和家庭问题也一直是中国文化的组成部分之一。我今天想谈一谈中国的"小皇帝"。这既是一个家庭问题，也是一个社会问题。我想和大家说一说中国的小皇帝有什么特点，这个现象在中国文化中有什么样的意义。

小皇帝的英文意思是 little emperor，指的是中国的独生子女们。由于中国的计划生育政策，现在的中国家庭，一般都只有一个孩子。爷爷、奶奶、外公、外婆、妈妈、爸爸，总共六个大人围着一个小孩转，想一想就知道这个小孩有多受宠爱了。大人们，尤其是爷爷奶奶们经常会尽力满足小皇帝的一切要求，要什么给什么，做错了也舍不得批评。这样的环境中长大的孩子，没有什么机会和其他小朋友分享，也没有什么机会独立照顾自己，更不用说适应各种有挑战性的环境了。

在中国，没有人不知道小皇帝的现象，而且小皇帝的问题已经成为了社会问题。不听人劝、脾气不好都算小事，吸毒打架什么的都有，出了问题就找爸爸，到最后有的还走上了犯罪的道路。前段时间就有一个叫李天一的孩子，父母都是有名的歌唱家，就因为犯罪进了监狱。

而在美国或其他国家，我们也可以接触到很多从中国来的小皇帝留学生。因为从小习惯了被人捧着哄着，他们不想学习就不学，开着名车乱花钱，在国际上造成的负面影响特别大。没有责任感和协作精神的孩子，最终不可能成才。

说实在的，现在中国的小皇帝越来越多，名声越来越坏，我也希望中国人可以正视这个问题，解决这个问题。

Traditional Chinese

中國是有著五千年歷史和文明的國家。中國的社會和家庭問題也一直是中國文化的組成部分之一。我今天想談一談中國的"小皇帝"。這既是一個家庭問題，也是一個社會問題。我想和大家説一説中國的小皇帝有甚麼特點，這個現象在中國文化中有甚麼樣的意義。

小皇帝的英文意思是 little emperor，指的是中國的獨生子女們。由於中國的計劃生育政策，現在的中國家庭，一般都只有一個孩子。爺爺、奶奶、外公、外婆、媽媽、爸爸，總共六個大人圍著一個小孩轉，想一想就知道這個小孩有多受寵愛了。大人們，尤其是爺爺奶奶們經常會盡力滿足小皇帝的一切要求，要甚麼給甚麼，做錯了也捨不得批評。這樣的環境中長大的孩子，沒有甚麼機會和其他小朋友分享，也沒有甚麼機會獨立照顧自己，更不用説適應各種有挑戰性的環境了。

在中國，沒有人不知道小皇帝的現象，而且小皇帝的問題已經成為了社會問題。不聽人勸、脾氣不好都算小事，吸毒打架甚麼的都有，出了問題就找爸爸，到最後有的還走上了犯罪的道路。前段時間就有一個叫李天一的孩子，父母都是有名的歌唱家，就因為犯罪進了監獄。

而在美國或其他國家，我們也可以接觸到很多從中國來的小皇帝留學生。因為從小習慣了被人捧著哄著，他們不想學習就不學，開著名車亂花錢，在國際上造成的負面影響特別大。沒有責任感和協作精神的孩子，最終不可能成才。

說實在的，現在中國的小皇帝越來越多，名聲越來越壞，我也希望中國人可以正視這個問題，解決這個問題。

English translation

China is a country with 5,000 years of history and civilization. Family and societal issues in China are always a part of Chinese culture. I am going to introduce "little emperors" in China today. Little emperor is not only a family issue but also a societal issue. I am going to discuss the characters of little emperors and what the significance of this phenomenon will be.

"Little Emperor" is what we call it in English, and the term is used for the only child in a family in China. Due to the one-child policy, Chinese families typically have only one child. That means there are four grandparents and two parents taking care of one child. Think about how much love and care the child will get! The adults, especially the grandparents, will try everything to satisfy the little emperor, no matter what the child wants. They tend not to criticize even if the child does something wrong. Growing up in this kind of environment, the child won't have many opportunities to share or to become independent, not to mention handling challenges.

The phenomenon of little emperors is well-known in China, and it became a societal issue. Those little emperors do not listen to others, have bad tempers, or even become addicted to drugs and fight physically. They are used to letting their parents handle problems, and some of them end up breaking the law. For example, a boy named Li Tian Yi, whose parents are both famous singers in China, broke the law and went to jail.

There are a lot of little emperors studying in the United States or other countries. Since they were spoiled when they were little, they probably just drive expensive cars and fling money around instead of studying hard. They have caused a very negative influence internationally. The child without a sense of responsibility and teamwork will never succeed.

To be honest, more and more little emperors from China have caused a bad reputation to form. I hope that China can face this issue directly and solve it. The positive Chinese culture is worth promoting.

Explanation

The topic selected of the "little emperor" is definitely not an easy one. It involves a negative element in Chinese culture. The vocabulary used here may be difficult and you may not have a lot of knowledge or understanding about this issue. Review the English translation of the sample answer and compare it with the sample cultural presentations in Chapter 11. Did you find out that you still are able to easily use the template you have prepared?

For the sample answer, let's walk through the process of adjusting your cultural presentation template to the topic:

1. Introduction: Your opening paragraph probably doesn't need much adjustment.

2. Features: The characteristics of a little emperor are what you need to know before the exam to be able to discuss them here. Think about what kind of privilege an emperor possesses. Describe it.

3. Personal experience: Your first sentence should work for every topic. Then add a couple of examples to elaborate. You do not need to discuss this in as much detail as in the sample answer. The example in the sample answer is actually a real case, but you may use one you make up. Anyway, you have no doubt heard about similar stories from other cultures.

4. Global significance: The statement "have caused a very negative influence internationally" is essential. You should address the global significance of the topic in some way.

5. Conclusion: You should add the concluding paragraph to your template options and memorize the expressions so you can use them.

Scoring and Interpreting Your Results

For multiple-choice questions, the simple number of correct answers you have can be used to convert to your AP score.

For free-response questions, it's not as easy for you to figure out what exactly your score could be. Here is a simple checklist to give you a general idea about how you did on the free-response questions so you can score them yourself.

Scoring Checklist

1. Did you answer all the basic questions?
   Yes. Your score may be 3 and above. Otherwise your score may be 2 or below 2.
2. Was your answer understandable and logical to the reader or listener?
   Yes. Your score may be 4 and above.
3. Was your answer well structured, with rich language usage and minor errors?
   Yes. Your score may be 5 and above.

To see what you might have done if this had been the actual AP exam, you may convert your answers to a rough AP score using the following worksheet. This is a method for estimating your score and the results do not guarantee that you will do similarly on the actual AP exam.

Section I: Multiple Choice

Rejoinders: (number correct) ÷15 × 0.10 = _____

Listening Selections: (number correct) ÷ (total number) × 0.15 = _____

Reading: (number correct) ÷ (total number) × 0.25 = _____

Section II: Free Response

Story Narration: (score yourself on a scale of 1 to 6) ÷ 6 × 0.15 = _____

E-mail Response: (score yourself on a scale of 1 to 6) ÷ 6 × 0.10 = _____

Conversation: (score yourself on a scale of 1 to 6) ÷ 36 × 0.10 = _____

Cultural Presentation: (score yourself on a scale of 1 to 6) ÷ 6 × 0.15 = _____

Total Score for Sections I and II = _____

Total Points for Sections I and II = _____ × 120 = _____

AP Chinese Language and Cultural Practice Test 2

Using the Practice Test

This practice test closely resembles the actual AP Chinese Language and Culture exam. Take this test to experience what the real test will be like. This practice test is especially valuable in helping to

- Familiarize yourself with the AP exam
- Learn to pace yourself within the time limits of the exam
- Practice the strategies you've learned in this book
- Build your test-taking confidence

How to Take the Practice Test

To get the most out of this diagnostic exam, you should try to simulate actual test-taking conditions as much as possible. Here are some tips that will help you:

- Plan to take the two-hour exam without interruption.
- Answer the questions within the required time limits in each section.
- Follow the instructions carefully.
- For the listening section of the test (Section I, Part A) and the conversation (Section II, Part B), you will find the audio content on the accompanying CD-ROM.
- Tear out the answer sheet provided (see the next page). Grid-in your answers for Section I (multiple choice) on this answer sheet. Or, if you wish, write your answers on scratch paper and take this test again later.
- Practice using the strategies you've learned in this book.

You may find this practice test to be slightly harder than the actual test. This slightly greater degree of difficulty will better prepare you for the actual test.

After the Test

- Check your work against the correct answers provided for the multiple-choice questions. Read the explanations, not only for the questions you missed, but for all those for which you weren't sure what the correct answer was.
- Read the explanations for all the free-response questions and compare your answers to the sample ones. Do over the ones you had difficulty with to learn from your mistakes.
- Look up the vocabulary words you had difficulty with on the test and note anything else you had trouble with when taking the exam.
- At the very end of the answers and explanations for this practice test, you'll find a score conversion sheet. Use this to determine a rough AP score; this will give you a rough idea of how you might do on the test if you took it today.
- Review the specific strategies if you found any section of this practice test challenging.
- You can reuse the self-evaluation worksheets at the end of Chapter 4 to analyze your performance on this practice test. Use the suggestions on these worksheets if you feel you need more practice.

AP Chinese Language and Culture Practice Test 2—Multiple Choice

ANSWER SHEET

Part A: Listening

1 Ⓐ Ⓑ Ⓒ Ⓓ　13 Ⓐ Ⓑ Ⓒ Ⓓ　25 Ⓐ Ⓑ Ⓒ Ⓓ
2 Ⓐ Ⓑ Ⓒ Ⓓ　14 Ⓐ Ⓑ Ⓒ Ⓓ　26 Ⓐ Ⓑ Ⓒ Ⓓ
3 Ⓐ Ⓑ Ⓒ Ⓓ　15 Ⓐ Ⓑ Ⓒ Ⓓ　27 Ⓐ Ⓑ Ⓒ Ⓓ
4 Ⓐ Ⓑ Ⓒ Ⓓ　16 Ⓐ Ⓑ Ⓒ Ⓓ　28 Ⓐ Ⓑ Ⓒ Ⓓ
5 Ⓐ Ⓑ Ⓒ Ⓓ　17 Ⓐ Ⓑ Ⓒ Ⓓ　29 Ⓐ Ⓑ Ⓒ Ⓓ
6 Ⓐ Ⓑ Ⓒ Ⓓ　18 Ⓐ Ⓑ Ⓒ Ⓓ　30 Ⓐ Ⓑ Ⓒ Ⓓ
7 Ⓐ Ⓑ Ⓒ Ⓓ　19 Ⓐ Ⓑ Ⓒ Ⓓ　31 Ⓐ Ⓑ Ⓒ Ⓓ
8 Ⓐ Ⓑ Ⓒ Ⓓ　20 Ⓐ Ⓑ Ⓒ Ⓓ　32 Ⓐ Ⓑ Ⓒ Ⓓ
9 Ⓐ Ⓑ Ⓒ Ⓓ　21 Ⓐ Ⓑ Ⓒ Ⓓ　33 Ⓐ Ⓑ Ⓒ Ⓓ
10 Ⓐ Ⓑ Ⓒ Ⓓ　22 Ⓐ Ⓑ Ⓒ Ⓓ　34 Ⓐ Ⓑ Ⓒ Ⓓ
11 Ⓐ Ⓑ Ⓒ Ⓓ　23 Ⓐ Ⓑ Ⓒ Ⓓ　35 Ⓐ Ⓑ Ⓒ Ⓓ
12 Ⓐ Ⓑ Ⓒ Ⓓ　24 Ⓐ Ⓑ Ⓒ Ⓓ

Part B: Reading

1 Ⓐ Ⓑ Ⓒ Ⓓ　13 Ⓐ Ⓑ Ⓒ Ⓓ　25 Ⓐ Ⓑ Ⓒ Ⓓ
2 Ⓐ Ⓑ Ⓒ Ⓓ　14 Ⓐ Ⓑ Ⓒ Ⓓ　26 Ⓐ Ⓑ Ⓒ Ⓓ
3 Ⓐ Ⓑ Ⓒ Ⓓ　15 Ⓐ Ⓑ Ⓒ Ⓓ　27 Ⓐ Ⓑ Ⓒ Ⓓ
4 Ⓐ Ⓑ Ⓒ Ⓓ　16 Ⓐ Ⓑ Ⓒ Ⓓ　28 Ⓐ Ⓑ Ⓒ Ⓓ
5 Ⓐ Ⓑ Ⓒ Ⓓ　17 Ⓐ Ⓑ Ⓒ Ⓓ　29 Ⓐ Ⓑ Ⓒ Ⓓ
6 Ⓐ Ⓑ Ⓒ Ⓓ　18 Ⓐ Ⓑ Ⓒ Ⓓ　30 Ⓐ Ⓑ Ⓒ Ⓓ
7 Ⓐ Ⓑ Ⓒ Ⓓ　19 Ⓐ Ⓑ Ⓒ Ⓓ　31 Ⓐ Ⓑ Ⓒ Ⓓ
8 Ⓐ Ⓑ Ⓒ Ⓓ　20 Ⓐ Ⓑ Ⓒ Ⓓ　32 Ⓐ Ⓑ Ⓒ Ⓓ
9 Ⓐ Ⓑ Ⓒ Ⓓ　21 Ⓐ Ⓑ Ⓒ Ⓓ　33 Ⓐ Ⓑ Ⓒ Ⓓ
10 Ⓐ Ⓑ Ⓒ Ⓓ　22 Ⓐ Ⓑ Ⓒ Ⓓ　34 Ⓐ Ⓑ Ⓒ Ⓓ
11 Ⓐ Ⓑ Ⓒ Ⓓ　23 Ⓐ Ⓑ Ⓒ Ⓓ　35 Ⓐ Ⓑ Ⓒ Ⓓ
12 Ⓐ Ⓑ Ⓒ Ⓓ　24 Ⓐ Ⓑ Ⓒ Ⓓ

AP Chinese Language and Cultural Practice Test 2

Section I: Multiple-Choice Questions

Section I, Part A: Listening

Track 23

Rejoinders

You will hear several short or incomplete conversations in Chinese. The answer choices will be read to you instead of appearing on your computer screen. After listening to the conversation and its four possible continuations, you will choose the response that is the most logical and culturally appropriate to complete the conversation. Mark the letter of your answer choice on the answer sheet. You have **five seconds** to choose the answer and you cannot go back to check or change it after the five seconds are up.

The listening tracks for the questions are provided on the CD-ROM accompanying this book. After you are done with the test, you may refer to the written script for the conversations and answer choices, which can be found starting on page 285. On the actual test, no script is provided.

1. (A) (B) (C) (D)
2. (A) (B) (C) (D)
3. (A) (B) (C) (D)
4. (A) (B) (C) (D)
5. (A) (B) (C) (D)
6. (A) (B) (C) (D)
7. (A) (B) (C) (D)
8. (A) (B) (C) (D)

9. (A) (B) (C) (D)
10. (A) (B) (C) (D)
11. (A) (B) (C) (D)
12. (A) (B) (C) (D)
13. (A) (B) (C) (D)
14. (A) (B) (C) (D)
15. (A) (B) (C) (D)

Track 24

Listening Selections

You will hear some audio selections in Chinese. For each selection, you will be told if it will play once or twice. You will not be able to see the questions until the audio selection is completed. Therefore, note taking is crucial in this part of the exam. You will have 12 seconds to choose the response that best answers each question. You cannot go back to check or change your answer after the 12 seconds are up. Mark the letter of your answer choice on the answer sheet.

The listening tracks for the questions are provided on the CD-ROM accompanying this book. After you are done with the test, you may refer to the written script for the listening selections, which can be found starting on page 292. On the actual test, no script is provided.

Announcement (Selection plays twice.)
Do not read the following questions until the audio selection has been completed.

16. Where would the announcement be heard?

    (A) On an airplane
    (B) In an office building
    (C) In a classroom
    (D) On a travel site

17. This announcement asks passengers to

    (A) stay on the bus.
    (B) get off the bus without luggage.
    (C) get on the bus with luggage.
    (D) get off the bus without important belongings.

18. What is the time for the passengers to come back?

    (A) 11:30
    (B) 11:45
    (C) 12:00
    (D) 2:00

Voice Message (Selection plays twice.)
Do not read the following questions until the audio selection has been completed.

19. What was *not* originally planned by the speaker?

    (A) Buy a black jacket
    (B) Buy a blue jacket
    (C) Go to the Forest Park
    (D) Play baseball

20. What caused the change of meeting location?

    (A) The need to change the color of the jacket
    (B) Not getting the phone call.
    (C) The change in the schedule for the meeting
    (D) The possibility of rain

21. Where will they meet at Forest Park if the location is changed?

    (A) In the park
    (B) At the gate
    (C) In the hotel hall
    (D) Not mentioned

22. What will the speaker possibly do tonight?

    (A) Send address and travel plans
    (B) Buy a blue jacket
    (C) Go to Forest Park
    (D) Call again

School Conversation (Selection plays one time.)
Do not read the following questions until the audio selection has been completed.

23. The woman is asking

    (A) to make up a test.
    (B) for a two-day leave.
    (C) for an appointment with the teacher.
    (D) to practice for the concert.

24. What will happen tomorrow?

(A) The unit test
(B) Studying in the library
(C) Studying in the office
(D) The make-up test

25. Why does the woman ask for leave?

(A) She is sick.
(B) She is afraid of taking a test.
(C) She is going to a violin concert.
(D) She is going to the library.

Instructions (Selection plays twice.)
Do not read the following questions until the audio selection has been completed.

26. What is the primary purpose of this instruction?

(A) To give directions to a location
(B) To learn how to take the subway
(C) To learn how to take a bus
(D) To learn how to make a phone call

27. Which subway line should be taken?

(A) Line 7
(B) Line 3
(C) Line 6
(D) Line 2

28. Which of the following can be inferred from the instruction?

(A) The subway is free.
(B) Coins are needed to buy subway tickets.
(C) You cannot find Xiao Yan's home.
(D) The subway station is far from the bus station.

Radio Report (Selection plays one time.)
Do not read the following questions until the audio selection has been completed.

29. What is the main theme of the report?

(A) Chinese culture
(B) American culture
(C) Education
(D) The college application

30. Chinese parents

(A) prefer that their children enroll in a famous college.
(B) don't care about their child's major.
(C) believe their child's interests are most important.
(D) hope their children learn everything.

31. American parents

(A) want their children to be famous.

(B) want their children to go into a money-making career.

(C) want their kids to go to a famous school.

(D) believe in the whole development of their children.

Job Interview (Selection plays one time.)
Do not read the following questions until the audio selection has been completed.

32. The woman started to do volunteer work

(A) on weekends.

(B) the first year of high school.

(C) in the summer.

(D) with this job.

33. What kind of volunteer work hasn't the woman done before?

(A) Work as an administrative assistant

(B) Interpret for patients

(C) Teach computer

(D) Take care of elders

34. What quality or qualities is the senior center looking for in a candidate?

(A) Good computer skills

(B) Good at English

(C) Patience and passion

(D) Availability of 6 hours weekly

35. Which of the following schedules would *not* work for the woman?

(A) Saturday morning

(B) Friday afternoon

(C) Saturday afternoon

(D) Sunday morning

Section I, Part B: Reading (60 minutes)

Read each passage and then choose the answer choice that best answers each question. You can switch between simplified Chinese and traditional Chinese. You are allowed to mark key words and move back and forth between questions to check or change your answers. There is no time limit for each question, but you will need to finish all the questions within 60 minutes. On the actual test a clock on the computer screen will show how much time remains. For this test, you will need to time yourself.

Read this e-mail:

Simplified Chinese

发件人：杨洋

收件人：李珞

邮件主题：礼物

发件时间：3月27日

杨洋，

你好！感谢你邀请我参加你们学校一年一度的踏青活动，这是我第一次在天马山效游和野餐呢！我妈妈也特别喜欢我带回来的礼物，就是那顶帽子，踏青时抽奖得到的，她经常戴着。还有啊，告诉你一个秘密，她也为你准备了一个小礼物，请告诉我你具体的通讯地址。我就盼望着暑假早点来，这样就可以陪你去参观我们学校。我们新建的科学实验楼可漂亮呢，比从前那一幢大多了，也高多了。

祝一切顺利。

李珞

Traditional Chinese

發件人：楊洋

收件人：李珞

郵件主題：禮物

發件時間：3月27日

楊洋，

你好！感謝你邀請我參加你們學校一年一度的踏青活動，這是我第一次在天馬山效游和野餐呢！我媽媽也特別喜歡我帶回來的禮物，就是那頂帽子，踏青時抽獎得到的，她經常戴著。還有啊，告訴你一個秘密，她也為你準備了一個小禮物，請告訴我你具體的通訊地址。我就盼望著暑假早點來，這樣就可以陪你去參觀我們學校。我們新建的科學實驗樓可漂亮呢，比從前那一幢大多了，也高多了。

祝一切順利。

李珞

1. The purpose of the e-mail is to

   (A) buy a hat for a friend.
   (B) invite a friend to go on a hike and have a picnic.
   (C) show thanks to a friend.
   (D) introduce a new school.

2. What does the mother of the sender feel about the gift she received?

   (A) She is embarrassed.
   (B) She is very happy.
   (C) She doesn't like the gift.
   (D) She wants another gift.

3. The writer asks his friend to provide

   (A) an invitation to visit his school.
   (B) his availability in summer.
   (C) a hat as a gift to his mom.
   (D) his address so that his mom can send a gift.

4. What does the writer recommend according to the e-mail?

   (A) They should go hiking.
   (B) His friend should visit his school.
   (C) His friend should give a gift to his mom.
   (D) They should have a picnic again.

Read this letter:

Simplified Chinese

发信人：珠理

收信人：康先生

康先生，

您好。

我去年参加了"汉语桥"世界中学生中文比赛，幸运地拿到了三等奖，也获得了在中国研修一学期汉语的机会。我特别希望能申请到贵校学习，提高中文水平。我想了解一下要准备哪些材料和填写哪些表格。在学校附近我有一位教英文的朋友，可以住到她家，周末和假期还有机会到她所在的培训中心打工。如果可能的话，我还希望学习时间可以延长到一年，我父母非常愿意负担第二个学期的费用。

祝您身体健康，工作顺利。谢谢。

珠理

Traditional Chinese

發信人：珠理

收信人：康先生

康先生，

您好。

我去年參加了"漢語橋"世界中學生中文比賽，幸運地拿到了三等獎，也獲得了在中國研修一學期漢語的機會。我特別希望能申請到貴校學習，提高中文水平。我想瞭解一下要準備哪些材料和填寫哪些表格。在學校附近我有一位教英文的朋友，可以住到她家，週末和假期還有機會到她所在的培訓中心打工。如果可能的話，我還希望學習時間可以延長到一年，我父母非常願意負擔第二個學期的費用。

祝您身體健康，工作順利。謝謝。

珠理

5. What is the purpose of this letter?

(A) Ask for information about the application process

(B) Register to participate in a Chinese competition

(C) Find a place in a residence hall

(D) Apply for financial aid

6. What is the scholarship for?

(A) To study in China for a year

(B) To pay for rent

(C) To study in China for a semester

(D) To work in a training center

7. The writer plans to stay in China and

(A) study for one semester.

(B) study for one year.

(C) teach for one semester.

(D) teach for one year.

Read this sign:

Simplified Chinese

水是生命之源，请您节约用水。

Traditional Chinese

水是生命之源，請您節約用水。

8. The purpose of the sign is to

   (A) stop people from wasting water.
   (B) give notice to people about access.
   (C) warn people about a danger.
   (D) post the penalty of breaking a law.

9. The sign is most likely posted

   (A) in an office.
   (B) in a restroom.
   (C) in a post office.
   (D) outside a store.

Read this brochure:

Simplified Chinese
康飞旅行社
畅销路线：
桂林三日游 278元
海南三亚双飞五日游 1290元
昆明大理丽江双飞六日游 1580元
北京双卧七日游 1280元
精品路线：
皇龙峡漂流一日游 178元
含门票、车费、中餐、景区保险和优秀导游服务
为节省您的时间，请务必带上有效身份证件办理旅行手续

Traditional Chinese
康飛旅行社
暢銷路線：
桂林三日游 278元
海南三亞雙飛五日游 1290元
昆明大理麗江雙飛六日游 1580元
北京雙臥七日游 1280元
精品路線：
皇龍峽漂流一日游 178元
含門票、車費、中餐、景區保險和優秀導遊服務
為節省您的時間，請務必帶上有效身份證件辦理旅行手續

10. The brochure is most likely given to the customers who want to

- (A) travel in China.
- (B) travel in different countries.
- (C) book a hotel.
- (D) book a flight.

11. What is covered in the trip to Sanya, Hainan?

- (A) A three-day trip with round-trip train tickets
- (B) A five-day trip with round-trip train tickets
- (C) A five-day trip with a one-way plane ticket
- (D) A five-day trip with round-trip plane tickets

12. What benefit is *not* included in the specially recommended trip to Huang Long Gorge?

- (A) A river rafting ticket
- (B) A free hotel
- (C) A free lunch
- (D) A tour guide

13. According to the brochure, what is required to enjoy the service?

- (A) Booking a hotel
- (B) Buying insurance
- (C) A valid ID
- (D) Hiring a tour guide

Read this advertisement:

Simplified Chinese
滨城电脑中心
日夜开班 随到随学
包学包会 推荐工作
军人凭证费用减半
地址：书馆路72号二楼
电话：7890–5346 罗小姐

Traditional Chinese
濱城電腦中心
日夜開班 隨到隨學
包學包會 推薦工作
軍人憑證費用減半
地址：書館路72號二樓
電話：7890–5346 羅小姐

14. The advertisement is placed by

- (A) a training center.
- (B) a computer store.
- (C) a job agency.
- (D) a bookstore.

15. The purpose of the advertisement is to recruit

    (A) customers to buy computers.
    (B) candidates for employment.
    (C) students to learn computer.
    (D) soldiers.

16. According to the advertisement, who will most likely get the discount?

    (A) Students
    (B) Someone with experience
    (C) Seniors
    (D) Soldiers

Read this poster:

Simplified Chinese

商住两用房一套出租，潮流街区，145平方米，三室两厅，高档装修，拎包可入住，亦适合办公、网吧、美容美发等。
有意者请致电 8259–7638 （早八点前及晚八点后关机，恕不接听来电）

Traditional Chinese

商住兩用房一套出租，潮流街區，145平方米，三室兩廳，高檔裝修，拎包可入住，亦適合辦公、網吧、美容美髮等。
有意者請致電 8259–7638 （早八點前及晚八點後關機，恕不接聽來電）

17. The purpose of the poster is to

    (A) sell a business.
    (B) rent out a unit.
    (C) seek a business partner.
    (D) promote a business.

18. Which one of the following statements is true according to this advertisement?

    (A) The rental unit could not be used as a residence.
    (B) The rental unit has three rooms in total.
    (C) The rental unit could be used as a beauty salon.
    (D) The rental unit is not furnished.

19. The poster says calls will be taken

    (A) before 8:00 p.m.
    (B) after 8:00 p.m.
    (C) before 8:00 a.m.
    (D) only at 8:00 p.m.

Read this flyer:

Simplified Chinese
事达搬家公司
快捷和安全是我们的服务宗旨
专业空调移机 专业钢琴搬运

315消费者信得过单位
工作时间：早上6:00至晚上11:00

Traditional Chinese
事達搬家公司
快捷和安全是我們的服務宗旨
專業空調移機 專業鋼琴搬運
315消費者信得過單位
工作時間：早上6:00至晚上11:00

20. The purpose of this flyer is to

    (A) promote a piano company.
    (B) promote a moving company.
    (C) promote an express delivery company.
    (D) promote the sale of air conditioners.

21. What is *not* listed in the promotion?

    (A) That the company is trusted by customers
    (B) That the company fixes air conditioners and pianos
    (C) That the company's service is safe
    (D) The company can start to work at 6:00 a.m.

Read these instructions:

Simplified Chinese
由于施工需要，星球大战展入口临时从东门改到北门，请各位游客向左绕行，
下一路口右转。
本展门票当天有效，票价成人二十元，老年人和学生凭证减半。
本展部分展区允许拍照、录像，但须预先申请许可证并不准使用闪光灯。
禁止携带任何食品饮料入场。
如需获得地图，请直接在购票处索取。
本展提供星球大战纪念册，限量发行，售完为止。

Traditional Chinese
由於施工需要，星球大戰展入口臨時從東門改到北門，請各位遊客向左繞行，
下一路口右轉。
本展門票當天有效，票價成人二十元，老年人和學生憑證減半。
本展部分展區允許拍照、錄像，但須預先申請許可證並不准使用閃光燈。
禁止攜帶任何食品飲料入場。
如需獲得地圖，請直接在購票處索取。
本展提供星球大戰紀念冊，限量發行，售完為止。

22. The entrance to the *Star Wars* exhibition is moved to

    (A) the north gate.
    (B) the south gate.
    (C) the east gate.
    (D) the west gate.

23. The instructions are primarily about

    (A)   the movie *Star Wars*.
    (B)   entering an exhibition.
    (C)   organizing an exhibition.
    (D)   buying books about *Star Wars*.

24. According to the instructions, the cost for a senior citizen to see the exhibition is

    (A)   free.
    (B)   20 yuan.
    (C)   10 yuan.
    (D)   not mentioned.

25. Which statement is true according to the information provided?

    (A)   No video recording is allowed in the exhibition.
    (B)   Only drinks can be brought in.
    (C)   The souvenir album is sold out.
    (D)   A map can be bought at the ticket office.

Read this article:

Simplified Chinese

根据高等院校关于开设文学欣赏课程的提议，燕京大学将外国文学欣赏课纳入每个大学生的必修课程中。

一直以来，中国大学提供的课程绝大部分都与专业相关，学生极少有机会对其他领域的东西进行了解和研究。与欧美大学生比较，中国的大学生在音乐、美术、文学等方面缺少起码的了解。这种方式培养不出全面的人才。

整个世界正在向全球化方向发展，简单的专业技术人员往往缺乏人文科学方面的体验，尤其是关于其他文化的知识。文学欣赏课的教材将以各种有代表性的外国文学作品为主，也会加入部分中国古典文学和现代文学作品作为比较。学生在学习过程中的比较与反思可以帮助他们更好地认识自己的文化，同时深入了解其他国家的价值观和社会意识。

从目前情况来看，实现这一计划的困难并不在于师资，而是来自于当今大学生对文学欣赏课程的误解和轻视。加强这方面的推广与宣传是成功的关键。

Traditional Chinese

根據高等院校關於開設文學欣賞課程的提議，燕京大學將外國文學欣賞課納入每個大學生的必修課程中。

一直以來，中國大學提供的課程絕大部分都與專業相關，學生極少有機會對其他領域的東西進行瞭解和研究。與歐美大學生比較，中國的大學生在音樂、美術、文學等方面缺少起碼的瞭解。這種方式培養不出全面的人才。

整個世界正在向全球化方向發展，簡單的專業技術人員往往缺乏人文科學方面的體驗，尤其是關於其他文化的知識。文學欣賞課的教材將以各種有代表性的外國文學作品為主，也會加入部分中國古典文學和現代文學作品作為比較。學生在學習過程中的比較與反思可以幫助他們更好地認識自己的文化，同時深入瞭解其他國家的價值觀和社會意識。

從目前情況來看，實現這一計劃的困難並不在於師資，而是來自於當今大學生對文學欣賞課程的誤解和輕視。加強這方面的推廣與宣傳是成功的關鍵。

26. Which of the following is mentioned in the article as a change?

    (A)   Adding a foreign literature appreciation course
    (B)   Adding a Chinese literature appreciation course
    (C)   Promoting literature appreciation in China
    (D)   Promoting literature appreciation overseas

27. How do Chinese students differ from students in the United States according to the article?

    (A)   Chinese students learn more music.
    (B)   Only students in the United States take literature courses.
    (C)   U.S. students love literature appreciation.
    (D)   Chinese students have less chance to study literature.

28. Which of the following is *not* included in the learning materials according to the article?

    (A)   Representative novels from other countries
    (B)   Works of classical Chinese literature
    (C)   Works of modern Chinese literature
    (D)   Textbooks from other countries

29. The biggest obstacle to this plan is

    (A)   funding to implement the plan of adding literature appreciation.
    (B)   changing the stereotype students have of literature appreciation.
    (C)   the limited number of instructors specializing in literature appreciation.
    (D)   the lack of learning materials on literature appreciation.

Read this short story:

Simplified Chinese

正月十五是春节过后的第一个月圆之日，也是深受中国人所喜爱的元宵节，既热闹又有趣。按中国民间的传统，家家都会在元宵节点起各种各样的灯庆贺。欣赏完了白天的踩高跷、划旱船、扭秧歌、舞龙舞狮等，晚上一家人会坐在一起津津有味地吃元宵。吃完以后，大家开始走出家门游玩。有的人猜灯谜，有的人放焰火，还有的人成群结队地在河边放花灯。

Traditional Chinese

正月十五是春節過後的第一個月圓之日，也是深受中國人所喜愛的元宵節，既熱鬧又有趣。按中國民間的傳統，家家都會在元宵節點起各種各樣的燈慶賀。欣賞完了白天的踩高蹺、劃旱船、扭秧歌、舞龍舞獅等，晚上一家人會坐在一起津津有味地吃元宵。吃完以後，大家開始走出家門遊玩。有的人猜燈謎，有的人放焰火，還有的人成群結隊地在河邊放花燈。

30. The story begins with

    (A)   a brief introduction to the Yuan Xiao festival.
    (B)   eating Yuan Xiao dumplings.
    (C)   a story of the Yuan Xiao festival.
    (D)   the activities of the Yuan Xiao festival.

31. Which daytime activity is popular during the Yuan Xiao festival according to the story?

    (A)   Eating Yuan Xiao dumplings
    (B)   The dragon dance and the lion dance
    (C)   Setting off fireworks
    (D)   Playing lantern riddles

32. Why did Dong Fang Shuo talk to the girl named Yuan Xiao?

    (A)   The girl worked for the emperor.
    (B)   The girl was in the emperor's palace.
    (C)   He fell in love with the girl.
    (D)   He was curious why the girl was crying.

33. Which of the following is true about the girl Yuan Xiao?

    (A)   She loved sending out the festival lantern.
    (B)   She loved her parents and missed them.
    (C)   She wanted to be with Dong Fang Shuo.
    (D)   She never got a chance to see her parents.

34. How did the emperor feel after he heard the story made up by Dong Fang Shuo?

    (A)   He was afraid.
    (B)   He was happy.
    (C)   He was angry.
    (D)   He was sad.

35. Which of the following is true according to the story?

    (A)   Chinese people eat moon cakes during the Yuan Xiao festival.
    (B)   Chinese people set fire and burn things during the Yuan Xiao festival.
    (C)   The Yuan Xiao festival is held on a day with a full moon.
    (D)   Yuan Xiao is the name of an emperor in China.

Section II: Free-Response Questions

Section II, Part A: Writing

Story Narration

You will have 15 minutes to finish the task of story narration. On the real test there will be a clock on your screen telling you how much time is left. For this practice test, you will need to time yourself.

Based on the four pictures provided, you need to write a coherent story with a beginning, a middle, and an ending. On the test you will need to type your answer using either the preset input of Microsoft IME or Microsoft New Phonetic IME system to type Chinese characters. You can switch between simplified Chinese and traditional Chinese.

The following four pictures present a story. Imagine you are telling the story to a friend. Write a complete story as suggested by the pictures. Give your story a beginning, a middle, and an ending.

E-mail Response

You will have 15 minutes to read an e-mail message from a specific person and type a response. On the real test there will be a clock on your screen telling you how much time is left. For this practice test, you will need to time yourself.

On the test you will need to type your response using the preset input of Microsoft IME or Microsoft New Phonetic IME system to type Chinese characters. You can switch between simplified Chinese and traditional Chinese.

Read this e-mail from a friend and then type a response.

Simplified Chinese

发件人：常明明

邮件主题：学习方法

小路，

你好！老师要我们收集各种适合自己的学习方法并做一个报告，可是我不知道该怎么写。你认为什么是最有益的学习方法？我需要改进哪些地方？还有，除了学习方法以外，你觉得对于一个优秀的学生，还应该具备哪些方面的技能？我想听听你的意见，谢谢。

Traditional Chinese

發件人：常明明

郵件主題：學習方法

小路，

你好！老師要我們收集各種適合自己的學習方法並做一個報告，可是我不知道該怎麼寫。你認為甚麼是最有益的學習方法？我需要改進哪些地方？還有，除了學習方法以外，你覺得對於一個優秀的學生，還應該具備哪些方面的技能？我想聽聽你的意見，謝謝。

Section II, Part B: Speaking

Track 25

Conversation

In this part of the exam, you will participate in a simulated conversation by responding to questions you will hear. The questions are based on a particular topic in a conversation with a particular person. There will be six 20-second pauses in the conversation during which you need to speak a response to the question(s) you've been asked. On the actual test, your 20-second response will be recorded and graded later.

You will have a conversation with Jing Jing, a friend you met in a Chinese summer camp, about your Chinese learning experience.

Cultural Presentation

In this part of the exam, you will make a presentation on a cultural topic you are given. You will have four minutes to prepare and then two minutes to make your oral presentation. On the actual test, your two-minute presentation will be recorded and then graded later. There will be a clock on your computer screen telling you how much time is left on the real test. For this practice test, you will need to time yourself.

Choose one traditional sport or activity in China, such as Jian Zi (Chinese Hacky Sack), Wei Qi, martial arts, or dragon boat race. In your presentation, describe the sport or activity in detail and explain its significance.

STOP. END OF PRACTICE TEST 1

Scripts for the Audio Portions of the Test

Script for Section I, Part A: Listening Rejoinders

Question #1

Simplified Chinese

Woman: 你怎么穿这么少？今天零下五度啊。

Man:

    (A) 我特别喜欢这身衣服。

    (B) 啊？零下五度？怎么这么热？

    (C) 我哪知道啊，早上出门还挺暖和的。

    (D) 是啊，今天就是热，我早就想脱掉外套了。

Traditional Chinese

Woman: 你怎麼穿這麼少？今天零下五度啊。

Man:

    (A) 我特別喜歡這身衣服。

    (B) 啊？零下五度？怎麼這麼熱？

    (C) 我哪知道啊，早上出門還挺暖和的。

    (D) 是啊，今天就是熱，我早就想脫掉外套了。

Question #2

Simplified Chinese

Woman: 昨天你去哪儿了？我打了好几个电话都没有找到你。

Man: 我头很痛，先去看了医生，然后去了一趟邮局。

Woman:

    (A) 原来你在邮局接的电话，怪不得那么吵。

    (B) 那你现在头还痛吗？

    (C) 你为什么不给我留言呢？

    (D) 你打电话有什么事吗？

Traditional Chinese

Woman: 昨天你去哪兒了？我打了好幾個電話都沒有找到你。

Man: 我頭很痛，先去看了醫生，然後去了一趟郵局。

Woman:

    (A) 原來你在郵局接的電話，怪不得那麼吵。

    (B) 那你現在頭還痛嗎？

    (C) 你為甚麼不給我留言呢？

    (D) 你打電話有甚麼事嗎？

Question #3

Simplified Chinese

Woman: 我总算明白小钟为什么成绩好了。他每天都呆在图书馆看书。

Man:

(A) 他成绩不好，谁成绩好呀？
(B) 小钟在图书馆等你吗？
(C) 是啊，所以我的成绩很好。
(D) 他就是聪明，天天玩，成绩还是好。

Traditional Chinese

Woman: 我總算明白小鐘為甚麼成績好了。他每天都呆在圖書館看書。

Man:

(A) 他成績不好，誰成績好呀？
(B) 小鐘在圖書館等你嗎？
(C) 是啊，所以我的成績很好。
(D) 他就是聰明，天天玩，成績還是好。

Question #4

Simplified Chinese

Man: 新买的游戏你到底放哪儿了？我怎么找也找不到。

Woman: 昨天我还看到在沙发左边的茶几上呢，难道你没看到吗？

Man:

(A) 原来你买了新沙发。
(B) 你也喜欢喝茶，跟我一样。
(C) 我没注意看，马上再去找找。
(D) 对不起，我不知道你想玩，早收起来了。

Traditional Chinese

Man: 新買的遊戲你到底放哪兒了？我怎麼找也找不到。

Woman: 昨天我還看到在沙發左邊的茶几上呢，難道你沒看到嗎？

Man:

(A) 原來你買了新沙發。
(B) 你也喜歡喝茶，跟我一樣。
(C) 我沒注意看，馬上再去找找。
(D) 對不起，我不知道你想玩，早收起來了。

Question #5

Simplified Chinese

Man: 都几点了，你怎么才来？晚了半小时，真把我急死了。

Woman:

(A) 我的表慢了，实在对不起。
(B) 你难道不知道打车吗？这么晚才到。
(C) 我等你好长一段时间了，下次你至少先给我打个电话。
(D) 不要紧，一会儿就好了。

Traditional Chinese

Man: 都幾點了，你怎麼才來？晚了半小時，真把我急死了。

Woman:

    (A) 我的表慢了，實在對不起。

    (B) 你難道不知道打車嗎？這麼晚才到。

    (C) 我等你好長一段時間了，下次你至少先給我打個電話。

    (D) 不要緊，一會兒就好了。

Question #6

Simplified Chinese

Woman: 今天公园有万圣节游乐会，你觉得我们扮什么比较好玩？

Man: 那么多人，我会想去？还不如在家睡觉呢。

Woman:

    (A) 原来你一直在家睡觉啊。

    (B) 好，我们七点钟去，那时候人最多。

    (C) 我也想去，肯定很棒。

    (D) 睡觉有什么好？还是去玩吧。

Traditional Chinese

Woman: 今天公園有萬聖節遊樂會，你覺得我們扮甚麼比較好玩？

Man: 那麼多人，我會想去？還不如在家睡覺呢。

Woman:

    (A) 原來你一直在家睡覺啊。

    (B) 好，我們七點鐘去，那時候人最多。

    (C) 我也想去，肯定很棒。

    (D) 睡覺有甚麼好？還是去玩吧。

Question #7

Simplified Chinese

Man: 这次我数学考了九十三分，说起来都是因为你帮我复习，真不知道应该怎么感谢你才好。

Woman:

    (A) 倒也是，有了你的帮助，我学习起来轻松多了。

    (B) 没关系，下次认真点就好了。

    (C) 看你说得那么客气，其实我也没做什么。

    (D) 今天没时间了，我得考完以后再谢你。

Traditional Chinese

Man: 這次我數學考了九十三分，說起來都是因為你幫我復習，真不知道應該怎麼感謝你才好。

Woman:

    (A) 倒也是，有了你的幫助，我學習起來輕鬆多了。

    (B) 沒關係，下次認真點就好了。

    (C) 看你說得那麼客氣，其實我也沒做甚麼。

    (D) 今天沒時間了，我得考完以後再謝你。

Question #8

Simplified Chinese

Woman: 我和陈同说好了下午三点一起做研究报告，可他没有来。我的部分早就做完了，他的还没写一半，明天上课够呛。

Man: 陈同的性子就是慢，还好我没有和他分在一组。

Woman:

    (A) 太过份了，你怎么不早点写完？

    (B) 这下我可真够麻烦的。

    (C) 哪儿的话呀，他做得可快呢。

    (D) 别难过，下次一定要努力。

Traditional Chinese

Woman: 我和陳同說好了下午三點一起做研究報告，可他沒有來。我的部分早就做完了，他的還沒寫一半，明天上課夠嗆。

Man: 陳同的性子就是慢，還好我沒有和他分在一組。

Woman:

    (A) 太過份了，你怎麼不早點寫完？

    (B) 這下我可真夠麻煩的。

    (C) 哪兒的話呀，他做得可快呢。

    (D) 別難過，下次一定要努力。

Question #9

Simplified Chinese

Woman: 我赶着去看古典音乐会，你反正不想去，有时间把家里的水管修一下吧。

Man:

    (A) 为什么你自己不修？

    (B) 我去不了音乐会，太可惜了。

    (C) 你喜欢修水管，我喜欢看音乐会，正好。

    (D) 你为什么一定要去看摇滚音乐会？

Traditional Chinese

Woman: 我趕著去看古典音樂會，你反正不想去，有時間把家裡的水管修一下吧。

Man:

    (A) 為甚麼你自己不修？

    (B) 我去不了音樂會，太可惜了。

    (C) 你喜歡修水管，我喜歡看音樂會，正好。

    (D) 你為甚麼一定要去看搖滾音樂會？

Question #10

Simplified Chinese

Man: 怎么样，行李超重了吧？都说了要少带点礼物。

Woman: 看把你急的。这是国际航班，每人可以带两件行李，每件不超过五十磅就行了。

Man:

    (A) 你说得对，我经常搭国际航班。

    (B) 你哪个箱子都超过了五十磅。

    (C) 反正我都得带上，该交多少交多少。

    (D) 幸好你的箱子都超过了五十磅。

Traditional Chinese

Man: 怎麼樣，行李超重了吧？都説了要少帶點禮物。

Woman: 看把你急的。這是國際航班，每人可以帶兩件行李，每件不超過五十磅就行了。

Man:

    (A) 你説得對，我經常搭國際航班。

    (B) 你哪個箱子都超過了五十磅。

    (C) 反正我都得帶上，該交多少交多少。

    (D) 幸好你的箱子都超過了五十磅。

Question #11

Simplified Chinese

Woman: 张伯伯感冒了好几天，最后住院了你知道吗？

Man: 不会那么严重吧？吃药打针都不行，非得住院啊？

Woman:

    (A) 是啊，你怎么不到医院来看我？

    (B) 是啊，我也没想到会那么严重。

    (C) 没错，不严重，所以不需要住院。

    (D) 吃药打针对治疗感冒很有效的。

Traditional Chinese

Woman: 張伯伯感冒了好幾天，最後住院了你知道嗎？

Man: 不會那麼嚴重吧？吃藥打針都不行，非得住院啊？

Woman:

    (A) 是啊，你怎麼不到醫院來看我？

    (B) 是啊，我也沒想到會那麼嚴重。

    (C) 沒錯，不嚴重，所以不需要住院。

    (D) 吃藥打針對治療感冒很有效的。

Question #12

Simplified Chinese

Man: 我的运气实在是太差了，这次考试又没拿到驾照。还是趁着上午人不多才去考的呢，仍然没过。

Woman: 光在停车场练习怎么行，你得上路练，习惯了就不会紧张。

Man:

(A) 哦，他们会把驾照寄给你的。
(B) 怪不得你拿到了驾照，上午开车是比较容易。
(C) 是啊，停车场练习驾驶很有用。
(D) 我就是不怎么敢上路练习。

Traditional Chinese

Man: 我的運氣實在是太差了，這次考試又沒拿到駕照。還是趁著上午人不多才去考的呢，仍然沒過。

Woman: 光在停車場練習怎麼行，你得上路練，習慣了就不會緊張。

Man:

(A) 哦，他們會把駕照寄給你的。
(B) 怪不得你拿到了駕照，上午開車是比較容易。
(C) 是啊，停車場練習駕駛很有用。
(D) 我就是不怎麼敢上路練習。

Question #13

Simplified Chinese

Man: 这菜钱多算了二十块，你得跟餐馆经理谈一谈。咱们吃什么都不能吃亏。

Woman:

(A) 你说得对，这家餐馆很便宜。
(B) 你只有二十块钱？算了，我请客。
(C) 是啊，我也不喜欢吃亏。
(D) 我下次一定多叫些人来吃。

Traditional Chinese

Man: 這菜錢多算了二十塊，你得跟餐館經理談一談。咱們吃甚麼都不能吃虧。

Woman:

(A) 你說得對，這家餐館很便宜。
(B) 你只有二十塊錢？算了，我請客。
(C) 是啊，我也不喜歡吃虧。
(D) 我下次一定多叫些人來吃。

Question #14

Simplified Chinese

Woman: 听说这次比赛你们班得了第一名，恭喜恭喜！
Man:

    (A) 别逗了，是倒数第一！
    (B) 你们班拿到了第一啊，难怪你今天这么高兴。
    (C) 你什么时候参加的比赛？
    (D) 一直没见到你，原来你是去比赛了！

Traditional Chinese

Woman: 聽說這次比賽你們班得了第一名，恭喜恭喜！
Man:

    (A) 別逗了，是倒數第一！
    (B) 你們班拿到了第一啊，難怪你今天這麼高興。
    (C) 你甚麼時候參加的比賽？
    (D) 一直沒見到你，原來你是去比賽了！

Question #15

Simplified Chinese

Woman: 看你这一身脏的，是不是摔跤了？
Man: 没办法，我的车坏了，大热天的挤公交，真受不了。
Woman:

    (A) 先休息一下吧。摔得痛不痛？
    (B) 天天开车的人，突然一下子要坐公交车，是挺不习惯的。
    (C) 我帮你把车开过来。
    (D) 那我能不能借你的车用一下？拜托了！

Traditional Chinese

Woman: 看你這一身臟的，是不是摔跤了？
Man: 沒辦法，我的車壞了，大熱天的擠公交，真受不了。
Woman:

    (A) 先休息一下吧。摔得痛不痛？
    (B) 天天開車的人，突然一下子要坐公交車，是挺不習慣的。
    (C) 我幫你把車開過來。
    (D) 那我能不能借你的車用一下？拜託了！

Script for Section I, Part A: Listening Selections

Track 24

Announcement
Narrator: Now you will listen to an announcement. This selection will be played twice.

Simplified Chinese

各位乘客，这里就是著名的河南嵩山少林寺，是联合国批准的世界文化遗产，也是中国武术文化的象征。请大家将行李留在车上，随身携带贵重物品下车参观。参观时间为两个小时，请于十一点三刻以前回来，我们将在十二点准时发车，继续今天的旅行。

Traditional Chinese

各位乘客，這裡就是著名的河南嵩山少林寺，是聯合國批准的世界文化遺產，也是中國武術文化的象徵。請大家將行李留在車上，隨身攜帶貴重物品下車參觀。參觀時間為兩個小時，請於十一點三刻以前回來，我們將在十二點準時發車，繼續今天的旅行。

Narrator: Now listen again.
[Repeat]
Narrator: Now answer the questions for this selection.

Voice Message
Narrator: Now you will listen to a voice message. This selection will be played only once.

Simplified Chinese

Woman: 史开，你好。对不起，我刚才正在开会，所以不能接听你的电话。你要买的外套已经没有蓝色的了，不过还有黑色的。如果仍然需要，我可以帮你订。我们下个星期天去森林公园的计划没变吧？早上八点在公园门口等，对吗？这个季节下雨天特别多，地点是不是改在森林宾馆大厅比较好呢？我现在马上就要去参加棒球训练，晚上十点才能回来，只能到那时候给你发地址和行程安排。我先走了，有什么问题请给我电话留言。

Traditional Chinese

Woman: 史開，你好。對不起，我剛才正在開會，所以不能接聽你的電話。你要買的外套已經沒有藍色的了，不過還有黑色的。如果仍然需要，我可以幫你訂。我們下個星期天去森林公園的計劃沒變吧？早上八點在公園門口等，對嗎？這個季節下雨天特別多，地點是不是改在森林賓館大廳比較好呢？我現在馬上就要去參加棒球訓練，晚上十點才能回來，只能到那時候給你發地址和行程安排。我先走了，有什麼問題請給我電話留言。

Narrator: Now answer the questions for this selection.

School Conversation
Narrator: Now you will listen to a conversation between a teacher and a student. This selection will be played only once.

Simplified Chinese

Woman: 秦老师，我明天和后天都不能来上课，您可不可以告诉我这两天的功课有哪些？
Man: 明天就是单元测试，你最好不要缺课。

Woman: 我也没有办法啊，我明天得去纽约参加小提琴演奏会，后天晚上才能回来。不过我星期五可以补考。
Man: 星期五什么时候？
Woman: 下午第六节课是我在图书馆的自习时间，我可以到您的办公室来找您。我保证这是最后一次，下一次表演时间就到暑假了。
Man: 那好吧。考试内容是第八课，你得抓紧时间准备。
Woman: 我在飞机上会认真复习的。
Man: 我知道这次演奏会对你很重要，不过作为一个高中生，学习更重要。

Traditional Chinese

Woman: 秦老師，我明天和後天都不能來上課，您可不可以告訴我這兩天的功課有哪些？
Man: 明天就是單元測試，你最好不要缺課。
Woman: 我也沒有辦法啊，我明天得去紐約參加小提琴演奏會，後天晚上才能回來。不過我星期五可以補考。
Man: 星期五什麼時候？
Woman: 下午第六節課是我在圖書館的自習時間，我可以到您的辦公室來找您。我保證這是最後一次，下一次表演時間就到暑假了。
Man: 那好吧。考試內容是第八課，你得抓緊時間準備。
Woman: 我在飛機上會認真複習的。
Man: 我知道這次演奏會對你很重要，不過作為一個高中生，學習更重要。

Narrator: Now answer the questions for this selection.

Instructions

Narrator: Now you will listen to someone giving instructions. This selection will be played twice.

Simplified Chinese

Woman: 小严，三点钟下课的话，你可以先在校门口赶上三点一刻的7路公交车。经过三站，在友谊百货商店下车。地铁站在公交站旁边，一眼就可以看到。然后坐去翠竹北的地铁二号线，票价是五块钱，如果没有硬币的话，可以到咨询处先换硬币再买票。大概是六站吧，田贝中学的后一站下。记得要从北门出，太白路出口，是太白路哦！出站台后左边是大地花园，我住大地花园西座1110号。如果实在找不到，记得给我打电话。

Traditional Chinese

Woman: 小嚴，三點鐘下課的話，你可以先在校門口趕上三點一刻的7路公交車。經過三站，在友誼百貨商店下車。地鐵站在公交站旁邊，一眼就可以看到。然後坐去翠竹北的地鐵二號線，票價是五塊錢，如果沒有硬幣的話，可以到諮詢處先換硬幣再買票。大概是六站吧，田貝中學的後一站下。記得要從北門出，太白路出口，是太白路哦！出站台後左邊是大地花園，我住大地花園西座1110號。如果實在找不到，記得給我打電話。

Narrator: Now listen again.
[Repeat]
Narrator: Now answer the questions for this selection.

Radio Report

Narrator: Now you will listen to a radio report. This selection will be played twice.

Simplified Chinese

Man: 各位听众，据唐人台报导，在昨日下午举行的子女教育座谈会中，与会代表和现场观众就中美家庭对孩子的教育问题进行了热烈的讨论。中国父母"望子成龙，望女成凤"的理念普遍存在，对孩子的学习成绩非常重视，名牌大学和赚钱的专业是他们的目标。美国父母大多认为孩子的性格和兴趣爱好更为重要，希望孩子全面发展，对考上名牌大学与否没有特别要求。请大家继续关注唐人新闻。

Traditional Chinese

Man: 各位聽眾，據唐人台報導，在昨日下午舉行的子女教育座談會中，與會代表和現場觀眾就中美家庭對孩子的教育問題進行了熱烈的討論。中國父母"望子成龍，望女成鳳"的理念普遍存在，對孩子的學習成績非常重視，名牌大學和賺錢的專業是他們的目標。美國父母大多認為孩子的性格和興趣愛好更為重要，希望孩子全面發展，對考上名牌大學與否沒有特別要求。請大家繼續關注唐人新聞。

Narrator: Now listen again.

[Repeat]

Narrator: Now answer the questions for this selection.

Job Interview

Narrator: Now you will listen to a job interview. This selection will be played twice.

Simplified Chinese

Man: 你有哪些做志愿者的工作经验？
Woman: 从高一开始，我每年暑假都会做义工，主要是在医院接待病人，帮英文不好的人做翻译等等。有时候周末也会去一些非盈利性社团，教电脑啊，照顾老人小孩啊，跟您现在的这份工作很相似。我没在公司工作过。
Man: 我们老年公寓有些住户脾气不太好，需要很大的耐心。你有哪些能力让我们优先考虑你呢？
Woman: 我对人一直很热情，在从前的工作中也接触过很多老人，为他们组织过很多活动，和他们相处得非常愉快。当然，我也遇到过喜欢生气的，我的经验就是把他们当成小孩，多交流，多听，找到他们生气的原因，问题就容易解决了。
Man: 我们要求志愿者每周至少工作四个小时，你周末也可以工作吗？
Woman: 完全可以，除星期六早上以外，其他时间我都有空。

Traditional Chinese

Man: 你有哪些做志願者的工作經驗？
Woman: 從高一開始，我每年暑假都會做義工，主要是在醫院接待病人，幫英文不好的人做翻譯等等。有時候週末也會去一些非盈利性社團，教電腦啊，照顧老人小孩啊，跟您現在的這份工作很相似。我沒在公司工作過。
Man: 我們老年公寓有些住戶脾氣不太好，需要很大的耐心。你有哪些能力讓我們優先考慮你呢？
Woman: 我對人一直很熱情，在從前的工作中也接觸過很多老人，為他們組織過很多活動，和他們相處得非常愉快。當然，我也遇到過喜歡生氣的，我的經驗就是把他們當成小孩，多交流，多聽，找到他們生氣的原因，問題就容易解決了。
Man: 我們要求志願者每週至少工作四個小時，你週末也可以工作嗎？
Woman: 完全可以，除星期六早上以外，其他時間我都有空。

Narrator: Now listen again.

[Repeat]

Narrator: Now answer the questions for this selection.

Track 25

Script for Section II, Part B: Conversation

Narrator: You will have a conversation with Feng Qing, a reporter from a newspaper, who is interviewing high school students about their Chinese cultural experience.

Simplified Chinese

1. 你是第一次参加中文夏令营吗？你为什么想参加中文夏令营？
2. 在夏令营学了很多成语，你印象最深的是哪一句？
3. 中国人日常生活中喜欢用一些俗语歇后语什么的，请你举个例子。
4. 看电影可以帮助学生练习中文和了解中国文化。你最喜欢哪一部中国电影？这部电影让你对中国文化有了什么新的认识？
5. 学中文难吗？你对初学者有什么建议？
6. 你打算在大学继续学中文吗？你觉得学习中文有什么好处？

Traditional Chinese

1. 你是第一次參加中文夏令營嗎？你為甚麼想參加中文夏令營？
2. 在夏令營學了很多成語，你印象最深的是哪一句？
3. 中國人日常生活中喜歡用一些俗語歇後語甚麼的，請你舉個例子。
4. 看電影可以幫助學生練習中文和瞭解中國文化。你最喜歡哪一部中國電影？這部電影讓你對中國文化有了甚麼新的認識？
5. 學中文難嗎？你對初學者有甚麼建議？
6. 你打算在大學繼續學中文嗎？你覺得學習中文有甚麼好處？

Answers and Explanations for Section I

Here are the correct answers with complete explanations. Check your answers on the practice test. Look at the explanations not only for the ones you missed but also for all those that you were unsure about and could have missed.

Answers and Explanations for the Listening Rejoinders

Answers

1. C	6. D	11. B
2. B	7. C	12. D
3. A	8. B	13. C
4. C	9. A	14. A
5. A	10. B	15. B

Explanations

Look back at "Strategies for the Listening Rejoinders" in Chapter 5. Did you remember all the strategies and use them effectively?

1. (C) The woman asks why the man is dressed so lightly. She states that the temperature today is 5 degrees below freezing. So the answers should continue the logic of being cold, which is (C). In China, Celsius is used for temperature instead of Fahrenheit.

2. (B) The woman states that she called the man several times but didn't find him. The man says that he got a headache so he went to see the doctor first and then to the post office.

3. (A) The woman says that she figured out why someone is doing very well academically. The reason is studying in the library every day. The answer should continue the logic, which excludes (B) and (C). Choice (D) would be a great response if it didn't say "plays every day." 他成绩不好，谁成绩好呀（他成績不好，誰成績好呀） is a commonly used expression to emphasize, for example: If he is not great, who would be great?

4. (C) The man asks for where the woman put the newly purchased game. The woman says that she saw it on the table by the sofa. The answer should match the logic of the game on the table, which is answer (C).

5. (A) The man is complaining that the woman was late. The answer of the woman should explain the situation, which is: "My watch is slow. Sincerely sorry."

6. (D) The woman asks what to wear for Halloween; the man answers that he prefers staying home and sleeping. Pay attention to the tone from the man. "So many people, I want to go?" 那么多人，我会想去？（那麼多人，我會想去？） means "How can I want to go?" instead of that he really wants to go.

7. (C) The man shows his thanks to the woman because he obtained a high score on the math test after the woman helped him. So the answer should continue the logic. "See you are too polite." 看你说得那么客气（看你説得那麼客氣）.

8. (B) The woman complains that her partner Chen Tong didn't finish the group project. The man emphasized that Chen Tong is slow. The answer should continue this logic. Choice (A) is what the woman should tell Chen Tong instead of the man. Choice (C) is inconsistent with the fact that Chen Tong is slow. Choice (D) doesn't make sense. Learn these two commonly used set phrases: "unbearable, terrible" 够呛（夠嗆） and "really troublesome" 真够麻烦的（真夠麻煩的）.

9. (A) The woman says that she is going to the classical music concert and asks the man to fix the plumbing since he doesn't want to go. Choice (D) is incorrect because the conversation is about classical music instead of a rock and roll concert. Choice (B) "It's a pity that I could not go" is not true since the man doesn't want to go. Choice (C) "You like fixing plumbing and I like going to a concert, great!" isn't consistent with the conversation.

10. (B) This topic is about overweight luggage. The man worries that the luggage is overweight; the woman explains that it is an international flight and the maximum is 50 pounds per piece of luggage. The man thinks that both cases are more than 50 pounds. Note that "lucky" is 幸好.

11. (B) The woman says that uncle Zhang is in the hospital. The man is surprised. The answer should continue this logic. Choices (A) and (C) don't continue it, and (D) provides contradictory information.

12. (D) The man is frustrated at not passing the driver's license test. The woman suggests that he should practice on the road instead of the parking lot. Choices (A) and (B) are incorrect because they are based on the premise that the man got his license. Choice (C) is incorrect because it provides the opposite logic that the "parking lot is good for driving practice."

13. (C) The man says that the bill was incorrect. He used a very popular expression in Chinese: "Can be taken whatever but not taken advantage of." 吃什么都不能吃亏（吃什麼都不能吃虧）. There are a lot of interesting proverbs and slams related to 吃, such as:

吃女人豆腐 take advantage of woman

吃不消 cannot handle

吃不准 not so sure

14. (A) The woman congratulates the man for being first in a competition. The man explains that actually it was first from the bottom.

15. (B) The woman wonders whether the man fell down, since his clothes are kind of dirty. The man explains that his car was broken and he had to take the bus. The answer should continue the logic of a broken car and taking the bus. "The person used to driving daily will find it inconvenient taking buses." Note that "not used to, not convenient" is 挺不习惯的（挺不習慣的）.

Answers and Explanations for the Listening Selections

Look back at "Strategies for the Listening Selections" in Chapter 6. Did you remember all the strategies and use them effectively? How did you do on note taking? Remember that you will need to take notes when you listen to the selections, because you won't see the questions until the audio selection is finished.

Answers

16. D	**23.** B	**30.** A
17. B	**24.** A	**31.** D
18. B	**25.** C	**32.** B
19. A	**26.** A	**33.** A
20. D	**27.** D	**34.** C
21. C	**28.** B	**35.** A
22. A	**29.** C	

Explanations

16. (D) 车（車）was mentioned several times; you can guess that it is a place to visit.

17. (B) Note that "get off" is 下车（下車）. "Leave the luggage in the bus" is 将行李留在车上（將行李留在車上）.

18. (B) It's easy to choose the incorrect answer of (C), since the last number mentioned in the audio selection is often the correct choice. However, the question asks for the time to "come back" instead of "leave"; it is 11:45.

19. (A) This is a relatively difficult question since the four choices are spread out through the whole selection. Play attention to (A) and (B) since they share the same structure. The voice message mentioned that there were only black ones left so you can guess that A is correct.

20. (D) The reason of the change of meeting location, by common sense, will be (D). Others are not logical.

21. (C) Since there is a change of location, the location mentioned last is usually correct: "hotel hall" 宾馆大厅（賓館大廳）.

22. (A) The voice message clearly states that the speaker will "send address and travel plans to you" 给你发地址和行程安排（給你發地址和行程安排）.

23. (B) "I cannot attend class tomorrow and the day after tomorrow" is 我明天和后天都不能来上课（我明天和後天都不能來上課）.

24. (A) "Tomorrow is the date for unit test" is 明天就是单元测试（明天就是單元测試）.

25. (C) "Violin concert" is 小提琴演奏会（小提琴演奏會），表演.

26. (A) This is an easy one. Hearing so many familiar phrases related to transportation and road, you should select (A).

27. (D) Be sure to take notes. You should have noted down the number and the corresponding information.

28. (B) Did you hear something about money? Yes, so (A) is incorrect, and (B) is correct.

29. (C) This is an easy question. Note that "children's education" is 子女教育.

30. (A) The goal of Chinese parents is to send their kids to a famous college or to make money. Making money isn't a choice, so that leaves (A).

31. (D) The last part of this selection states that "American parents hope their kids get the whole development" 美国父母……他们希望孩子全面发展（美國父母……他們希望孩子全面發展）.

32. (B) The woman states: "since the first year of high school" 从高一开始（從高一开始）.

33. (A) You heard choices (B), (C), and (D) in the selection. However, there was no mention of (A) an administrative assistant, so this is the one answer choice she has not done before.

34. (C) It's not easy to recognize "patience" 耐心 and passion.

35. (A) The only part mentioning time is at the end. She states: "except for Saturday morning" 除星期六早上以外. The answer is (A).

Answers and Explanations for Reading Comprehension

Look back at "Strategies for Reading Comprehension" in Chapter 7. Did you remember all the strategies and use them effectively? Which ones do you still need to work on?

Answers

1. C	**13.** C	**25.** C
2. B	**14.** A	**26.** A
3. D	**15.** C	**27.** D
4. B	**16.** D	**28.** D
5. A	**17.** B	**29.** B
6. C	**18.** C	**30.** A
7. B	**19.** A	**31.** B
8. A	**20.** B	**32.** D
9. B	**21.** B	**33.** B
10. A	**22.** A	**34.** A
11. D	**23.** B	**35.** C
12. B	**24.** C	

Explanations

1. (C) The first sentence states "thank you for…" 感谢你（感謝你）. Here's another strategy you can use since the question is asking for the purpose: You know the purpose must be related to the recipient (you). Therefore, the purpose should sit in a sentence of "verb + you." For the first half of the message, the only phrase of "verb + you" is 感谢你（感謝你）.

2. (B) The e-mail didn't state directly what she feels about the gift. However, the phrase of "especially like" 特别喜欢（特別喜歡）indicates that she is very happy.

3. (D) You have learned the strategy of paying attention to the content after "的," which may be subjects or objects. Here "detailed address" is 的具体地址（的具體地址）.

4. (B) The last part of the e-mail is about "visiting the sender's school" 参观我们学校（參觀我們學校）.

5. (A) Please review the explanation for Question #1. Normally, you would look for the construction "verb + you" here as well. However, there is no "you" in or around the beginning part; instead, it is "your honorable school" 贵校（貴校）. This is how Chinese write formal letters. 贵（貴）is used for courtesy. The phrase "I hope" 我希望 is the one to locate in this sentence of purpose. The purpose is "application" 申请（申請）.

6. (C) To find the sentence about the "scholarship" 奖学金（獎學金）, normally you would try to find the Chinese characters. But in this case, they are actually not in the letter. However, based on the four choices, you know it is probably a decision between (A) and (C) since they share the same structure. The first sentence mentioned "one semester," which is answer (C).

7. (B) Anything with numbers is great because the numbers can help you locate the sentences for the answer. The writer hopes to study for one year, and her parents are willing to pay for her second semester.

8. (A) It's about water, of course. The only choice mentioning water is (A).

9. (B) You may not know the meaning of 节约（節約）, which means "save." However, you know "use water" 用水. The six characters are "Please _____ using water." Common sense tells you the blank would be about saving water or being cautious when using water and this sign would most likely be in a restroom.

10. (A) It's about travel in China because the trip destinations are all cities in China.

11. (D) Remember that province will be in front of city, so you were looking for "Hainan, Sanya." Sanya and Hainan—at least you can figure out two characters: 三 and 海. Therefore, you know the question is asking about the trip of 1290 yuan. Note that "round trip by air" is 双飞（雙飛）and "one-way trip by train" is 单卧（單臥）.

12. (B) The "draft ticket" 门票（門票）, "lunch" 中餐, and "tour guide" 导游（導遊）were included.

13. (C) A "valid ID" is 有效身份证件（有效身份證件）.

14. (A) The first line states that it is a computer center. The second line states that there are classes and learning. Therefore, (A) is correct.

15. (C) Refer to the explanation for Question #14.

16. (D) Note that "half price" is 减半（減半）. You may not know 军人（軍人）means "solider," but you probably know the characters for the other three choices. Since there is no mention of the other three choices, the answer has to be "soldier."

17. (B) The phrase "for rent" is 出租. From "three bedrooms, one living room, one dining room" 三室两厅（三室兩廳）, you know it is a rental unit.

18. (C) This type of poster is typical in China. You need to be aware of customary Chinese practices on a poster, which are often more pictographic than straightforward. "Both for commercial or for residence" is 商住两用（商住兩用）. "Can live in with your bag" 拎包可入住 indicates that it is well furnished. Thus, the only choice that is true is (C).

19. (A) Use common sense and look for numbers. You can locate the sentence and get the answer easily.

20. (B) "Moving company" is 搬家公司.

21. (B) The company moves air conditioners and pianos instead of fixing them.

22. (A) The instructions say "Enter by the north gate instead of the east gate": 从东门改到北门（從東門改到北門）.

23. (B) Even if you do not know 展 means "exhibition," Question #22 already told you it's an exhibition so you can eliminate choices (A) and (D). Since the instructions talk about a ticket fee, you know the instructions are about getting into the exhibit rather than (C).

24. (C) You'll notice 减半（減半） again; it means "half the price."

25. (C) "Which of the following is true/false?" questions always test your patience. Locate the choices in the selection and eliminate the incorrect choices.

26. (A) The first paragraph states the answer clearly.

27. (D) To locate the answer in the selection, the key phrase to look for is "compared to the college students in the Europe and the United States" 与欧美大学生比较（與歐美大學生比較）. The article is usually the most difficult reading selection on the test. If you are not sure about an answer, always read the sentences before and after the sentence with the answer. Sometimes understanding the context will make it easier to understand the sentence.

28. (D) (A), (B), and (C) are mentioned together in the middle of Paragraph 3. That makes (D) the only answer choice not included.

29. (B) The last paragraph of the article states the answer. "Misunderstanding and neglecting" is 误解和轻视（誤解和輕視）.

30. (A) Some students may choose (D) since a big part of Paragraph 1 is about the activities. But the question asks for "begins with," and the paragraph begins with a brief introduction to the Yuan Xiao festival (A).

31. (B) Use "daytime" as a key word to locate the sentence with the answer. Although there are a number of daytime activities listed that you probably have no idea what they are, you do know "the dragon dance and the lion dance." That's good enough for you to choose the correct answer.

32. (D) "Cry" is 哭.

33. (B) The whole story of Yuan Xiao is about helping her get out to see her parents.

34. (A) According to the story, "the emperor was scared after he heard this story" 皇帝听了这个故事非常害怕（皇帝聽了這個故事非常害怕）.

35. (C) Moon cakes (A) are for moon festival; you can eliminate this answer. Choice (B) is not true, instead Chinese people put up lanterns to stand for fire; "Just like there is a fire" is 好像满城大火一样（好像滿城大火一樣）. Finally, eliminate choice (D) Yuan Xiao is the girl's name, not an emperor's.

Section II: Free-Response Questions

For the free-response questions, it's not hard to get a score of 4 as long as you answered each question and completed each task. In this section are sample answers at a level of 5 or above. These are followed by an English translation of the sample answer and an explanation of the answer.

Answer and Explanation for the Story Narration

Look back at "Strategies for the Story Narration" in Chapter 8. Did you remember all the strategies and use them effectively? Which ones do you still need to work on?

Sample Answer

Simplified Chinese

小李要飞去美国开会，开开心心地和他的妻子小王说再见。他带上行李，坐出租车来到了机场。在等着办登机手续的时候，小李突然发现找不到自己的护照了，急得一拍头：这下坏了！他赶忙给小王打电话："糟糕！护照怕是掉在家里了。你帮我找找！好不好？"小王找到了护照赶到机场，交到了小李手上。"幸好还来得及！"小李不好意思地笑了，再次和妻子告别。 (Level 6)

Traditional Chinese

小李要飛去美國開會，開開心心地和他的妻子小王說再見。他帶上行李，坐出租車來到了機場。在等著辦登機手續的時候，小李突然發現找不到自己的護照了，急得一拍頭：這下壞了！他趕忙給小王打電話："糟糕！護照怕是掉在家裡了。你幫我找找！好不好？"小王找到了護照趕到機場，交到了小李手上。"幸好還來得及！"小李不好意思地笑了，再次和妻子告別。 (Level 6)

English translation

Xiao Li is flying to the United States for a conference. He bid farewell to his wife Xiao Wang and went to the airport by taxi, taking his luggage with him. When Xiao Li was checking in, he found out that he didn't have his passport. He patted his head and said to himself, "Oh, Great!" Xiao Li called Xiao Wang immediately: "What a mess! I probably left my passport at home. Can you help me by looking for it?" Xiao Wang found his passport and rushed to the airport. She handed him the passport. "Lucky that I still have time!" Xiao Li said. Embarrassed, Xiao Li smiled and said goodbye to his wife.

Explanation

Based on the four pictures, the storyline is: The man with luggage was leaving the woman while the taxi waited. The man found out that he didn't have the passport at the airport. Then he made a phone call to the woman. The woman handed the passport to him at the airport.

For this prompt, there are a lot of factors that could keep you from scoring a 6. The most common mistakes would be missing an important action in the pictures or not providing all the transitional elements for the logic of the four pictures. Pay attention to the following details:

- For Picture #1, mention the taxi. It's a good idea to also mention the luggage since it is in the picture.
- For Picture #2, describe that he was patting his head.

- For Picture #3, writing a dialogue is probably much easier than writing a long explanation of the incident.
- For Picture #4, explain all the events including that the woman found the passport, brought it to the airport, and handed it to the man so that the story makes sense.

Answer and Explanation for the E-mail Response

Look back at "Strategies for the E-mail Response" in Chapter 9. Did you remember all the strategies and use them effectively? Which ones do you still need to work on?

Sample Answer

Simplified Chinese

常明明，

你好！好久没和你联系了，收到你的电子邮件很开心。

你想确定最有益的学习方法是什么，每个人的看法都不一样。有的人喜欢背诵学习资料，有的人喜欢练习解决问题。但无论如何，最好的学习方法应当包括了解自己的学习目的和正确运用时间管理。也就是先知道自己要做什么，然后要有好的计划。如果计划得当，就可以节省很多时间。要是不清楚自己的目的，再怎么努力都不能达到最佳效果。我记得你说过你不喜欢做计划，这样的话，你常常要浪费时间想这个时候该学什么，是不是还经常会忘记交作业的最后期限？所以你应该养成做计划的习惯。

一个优秀的学生，除了学习方法好以外，首先是要有很好的应用技能，把学的东西真正用到生活中。其次要注意的是社交能力和与其他同学合作的能力。另外，也不要忘了全面发展，因为音乐、体育、美术等这些方面的学习同样重要。

我的看法不一定对，你还可以咨询一下你的老师和同学，听听他们的建议。

祝一切顺利。

小路

Traditional Chinese

常明明，

你好！好久沒和你聯繫了，收到你的電子郵件很開心。

你想確定最有益的學習方法是甚麼，每個人的看法都不一樣。有的人喜歡背誦學習資料，有的人喜歡練習解決問題。但無論如何，最好的學習方法應當包括瞭解自己的學習目的和正確運用時間管理。也就是先知道自己要做甚麼，然後要有好的計劃。如果計劃得當，就可以節省很多時間。要是不清楚自己的目的，再怎麼努力都不能達到最佳效果。我記得你說過你不喜歡做計劃，這樣的話，你常常要浪費時間想這個時候該學甚麼，是不是還經常會忘記交作業的最後期限？所以你應該養成做計劃的習慣。

一個優秀的學生，除了學習方法好以外，首先是要有很好的應用技能，把學的東西真正用到生活中。其次要注意的是社交能力和與其他同學合作的能力。另外，也不要忘了全面發展，因為音樂、體育、美術等這些方面的學習同樣重要。

我的看法不一定對，你還可以咨詢一下你的老師和同學，聽聽他們的建議。

祝一切順利。

小路

English translation

Chang Ming Ming,

Long time, no see. I am very glad to receive your e-mail.

You want to know the best way to learn. Everybody has his own opinion. Some of them enjoy reciting the materials, and some of them practice problem solving. No matter what you prefer, the best learning strategy should include understanding your learning goals and having good time management skills. That means you should know exactly what you need to do, and then plan scientifically. A good plan can save you a lot of time. If you are not sure about your goal, however hard you try you may not have the best result. I remember that you said you didn't like planning. If this is the case, you often have to waste time figuring out what to do. Do you often forget the due dates of your assignments as well? Then I think you should make planning a good habit.

Besides good learning strategy, an excellent student should have good application skills, using what he or she has learned in daily life. Second, the student should pay attention to his or her social skills and teamwork skills. Also, do not forget developing other talents because learning in music, sports, and arts is also important.

This is just my personal opinion. You should consult your teachers or classmates and ask for their suggestions.

Hope everything goes well.

Xiao Lu

Explanation

First, what do you write? The two questions are obvious, but note that there are two parts to the first question: what the best learning strategy is and what the sender needs to improve. The second question expands this to what is important to be an excellent student.

The second step in writing your response is to apply your prepared template. The sample answer provides a thorough adaptation of a prepared template to the specific questions in this e-mail message. You do not need to write in such detail in the real exam. You can "fill in the blanks" by adding the content from the e-mail message. There are actually only two basic components of your reply:

1. The importance of goal setting and planning
2. The other requirements to being a good student—applying what you have learned, teamwork, and developing a variety of talents

If you had trouble, review the skill-building exercises in Chapter 9 to build or improve your template. Analyze the sample answer. Did you see how the sample answer applies the template smoothly? What adjustments to the template were made in the answer?

Answers and Explanations for the Conversation

Look back at "Strategies for the Conversation" in Chapter 10. Did you remember all the strategies and use them effectively? Which ones do you still need to work on?

Sample Answers

In this part of the exam, you are required to answer six questions about your Chinese learning experience in a conversation with a friend you met in a Chinese summer camp. A rather detailed set of answers is provided for your reference. On the actual exam, an answer scored 5 or 6 generally consists of four to six short sentences.

Simplified Chinese

1. 你是第一次参加中文夏令营吗？你为什么想参加中文夏令营？

Is this the first time you attended a Chinese summer camp? Why do you want to participate?

我是第一次参加中文夏令营。我学中文已经三年多了，一直很想在一个全中文的环境中提高自己的水平，也想有机会来中国练习中文。这次夏令营可以满足我最大的愿望。同时，我有同学参加了去年的夏令营，都说特别好，所以我就来了。

2. 在夏令营学了很多成语，你印象最深的是哪一句？

You have learned a lot of Chinese idioms in the summer camp. Which one is the most impressive to you?

我印象最深的一句成语是"乱七八糟"，它的英文意思是very messy。我觉得这句成语什么时候什么地方都可以用，用起来很好玩。我的卧室是乱七八糟的，我的作业也是乱七八糟的，我的头发更是乱七八糟，我不喜欢乱七八糟的朋友，我说了这么一大段乱七八糟的……

3. 中国人日常生活中喜欢用一些俗语歇后语什么的，请你举个例子。

Chinese people enjoy using proverbs in daily life. Please provide an example.

中国人日常生活中喜欢用俗语，我印象最深的一句是"饭后百步走，活到九十九"。这句话的意思是说，吃完饭后走一百步，就可以活得很久，很长寿。我觉得这一句话中含着很深的道理，健康和养生是密不可分的，吃完饭活动一下，消化好，也不容易长胖。

4. 看电影可以帮助学生练习中文和了解中国文化。你最喜欢哪一部中国电影？这部电影让你对中国文化有了什么新的认识？

Watching movies helps students to practice Chinese and understand Chinese culture. What is your favorite Chinese movie? What new cultural understanding did this movie provide?

我最喜欢的电影是《白蛇传说》。老实说，我从前认为中国人相当传统，不会有什么特别离奇的神话。看过白蛇传说才对中国文化有了新的认识。想一想啊，一个人和一条蛇相爱，居然还结婚生了孩子，真的是不可思议。原来中国人也非常浪漫，中国文化的包容性太强了。

5. 学中文难吗？你对初学者有什么建议？

Is learning Chinese hard? What suggestions do you have for beginners?

学中文不难。对初学者来说，第一是要把发音练好，不管花多少时间，一定要掌握正确的声调。第二是要多认汉字。其实认字很好玩的，很多汉字其实就象画一样，可以根据它们的形状猜意思。第三嘛，当然是要多找中国人交流，每天说十分钟，三年就可以说得很流利了。

6. 你打算在大学继续学中文吗？你觉得学习中文有什么好处？(20 seconds)

Will you continue learning Chinese in college? In your opinion, what benefits will learning Chinese provide?

我在大学当然会继续学中文。我已经学了四年了，交了很多好朋友，而且我相信朋友会越来越多，因为全世界有四分之一的人在说中文。同时，中国现在发展很快，学中文将来会有更多的机会。还有啊，我去过中国，特别喜欢那里的文化，中国人都很友善，我想大学毕业以后住在中国。

Traditional Chinese

    1. 你是第一次參加中文夏令營嗎？你為甚麼想參加中文夏令營？
Is this the first time you attended a Chinese summer camp? Why do you want to participate?

我是第一次參加中文夏令營。我學中文已經三年多了，一直很想在一個全中文的環境中提高自己的水平，也想有機會來中國練習中文。這次夏令營可以滿足我最大的願望。同時，我有同學參加了去年的夏令營，都說特別好，所以我就來了。

    2. 在夏令營學了很多成語，你印象最深的是哪一句？
You have learned a lot of Chinese idioms in the summer camp. Which one is the most impressive to you?

我印象最深的一句成語是"亂七八糟"，它的英文意思是very messy。我覺得這句成語甚麼時候甚麼地方都可以用，用起來很好玩。我的臥室是亂七八糟的，我的作業也是亂七八糟的，我的頭髮更是亂七八糟，我不喜歡亂七八糟的朋友，我說了這麼一大段亂七八糟的……

    3. 中國人日常生活中喜歡用一些俗語歇後語甚麼的，請你舉個例子。
Chinese people enjoy using proverbs in daily life. Please provide an example.

中國人日常生活中喜歡用俗語，我印象最深的一句是"飯後百步走，活到九十九"。這句話的意思是說，吃完飯後走一百步，就可以活得很久，很長壽。我覺得這一句話中含著很深的道理，健康和養生是密不可分的，吃完飯活動一下，消化好，也不容易長胖。

    4. 看電影可以幫助學生練習中文和瞭解中國文化。你最喜歡哪一部中國電影？這部電影讓你對中國文化有了甚麼新的認識？
Watching movies helps students to practice Chinese and understand Chinese culture. What is your favorite Chinese movie? What new cultural understanding did this movie provide?

我最喜歡的電影是《白蛇傳説》。老實説，我從前認為中國人相當傳統，不會有甚麼特別離奇的神話。看過白蛇傳説才對中國文化有了新的認識。想一想啊，一個人和一條蛇相愛，居然還結婚生了孩子，真的是不可思議。原來中國人也非常浪漫，中國文化的包容性太強了。

    5. 學中文難嗎？你對初學者有甚麼建議？
Is learning Chinese hard? What suggestions do you have for beginners?

學中文不難。對初學者來説，第一是要把發音練好，不管花多少時間，一定要掌握正確的聲調。第二是要多認漢字。其實認字很好玩的，很多漢字其實就象畫一樣，可以根據它們的形狀猜意思。第三嘛，當然是要多找中國人交流，每天説十分鐘，三年就可以説得很流利了。

    6. 你打算在大學繼續學中文嗎？你覺得學習中文有甚麼好處？(20 seconds)
Will you continue learning Chinese in college? In your opinion, what benefits will learning Chinese provide?

我在大學當然會繼續學中文。我已經學了四年了，交了很多好朋友，而且我相信朋友會越來越多，因為全世界有四分之一的人在説中文。同時，中國現在發展很快，學中文將來會有更多的機會。還有啊，我去過中國，特別喜歡那裡的文化，中國人都很友善，我想大學畢業以後住在中國。

Scoring Guidelines

Review in your mind your answers to each of the six questions. To get a high score, your answers need to meet the following characteristics:

- Did you address the questions thoroughly with details?
- Did you have smooth sentence connections?
- Did your answers have a natural pace with a minimum of repetitions/hesitations?
- Did you use correct pronunciation and register?
- Did your answers show good vocabulary usage with minimal grammatical errors?

Answer and Explanation for the Cultural Presentation

Look back at "Strategies for the Cultural Presentation" in Chapter 11. Did you remember all the strategies and use them effectively? Which ones do you still need to work on?

Sample Answer

Simplified Chinese

中国是有着五千年历史和文明的国家。中国式的体育运动和活动也一直是中国文化的组成部分。我今天想介绍一种中国著名的体育运动，这种运动是武术。我想和大家谈谈中国武术为什么很重要，有什么样的特点和意义。

武术的英文意思是 martial arts，对大多数中国人来说，就是他们常说的功夫。中国功夫在全世界都非常有名。我特别喜欢看各种各样的功夫电影，像李小龙啊，成龙啊，李连杰啊，他们展现的中国武术各有特点。我自己也练习中国武术，就像体育运动一样，我学的是太极剑，每天练习二十分钟后，一整天都不会觉得疲倦。

武术是一种全身运动，对身体健康很有好处。更重要的是，武术能够锻炼人的心志和毅力，培养人勤奋、勇敢、刻苦的精神；还可以交到很多的朋友，在中国，每天早上都有很多人在公园里练习中国武术，年轻人、老年人都有，练剑啊，功夫扇啊，打太极拳啊什么的；功夫在美国也特别流行，到处都有中国武术学习中心。武术成为传播中国文化的桥梁，为世界带来友谊与和平。

中国武术是中国文化不可缺少的部分。说实在的，我这个武术迷一直想去中国河南的少林寺看看。那是中国武术的故乡，和其他的武术爱好者一起交流进步，肯定很值得。

Traditional Chinese

中國是有著五千年歷史和文明的國家。中國式的體育運動和活動也一直是中國文化的組成部分。我今天想介紹一種中國著名的體育運動，這種運動是武術。我想和大家談談中國武術為甚麼很重要，有甚麼樣的特點和意義。

武術的英文意思是 martial arts，對大多數中國人來說，就是他們常說的功夫。中國功夫在全世界都非常有名。我特別喜歡看各種各樣的功夫電影，像李小龍啊，成龍啊，李連傑啊，他們展現的中國武術各有特點。我自己也練習中國武術，就像體育運動一樣，我學的是太極劍，每天練習二十分鐘后，一整天都不會覺得疲倦。

武術是一種全身運動，對身體健康很有好處。更重要的是，武術能夠鍛鍊人的心志和毅力，培養人勤奮、勇敢、刻苦的精神；還可以交到很多的朋友，在中國，每天早上都有很多人在公園裡練習中國武術，年輕人、老年人都有，練劍啊，功夫扇啊，打太極拳啊甚麼的；功夫在美國也特別流行，到處都有中國武術學習中心。武術成為傳播中國文化的橋梁，為世界帶來友誼與和平。

中國武術是中國文化不可缺少的部分。說實在的，我這個武術迷一直想去中國河南的少林寺看看。那是中國武術的故鄉，和其他的武術愛好者一起交流進步，肯定很值得。

English Translation

China is a country with 5,000 years of history and civilization. Traditional Chinese sports and activities are always a part of Chinese culture. I am going to introduce a famous Chinese sport today: Chinese martial arts. I am going to discuss why Chinese martial arts are important and what the significance of Chinese will be.

"Chinese martial arts" is what we call it in English. To most Chinese, it is Kung Fu. Chinese Kung Fu is very popular worldwide. I love watching all kinds of Kung Fu movies, such as movies with Bruce Lee, Jackie Chan, Jet Li, and so on. They presented different features of Chinese Kung Fu. I myself practice Chinese martial arts. It is just like sports. I learned Taiji sword. I practice twenty minutes each day, which helps me to stay energetic.

Martial arts is an exercise for the whole body, which benefits health. More importantly, practicing martial arts can reinforce persistence and will, and help you make a lot of great friends. In China, there are a lot of people practicing martial arts in the morning, older people and young. They practice swords, Kung Fu fan, Taiji, and so on. Chinese martial arts is popular in China as well with training centers everywhere. As the bridge of Chinese culture, martial arts plays a role in connecting the world with friendship and peace.

Chinese martial arts is an essential part of Chinese culture. I am a Kung Fu fan and have always wanted to visit Shao Lin Temple in Henan, China, which is the hometown of Chinese martial arts. Communicating with other Kung Fu fans and improving my skills would be a great experience. Chinese martial arts is part of Chinese culture worth promoting.

Explanation and Tips

This topic is typical of what you'll find on the exam. It's good to know something about the topic of Chinese martial arts because you can use this not only for presentations about sports and cultural activities, but also for diverse topics such as a movie about Chinese culture (Karate Kid, Shao Lin Soccer), a celebrity in China (Jackie Chan, Jet Li), or even UNESCO World Heritage sites in China (Shao Lin Temple).

Selecting some subjects for the presentation is important preparation. Catalog the subjects you have practiced and try to reduce these to a smaller number that can be adapted broadly to different presentation topics. Here are some ideas:

When preparing for the subject of the Chinese spring festival, you can focus on the topics of

1. Food: 饺子（餃子）
2. A holiday: 春节（春節）
3. An ancient story: 年的故事
4. Chinese philosophy: 合家团圆（合家團圓）
5. Folk customs: 守岁，合家团圆（守歲，合家團圓）
6. Inventions: 烟花，焰火（煙花，焰火）

When preparing for the subject of the Great Wall of China, you can focus on the topics of

1. Architecture
2. Famous people in ancient times: 秦始皇
3. An ancient story: 孟姜女哭长城（孟姜女哭長城）
4. A landmark
5. A travel site

When preparing for the subject of 四合院, you can focus on the topics of

1. Architecture
2. Family structure: 家族
3. A travel site: 北京
4. Taboos: 风水，颜色，数字（風水，顏色，數字）

Scoring and Interpreting Your Results

For multiple-choice questions, the simple number of correct answers you have can be used to convert to your AP score.

For free-response questions, it's not as easy for you to figure out what exactly your score could be. Here is a simple checklist to give you a general idea about how you did on the free-response questions so you can score yourself.

Scoring Checklist

1. Did you answer all the basic questions?
   Yes. Your score may be 3 and above. Otherwise your score may be 2 or below 2.
2. Was your answer understandable and logical to the reader or listener?
   Yes. Your score may be 4 and above.
3. Was your answer well structured, with rich language usage and minor errors?
   Yes. Your score may be 5 and above.

To see what you might have done if this had been the actual AP exam, you may convert your answers to a rough AP score using the following worksheet. This is a method for estimating your score and the results do not guarantee that you will do similarly on the actual AP exam.

Section I: Multiple Choice

Rejoinders: (number correct) ÷15 × 0.10 = _____

Listening Selections: (number correct) ÷ (total number) × 0.15 = _____

Reading: (number correct) ÷ (total number) × 0.25 = _____

Section II: Free Response

Story Narration: (score yourself on a scale of 1 to 6) ÷ 6 × 0.15 = _____

E-mail Response: (score yourself on a scale of 1 to 6) ÷ 6 × 0.10 = _____

Conversation: (score yourself on a scale of 1 to 6) ÷ 36 × 0.10 = _____

Cultural Presentation: (score yourself on a scale of 1 to 6) ÷ 6 × 0.15 = _____

Total Score for Sections I and II = _____

Total Points for Sections I and II = _____ × 120 = _____

Appendixes

Functional Grammar for Smooth Writing
Useful Expressions for Smooth Speaking
Frequently Used Vocabulary in Reading and Listening
Useful Websites

FUNCTIONAL GRAMMAR FOR SMOOTH WRITING

It's not too difficult to do a good job in writing in regard to the scoring guidelines (rubrics) of "task completion" and appropriate "delivery," but the rubric of "language use" requires a "wide range of grammatical structures." Reviewing the grammar in a "functional" way is an effective and efficient way to grasp a wide range of grammatical structures in a short time.

Why Learn Functional Grammar?

Different languages follow different grammatical systems. Different authorities label the systems in different ways. Different teachers teach grammar in different ways. All of this may not only cause confusion for learners, but also mislead the learner to an obsession with rules of mechanics instead of language proficiency.

Language is the tool for communication. However a language looks or sounds, it is used to achieve the function of communication. The grammar learning method you will use in this book is based on applying sentences to functions. That is why I call it "functional grammar"—the syntax is cataloged by the function.

What Is Functional Grammar?

Forget the ways you have learned about sentence structure. Think from the beginning. Let's make this simple.

How Many Types of Sentences Exist in a Language?

The answer is only two: the simple sentence and the nonsimple sentence. A simple sentence, or an independent clause, is normally one subject and one verb, no matter how long it is or how much description has been added.

Samples: Romeo loves Juliet.

The handsome, brave Romeo loves the beautiful, sweet, kind Juliet this hot and sunny summer.

How Many Types of Nonsimple Sentences in a Language?

Complex sentences, compound sentences, complex *and* compound sentences, or... Stop! The answer is still just two.

First, think about what you want to say. Regarding nonsimple questions, or those with two or more clauses, there are only two kinds of functions for the relationships between clauses: parallel or interacted.

Parallel: Romeo loves Juliet, and Juliet loves Romeo.
Interacted: Because Romeo loves Juliet, Juliet loves Romeo.

How Many Types of Functions Can Nonsimple Sentences Have?

There are nine different functions expressed by the relationship between two independent clauses. Let's mark the clauses as A and B.

For a Parallel Relationship

Function 1: A and B
Romeo loves Juliet, and Juliet loves Romeo, too.

Function 2: A or B
Romeo loves Juliet, or Juliet loves Romeo?

Function 3: A but B
Romeo loves Juliet, but Juliet doesn't love Romeo.

Function 4: Emphasize B (not only A, but also B).
Not only does Romeo love Juliet, but Juliet also loves Romeo.

For an Interactive Relationship

Function 5: A is the condition.
As long as Romeo loves Juliet, Juliet will love Romeo.

Function 6: A is the hypothesis.
If Romeo loves Juliet, Juliet will love Romeo.

Function 7: A is the reason.
Because Romeo loves Juliet, Juliet loves Romeo.

Function 8: B is the goal.
Romeo loves Juliet, in order that Juliet will love Romeo.

Have you found out that Functions 5 and 6 could be cataloged together? Functions 7 and 8 could also be cataloged together. However, separating them can be more specific, and thus more useful, in fulfilling the exact function you want to express in writing.

Function 9: A first, B second. The relationship of A and B could be either parallel or interacted.
Romeo loves Juliet first, then Juliet loves Romeo.

Are You Kidding? Only Nine Functions of Sentences? What About the Complicated Literature Pieces?

They still follow our rules of functional grammar. Let's take one of Shakespeare's famous quotes as an example:

To be or not to be?
Function 2!

There may be a few exceptions for these nine functions which are not included here. But, remember, you are preparing for the AP Chinese exam. These nine functions solve 99.9% of the issues in writing sentences; we can leave the other 0.1% for scholars.

How to Apply Functional Grammar

Choose two conjunction phrases for each function. One could be a popular one, and the other could be less popular but authentic so that it expresses your skills of advanced-level writing. We don't need to cover all the possible expressions. Practicing 18 phrases selected by you is a great solution.

Simplified Chinese

FUNCTIONS	USEFUL PHRASES
1. A = B	既……又……, 还, 也, 同样, 不是……而是……, 是……不是……
	一方面……（另）一方面……, 一边……一边……
	有的……有的……
	* 要在中文AP考试取得成功, 一方面是要多练习, 另一方面是要学习正确的考试方法。
2. A or B	要么……要么……, 是……还是……,不是……就是……,
	与其……不如……, 宁可……也（决）不……
	* 与其等到AP考试时着急, 不如现在用这本书好好复习。
3. A but B	虽然……但是/不过……, 尽管……可是……, **竟然, 居然**
	* If you use 虽然……却……, the subject needs to be in front of 却.
	虽然小王没来, 不过小李来了。
	虽然小王没来, 小李<u>却</u>来了。
4. Emphasize B	不但/不仅/不光……而且/还……,
	尚且……更何况/更不用说……
	* 他尚且不担心AP考试, 更不用说我了。
5. A is the condition	只要……就……, 只有……才……, 除非……才……
	无论/不管/不论……也/都/还……
	* 无论怎么样, 我都不想现在就睡觉。
	Tip: If you do not know how to freely use the expression of "no matter what/how/whether," just use 无论怎么样.
6. A is the hypothesis	如果/假如/倘若/若/要是/要……就/那么/便/那就……,
	即使/就算/哪怕/即便/纵使……也/还/还是……
	* 即使你从小就说中文, 你还是应该准备一下AP考试。
7. A is the reason	因为/由于……所以, ……因此……, 之所以……是因为……,
	既然……就/可见……
	* 既然打算考AP中文, 就应该开始准备。
8. B is the goal	为了……, 为的是……,
	negative: 以免……, 免得……
	* 小王七点就来了, 以免让小李等。
9. A first, B second	首先……接着/其次……然后……最后
	第一……接下来……还有……
	* 首先……其次……cannot be used for sequence.
	首先, 我喜欢唱歌, 其次喜欢跳舞。
	今天晚上我一直在忙。首先我唱了三首歌, 其次我跳了一会儿舞。✘
	今天晚上我一直在忙。首先我唱了三首歌, <u>然后</u>我跳了一会儿舞。✔

Traditional Chinese

FUNCTIONS	USEFUL PHRASES
1. A = B	既……又……，還，也，同樣，不是……而是……，是……不是……
	一方面……（另）一方面……，一邊……一邊……
	有的……有的……
	* 要在中文AP考試取得成功，一方面是要多練習，另一方面是要學習正確的考試方法。
2. A or B	要麼……要麼……，是……還是……，不是……就是……，
	與其……不如……，寧可……也（決）不……
	* 與其等到AP考試時著急，不如現在用這本書好好復習。
3. A but B	雖然……但是/不過……，儘管……可是……，竟然，居然
	* If you use 雖然……卻……, the subject needs to be in front of 卻.
	雖然小王沒來，不過小李來了。
	雖然小王沒來，小李卻來了。
4. Emphasize B	不但/不僅/不光……而且/還……，
	尚且……更何況/更不用說……
	* 他尚且不擔心AP考試，更不用說我了。
5. A is the condition	只要……就……，只有……才……，除非……才……
	無論/不管/不論……也/都/還……
	* 無論怎麼樣，我都不想現在就睡覺。
	Tip: If you do not know how to freely use the expression of "no matter what/how/whether," just use 無論怎麼樣.
6. A is the hypothesis	如果/假如/倘若/若/要是/要……就/那麼/便/那就……，
	即使/就算/哪怕/即便/縱使……也/還/還是……
	* 即使你從小就說中文，你還是應該準備一下AP考試。
7. A is the reason	因為/由於……所以，……因此……，之所以……是因為……，
	既然……就/可見……
	* 既然打算考AP中文，就應該開始準備。
8. B is the goal	為了……，為的是……，
	negative: 以免……，免得……
	* 小王七點就來了，以免讓小李等。
9. A first, B second	首先……接著/其次……然後……最後
	第一……接下來……還有……
	* 首先……其次……cannot be used for sequence.
	首先，我喜歡唱歌，其次喜歡跳舞。
	今天晚上我一直在忙。首先我唱了三首歌，其次我跳了一會兒舞。✗
	今天晚上我一直在忙。首先我唱了三首歌，然後我跳了一會兒舞。✓

How to Refine Your Advanced-Level Writing Skills

Functional grammar helps you write nonsimple sentences logically at an advanced level in a couple of hours. However, functional grammar is not able to solve the problem for someone who finds writing a simple sentence difficult. Chinese learning is a long-term and accumulative process. The good news is that the AP Chinese writing section doesn't test how complicated your sentences are. You can easily elaborate a sentence of subject + verb + object (S + V + O) to make your writing reach the AP level of 6 while minimizing grammatical errors. You are not writing a publishable book of literature in Chinese.

As stated earlier in this book, adding descriptive elements to simple sentences fulfills the requirement of rich language usage in the AP exam. How do you elaborate a simple sentence to achieve an advanced level? You just need to add all or some of the elements: time, location, adjectives, adverbs, weather, feelings/facial expressions, and so on. Learn to do this first, and then apply functional grammar.

1. S + V + O
   我见到了小明。
   （我見到了小明。）

I saw Xiao Ming.

2. Add time, location, adjectives, adverbs, weather, feelings/facial expressions.
   今天下午天气很好，我在图书馆突然见到了最好的朋友小明，我很高兴。
   （今天下午天氣很好，我在圖書館突然見到了最好的朋友小明，我很高興。）

The weather was nice this afternoon. I met my best friend Xiao Ming by accident at the library. I was happy.

3. Apply functional grammar.
   因为今天下午天气很好，所以我去了图书馆。我突然见到了我最好的朋友小明，他也看到了我。不但我很高兴，小明也很高兴："如果我没来图书馆，就不会见到你了。"
   （因為今天下午天氣很好，所以我去了圖書館。我突然見到了我最好的朋友小明，他也看到了我。不但我很高興，小明也很高興："如果我沒來圖書館，就不會見到你了。"）

Because the weather was nice this afternoon, I went to the library. Suddenly I saw my best friend Xiao Ming, and he saw me as well. Not only was I happy, but so was Xiao Ming: "If I hadn't come to the library, I would not have seen you here!"

USEFUL EXPRESSIONS FOR SMOOTH SPEAKING

The phrases we learned for functional grammar in writing are highly recommended for speaking as well. In addition, there are authentic and powerful set expressions for you to speak as a native and win yourself some time in the exam. Here are some popular and useful ones; catalog them for easier usage. Feel free to organize them in your preferred way. Again, keep in mind that you do not need to memorize all of them. Choose your favorite expressions and practice using them daily!

Describing Time

after that	那以后（那以後）
later, afterward	后来（後來）
soon	不久
soon/shortly after	……之后不久（之後不久）
at last	终于（終於）
lately	近来（近來）
recently	最近
since then	从那时起（從那時起）
until now	直到现在（直到現在）
after a while	一会儿，过了一会儿（一會兒，過了一會兒）
once, as soon as	一……就……
right away, immediately	立即，马上，立刻（立即，馬上，立刻）
at the same time	在此期间，同时（在此期間，同時）
suddenly, all of a sudden	突然

Describing Position

in front of	在……前面
at the back of	在……后面（在……後面）
below	在……下方
above	在……上方
in the middle of	在……中间（在……中間）
at the bottom of	在……底部
on top of	在……顶部（在……頂部）
across	在……的另一边
around	在……周围（在……周圍）
nearby	在……附近
opposite to	与……相对（與……相對）
close to	靠近
on the right/left	在右/左边（在右/左邊）
to the right/left	朝右/左

Comparing

comparatively	比较起来（比較起來）
like	像……，像……一样（像……，像……一樣）

similarly	同样地（同樣地）
in the same way	以相同的方式
on the contrary	正相反
different from	与……不同（與……不同）
not exactly like	并不完全是（並不完全是）

Giving an Example or Emphasizing Something

for example	例如……，举个例子吧（例如……，舉個例子吧）
such as	如……
take … for example	拿……来说（拿……來说）
especially	特别是，尤其是
favorite	我最喜欢的是（我最喜歡的是）
in fact/as a matter of fact	事实上（事實上）
in other words	换句话说（換句話说）
that is	也就是说（也就是说）
in that case	那样的话（那樣的話）
to be more exact	更确切地说（更確切地说）

Summarizing

in conclusion	总的来说，一句话，总而言之（總的來说，一句話，總而言之）
it is well known that	大家都知道，众所周知（大家都知道，眾所周知）
it is clear that	很显然（很顯然）
as has been mentioned	正如所提到的
generally speaking	一般说来（一般説來）
taking everything into consideration	从总体来看（從總體來看）
I think	我认为，我觉得，我的看法是（我認為，我覺得，我的看法是）
as far as I know	据我所知（據我所知）
in my opinion	依我看来（依我看來）
by the way	顺便说（順便说）
I am afraid	我恐怕
to tell the truth	说实话（説實話）
to be honest	老实说（老實説）
in fact	事实上（事實上）

FREQUENTLY USED VOCABULARY IN READING AND LISTENING

How much vocabulary should you know to succeed on the AP Chinese exam? The more vocabulary you know, the more easily you can apply strategies in the actual exam. Learning all the vocabulary of the lists here can prepare you very well for the AP Chinese exam.

Lists of frequently used vocabulary were provided in Chapters 6 and 7 for the listening sections and the reading selections. So why does a frequently used list of vocabulary appear in the appendix when you have those lists already—because there is an important feature of the Chinese language: radicals. Radicals are similar to prefixes and suffixes in English, but they are much more powerful and crucial to improving your Chinese literacy. They indicate the meanings of a character.

Here you'll find the frequently used vocabulary that students may find difficult. Feel free to collect more based on your own learning. You may try to guess the meaning first, and then use the Pinyin to search or confirm if there is any confusion. The slight change of radicals between simplified and traditional Chinese should not affect your learning.

亻：Related to People
休息、退休、身体、具体、健康、健身房、付款、跳楼价、大减价、讨价还价、便宜、兵马俑、风俗习惯、保护、保险、保重、保修期、装修、修理、修改、必修课、选修课、机票代理、相信、信用卡、假期、放假、停车、传统、方便
（休息、退休、身體、具體、健康、健身房、付款、跳樓價、大減價、討價還價、便宜、兵馬俑、風俗習慣、保護、保險、保重、保修期、裝修、修理、修改、必修課、選修課、機票代理、相信、信用卡、假期、放假、停車、傳統、方便）

xiūxi, tuìxiū, shēntǐ, jùtǐ, jiànkāng, jiànshēnfáng, fùkuǎn, tiào lóu jià, dà jiǎn jià, tǎojiàhuánjià, piányi, bīngmǎyǒng, fēngsú xíguàn, bǎohù, bǎoxiǎn, bǎozhòng, bǎoxiū qī, zhuāngxiū, xiūlǐ, xiūgǎi, bìxiū kè, xuǎnxiū kè, jīpiào dàilǐ, xiāngxìn, xìnyòngkǎ, jiàqī, fàngjià, tíngchē, chuántǒng, fāngbiàn

宀：A Closed Room, a Place with Roof, Family
教室、宿舍、室友、电脑室、办公室、卧室、急诊室、阅览室、三室两厅、公寓、顾客、乘客、旅客、客气、故宫、寄信、元宵、夜宵、秘密、宇宙、肯定、一定、确定
（教室、宿舍、室友、電腦室、辦公室、臥室、急診室、閱覽室、三室兩廳、公寓、顧客、乘客、旅客、客氣、故宮、寄信、元宵、夜宵、秘密、宇宙、肯定、一定、確定）

jiàoshì, sùshè, shìyǒu, diànnǎo shì, bàngōngshì, wòshì, jízhěn shì, yuèlǎn shì, sānshì liǎng tīng, gōngyù, gùkè, chéngkè, lǚkè, kèqì, gùgōng, jì xìn, yuánxiāo, yèxiāo, mìmì, yǔzhòu, kěndìng, yīdìng, quèdìng

穴：Cave
空气、空调、窗户、穿过、贫穷、研究
（空氣、空調、窗戶、穿過、貧窮、研究）

kōngqì, kōngtiáo, chuānghu, chuānguò, pínqióng, yánjiū

厂、户、广、尸：House, Bigger Space or Huge Room, Half-Closed Room

餐厅、野餐、楼房、窗户、客厅、厨房、厕所、饭厅、车库、走廊、病房、订房间、退房、房地产租赁、雇用、解雇、广场、商店、零售店、便利店、座位、咖啡屋、居民、邻居

（餐廳、野餐、樓房、窗戶、客廳、廚房、廁所、飯廳、車庫、走廊、病房、訂房間、退房、房地產租賃、雇用、解雇、廣場、商店、零售店、便利店、座位、咖啡屋、居民、鄰居）

cāntīng, yěcān, lóufáng, chuānghu, kètīng, chúfáng, cèsuǒ, fàntīng, chēkù, zǒuláng, bìngfáng, dìngfáng jiān, tuì fáng, fángdìch ǎn zūlìn, gùyòng, jiěgù, guǎngchǎng, shāngdiàn, língshòu diàn, biànlì diàn, zuòwèi, kāfēi wū, jūmín, línjū

阝：Geography, Area, Administrational Area

影院、学院、医院、大专院校、商学院、工学院、四合院、邮局、邮票、邮费、邻居、附近、郊游、陪同、首都、消防、限制、限量、教育部

（影院、學院、醫院、大專院校、商學院、工學院、四合院、郵局、郵票、郵費、鄰居、附近、郊遊、陪同、首都、消防、限制、限量、教育部）

y ǐngyuàn, xuéyuàn, yīyuàn, dàzhuān yuànxiào, shāng xuéyuàn, gōng xuéyuàn, sìhéyuàn, yóujú, yóupiào, yóufèi, línjū, fùjìn, jiāoyóu, péitóng, shǒudū, xiāofáng, xiànzhì, xiànliàng, jiàoyù bù

木：Something Related to Wood

衣柜、书桌、椅子、教学楼、科学楼、实验楼、行李架、大排档、机器、录音机、机会

（衣櫃、書桌、椅子、教學樓、科學樓、實驗樓、行李架、大排檔、機器、錄音機、機會）

yīguì, shūzhuō, yǐzi, jiàoxué lóu, kēxué lóu, shíyàn lóu, xínglǐ jià, dà páidàng, jīqì, lùyīnjī, jīhuì

艹：Grass

花草、茶几、吃药、火药、蔬菜、荤菜

（花草、茶几、吃藥、火藥、蔬菜、葷菜）

huāc ǎo, chájī, chī yào, hu ǒyào, shūcài, hūncài

竹：Bamboo

签证、风筝、筷子、园林建筑、策划、管理、铅笔、蜡笔、钢笔、简单

（簽證、風箏、筷子、園林建築、策劃、管理、鉛筆、蠟筆、鋼筆、簡單）

qiānzhèng, fēngzheng, kuàizi, yuánlín jiànzhù, cèhuà, gu ǎnl ǐ, qiānb ǐ, làb ǐ, gāngb ǐ, ji ǎndān

冫：Cold, Freezing, Water

氵：Water, Move

冰冻、冰箱、寒冷、冰淇淋、决定、决赛、
清洁卫生、取消、流行、表演、演奏、血液、湖泊、海滩、河、加油、旅游

（冰凍、冰箱、寒冷、冰淇淋、決定、決賽、
清潔衛生、取消、流行、表演、演奏、血液、湖泊、海灘、河、加油、旅遊）

bīngdòng, bīngxiāng, hánlěng, bīngqílín, juédìng, juésài, qīngjié wèishēng, qǔxiāo, liúxíng, bi ǎoyǎn, yǎnzòu, xiěyè, húpō, hǎitān, hé, jiāyóu, lǚyóu

灬: **Cook**
煎熬、热烈、煮、蒸、烧焦
（煎熬、熱烈、煮、蒸、燒焦）

jiān'áo, rèliè, zhǔ, zhēng, shāo jiāo

火：**Fire**
发烧、烧烤、烧焦、麻烦、灯笼、灯迷、灶王爷、炒菜、锻炼、烟火、灭火
（發燒、燒烤、燒焦、麻煩、燈籠、燈迷、灶王爺、炒菜、鍛鍊、煙火、滅火）

fāshāo, shāokǎo, shāojiāo, máfan, dēnglóng, dēng mí, zào wángye, chǎocài, duànliàn, yānhuǒ, mièhuǒ

讠、言：**Speak, Language**
证件、证明、身份证、许可证、移民签证、翻译与公证、会计、考试、面试、试用期、登记、培训、评论、建议、洽谈、申请、记者、采访、平面设计、课堂、讲解、诚征、计划、应该、告诉、成语、俗语、认识
（證件、證明、身份證、許可證、移民簽證、翻譯與公證、會計、考試、面試、試用期、登記、培訓、評論、建議、洽談、申請、記者、採訪、平面設計、課堂、講解、誠徵、計劃、應該、告訴、成語、俗語、認識）

zhèngjiàn, zhèngmíng, shēnfèn zhèng, xǔkě zhèng, yímín qiānzhèng, fānyìyǔ gōngzhèng, kuàijì, kǎoshì, miànshì, shìyòng qī, dēngjì, péixùn, pínglùn, jiànyì, qiàtán, shēnq ǐng, jìzhě, cǎifǎng, píngmiàn shèjì, kètáng, ji ǎngjiě, chéngzhēng, jìhuà, yīnggāi, gàosu, chéngyǔ, súyǔ, rènshi

口：**Something Related to Mouth or Sound**
咳嗽、嗓子疼、吃药、口味、交响乐、影响、喧哗、呼吸、吸引、打听
（咳嗽、嗓子疼、吃藥、口味、交響樂、影響、喧嘩、呼吸、吸引、打聽）

késou, sǎngzi téng, chīyào, kǒuwèi, jiāoxi ǎngyuè, yǐngxiǎng, xuānhuá, hūxī, xīyǐn, dǎtīng

囗：**Land, Circle, Around**
国籍、出国留学、围绕、困难、固定、园林、公园
（國籍、出國留學、圍繞、困難、固定、園林、公園）

guójí, chūguó liúxué, wéirào, kùnnán, gùdìng, yuánlín, gōngyuán

饣（食）、食：**Food, Eat**
餐厅、食品、饮食、饮料、饭馆、月饼、博物馆、图书馆、展览馆
（餐廳、食品、飲食、飲料、飯館、月餅、博物館、圖書館、展覽館）

cāntīng, shípǐn, yǐnshí, yǐnliào, fànguǎn, yuèbǐng, bówùguǎn, túshū guǎn, zhǎnlǎn guǎn

米：**Rice, Resource**
粽子、蛋糕、糕饼店、饮料、颜料、材料、资料
（粽子、蛋糕、糕餅店、飲料、顏料、材料、資料）

zòngzi, dàngāo, gāobǐng diàn, yǐnliào, yánliào, cáiliào, zīliào

礻、示：**(A) Show, Warn; (B) Things Related to God, Worship, Fortune, Group**
车祸、幸福、祝福、神仙、礼物、礼仪、社会、社区、展示、禁止、严禁、电影票、机票
（車禍、幸福、祝福、神仙、禮物、禮儀、社會、社區、展示、禁止、嚴禁、電影票、機票）

chēhuò, xìngfú, zhùfú, shénxiān, lǐwù, lǐyí, shèhuì, shèqū, zhǎnshì, jìnzhǐ, yánjìn, diànyǐng piào, jīpiào

忄 : Feeling

遗憾、感情、恨、愉快、尽快、忙、担忧、怕、恐怕、可惜、事情

（遺憾、感情、恨、愉快、盡快、忙、擔憂、怕、恐怕、可惜、事情）

yíhàn, gǎnqíng, hèn, yúkuài, jǐnkuài, máng, dānyōu, pà, kǒngpà, kěxī, shìqing

心: Thoughts

感觉、感动、感谢、感冒、思想、想法、主意、注意、意思、意见、考虑、担心、耐心、宁愿、念完高中

（感覺、感動、感謝、感冒、思想、想法、主意、注意、意思、意見、考慮、擔心、耐心、寧願、念完高中）

gǎnjué, gǎndòng, gǎnxiè, gǎnmào, sīxiǎng, xiǎngfǎ, zhǔyì, zhùyì, yìsi, yìjiàn, kǎolǜ, dānxīn, nàixīn, nìngyuàn, niànwán gāozhōng

贝(貝)：Money, Business, Shop

购物中心、百货商场、售货员、交费、免费、花费、邮费、退货、贵重、期货、胜败、贷款、租赁、负责、欣赏、比赛、赚钱

（購物中心、百貨商場、售貨員、交費、免費、花費、郵費、退貨、貴重、期貨、勝敗、貸款、租賃、負責、欣賞、比賽、賺錢）

gòuwù zhōngxīn, bǎihuò shāngchǎng, shòuhuòyuán, jiāo fèi, miǎnfèi, huāfèi, yóufèi, tuìhuò, guìzhòng, qīhuò, shèngbài, dàikuǎn, zūlìn, fùzé, xīnshǎng, bǐsài, zhuànqián

日：A. Sun, Light; B. Time; C. Warm

睡醒、早晨、最晚、时间、按时、时尚、临时、温暖

（睡醒、早晨、最晚、時間、按時、時尚、臨時、溫暖）

shuì xǐng, zǎochén, zuì wǎn, shíjiān, àn shí, shíshàng, línshí, wēnnuǎn

月：A. Moon, Light; B. Time; C. Body

学期、期限、保修期、保质期、过期、暑期工、假期、拉肚子、服务、舒服、说服、肥胖、京剧脸谱、肩膀、明星、服装、服饰

（學期、期限、保修期、保質期、過期、暑期工、假期、拉肚子、服務、舒服、説服、肥胖、京劇臉譜、肩膀、明星、服裝、服飾）

xuéqī, qīxiàn, bǎoxiū qī, bǎozhìqī, guòqī, shǔqī gōng, jiàqī, lādùzi, fúwù, shūfu, shuōfú, féipàng, jīngjù liǎnpǔ, jiānbǎng, míngxīng, fúzhuāng, fúshì

疒：Illness

病、头疼、嗓子疼、肚子疼、疼痛、针灸理疗、疾病、疲劳、疲倦

（病、頭疼、嗓子疼、肚子疼、疼痛、針灸理療、疾病、疲勞、疲倦）

bìng, tóuténg, sǎngzi téng, dùziténg, téngtòng, zhēnjiǔ lǐliáo, jíbìng, píláo, píjuàn

扌、手: Hands, Action

报告、报导、预报、报纸、打工、打针、招聘、摄影、小提琴、摇滚乐、挂号、挂失、指南针、抽奖、推迟、保护、找钱、携带、托运、拜托、搬家、盲人按摩、太极拳、挣钱、拍照、拍摄、执照、收拾、打算、坚持、支持、安排、推荐、提供

（報告、報導、預報、報紙、打工、打針、招聘、攝影、小提琴、搖滾樂、掛號、掛失、指南針、抽獎、推遲、保護、找錢、攜帶、托運、拜託、搬家、

盲人按摩、太極拳、掙錢、拍照、拍攝、執照、收拾、打算、堅持、支持、安排、推薦、提供）

bàogào, bàodǎo, yùbào, bàozhǐ, dǎgōng, dǎzhēn, zhāopìn, shèyǐng, xiǎotíqín, yáogǔnyuè, guàhào, guàshī, zhǐnánzhēn, chōují ǎng, tuīchí, bǎohù, zhǎoqián, xiédài, tuōyùn, bàituō, bānjiā, mángrén ànmó, tàijí quán, zhèng qián, pāizhào, pāishè, zhízhào, shōushi, dǎsuàn, jiānchí, zhīchí, ānpái, tuījiàn, tígōng

足: Feet, Walk
践踏、踩、道路、涉足、足够、跑、跳、舞蹈、跟、距离
（踐踏、踩、道路、涉足、足夠、跑、跳、舞蹈、跟、距離）

jiàntà, cǎi, dàolù, shèzú, zúgòu, pǎo, tiào, wǔdǎo, gēn, jùlí

辶: Walk, Run, Conduct, Pass
追星族、球迷、快递、客运、货运、交通运输、违反、名胜古迹、附近、抄近道、通道、水电管道、中国制造、邀请、欢迎、直达、达到、通讯、难过、迷路、出远门、选
（追星族、球迷、快遞、客運、貨運、交通運輸、違反、名勝古蹟、附近、抄近道、通道、水電管道、中國製造、邀請、歡迎、直達、達到、通訊、難過、迷路、出遠門、選）

zhuīxīng zú, qiúmí, kuàidì, kèyùn, huòyùn, jiāotōng yùnshū, wéifǎn, míngshèng gǔjī, fùjìn, chāo jìndào, tōngdào, shuǐdiàn guǎndào, zhōngguó zhìzào, yāoqǐng, huānyíng, zhídá, dádào, tōngxùn, nánguò, mílù, chū yuǎnmén, xuǎn

走：Pass
赶快、追赶、超重、超越、兴趣、起来
（趕快、追趕、超重、超越、興趣、起來）

gǎnkuài, zhuīgǎn, chāozhòng, chāoyuè, xìngqù, qǐlái

力：Power, Labor
服务、联系业务、务必、成功、用功、参加、能力、鼓励、劳动、疲劳
（服務、聯繫業務、務必、成功、用功、參加、能力、鼓勵、勞動、疲勞）

fúwù, liánxì yèwù, wùbì, chénggōng, yònggōng, cānjiā, nénglì, gǔlì, láodòng, píláo

土：Ground, Mud, Earth
地理、环境、体育场、运动场、广场、游乐场、操场、赛场、入场券、机场、长城、天坛、城市、少林寺、基地、地址、填好表格、坚持
（地理、環境、體育場、運動場、廣場、遊樂場、操場、賽場、入場券、機場、長城、天壇、城市、少林寺、基地、地址、填好表格、堅持）

dìlǐ, huánjìng, tǐyùchǎng, yùndòngchǎng, guǎngchǎng, yóulè chǎng, cāochǎng, sàichǎng, rùchǎng quàn, jīchǎng, chángchéng, tiāntán, chéngshì, shàolínsì, jīdì, dìzhǐ, tián hǎo biǎogé, jiānchí

纟、糸：Silk, Thread, Line, Path
造纸、家庭纠纷、组织、网络、地铁三号线、路线、经过、经历、经验、曾经、结婚、结束、继续、练习、联系、关系、紧张、累
（造紙、家庭糾紛、組織、網絡、地鐵三號線、路線、經過、經歷、經驗、曾經、結婚、結束、繼續、練習、聯繫、關係、緊張、累）

zàozhǐ, jiātíng jiūfēn, zǔzhī, wǎngluò, dìtiě sān hào xiàn, lùxiàn, jīngguò, jīnglì, jīngyàn, céngjīng, jiéhūn, jiéshù, jìxù, liànxí, liánxì, guānxì, jǐnzhāng, lèi

女：**Female**

婚姻、嫁娶、夫妻、妇女、老弱妇孺、妨碍、媒体
（婚姻、嫁娶、夫妻、婦女、老弱婦孺、妨礙、媒體）

hūnyīn, jiàqǔ, fūqī, fùnǚ, lǎoruò fùrú, fáng'ài, méitǐ

钅、金：**Metal**

打针、指南针、找钱、零钱、金融、奖学金、奖金、现金、地铁、钟点工、锻炼
（打針、指南針、找錢、零錢、金融、獎學金、獎金、現金、地鐵、鐘點工、鍛鍊）

dǎzhēn, zhǐnánzhēn, zhǎoqián, língqián, jīnróng, jiǎngxuéjīn, jiǎngjīn, xiànjīn, dìtiě, zhōngdiǎngōng, duànliàn

---

Another Strategy to Organize and Learn Vocabulary

Did you notice that we combined another strategy catalog to the vocabulary? Yes, we purposely organized some vocabulary including the same characters together for better memorization. You may try this method as well. For example:

术：美术、艺术、武术、学术、战术、科学技术，etc.

術：美術、藝術、武術、學術、戰術、科學技術，etc.

学：学期、学生、留学生、数学、化学、学院、奖学金、助学金、学分、学习成绩，etc.

學：學期、學生、留學生、數學、化學、學院、獎學金、助學金、學分、學習成績，etc.

After practicing the chunked vocabulary by radicals, you should continue to develop your vocabulary bank by themes in order to improve your skills of deducing the meaning under unrehearsed circumstances.

You will find the AP Chinese vocabulary list organized by themes in this link: https://quizlet.com/join/tHJp9DZSq. Here are some tips for you to make the most of the vocabulary list.

- If you need to enhance listening skills, approach the quizlet vocabulary by clicking the sound icon. This will help your intake by ear.
- Use the "quiz" function to do a self-check. Click "options" at the lower left corner. When a window pops up, only check "multiple choice" and change the number. This will help you to practice all the vocabulary efficiently.
- If you need to improve your typing skills at the same time, then use the "gravity" function.
- Create your own quizlet vocabulary set and collect the difficult vocabulary you want to review later.
- If you prefer dividing the big thematic vocabulary banks into smaller parts, you may organize them by topics, antonyms, synonyms, and so on. Some vocabulary or topics can be cataloged into more than one theme. The samples are provided below.

Theme 1 Families and Societies

Simplified Chinese

FAMILY MEMBERS	EDUCATION RELATED	SOCIETY RELATED
独生子女	望子成龙	政府
计划生育	望女成凤	政策
开放二胎	压力	讨论
家庭	控制	受到
四世同堂	长辈	条件
四二一家庭	晚辈	体会
美满	宠爱	相处
幸福	溺爱	新闻
家教	宝贝	赚钱
传宗接代	皇帝	存钱
长幼有序	自私	收入
孝顺	孤独	零用钱
尊重	弱点	省（下来）
尊敬	青少年	衣食住行
关照	良好教育	贫穷
关系	指出	富裕
归来	指导	放心
称呼	心事	分别
出生	心情	家务
父母	校内	家乡
侄女	校外	故乡
爷爷	知识	接风
奶奶	闹别扭	饯行
大人	可靠	接近
家长	道理	解释
儿童	乖	理解
童年	管	了解
姑妈	教育	联系
家长	厉害	矛盾
结婚	虎妈	实用性

(Continued)

FAMILY MEMBERS	EDUCATION RELATED	SOCIETY RELATED
姐妹	育儿	社会
兄弟	起跑线	生活
舅舅(妈)	奖学金	熟悉
老年	棍棒教育	思考
老太太	发展	思想
年轻（人）	展示	握手
姥爷	经验	礼物
陪	证明	街道
夫妻	害羞	超市
妻管炎	坚定	有害无益
未婚妻	勇气	成语
妻子	不知不觉	俚语
丈夫	挑战性	上街
嫂子	进步	购物
孙女	队友	空闲
孙子	做瑜伽	开玩笑
亲戚		逛
相处		谈天说地
拥抱		老式
		快餐
		筷子

Traditional Chinese

FAMILY MEMBERS	EDUCATION RELATED	SOCIETY RELATED
獨生子女	望子成龍	政府
計劃生育	望女成鳳	政策
開放二胎	壓力	討論
家庭	控制	受到
四世同堂	長輩	條件
四二一家庭	晚輩	體會
美滿	寵愛	相處
幸福	溺愛	新聞
家教	寶貝	賺錢
傳宗接代	皇帝	存錢
長幼有序	自私	收入
孝順	孤獨	零用錢
尊重	弱點	省（下來）
尊敬	青少年	衣食住行
關照	良好教育	貧窮
關系	指出	富裕
歸來	指導	放心
稱呼	心事	分別
出生	心情	家務
父母	校內	家鄉
侄女	校外	故鄉
爺爺	知識	接風
奶奶	鬧別扭	餞行
大人	可靠	接近
家長	道理	解釋
兒童	乖	理解
童年	管	了解
姑媽	教育	聯系
家長	厲害	矛盾
結婚	虎媽	實用性

(Continued)

FAMILY MEMBERS	EDUCATION RELATED	SOCIETY RELATED
姐妹	育兒	社會
兄弟	起跑線	生活
舅舅(媽)	獎學金	熟悉
老年	棍棒教育	思考
老太太	發展	思想
年輕（人）	展示	握手
姥爺	經驗	禮物
陪	証明	街道
夫妻	害羞	超市
妻管炎	堅定	有害無益
未婚妻	勇氣	成語
妻子	不知不覺	俚語
丈夫	挑戰性	上街
嫂子	進步	購物
孫女	隊友	空閑
孫子	做瑜伽	開玩笑
親戚		逛
相處		談天説地
擁抱		老式
		快餐
		筷子

Theme 2 Public and Personal Identities

Simplified Chinese

FESTIVALS	PERSONAL IDENTITY	SCHOOL LIFE	OCCUPATION
传统	背景	选择	不断
风俗	身份	参加	病人
福	表现	参观	工作人员
感恩节	性格	读书	成功
咕噜肉	条件	队员	成绩
红包	部	教育	成为
火锅	出版	教授	成人
农历	民族	留学生	大人
团圆	人才	交换生	教师
酒	银行	高中	服务员
联欢会	感觉	初中	飞行员
聚会	感情	科	工程师
晚会	钢琴	望子成龙 (T1)	律师
气氛	冠军	望女成凤 (T1)	师傅
清淡	国家	英语	发展
清蒸	国外	哲学	翻译
庆祝	海龟	新生	公共场所
祝贺	海外	影响	公平
热闹	想念	申请	贡献
元宵节	故乡	顺利	基础
月饼	骄傲	说服	机会
正月	开朗	学有所成	接受
粽子	考虑	压力	经理
欣赏	可靠	一干二净	厉害
盐	可怕	管	录用
传播	跨国	管理学院	落伍
茶艺	老百姓	工学院	满意
象征	老外	提条件	面积
赏月	情况	学分	陌生
特制	缺点	学位	墨西哥

(Continued)

FESTIVALS	PERSONAL IDENTITY	SCHOOL LIFE	OCCUPATION
嫦娥	讨论	奖学金	农村
故乡	讨厌	博士	欧洲
品种	体贴	硕士	提(高)
祝愿	伟大	系	推销
彩球	吓人	小学	上班
点燃	嫌	校内	相信
火腿	优秀	校外	想法
风调雨顺	优点	研究	整天
除夕	幽默	研究生	知音
对联	友谊	事业	规定
交好运	真心	毕业	重视
压岁钱	着急	职业	众人
合家团圆	心事	学业	自由
改变	心情	课外兴趣小组	做法
生肖	态度	义工	碰见
猜灯谜	习惯	倍	活力
属	重男轻女	计时	
奖品	特长	标准	
长假			
鞭炮/ 爆竹			

Traditional Chinese

FESTIVALS	PERSONAL IDENTITY	SCHOOL LIFE	OCCUPATION
傳統	背景	選擇	不斷
風俗	身份	參加	病人
福	表現	參觀	工作人員
感恩節	性格	讀書	成功
咕嚕肉	條件	隊員	成績
紅包	部	教育	成為
火鍋	出版	教授	成人
農曆	民族	留學生	大人
團圓	人才	交換生	教師
酒	銀行	高中	服務員
聯歡會	感覺	初中	飛行員
聚會	感情	科	工程師
晚會	鋼琴	望子成龍 (T1)	律師
氣氛	冠軍	望女成鳳 (T1)	師傅
清淡	國家	英語	發展
清蒸	國外	哲學	翻譯
慶祝	海龜	新生	公共場所
祝賀	海外	影響	公平
熱鬧	想念	申請	貢獻
元宵節	故鄉	順利	基礎
月餅	驕傲	説服	機會
正月	開朗	學有所成	接受
粽子	考慮	壓力	經理
欣賞	可靠	一干二淨	厲害
鹽	可怕	管	錄用
傳播	跨國	管理學院	落伍
茶藝	老百姓	工學院	滿意
象征	老外	提條件	面積
賞月	情況	學分	陌生
特制	缺點	學位	墨西哥

(Continued)

FESTIVALS	PERSONAL IDENTITY	SCHOOL LIFE	OCCUPATION
嫦娥	討論	獎學金	農村
故鄉	討厭	博士	歐洲
品種	體貼	碩士	提(高)
祝願	偉大	系	推銷
彩球	嚇人	小學	上班
點燃	嫌	校內	相信
火腿	優秀	校外	想法
風調雨順	優點	研究	整天
除夕	幽默	研究生	知音
對聯	友誼	事業	規定
交好運	真心	畢業	重視
壓歲錢	著急	職業	眾人
合家團圓	心事	學業	自由
改變	心情	課外興趣小組	做法
生肖	態度	義工	碰見
猜燈謎	習慣	倍	活力
屬	重男輕女	計時	
獎品	特長	標准	
長假			
鞭炮/ 爆竹			

Theme 3 Beauty and Aesthetics

Simplified Chinese

APPRECIATION	GEOGRAPHY	HISTORICAL SITES	MARTIAL ARTS	ENTERTAINMENT
风景	河流	名胜古迹	太极拳	电视剧
寒假	长江	兵马俑	武术	电影院
路线	黄河	博物馆	艺术	动作
马路	面积	长城	阴阳	演唱会
铁路	农村	朝代	功夫	音乐会
公路	城市	游览点	联系	门票
高速公路	高原	历史	起源	人山人海
办公室	平原	故宫	奥运	演员
四季如春	沙漠	宫殿	翻译	银行
亚洲	山脉	紫禁城	项目	杂志
到处	沿海一带	中国城	影响	出版
餐馆	海滩	奇怪	广播电台	画画
饭店	海洋	购物	强身健体	爬山
饭馆	省会	古老	修身养性	减肥
宾馆	地道	挂(着)	专程	健身房
旅馆	地理	摆着	流传	牛仔裤
旅客	地形	纪念品	吸引	身材
旅游	广州	旗袍	宝贵	时髦
导游	昆明	墙	遗产	毯子
美丽	南京	圈	精华	套装
体贴	天津	丝绸	结合	特色
卧铺	深圳	假山	独特	杂志
展览馆	新疆	石头	逐步	早晨
展厅	纬度	石林	寺院	哲学
	温度	园林		枕头
	湿	塔		
	干	熊猫		

Traditional Chinese

APPRECIATION	GEOGRAPHY	HISTORICAL SITES	MARTIAL ARTS	ENTERTAINMENT
風景	河流	名勝古跡	太極拳	電視劇
寒假	長江	兵馬俑	武術	電影院
路線	黃河	博物館	藝術	動作
馬路	面積	長城	陰陽	演唱會
鐵路	農村	朝代	功夫	音樂會
公路	城市	游覽點	聯系	門票
高速公路	高原	歷史	起源	人山人海
辦公室	平原	故宮	奧運	演員
四季如春	沙漠	宮殿	翻譯	銀行
亞洲	山脈	紫禁城	項目	雜志
到處	沿海一帶	中國城	影響	出版
餐館	海灘	奇怪	廣播電台	畫畫
飯店	海洋	購物	強身健體	爬山
飯館	省會	古老	修身養性	減肥
賓館	地道	挂(著)	專程	健身房
旅館	地理	擺著	流傳	牛仔褲
旅客	地形	紀念品	吸引	身材
旅游	廣州	旗袍	寶貴	時髦
導游	昆明	牆	遺產	毯子
美麗	南京	圈	精華	套裝
體貼	天津	絲綢	結合	特色
臥鋪	深圳	假山	獨特	雜志
展覽館	新疆	石頭	逐步	早晨
展廳	緯度	石林	寺院	哲學
	溫度	園林		枕頭
	濕	塔		
	干	熊貓		

Theme 4 Science and Technology

Simplified Chinese

INTERNET RELATED	OTHER TECHNOLOGY
博客	新鲜
网络	热水器
微信	空调
支付宝	冰箱
利弊	电车
软件	计程车
影响	船
上瘾	火车
网站	自行车
网上银行	申请
下载	设计
游戏	烘干机
短消息	洗衣机
电子邮件	新闻
发短信	发电
科学	发明
技术	文明
数位	先进
资料	活字印刷
自助服务	火药
语音信箱	指南针
查询	造纸
用户	记载
密码	纬度
低头族	太阳
手机	太阳能
信号	

Traditional Chinese

INTERNET RELATED	OTHER TECHNOLOGY
博客	新鮮
網絡	熱水器
微信	空調
支付寶	冰箱
利弊	電車
軟件	計程車
影響	船
上癮	火車
網站	自行車
網上銀行	申請
下載	設計
游戲	烘干機
短消息	洗衣機
電子郵件	新聞
發短信	發電
科學	發明
技術	文明
數位	先進
資料	活字印刷
自助服務	火藥
語音信箱	指南針
查詢	造紙
用戶	記載
密碼	緯度
低頭族	太陽
手機	太陽能
信號	

Theme 5 Contemporary Life

Simplified Chinese

SHOPPING	FOOD	LODGING	TRANSPORTATION	FRIENDS
标准	盒饭	搬家	帮忙	开朗
贷款	零食	存款	帮助	开玩笑
价格	饮食	打交道	超市	抱怨
价钱	快餐	打呼噜	出差	吵架
减轻	香	栋	出发	吹（了）
金融	嫩	钥匙	短期	生气
省钱	家庭	时髦	锻炼	道理
赚钱	垃圾	时代	健身	道歉
零用钱	酸	适合	爱好	答应
现金	甜	适应	安全	丢三拉四
信用卡	苦	轻松	散步	逗
名牌	辣	生活	退休	迟到
毛衣	咸	文具	经验	分手
毛巾	菜系	文学	礼物	读书
被子	餐桌	文章	讨论	交朋友
毯子	礼仪	数字	谈	反对
T恤衫	上座	负担	将来	态度
衣柜	抢先	工资	主意	过节
日用品	付帐	出生	主要	碰见
牙膏	蔬菜	屋子	爬山	建议
卫生纸	营养	家具	麻将	意见
物美价廉	均衡	理解	亲眼（看到）	事情
纯棉	卡路里	领导	良好	嫌
欠	酱油	减轻	房地产	敢
收入	醋	邻居	押金	害
免费	蛋白质	感觉	落伍	劝
	外卖	感情		考虑
	有益健康			马虎

Traditional Chinese

SHOPPING	FOOD	LODGING	TRANSPORTATION	FRIENDS
標准	盒飯	搬家	幫忙	开朗
貸款	零食	存款	幫助	开玩笑
價格	飲食	打交道	超市	抱怨
價錢	快餐	打呼嚕	出差	吵架
減輕	香	棟	出發	吹（了）
金融	嫩	鑰匙	短期	生气
省錢	家庭	時髦	鍛煉	道理
賺錢	垃圾	時代	健身	道歉
零用錢	酸	適合	愛好	答应
現金	甜	適應	安全	丢三拉四
信用卡	苦	輕鬆	散步	逗
名牌	辣	生活	退休	迟到
毛衣	咸	文具	經驗	分手
毛巾	菜系	文學	禮物	读书
被子	餐桌	文章	討論	交朋友
毯子	禮儀	數字	談	反对
T恤衫	上座	負擔	將來	态度
衣櫃	搶先	工資	主意	过节
日用品	付帳	出生	主要	碰见
牙膏	蔬菜	屋子	爬山	建议
衛生紙	營養	家具	麻將	意见
物美價廉	均衡	理解	親眼（看到）	事情
純棉	卡路裡	領導	良好	嫌
欠	醬油	減輕	房地產	敢
收入	醋	鄰居	押金	害
免費	蛋白質	感覺	落伍	劝
	外賣	感情		考虑
	有益健康			马虎

Theme 6 Global Challenges

Simplified Chinese

ENVIRONMENT	ECONOMICS	CHALLENGES
保护	金融	变化
保留	贷款	结婚生子
白色污染	税	政府
地球	压力	留守儿童
倒垃圾	单位	社会问题
空气	抵押	世界公民
质量	房地产泡沫	看法
不堪设想	投资	想法
自由	理财	发达
大自然	风险	发展中
车辆	股票	改革开放
交通拥挤	市场	事故
堵塞	赚钱	交流
环境	存钱	解决
回收	经济	决定
化学成分	利息	妇女地位
节约用水	贸易	女性
利用	企业	贫穷
瓶装水	签合同	平等
条件	剩余	公平
暖气	剩下（来）	取得
危机	工资	取之不得
吸烟	收入	时代
享受	薪水	世纪
受到	同工同酬	统一
严肃	竞争	稳定
严重	消费	跌
严禁…	增加	摔
一次性	减少	退休
逐渐	接近	老龄化
现象	意见/主意	城市化
恐怕	同意	人口密集
进入	赞成	集中
进行	提供	新兴，新型

Traditional Chinese

ENVIRONMENT	ECONOMICS	CHALLENGES
保護	金融	變化
保留	貸款	結婚生子
白色污染	稅	政府
地球	壓力	留守兒童
倒垃圾	單位	社會問題
空氣	抵押	世界公民
質量	房地產泡沫	看法
不堪設想	投資	想法
自由	理財	發達
大自然	風險	發展中
車輛	股票	改革開放
交通擁擠	市場	事故
堵塞	賺錢	交流
環境	存錢	解決
回收	經濟	決定
化學成分	利息	婦女地位
節約用水	貿易	女性
利用	企業	貧窮
瓶裝水	簽合同	平等
條件	剩余	公平
暖氣	剩下（來）	取得
危機	工資	取之不得
吸煙	收入	時代
享受	薪水	世紀
受到	同工同酬	統一
嚴肅	競爭	穩定
嚴重	消費	跌
嚴禁…	增加	摔
一次性	減少	退休
逐漸	接近	老齡化
現象	意見/主意	城市化
恐怕	同意	人口密集
進入	贊成	集中
進行	提供	新興，新型

Exam Registration

- https://apstudents.collegeboard.org/register-for-ap-exams
  You can find the answers to questions about registration with this link.

AP Chinese Course and Exam Description, Scoring Guidelines, and Practice Materials

- https://apcentral.collegeboard.org/courses/ap-chinese-language-and-culture/exam
  You can find the newest version (2019) of the AP Chinese Course and Exam Description (CED), as well as the scoring guidelines, with this link. The new CED provides detailed guidance and resources for AP Chinese exam preparation.

- https://myap.collegeboard.org/login
  You can use this to register for the AP exam, access AP Classroom assignments from your teachers, and get feedback on your performance.

Previous AP Language and Culture Exams

- https://apcentral.collegeboard.org/courses/ap-chinese-language-and-culture/exam/past-exam-questions?course=ap-chinese-language-and-culture
  The most useful information you can find on this website is the actual free-response questions that were used on previous AP Chinese Language and Culture exams. You'll also find sample answers with explanations for these questions.

- http://apcentral.collegeboard.com/apc/public/courses/teachers_corner/205159.html
  Here you'll find the actual multiple-choice questions from the 2007 AP Chinese and Culture exam. Practice with these to experience the test.

Tools You Can Use

- https://quizlet.com/join/tHJp9DZSq
  This quizlet link provides useful resources related to this book, such as templates, samples, and vocabulary banks by themes, etc.

- http://translate.google.com/
  Vocabulary (characters), English and Pinyin.

Authentic Chinese Learning Resources

1. http://www.youtube.com/

YouTube. Of course! Type in *Chinese* to search any topic you would like to watch. Practice your note-taking skills as well.

2. http://cul.chinese.cn/index.html

Confucius Institute Online. This is an excellent place to gain cultural knowledge in Chinese. You can find idioms, stories, and Chinese learning programs by levels.